U.S. Peacefare

U.S. Peacefare

Organizing American Peace-Building Operations

Dane F. Smith, Jr.

Published in cooperation with the Center for Strategic and International Studies,
Washington D.C.

Praeger Security International

 PRAEGER

AN IMPRINT OF ABC-CLIO, LLC
Santa Barbara, California • Denver, Colorado • Oxford, England

Library of Congress Cataloging-in-Publication Data

Smith, Dane F.
    U.S. peacefare : organizing American peace-building operations / Dane F. Smith, Jr.
      p. cm.
    "Published in cooperation with the Center for Strategic and International Studies,
Washington D.C."
    Includes bibliographical references and index.
    ISBN 978–0–313–38262–8 (hard copy : alk. paper) — ISBN 978–0–313–38263–5 (ebook)
  1. Peace-building—United States. 2. National security—United States. 3. United States—
Foreign relations. 4. United States—Politics and government. I. Title.
JZ5584.U6 S6   2010
327.1'720973—dc22   2009050893

ISBN: 978–0–313–38262–8
EISBN: 978–0–313–38263–5

14 13 12 11 10   1 2 3 4 5

This book is also available on the World Wide Web as an eBook.
Visit www.abc-clio.com for details.

Praeger
An Imprint of ABC-CLIO, LLC

ABC-CLIO, LLC
130 Cremona Drive, P.O. Box 1911
Santa Barbara, California 93116-1911

This book is printed on acid-free paper ∞

Manufactured in the United States of America

To Judy

who joined me on excursions in peace-building in the Peace Corps and Foreign Service, wife, mother of my children, lover, and best friend, with deepest gratitude.

Contents

viii   Contents

Preface

This study had its origin in a course I was asked to teach at American University to acquaint students with the roles of various U.S. government agencies in dealing with international conflict. I had gained a direct acquaintance with some of those roles a decade earlier as Special Presidential Envoy for Liberia. When I undertook the course, I assumed that I could draw on extensive analysis of the organization, operations and effectiveness of the individual agencies, to which I could add my personal experience as a diplomat. I quickly discovered that was not the case. There is plenty of material on the application of the tools of peace-building in the field of conflict and on individual country cases, but relatively little on the agencies themselves.

In 2002 the Center for Strategic and International Studies (CSIS) established the Post-Conflict Reconstruction Project. Focusing on the full spectrum of conflict-related concerns, from early warning and conflict prevention to rebuilding shattered societies, it has studied closely the pillars of reconstruction in conflict-riven states. It has become a leading source for authoritative analysis, evaluation, and recommendations both for fragile states and for post-conflict reconstruction. Project Codirectors Frederick Barton and Karin von Hippel encouraged me to write a book on the agencies involved with international conflict and the interagency coordination process. It is hoped that such a volume will complement the outstanding study on the modalities of post-conflict reconstruction published by CSIS in 2004: Robert C. Orr, ed., *Winning the Peace: An American Strategy for Post-Conflict Reconstruction*.

After a review of the historical roots of American peacefare, the study examines five key bureaucratic entities involved in peace-building. The analysis is Washington-centered, focused on organization and the interagency process, and gives relatively little space to overseas implementation. It is based largely on more than 120 interviews with current and previous government officials. The study begins with the National Security Council (NSC), covering the Cabinet-level officials meeting with the President as a council, as well as the NSC staff, which serves as the foreign policy/national security staff of the President. It goes on to consider the role of the State Department, exercised both through the diplomacy of its geographic bureaus and the specialized programs of certain functional bureaus. A separate chapter is devoted to the State Department's new formal mechanism for coordination, the Office of the Coordinator for Reconstruction and Stabilization. The following chapter outlines the zigzag route followed by the Defense Department under the Clinton and George W. Bush administrations in dealing with stability operations. USAID's increased attention to shaping foreign assistance and development to the dynamics of conflict is then chronicled. The survey of agencies ends with the unique and evolving role of the U.S. Institute of Peace, a nonpartisan body formally independent of the executive branch. The budget process for U.S. peacefare is traced through Function 150 (international affairs) and more cursorily through Function 050 (defense) to the actions of authorizing and appropriating committees in the Congress. The book ends with recommendations to the Obama administration for strengthening U.S. peacefare, drawing from the experience of the past two decades.

The study does not analyze the role of the intelligence community. Intelligence is important to foreign policy decisions, including those related to peace-building. However, the intelligence community has not been a major influence on the way the major agencies organize or on how they coordinate. The analysis also omits agencies such as the Departments of Justice, Commerce, and Agriculture. Their personnel and expertise may contribute to post-conflict reconstruction, but those departments do not treat peace-building as a major function. The role of the Justice Department in the post-conflict training of civilian police is briefly described in the chapter on the State Department, which has the policy lead in that sector. The role of U.S. government contractors, both for-profit firms and nongovernmental organizations (NGOs), is also not explored. Although State, Defense, and USAID all contract work in the peace-building sector, the contractors operate largely in the field and thus fall outside of this Washington-based study.

The work looks at U.S. peace-building directed toward civil wars. Since World War II, and particularly during the period since the end of the Cold War—the era which is the focus of analysis—the dominant mode of conflict has been wars within the territory of a single state. Governments of conflicted countries usually seek to fend off international interest in such conflicts by claiming they fall exclusively within the domestic jurisdiction of the state. Some civil conflicts by their nature are territorially self-contained. The international community—aside from voicing occasional concern about human rights—has generally refrained from taking an active interest, for example, in Tuareg violence in Mali and Niger and Muslim violence in southern Thailand, to say nothing of violent resistance within the homelands of great powers, as in the case of Ingushetia and Xinjiang. However, internal conflict often has serious international repercussions. Insurgents may purchase arms in neighboring countries. They may use neighboring territory as a rear base. They may be supported, sometimes surreptitiously, by neighboring governments. They may carry out raids on neighboring territory in search of tradable resources, supplies, and equipment, killing or injuring civilians or local security forces. The violence often generates large flows of refugees across borders. All these factors may make a civil war a matter of international concern, including for the United States.

Sometimes the violence is accompanied by horrific violations of human rights, including atrocities against identifiable groups, giving rise to charges of genocide. In the past 20 years, the international community has displayed an increasing tendency to claim the right of humanitarian intervention in such situations and to set aside claims of domestic jurisdiction. That tendency has increased the importance for the United States of dealing effectively with civil wars. Genocide in Rwanda and ethnic cleansing in the Balkans generated a debate—in which the United States played a major role—that eventuated in the articulation of "the responsibility to protect" (R2P) civilians from mass atrocities.[1] When individual states fail to meet that responsibility, protection becomes the collective responsibility of the international community. The concept of R2P was accepted by the UN World Summit in 2005, but huge difficulties remain in translating it into effective action, as illustrated by the many frustrations of U.S. multilateral diplomacy in Darfur.

The one exception to the exclusive internal conflict focus of this study is Iraq. Unlike in Afghanistan, where the United States intervened on the side of insurgents in a civil war in a Security Council-endorsed exercise of self-defense after the 9/11 attacks, the United States invaded Iraq and overthrew the regime. However, Iraq has figured so importantly in the U.S. government debate about modes of post-conflict reconstruction and in the formation of bureaucratic and field mechanisms for reconstruction and stabilization that it would make no sense to omit it from the analysis.

It is important to be explicit about the terminology used in this work.[2]

"Peace-building" is an umbrella term covering a range of actions to reduce conflict in general or to end specific conflicts. It includes conflict prevention measures, efforts to resolve ongoing conflicts, and post-reconstruction activities. It includes diplomacy, mediation or good offices, and specific measures for reconstruction and stabilization. Peace-building may also be done by individuals or NGOs, but this analysis is exclusively concerned with official peace-building.[3]

The neologism "peacefare" is synonymous with "peace-building."

"Peacekeeping" typically refers to operations by a military force acting with the consent of the parties to a conflict, pursuant to a cease-fire or other agreement between them. It is designed to monitor and facilitate implementation of the cease-fire or other agreement and to separate warring parties. It is normally authorized by the UN Security Council or a regional organization.

"Peace enforcement" refers to military actions or the threat of force authorized by the Security Council under Chapter VII of the UN Charter to force the compliance of one or more parties with the resolutions or sanctions approved by the Council.

Both peacekeeping and peace enforcement include civilian actions as part of the mission.

"Conflict prevention" consists of actions taken before a looming crisis to forestall or limit violence or to reach a solution before armed hostilities begin. It includes diplomatic initiatives but may also refer to social, economic, and political measures to prevent escalation into hostilities.

"Conflict resolution" refers to efforts to achieve a sustainable long-term solution to a violent conflict. Such efforts include activities ranging from third-party, nonofficial actions (Track II diplomacy) to bilateral and multilateral diplomacy and formal mediation.

"Post-conflict reconstruction" refers to efforts taken by outside actors to help national authorities build up a minimally capable state. It encompasses four key areas: security, governance and participation, justice and reconciliation, and social and economic well-being.[4] "Post-conflict reconstruction" is currently used interchangeably with "reconstruction and stabilization" (the preferred State Department term) and "stability operations" (the preferred Defense Department term). It has the same general meaning as the term "nation-building," favored by the Clinton administration, although "state-building" is a more accurate description of the process.[5] In the American approach to post-conflict reconstruction, democratization is almost inevitably a major objective and the creation or restoration of a free market economy is a *desideratum*.

* * *

I am indebted to Abdul Aziz Said, legendary professor, founder and former director of the Division of International Peace and Conflict Resolution at American University's School of International Service, the first to encourage the idea of a book. I have also appreciated the support of Prof. Ron Fisher, the current director, and Prof. Chuck Call, both of whom provided useful advice. At CSIS, Rick Barton and Karin von Hippel lent essential intellectual guidance and continuous backing for the enterprise. I received invaluable guidance and correctives from Laura A. Hall on the NSC and S/CRS, Timothy R. Shortley at the State Department, Dr. S. Tjip Walker at USAID, and Beth Ellen Cole at USIP. Leonard R. Hawley talked me through at length the peace-building approaches of the Clinton administration at the NSC, Defense, and State. Prof. I. M. Destler, Laura Hall, Harry W. Kopf, Len Hawley, Tjip Walker, Robert M. Perito, Chuck Ludlam, and Paula M.

Hirschoff read parts of the manuscript. Any errors are, of course, my own. Adam Lockyear at CSIS helped improve the sections on State and USAID, and Shannon Hayden of the Post-Conflict Reconstruction Project did me many kindnesses. James Dunton, Director of CSIS Publications, and Steve Catalano, Senior Editor, Praeger Security International, crafted the publication arrangements. Christy Anitha, Project Manager at Beacon PMG, skillfully guided the editorial process. Finally, thanks go to my wife, Judith Smith, who read parts of the text and provided that constant moral support that made the project possible.

Abbreviations

ACDA	Arms Control and Disarmament Agency
ACOTA	African Contingency Operations Training and Assistance
ACT	Advance Civilian Team (IMS)
AF	Bureau of African Affairs (State)
AFR	Bureau for Africa (USAID)
AFRICOM	U.S. African Command
ASFF	Afghanistan Security Forces Fund
ASG	Abu Sayyaf Group
AWG	Assistance Working Group (State/USAID)
CAC	Combined Arms Center (Fort Leavenworth)
CAF	Conflict Assessment Framework (USAID)
CALL	Center for Army Lessons Learned (Fort Leavenworth)
CAP	Center for Analysis and Prevention (USIP)
CCIF	Combatant Commander's Initiative Fund (Function 050)
CCO	Consortium for Complex Operations
CENTCOM	U.S. Central Command
CERP	Commander's Emergency Response Program (Function 050)
CFA	House Committee on Foreign Affairs
CIPA	Contributions to International Peacekeeping Activities (Function 150)
CIVPOL	civilian police training program
CMCR	Center for Mediation and Conflict Resolution (USIP)
CMM	Office of Conflict Management and Mitigation (USAID)
COCOM	U.S. combatant command
CPA	Coalition Provisional Authority (Iraq)
CPA	Comprehensive Peace Agreement (Sudan)
CR	Continuing Resolution
CRC-A	Civilian Response Corps—Active Component

CRC-C	Civilian Response Corps—Reserve
CRC-S	Civilian Response Corps—Standby Component
CSTC-Alpha	Combined Security Transition Command—Afghanistan
DA	Development Assistance (Function 150)
DART	Disaster Assistance Response Team
DASD	Deputy Assistant Secretary of Defense
DCHA	Bureau of Democracy, Conflict and Humanitarian Assistance (USAID)
DFID	Department for International Development (UK)
DG	Office of Democracy and Governance (USAID)
DNSA	Deputy National Security Advisor
DSCA	Defense Security Cooperation Agency
EEB	Bureau of Economic, Energy, and Business Affairs (State)
ECOWAS	Economic Community of West African States
ERMA	Emergency Refugee and Migration Assistance (Function 150)
ESF	Economic Support Fund (Function 150)
ETC	Education and Training Center (USIP)
EUCOM	U.S. European Command
EUR	Bureau of European and Eurasian Affairs (State)
F	Office of the Director Foreign Assistance (State/USAID)
FACT	Field Action Civilian Team (IMS)
FARC	Revolutionary Armed Forces of Colombia
FFP	Office of Food for Peace (USAID)
FMF	Foreign Military Financing (Function 150)
FSA	Freedom Support Act (Function 150)
FSI	Foreign Service Institute
GPOI	Global Peace Operations Initiative
HASC	House Armed Services Committee
HRDF	Human Rights and Democracy Fund (Function 150)
ICAF	Interagency Conflict Assessment Framework
ICITAP	International Criminal Investigative Training and Assistance Program (Justice)
IDA	International Disaster Assistance (Function 150)
IFOR	Implementation Force (NATO for Bosnia)
IGAD	Intergovernmental Authority on Development (Horn of Africa)
IMET	International Military Education and Training (Function 150)
IMS	Interagency Management System
INCLE	International Narcotics Control and Law Enforcement (Function 150)
INL	Bureau of International Narcotics and Law Enforcement Affairs (State)
IO	Bureau of International Organization Affairs (State)
IPC	Integrated Planning Cell (IMS)
ISAF	International Security Assistance Force (Afghanistan)
ISFF	Iraq Security Forces Fund (Function 050)
IWG	Interagency Working Group (Clinton administration)
JFCOM	U.S. Joint Forces Command

JIACG	Joint Interagency Coordination Group (U.S. geographic combatant commands)
JOpsC	Joint Operating Concept
KFOR	NATO Kosovo Force
LTTE	Liberation Tigers of Tamil Eelam
LURD	Liberians United for Reconstruction and Democracy
MILF	Moro Islamic Liberation Front (Philippines)
MINUSTAH	UN Stabilization Mission in Haiti
MME	major mission elements (IMS)
MNSTC-I	Multinational Security Transition Command—Iraq
MONUC	UN Mission in the Congo
MOOTW	military operations other than war
MRA	Migration and Refugee Assistance (Function 150)
MSP	Mission Strategic Plan (State)
MWI	Muslim World Initiative (USIP)
NEA	Bureau of Near Eastern Affairs (State)
NED	National Endowment for Democracy
NPS	Naval Post-Graduate School
NSA	National Security Advisor
NSC	National Security Council
NSPD	National Security Presidential Directive (Bush administration)
O&M	Operations and Maintenance (Function 050)
OHDACA	Overseas Humanitarian, Disaster Assistance and Civic Assistance (Function 050)
OIC	Organization of the Islamic Conference
OMB	Office of Management and Budget
ORHA	Office of Reconstruction and Humanitarian Assistance in Iraq
OSCE	Organization for Security and Cooperation in Europe
OSD	Office of the Secretary of Defense
OTI	Office of Transition Initiatives (USAID)
PCC	Policy Coordination Committee (NSC)
PCP&SO	Center for Post-Conflict Peace and Stability Operations (USIP)
PDD	Presidential Decision Directive (Clinton administration)
PFP	Philippine Facilitation Project (USIP)
PK&HA	Office of Peacekeeping and Humanitarian Assistance (DOD—Clinton administration)
PKO	Peacekeeping Operations (Function 150)
PKSOI	Peacekeeping and Stability Operations Institute (Army War College)
PM	Bureau of Political-Military Affairs (State)
PMAT	Pol-Mil Action Team, Bureau of Political-Military Affairs (State)
PRT	Provincial Reconstruction Team
QDR	quadrennial defense review
QNSR	quadrennial national security review
R&S	reconstruction and stabilization

ROMO	range of military operations
RSCMA	Reconstruction & Stabilization Civilian Management Act
S/CRS	Office of the Coordinator for Reconstruction and Stabilization (State)
S/I	Office of the Coordinator for Iraq (State)
SASC	Senate Armed Services Committee
SCA	Bureau of South and Central Asian Affairs (State)
SEED	Support for European Democracy (Function 150)
SFRC	Senate Foreign Relations Committee
SIGIR	Special Inspector General for Iraq Reconstruction
SO	Office of Stability Operations (DOD—Bush administration)
SOCOM	U.S. Special Operations Command
SO/LIC	Office of the Assistant Secretary for Special Operations/Low-Intensity Conflict (DOD)
SOLIC/IC	Office of the Assistant Secretary for Special Operations/Low-Intensity Conflict and Interdependent Capabilities (DOD—Bush administration)
SPLM/SPLA	Sudan People's Liberation Movement/Army
SSTRO	Stability, Security, Transition, and Reconstruction Operations
START	Stabilization and Reconstruction Task Force (Canada)
TI	Transition Initiatives (Function 150)
UNAMID	African Union/United Nations Hybrid operation in Darfur
UNITAF	Unified Task Force (Somalia)
UNOSOM I and II	United Nations Operation in Somalia
USIP	U.S. Institute of Peace
WFP	World Food Program
WHA	Bureau of Western Hemisphere Affairs (State)

CHAPTER 1

AN AMERICAN VOCATION FOR PEACE-BUILDING

> Our object . . . is to vindicate the principles of peace and justice . . . against selfish and autocratic power and to set up among the really free and self governed peoples of the world such a concert of purpose and of action as will henceforth insure the observance of those principles.
>
> —Woodrow Wilson

BEGINNINGS

At the end of the eighteenth century, securing peace was a matter of survival for a new state operating in the maelstrom of competition among Britain, France, and Spain for overseas territory and commercial dominance. Success in the Revolutionary War depended on an opportunistic alliance with France, taking advantage of its centuries-long deadly rivalry with Britain. Reflecting that reality, George Washington warned in his 1796 farewell address that the United States should have "as little political connection as possible" with the European powers and "steer clear of permanent alliances." The warning aimed not to isolate the new country from the rest of the world; freedom to trade was viewed as essential to future prosperity. Washington wanted to steer future leaders away from permitting the fragile state to be drawn into and torn apart by Europe's wars.[1]

Even during that early period, however, there was a minor current of interest in foreign peace-building. In 1792 Benjamin Rush, signer of the Declaration of Independence and elected delegate to the 1787 Constitutional Convention, proposed a "peace-office" for the United States. He lamented that such an institution had not been included in the new constitution and argued that "the principles of republicanism and Christianity are no less friendly to universal and perpetual peace than they are to universal and equal liberty."[2]

Within a few decades American leaders were consumed with continental expansion and were giving attention to Latin America. The struggles for independence there evoked sympathy. Many Americans saw the cause of the Spanish colonies as analogous to that of their own revolution and concluded that the United States should play a special role in the Western Hemisphere. That sentiment stemmed both from the desire to forestall European "balance of power" efforts to dominate the Latin American states politically and commercially and from the hope that the United States could itself acquire territory to the south. In 1823 President James Monroe announced that the territories of the Western Hemisphere "are henceforth not to be considered as subjects for future colonization by a European power." He added that the United States would consider any intervention by European powers supporting Spain's efforts to regain its colonies "as inimical to our peace and safety." At that moment the United States had neither the sea nor the land forces to back up this purportedly peace-building pronouncement.[3]

In two cases, the United States played a peace-building role in Latin American civil conflict in the nineteenth century. In 1857 civil war broke out in Mexico between conservatives, supported by the church and landowners, and the liberal reformist forces of Benito Juàrez. The Buchanan administration supported the Juàrez regime in hopes of securing a territorial cession. The conservatives looked to Europe for rescue and were willing to accept a European monarch. In 1861 British, French, and Spanish forces occupied Veracruz, and the French installed Maximilian, brother of the Austrian Emperor, as emperor. The European powers recognized the Mexican Empire. However, Juàrez's forces resisted, and it became clear that the puppet regime's survival depended on continued deployment of French troops. Washington, preoccupied with civil war and unwilling to provoke Spain or France into recognizing the Confederacy, contented itself with diplomatic protests. When the civil war ended, the protests were ratcheted up. In February 1866 Secretary of State William H. Seward warned that the presence of European armies in Mexico was a source of danger not only to the United States but to all the "republican states" in the Western Hemisphere. He demanded a date for French withdrawal.[4] Louis Napoleon's decision to remove French troops in 1867, leaving Maximilian to Juàrez's firing squad, was also prompted by the presence of 50,000 battle-tested American troops in Texas, in touch with Mexican republicans on the other side of the Rio Grande. Relative peace returned to Mexico for several decades.

In 1889 republican forces overthrew the imperial government of Brazil. The United States was the first state outside Latin America to recognize the republican government. Monarchists launched a counterrevolution in 1893. The United States refused to recognize the belligerent status of the monarchists and sent its own naval squadron, which faced off against warships of European powers sympathetic with the monarchists and intent on blockading American ships allegedly carrying contraband to the republicans. The refusal of the American command to accede to the blockade forced the European powers to reconsider recognizing the belligerency of the monarchists. The republicans triumphed, and civil war ended.[5]

These two episodes, particularly the Mexican case, "tremendously strengthened the stamina of the Monroe Doctrine and gathered for it immense popular approval," according to diplomatic historian Samuel F. Bemis, even though the Doctrine was not explicitly asserted in either case.[6] They helped lay the groundwork for a broader U.S. role in mediating disputes in Latin America, and the Doctrine became a wedge for assertion of a peace-building role in Latin America—for good or for ill.

Significant engagement in peace-building did not occur until the United States emerged as a world power. That historical milestone is associated with the Spanish-American War of 1898, when the United States acquired Puerto Rico, Guam, and the Philippines as colonies, completed the annexation of Hawaii, and provoked the independence of Cuba. It is also associated with the presidency of Theodore Roosevelt.

TEDDY ROOSEVELT AS PEACE-BUILDER

Theodore Roosevelt, a strong proponent of an interventionist foreign policy and initially an enthusiastic imperialist, is associated with the Roosevelt Corollary of the Monroe Doctrine. He asserted in 1904 that "adherence ... to the Monroe Doctrine may lead the United States, however reluctantly, in flagrant cases of ... wrongdoing or impotence, to the exercise of an international police power," if American rights were violated and foreign aggression loomed.[7] The corollary led subsequently to multiyear U.S. occupations of Cuba, Nicaragua, Haiti, and the Dominican Republic, prompted by internal disorders in these countries and default on their international debts.

Outside the Hemisphere, TR was the first American leader to take on an explicit peace-building role. He was the central figure in two significant cases.

During the nineteenth century the Qing dynasty weakened, and China became subject to frequent revolts and civil strife. Western powers and Japan eagerly sought concessions to control key ports and coastal territories. By contrast, the United States announced support for an Open Door, which called for respect for China's independence and for equal commercial opportunities in China for trading countries. Violence by the Boxers, militia forces encouraged by antiforeign elements at court and bent on expelling all foreigners, led to the massacre of missionaries and other foreigners. An international expedition in 1900 to relieve Western diplomatic outposts and insistence on Chinese government reparation opened China to further efforts at partition.

In 1904 Russia rebuffed a Japanese proposal that each have a free hand respectively in Manchuria and Korea. Japan then launched the Russo-Japanese War. Though Roosevelt initially sided with Japan, stunning Japanese victories persuaded him the Open Door could best be buttressed by a balance between the belligerents, not further Japanese successes. Despite their triumphs, the Japanese were overextended and wanted a peace agreement. They asked Roosevelt to use his good offices. Roosevelt convened a conference in Portsmouth,

New Hampshire. Under the Portsmouth Agreement of 1905, Russia disavowed territorial advantages in Manchuria and agreed to restore it "to the exclusive administration of China," although Japan received Russian mining and railroad concessions in the territory.[8] China was not a party to the Portsmouth Agreement, but relative internal peace was restored until the 1911 revolution brought an end to the Qing dynasty. Roosevelt demonstrated impressive skill as a diplomat and won the Nobel Peace Prize. U.S. interests were on the whole not enhanced, however, since the Japanese harbored lingering resentment over the settlement. Japan gave only lip service to the Open Door while expanding its political and commercial predominance in Manchuria.[9]

By 1900 Morocco, under pressure from interested European powers, was experiencing increasing internal disorder. The young Sultan 'Abd-al 'Aziz was plagued with tribal rebellion and popular discontent. A pretender set up a competing court on the Mediterranean coast. France and Spain used the turmoil to press their territorial designs. The British recognized the French sphere of interest in Morocco, as did Spain, bought off by recognition of its interests in northern Morocco. The Germans, who had recently acquired colonies in Africa, decided to oppose French sovereignty. Kaiser Wilhelm visited Tangier in early 1905. While expressing hope for continuation of a "free Morocco" under the authority of the Sultan and equality of commercial access, he was signaling that Germany wanted a role in any Moroccan arrangement. Berlin encouraged the Sultan to call for a conference to propose reforms, as an alternative to French demands for reorganization of security forces and state finances by France. The French intimated that war could break out. The Kaiser, carefully cultivated by Roosevelt during the early part of his presidency, asked the American to persuade France and Britain to accept a conference. Wilhelm indicated naively that Germany would accept "any decision [Roosevelt] considered fair and practical." The Germans got their conference—at Algeciras, Spain in 1906. Roosevelt worked out a compromise: the parties recognized the "sovereignty and independence" of the Sultan and "the integrity of his domains"; the police were placed under French and Spanish tutelage; control of the state bank was vested in several European powers; and the Open Door affirmed for foreign commerce.[10] The Moroccans were not consulted. The solution preserved peace among the European powers—if it was really threatened at all—but paved the way for a French protectorate over Morocco seven years later.

The acclaim that Roosevelt received for his diplomatic successes both at home and abroad, despite their long-term negative impact on the two countries most affected, whetted the appetite of some American leaders who saw the role of peace mediator as appropriate for a newly arrived "great power."

WILSONIAN PEACE-BUILDING

Woodrow Wilson was convinced that the United States had a vocation for peace—as "the light which shall . . . guide the feet of mankind to the goal of justice and liberty and peace."[11] A decade after TR's forays into mediation, Wilson launched a much more comprehensive American peace-building initiative, focused on emerging nations as well as recent belligerents. In attempting to secure a permanent peace at the end of World War I, Wilson wanted to make good on the rhetoric he had employed in bringing the United States into the conflict. In the war message to Congress affirming that "the world must be made safe for democracy," he sketched the outlines of a theory of peace-building:

[W]e shall fight for the things which we have always carried nearest our hearts—for democracy, for the rights of those who submit to authority to have a voice in their own governments, for the rights and liberties of small nations, for a universal dominion of right by such a concert of free peoples as shall bring peace and safety to all nations and make the world itself at last free.[12]

Wilson believed that international peace was basically dependent on the extension of the right of self-government to nations, large and small, and the protection of their independence and territorial integrity. Since the war had led to the collapse of empires—German, Austro-Hungarian, Russian and Ottoman—Wilson was mindful of self-government as it might apply to the unorganized remnants of these empires, particularly in Europe. He called for "security of life" and "an absolutely unmolested opportunity for autonomous development" for the nationalities of the Ottoman Empire. He invoked "a free, open-minded and absolutely impartial adjustment of all colonial claims," giving equal weight to the interests of the populations concerned and the equitable claims of the government whose title was to be determined. That did not mean an attack on the colonial empires of Britain and France, U.S. allies, but rather targeted colonies held by Germany. Wilson did not view the principles he advocated as self-implementing but considered them as requiring an association of nations to guarantee "political independence and territorial integrity to great and small states alike." A League of Nations, whose combined strength was greater than that of any single state or group of states, was essential to assure international justice and therefore to maintain the peace.[13] On several occasions, Wilson presented his proposed peace-building machinery as globalizing the Monroe Doctrine.

I am proposing, as it were, that the nations should with one accord adopt the doctrine of President Monroe as the doctrine of the world: that no nation should seek to extend its polity over any other nation or people, but . . . every people should be left free to determine its own polity, its own way of development, unhindered, unthreatened, unafraid, the little along with the great and powerful.[14]

Wilson was remarkably successful in his work as an international negotiator. The Treaty of Versailles reflected his input more than that of anyone else. In particular, the League of Nations Covenant provided for membership of "any fully self-governing State, Dominion or Colony." Decisions in the

League Assembly and more restricted Council required the agreement of all members present. Under the famous Article 10, League members undertook to "respect and preserve against external aggression the territorial integrity and existing political independence" of all members. Disputes likely to lead to a "rupture" of the peace and not subject to arbitration were to be submitted to the Council.

Wilson's vision of peace did not extend to League involvement in or application of measures for collective security to political strife within countries. A cornerstone provision of the Covenant was Article 15(8).

If the dispute between the parties is claimed by one of them, and is found by the Council, to arise out of a matter which by international law is solely within the jurisdiction of that Party, the Council ... shall make no recommendation as to its settlement.

Despite the Senate's rejection of the Versailles Treaty, Wilson introduced critical concepts into the future American approach to peace-building:

- Self-government is essential to sorting out issues of equity and justice and avoiding future violence; "peoples" must have a stake in their government;
- In dealing with the claims and agitations of peoples seeking self-government, the international community must give heavy weight to the interests of the populations concerned;
- Democracy is the normal test of whether self-government is taking place, elections are an important gauge of the legitimacy of an outcome and thus necessary to peace; and
- Collective international action is important in resolving disputes which may lead to war, many of which arise from internal political violence which impacts neighboring states.[15]

PEACE-BUILDING AFTER WORLD WAR II: ENEMY STATES

The task of peace-building for the Roosevelt and Truman administrations was a dual one, reconstructing Germany and Japan so as to eliminate future threats to peace from those powers and creating an international architecture to deal with threats to the peace from other sources.

Key to the approach to the defeated Axis powers were wartime summit decisions to secure unconditional surrender and carry out military occupation. They triggered the most extensive experiments in post-conflict reconstruction in history.

In Germany the Allies divided occupation responsibilities into zones, where each set up a military government. Cooperation broke down quickly between the Western allies and the Soviet Union but remained strong among the former.[16] The essential tasks were security, humanitarian assistance, civil administration, and reconstruction. Security was provided initially by the occupying armies. There was fear that renegade guerrillas drawn from German military forces would launch small-scale attacks on Allied forces.

The United States soon introduced a constabulary force of about 30,000, backed up by the 170,000 occupying troops remaining at the end of 1946. Humanitarian assistance focused on the feeding and care of 15 million German refugees from other parts of Europe. Civil administration concentrated at the outset on denazification, including the establishment of the Nuremberg Tribunal and sector-level tribunals run by Germans under Allied supervision. More gradually, following the dictate of the Potsdam Declaration, the Allied administration introduced democratic elections, starting with the county level and gradually extending to the state and national level. The first national election took place in 1949, but full sovereignty was not transferred in the Western sector until 1955.

Reconstruction was begun by the military governors of the occupation zones. U.S. military governor, General Lucius Clay, in particular, pressed for economic revival to reduce occupation costs. The United States provided billions of dollars in credits to Germany and other countries in Europe to finance the imports necessary for recovery, a flow which expanded significantly when the Marshall Plan was passed by the U.S. Congress in 1948.[17] The perceived Soviet threat to the Western sectors of Germany helped expand funding for recovery.

Although post-conflict policy for Japan was laid down at Potsdam, the U.S. role was much more predominant. Because of its central role in the final stages of the war with Japan, the United States, already frustrated by the division of authority in Germany, decided to take the lead.[18] A force of about 350,000 American troops was complemented initially by 45,000 British and Commonwealth troops. They oversaw demobilization of Japanese troops, which was actually carried out by renamed—and fully cooperative—Japanese Army and Navy ministries. Within five months of surrender, the Japanese armed forces were no more. The humanitarian task centered on providing food after the collapse of the food distribution system. American planners wanted to keep assistance at a minimum, but General MacArthur, Supreme Allied Commander, lobbied successfully to get the tonnage up, fearful that his political objectives would otherwise be hampered. Food aid, particularly for children, paid dividends in good will from the population.

The key issues for civil administration were how to govern—directly or through Japanese institutions—how to treat the emperor, and how to handle war crimes. Each was related to the objective of introducing democracy, an objective outlined in the Potsdam Declaration.[19] A shortage of U.S. personnel with language and governing skills led to a decision to use the existing government structure, while maintaining oversight. A staff of 4,000 reviewed all Japanese bureaucratic directives to ensure compliance with occupation policy but managed to keep its guidance sufficiently broad as to allow the Japanese latitude to manage in their own way. MacArthur and his staff became convinced, even before surrender, that the Emperor, despite his "war guilt," had to be retained as head of state because of the fanatic loyalty of his subjects.[20] The objective was to keep him as a symbol of the Japanese while vesting sovereign democratic authority in the Diet, the national parliament. One aspect of this approach was vigorously to prosecute war criminals, thereby separating the emperor, exempted from that group, from militarist leaders said to have duped him into war. In March 1946 MacArthur announced that the emperor and government of Japan would propose a new constitution to the Japanese people, a draft in fact largely written at MacArthur's headquarters.

Reconstruction policy focused on revival and reorganization of the Japanese economy. Initially the occupation concentrated on promoting equality of economic opportunity. The Japanese government was ordered to draft and enact a law guaranteeing workers the right to organize, strike, and bargain collectively. Thoroughgoing land reform doubled the share of farmers owning their own land. The occupation authorities had less success in breaking up the giant business oligopolies (*zaibatsu*). A total of 83 were broken down into their subsidiaries, but interlocking management and financial links were left largely intact. Actual revival of the Japanese economy came with the Korean War, as U.S. spending on Japanese exports soared.[21] The Korean conflict also expedited the end of the occupation. Worried about the threat from the "Sino-Soviet" bloc and seeing Japan as a potential ally, the Truman administration negotiated a Treaty of Peace and accompanying U.S.-Japan Security Treaty. Senate ratification in 1952 triggered formal transfer of sovereignty.

Post-conflict reconstruction in Germany and Japan applied to defeated enemy states and not to peace-building in countries engulfed by civil war. Nevertheless, the basic model used in these most extensive and successful examples of American peace-building, aided by unconditional surrender, has influenced subsequent efforts. The model of military-led reconstruction was applied only in Panama and Iraq, where the State Department and other civilian agencies initially took a backseat. Humanitarian assistance, particularly food aid, used to prevent starvation and gain good will for the occupiers, remains an element in virtually all reconstruction and stabilization (R&S) programs.[22] Demobilization and disarmament of armed groups is standard procedure. Complete elimination of the armed forces, at least for a significant period, successful in Japan and Germany, was attempted in Iraq but led to insurgency rather than internal peace. The introduction of democratic constitutionalism and elections is likewise a standard feature of post-conflict reconstruction.

PEACE-BUILDING AFTER WORLD WAR II: THE UNITED NATIONS

As World War II moved toward its close, there was consensus in the administration and Congress—in contrast to 1918—that the United States should take a leading role in creating an international architecture for peace-building.[23] Even so, President Roosevelt, mindful of Wilson's failures, avoided making public reference to a postwar organization of nations, while planning moved forward rapidly in the State Department on a draft constitution for such a body.[24] That planning process influenced in a fundamental way the United Nations Conference on International Organization (UNCIO) in San Francisco in April 1945. The U.S. delegation included Senate leaders, notably Republican Arthur Vandenberg, ranking minority member of the Foreign Relations Committee.

The UN system was set up fundamentally, though not entirely, as a system to prevent war.[25] It carried forward key principles from the League of Nations Covenant:

- All members shall settle their international disputes by peaceful means (2:3).
- All members shall refrain in their international relations from the threat or use of force against the territorial integrity or political independence of another state (2:4).
- Nothing in the Charter authorizes the United Nations to intervene in matters essentially within the domestic jurisdiction of any state (2:7).[26]

Chapter VI established a mechanism for "pacific settlement of disputes." The parties to any dispute likely to endanger peace shall "seek a solution by negotiation, enquiry, mediation, conciliation, arbitration, judicial settlement, resort to regional settlement or arrangements, or other peaceful means of their own choice." If they exhaust one or more of these remedies, they may avail themselves of the United Nations. Any UN member may bring up a dispute in the General Assembly or the Security Council. The General Assembly may inform the Security Council of "situations likely to endanger international peace and security." The Security Council, vested with the primary UN role on peace and security, may investigate a dispute to see if it endangers international peace and security and may make recommendations for a settlement. Chapter VI should be read in tandem with Article 99, which enables the Secretary-General to bring any matter to the attention of the Council he believes could threaten international peace and security.

The chapter represented the elaboration and broadening of peace-building mechanisms attempted over the previous half century, including mediation efforts of individuals like Theodore Roosevelt and a variety of techniques developed by the League.[27] American planners pressed successfully for giving a peace-building role to the General Assembly—and thus the entire UN membership—as a complement to the more decisive role of the Security Council.[28] The Charter thus reflects a certain democratization of peace-building by involving all self-governing states. It was in that sense a limited acknowledgment of the Wilsonian view that international peace was basically dependent on the extension of the right of self-government to nations, large and small, and their involvement in an international organization to keep the peace. It also marked the acceptance of broad multilateral diplomacy, exercised through debate open to all members, as one technique for peace-building.

Although Chapter VI today typically refers to traditional "peacekeeping," that term does not appear in the Charter. It emerged only in response to the 1956 Suez Crisis, when a "neutral" and "non-partial" UN Emergency Force

(UNEF) was dispatched with the consent of the parties to separate the armies of Israel and Egypt.[29]

Chapter VII. With the global violence of the previous decade looming large in international consciousness, the Charter set up a second mechanism for disputes crossing the threshold of violence or posing a significant threat to peace. Under Article 39, the Security Council determines the existence of a threat to or breach of peace or act of aggression. It makes recommendations or decides on measures to restore peace and security. It can call on the parties to take certain steps or impose economic sanctions on them. If it decides those measures are inadequate, it may authorize the deployment of armed forces as necessary to maintain or restore peace (Article 42). That is peace enforcement. Articles 43–47 anticipated the allocation by member states of military units to function under a Military Staff Committee guided by the Security Council, but those arrangements were never brought into effect. The Military Staff Committee exists, consisting of military representatives of the permanent members of the Security Council, but its role is limited to advising the Council on peacekeeping. In practice, when enforcement action has been attempted, it has been carried out by coalitions of willing states, with a Chapter VII mandate from the Security Council.[30]

For Roosevelt, who termed himself "a disillusioned Wilsonian," Chapter VII was the heart of a strengthened peace-building system. He was convinced that what was required was creation of "an international police power." In the words of Townsend Hoopes, FDR had "an ingrained belief in the primacy of the strong," who should exercise a "trusteeship of the powerful." By contrast, he considered that small nations, even those committed to peace, had no serious role to play in the policing function.[31] The international police power envisaged in Chapter VII, of course, depended on agreement among the "police chiefs."

Chapter VIII. The Charter also recognizes the importance of "regional arrangements" in maintaining or restoring peace. Article 52 enjoins regional bodies "consistent with the purposes and principles" of the United Nations "to make every effort to achieve pacific settlement of local disputes through such regional arrangements before referring them to the Security Council." The article was proposed by the United States under pressure from the Latin American countries, which sought a more robust regional security system than the periodic meetings of leaders and foreign ministers.[32] Article 53 authorized the Security Council to use regional arrangements for enforcement action but prohibited such action at the initiative of a regional body without Security Council approval. That provision buttressed the Monroe Doctrine, since the United States could exercise a veto in the Security Council over UN operations it might construe as outside intervention in the Americas. Over the next five decades a variety of regional arrangements emerged—e.g., the Organization of American States (OAS), the League of Arab States, the Organization of African Unity, the Association of Southeast Asian Nations, the European Union, plus smaller subregional groupings. Only a few of these organizations have played a role in peacekeeping.

PEACE-BUILDING IN A BIPOLAR WORLD

Although the United States was the major force shaping the UN Charter and its approach to conflict in the international arena, between 1949 and 1990 U.S. peace-building was primarily guided by the demands of the Cold War and its grand strategy of containment of the USSR and China. The conflicts to which the United States devoted most blood and treasure were Korea and Vietnam, at contested frontiers between Sino-Soviet and U.S. power. Both countries had been divided into Communist and non-Communist zones and successor states under international agreement.[33] There was active leftist insurgency in both South Korea and South Vietnam, but it had been effectively suppressed in the former by 1950. In each case, both sides wanted ultimate reunification, but on their own terms. Thus both the Korean and the Vietnam wars were in many respects internal conflicts, even though fighting crossed internationally recognized borders.

A North Korean offensive across the 38th parallel boundary, collapse of the South Korean forces, and occupation of Seoul led to U.S. military intervention. Washington sought UN Security Council endorsement of Chapter VII enforcement action against North Korea. A fortuitous Soviet boycott of Council sessions enabled passage of resolutions recommending assistance to the South in repelling the armed attack and contributions to a UN force led by the United States. When the Soviets returned to impose vetoes on further Council votes, the United States secured passage in the General Assembly of the Uniting for Peace Resolution, which authorized the Assembly, when the Council fails to meet its responsibility for a specific threat, to make recommendations for specific measures for the use of force to restore peace.[34] Astute use of the UN Charter enabled Washington to establish and maintain leadership of UN enforcement action on the Korean conflict. Although an offensive into North Korea was hurled back by Chinese entry into the war, ultimately leading to stalemate and armistice at the 38th parallel, the independence of South Korea was preserved.[35]

In the late 1950s the North Vietnamese government activated Viet Cong guerrilla cadres in the south and aided them militarily and logistically in their attacks on the Saigon government. The United States responded to South Vietnam's requests for assistance, first with military advisors and then with combat troops. With the Soviet Union and China arrayed on the side of North Vietnam and nonaligned Asia suspicious of or hostile to the American position, Washington made no formal effort to enlist the United Nations. Vietnam was discussed only cursorily in the Security Council and did not reach the agenda of the Assembly. Instead, the United States established a "coalition of the willing" with Australia, Canada, South Korea, the Philippines, New Zealand, and Thailand. Secretary-General U Thant urged the parties to negotiate a settlement, but his modest efforts encountered U.S. hostility or indifference.[36] The Paris Accords, which resulted in a cease-fire and the withdrawal of American forces, were negotiated outside the UN framework. Vietnam was forcibly reunited by North Vietnamese forces in 1975.

Although Chapters VI and VIII were originally envisaged as an international legal framework for dealing with disputes between states, each proved relevant to the resolution of internal conflicts which become internationalized because of their impact on neighboring states or the wider international community. In fact, after World War II the predominant mode of conflict became war taking place within the territory of a single state.[37] In particular, decolonization in Asia and Africa led to a host of disputes which either descended into internal political violence or threatened to do so. Washington was highly selective about involvement, weighing its interests carefully and giving particular attention to the impact of the conflict on the superpower balance. Nonetheless, drawing on a variety of diplomatic, institutional, and legal tools, the U.S. government was the most active mediator of international conflicts between 1945 and 1990.[38] Four additional examples give a flavor of the American approach.

Congo

The former Belgian Congo was the first African crisis for UN peacekeeping. The United States played a major role in decisions taken. Washington was worried that the Soviets would seize control of the heart of the African continent through radical nationalist leader Patrice Lumumba and his *Mouvement National Congolais* (MNC) party. Yet the Eisenhower administration had no sympathy for European financial interests trying to divide the Congo into European-controlled fiefdoms, particularly copper-rich Katanga. It feared the secession of Katanga, announced within days of independence in July 1960, would mobilize furious African leaders behind the Soviet Union. So it and the Kennedy administration strongly backed UN Secretary-General Dag Hammarskjold's effort to promote a united Congo, hoping that UN peacekeepers would buy time for integration efforts in the new state. ONUC, a peacekeeping force of African and Asian troops which eventually reached 20,000, began moving into Congo within days of the Congolese government's request for assistance.[39] The initial mandate of ONUC was to ensure withdrawal of Belgian forces and assist the government in maintaining law and order. It was later modified to include maintaining territorial integrity and political independence, forestalling civil war, and securing removal of all foreign military, including mercenaries, not under UN command.[40] ONUC ended the secession of Katanga in January 1963, and UN forces pulled out 17 months later. The first two U.S. ambassadors to the Congo, Clare Timberlake and Edmund Gullion, played a proconsular role in the new state.

Civilian political groups remained bitterly divided even after Katanga was reintegrated. Not long after the peacekeepers departed, leftist rebels captured Kisangani and set up a "people's republic." Numerous European and African hostages were slaughtered. In 1964 the United States air-dropped Belgian paratroops into Kisangani, routing the rebels and saving remaining hostages. There was widespread opposition to this intervention in Africa, and Congolese civilian leaders were further discredited.[41] From the chaos, a military leader emerged who caught the eye of those who wanted, above all, stability in the Congo. Lt. Col. Joseph Désiré Mobutu, first Congolese army chief of staff and already linked to Belgian and U.S. intelligence, demonstrated a decisiveness and articulateness that attracted positive attention in American policy circles. After brief military interventions in 1960 and 1964, he permanently seized power in November 1965. The United States, Belgium, and the United Nations made no significant objections. Seeing Mobutu as a bulwark against Soviet influence, the United States poured in assistance for decades, long after the Congolese leader's star was tarnished by staggering corruption. Aside from pressing periodically for economic reform, the U.S. government paid little more than lip service to promoting peaceful and democratic political change. The alliance with Mobutu continued into the 1990s but weakened with the end of the Cold War.

Cyprus

The agreements for decolonization of Cyprus in 1960 underwrote the territorial integrity of the island, entrenched in the constitution fixed proportions of Greeks and Turks in various parts of the government, and guaranteed human rights. The settlement left unresolved the demand of the Greek Cypriot population (80% of the population) for union with Greece and adamant opposition by the Turkish Cypriot minority. Constitutional revisions proposed by Greek Cypriot President Makarios aimed at union with Greece set off disorders on the island which brought Turkey and Greece to the brink of war in 1964. The Security Council then created a peacekeeping force, the United Nations Force in Cyprus (UNFICYP), to prevent a recurrence of fighting and restore law and order.[42] That force has been in Cyprus ever since. A deterioration of the situation in 1967 led to a Turkish invasion threat. Alarmed by the rapid deterioration of relations between two key NATO members on the eastern frontier of the alliance, President Lyndon Johnson appointed Cyrus Vance, later Secretary of State in the Carter administration, as his special envoy to promote negotiations among Greece, Turkey, and the Cypriot government. Those negotiations eventually foundered, leading to de facto partition of the island. Partition hardened in 1974 when a coup d'état by Greek Cypriots supporting union with Greece, abetted by some Greek support, led to a Turkish invasion, establishing Turkish Cypriot control over the northern part of the island. An informal cease-fire began later that year which has largely remained in effect ever since. Since 1974 the United States has provided assistance to the island "aimed at reunification of the island and designed to reduce tensions and promote peace and cooperation between the two communities on Cyprus."[43] Essentially unperturbed by the status quo of rough balance between Turkish and Greek interests, Washington did not attempt an activist role again until the end of the Cold War.

Ethiopia

In 1941 Britain pushed Italy out of Ethiopia, which it had conquered in the run-up to World War II, and out of Eritrea, the colony to the north it acquired in the 1890s. Emperor Haile Selassie reoccupied his throne, and the British temporarily took over the administration of Eritrea. The Emperor, a master diplomat, astutely lined up American support for uniting Eritrea with Ethiopia, arguing the ex-colony was historically part of the Ethiopian Empire. The prospects of a communications base in Eritrea, ideally situated for keeping an eye on Soviet activity in the Middle East, was an attractive selling point for Washington. Alliance with Washington was further cemented by the dispatch of 1,000 Ethiopian troops to fight under the UN flag in Korea. In 1950 the UN General Assembly, with U.S. support, resolved that Eritrea should "constitute an autonomous unit federated with Ethiopia under the sovereignty of the Ethiopian crown."[44]

Although there was relatively little resistance in Eritrea to the idea of association with Ethiopia at that time, the incompatibility between the Ethiopian system, where all authority lay with the Emperor, and the fledgling democratic system in Eritrea, adumbrated by the British after 1945, asserted itself almost immediately. The Crown pressured the Eritrean government to accede to tighter imperial control, bribing Eritrean leaders and co-opting them with high posts in Addis Ababa. Political parties disintegrated. Resistance engendered political killings and suppression of demonstrations with live fire.[45] In 1962 the Eritrean assembly voted to dissolve itself and make Eritrea a province of the Ethiopian Empire. Although any change in the status of Eritrea, as set forth in the General Assembly resolution, should have been debated by the United Nations, that body basically ignored the *fait accompli*.[46] Washington did not remonstrate.

Armed resistance began almost immediately in the outlying areas of Eritrea, gathering strength over the years. In 1973 the imperial government was overthrown, and the radical Marxist Derg (council) realigned Ethiopian foreign policy with Moscow. Massive Soviet military support enabled Ethiopian forces to regain the initiative temporarily in the late 1970s, but a decade later, the Derg was reeling from twin rebellions in Eritrea and Tigré, and Soviet support was withdrawn. Even during the Derg period, when Ethiopian foreign policy was bitterly hostile to the United States, Washington continued to support Ethiopian "territorial integrity," in deference to the wishes of the African states. In 1991 the Derg fell. The victorious Eritrean and Tigrean leadership met in London under U.S. sponsorship to agree that Eritrea might become independent after a referendum. Only at the end of the Cold War did the United States take on the role of peacemaker between Ethiopia and Eritrea.

Nigeria

Africa's most populous country came to independence in 1960 as a federal state with deeply chiseled regional divides between the populous North, under traditional Hausa-Fulani leadership, and the more educated West and East, where Yoruba and Igbo politicians held sway, respectively. Regional and federal elections administered by Britain, the colonial power, gave the preponderance of political power to the North. Sharply contested postindependence elections and charges of vote rigging contributed to a military coup in 1966 which killed mostly Northern political leaders and created the impression of Igbo leadership. A countercoup the same year killed Igbo officers and unleashed massacres of Igbo residents of the North. The Eastern military governor then declared the independence of that region as the Republic of Biafra. The rump Federal Military Government (FMG) suppressed the rebellion over a 30-month period. High civilian loss of life from starvation in the rebel area caused a global humanitarian outcry.

The outbreak of the civil war posed something of a dilemma for the United States, which was building a relationship with Africa's new giant. Major U.S. oil companies had operations off both the Midwest State, controlled by the FMG, and off the Eastern Region. There were doubts that Nigeria could survive as a single state and much sympathy among Americans for Biafra, which mounted an impressive public diplomacy campaign. At the outset, U.S. policymakers expressed determination to avoid American intervention in the dispute underlying the war. When the FMG asked to purchase U.S. arms to suppress the rebellion, Washington announced a weapons embargo toward both sides, angering Lagos and prompting a major Soviet sale of munitions, including MIG fighter planes.[47] However, Washington was not neutral. The United States announced its support for the territorial integrity of Nigeria and for the principle, enshrined in the Charter of the Organization of African Unity (OAU) that political boundaries of independent African states should not be changed by force.[48] The U.S. government held that the matter was an essentially African affair and most legitimately the province of the OAU. In response to cries from the American public for UN action, the Johnson administration reported that the African states were adamantly opposed to placing it on the UN agenda and would forestall an effective UN response.[49] The United States tried to draw a sharp distinction between political and humanitarian involvement in the conflict, and played a key role in establishing and supporting the relief effort. The Nixon administration maintained basically the same policy, a reasonably comfortable fit because the United States and the USSR were on the same side.

Nigeria's size and influence kept the conflict off the agenda of the General Assembly and the Security Council, but not off the regional agenda. In response to Nigeria's plea to the Secretary-General to avoid action to impair the sovereignty and integrity of Nigeria, U Thant said the Nigerian question should be regarded as "purely within" domestic jurisdiction. Although several African states, plus France and the Netherlands, called for UN action to bring about a negotiated solution, there was insufficient support. Instead, the locus of international political action was the OAU. Although Lagos initially opposed the regional body's involvement, it acquiesced in a resolution at the 1967 OAU summit which condemned "secession in any member state" and termed the conflict "an internal affair, the solution to which is primarily the responsibility of Nigerians themselves."[50] Emphasis on Nigerian domestic jurisdiction quietly eroded. Peace negotiations were held on three different occasions between Biafran and FMG delegations under the auspices of the OAU.[51] In that sense, the Nigerian conflict was "Africanized," with stress on finding a solution within the context of a single Nigeria. Biafra refused to concede that point, and the war continued until its surrender.[52]

PEACE-BUILDING SINCE 1989

In 1989 Soviet General Secretary Mikhail Gorbachev withdrew Soviet forces from Afghanistan. In Poland the Solidarity union was legalized. Demonstrations in East Germany destroyed the Berlin Wall. That eventful year coincided with the beginning of the first Bush administration. The elimination of Soviet military and political rivalry was confirmed by the dissolution of the USSR in 1992 and the emergence of Boris Yeltsin as the elected president of the Russian Federation. For the first time since World War II, the United States faced a new international situation: no interstate security threat and unquestioned U.S. global preeminence.

The past three presidencies have displayed sharply different policy tendencies toward internal conflicts with international repercussions.

George H. W. Bush: Aggression Halted, Civil War Peace-Building Eschewed

Bush and his primary foreign policy guide, National Security Advisor Brent Scowcroft, were hopeful that the changed situation could usher in a *new world order*—a period of successful resolution of long-standing international stability problems, characterized *inter alia* by successful peace-building. This view is apparent in Bush's statements to Congress in 1990 about Iraq's invasion of Kuwait.

We stand today at a unique and extraordinary moment. The crisis in the Persian Gulf, as grave as it is, also offers a rare opportunity to move toward an historic period of cooperation. Out of these troubled times, our . . . objective—a new world order—can emerge: a new era—freer from the threat of terror, stronger in the pursuit of justice, and more secure in the quest for peace. An era in which the nations of the world, East and West, North and South, can prosper and live in harmony. A hundred generations have searched for this elusive path to peace, while a thousand wars raged across the span of human endeavor. Today that new world is struggling to be born, a world quite different from the one we've known. A world where the rule of law supplants the rule of the jungle. A world in which nations recognize the shared responsibility for freedom and justice. A world where the strong respect the rights of the weak.[53]

In response to Iraq's flagrant violation of Article 2:4 of the UN Charter, President Bush assembled a broad coalition of 33 other countries, which contributed a quarter of the troops. The Bush administration worked hard and successfully to persuade the Russians and Chinese not to stand in the way. Consequently, the UN Security Council blessed Chapter VII enforcement action under Resolution 678.[54] The Gulf states, especially Saudi Arabia, financed about 40 percent of the war, and Japan and Germany about a quarter. The ground attack lasted only five days before Iraq accepted U.S. cease-fire terms. The administration had limited war aims: end the occupation of Kuwait, reduce Iraq's military capabilities, and reassert international law. It did not try to oust Saddam Hussein from power because it believed that, if U.S. forces entered Baghdad, the coalition would disintegrate. It also feared that Iraq might break up.[55] This was the exercise of predominant American military power in tandem with persuasive multilateral diplomacy, making skilled use of the UN machinery.

The Bush administration viewed Iraqi aggression against Kuwait as the first great test of "the new world order." It was actually, however, a throwback to the pre–Cold War situation in which the most serious danger to international peace was armed aggression by one state against another—exactly the situation Chapter VII of the UN Charter was designed for.[56] Instead, the road ahead was lined with civil conflicts dramatically bursting upon the international scene. The first Bush administration was reluctant to adopt a leadership role as peacemaker in these conflicts. Even in Somalia it attempted to restrict its operations to humanitarian assistance. It preferred to keep its attention focused on evolving a relationship with Russia supportive of that country's democratic opening and on managing the chill in relations with China after suppression of the Tiananmen Square democracy demonstrations in 1989.

1. Liberia is the African country with which the United States has had most continuous contact since the mid-nineteenth century. In the 1960s and 1970s the United States maintained a large embassy and a substantial aid program. In 1980 an indigenous group of noncommissioned army officers led by Samuel Doe violently overthrew the Americo-Liberian regime representing the long dominant minority descended from freed American slaves. The U.S. government kept the Doe regime out of Soviet and Libyan orbits through generous aid. After Doe rigged the 1985 elections and tightened repression, Washington became disenchanted. At the beginning of 1990, Charles Taylor, a former member of the Doe regime, launched an insurrection which reached the outskirts of the capital Monrovia by midyear. Fearing a bloodbath and long-term instability, the Assistant Secretary of State for African Affairs tried to arrange Doe's exile in nearby Togo. The Bush White House ordered the Assistant Secretary to desist, because the United States no

longer had a significant interest in Liberia's fate.[57] The result was a decade of civil war and instability for the entire subregion. Instead of exercising leadership, Washington backed diplomatically the decision by the West African countries, led by Nigeria, to deploy a force to Liberia, essentially to block Taylor from coming to power by military force.

2. Somalia. In 1991 Siad Barre, longtime Somali leader and U.S. ally since the 1980s, was driven from power. Central authority crumbled amidst the maneuverings of warlords. There was widespread killing of civilians, and starvation threatened 200,000. In 1992, the Bush administration, in its last months in office, took the lead at the United Nations in promoting Operation Restored Hope to provide humanitarian assistance, under the auspices of a unified task force (UNITAF), led by U.S. forces.[58] Thousands of lives were saved. The United Nations engaged both warlords and civilians in a modicum of political dialogue, but the United States made no effort to play a central political role in ending the conflict.

3. The Balkans. In 1980 the death of Marshall Tito released the nationalistic pressures he had suppressed in Yugoslavia for 35 years. Six years later Slobodan Milosevic gained power. His embrace of Serb nationalism led to declarations of independence from Yugoslavia—and Serbia—by Slovenia and Croatia in 1991 and Macedonia in 1992. The Bosnian government also declared independence in 1992, after a referendum, but Bosnian Serb representatives wanted to remain in Yugoslavia. With Serbia's support, the Bosnian Serbs launched armed attacks to divide Bosnia along ethnic lines and create a "greater Serbia." The Bush administration initially sought to persuade the Yugoslav parties to maintain the unity of the country. When they split off, however, the United States adopted a hands-off position, leaving the matter to the Europeans.[59] Fighting and atrocities continued.

4. Haiti. In 1990, Jean-Bertrand Aristide was overwhelmingly elected President of Haiti. He was overthrown the next year by dissatisfied army elements, supported by many of the country's economic elite. The coup contributed to a massive exodus of Haitians by boat, mostly to the United States. Over the next three years the OAS and the United Nations undertook various initiatives to end *de facto* military government. The Bush administration supported them but eschewed an active leadership role.

Bill Clinton: Experiments in Peace-Building

The Clinton administration initially de-emphasized traditional foreign affairs in favor of positioning the United States for long-term economic growth in a globalizing world. International politics quickly intruded. The Clinton response, including peace-building in the Global South, bore the marks of political experimentation. De-emphasizing foreign policy played into the hands of those in Congress who wished to reduce U.S. international commitments. Appropriations for the international affairs account dropped during Clinton's first six years, hampering his freedom of action.[60]

1. Somalia was the initial challenge. Despite the success of UNITAF on the humanitarian level, chief warlord Mohammed Farah Aideed and his militia soon began to intimidate the peacekeepers. Twenty-four Pakistani troops were murdered. The new Clinton administration decided to take a more aggressive approach. A new United Nations Operations in Somalia (UNOSOM II) sought to neutralize Aideed. During an October 1993 raid to seize him, led by U.S. Delta Force and Ranger units, two Black Hawk helicopters were shot down. Eighteen U.S. troops were killed, and some of the bodies were dragged through the streets of Mogadishu. The highly critical political and public reaction at home spooked the Clinton administration. U.S. forces were withdrawn in 1994 and remaining UN forces in 1995, leaving chaos. One critique charged that "it would be difficult to imagine . . . a more poorly executed and ill-timed 'hand-off' than the UNITAF-UNOSOM [II] transition. . . . Leadership, mandate and oversight were all changed, and while the mandate was more ambitious, the military resources available to support it were cut back severely."[61] At the close of 2008, there was still no single effective government in Somalia.

2. Rwanda. The Somalia experience created a Clinton administration allergy to African peace-building which shaped its response to Rwanda. Before independence in 1962 the Hutu population revolted, overthrowing the Tutsi monarchy. Belgian colonialists handed over power at independence to the Hutus, while 160,000 Tutsis fled to neighboring countries, most to Uganda. In 1990 Tutsis who had become part of the Ugandan army broke off and invaded Rwanda. The invaders established a base in-country. Inconclusive fighting led to a cease-fire and political talks with the Hutu president. Meanwhile, a Hutu extremist plot was brewing. In 1994 a plane carrying the president and his counterpart from Burundi was shot down while landing in Kigali, the signal for genocide against Tutsis and moderate Hutus. Over 800,000 died within three months, in spite of the presence of a 2,500 person UN force (UNAMIR). UNAMIR was charged with supervising the cease-fire but had no mandate to protect civilians. The U.S. administration stood by passively. The United Nations, rather than reinforcing UNAMIR, cut it by almost 90 percent. In June, under international pressure, the Security Council reversed itself and authorized a level of 5,500, but it was too late. The United States neither contributed troops nor provided lift for the additional troops. The genocide was eventually halted in June, when the Tutsi invader force defeated the Rwandan army. The Rwandan experience was such a blot on his administration's record that Bill Clinton, during a six-nation visit to Africa in 1998, made a special stop in Kigali to acknowledge that the United States and the international community had been too slow to act and "did not immediately call these crimes by their rightful name: genocide."[62]

3. Haiti marked a turning point for the administration. An initial misstep was ultimately redeemed by decisive multilateral action. International dissatisfaction with the military overthrow of the elected Aristide regime continued to grow after Clinton assumed office. The Security Council's threat of an oil

and arms embargo led to a negotiated agreement providing for Aristide's return and for UN peacekeepers, but, perhaps emboldened by Somalia and doubtful that there would be a resort to force, the military authorities refused to permit the lightly armed advance team to come ashore at Port-au-Prince.[63] Since the forces were coming under a Chapter VI exercise in peacekeeping, UN and U.S. officials were anticipating a permissive entry, but the image of the U.S. naval vessel being turned away was a humiliation for Clinton. Subsequently, in mid-1994 the United States persuaded the Security Council to shift to Chapter VII powers. The Council authorized member states "to use all necessary means" to facilitate the departure of Haiti's military leadership and to restore Haiti's constitutionally elected government to power.[64] The United States took the lead in forming a multinational force of 21,000 to carry out the UN's mandate. President Clinton dispatched a negotiating team led by former President Jimmy Carter to persuade Gen. Cedras and his military regime to step aside. In the end, however, notification that the 82nd Airborne Division was in the air convinced Cedras to accept exile, while Aristide returned to Port-au-Prince. That achievement did not end instability. Quarrels between Aristide and his successor, a dubious election in 2000 which brought Aristide back to the presidency, and gridlock for government business did not halt the gradual phasing out of U.S. and other military forces that same year. Although Haiti was not viewed at the time as a Clinton foreign policy success, it marked an important step in peace-building: first use of Chapter VII authority to restore democracy in an internal conflict with broad implications for the region—in this case the threat of massive refugee flows.[65]

4. The Balkans. The Clinton administration was more sympathetic than its predecessor to the Bosnian Muslim cause, but there was deep division within the administration about the wisdom of U.S. involvement. About 250,000 persons had died and another 2.7 million became refugees. In 1995 the Srebrenica massacre of thousands of Muslim prisoners galvanized Washington into becoming fully invested in a solution.[66] That effort also involved experimentation, but with more positive results. Diplomacy was coordinated with military operations.[67] U.S. air strikes against Bosnian Serb positions, combined with a ground offensive by Croat and Muslim armies, led to three weeks of high-pressure negotiations at an Ohio Air Force base.[68] The Dayton Accords divided Bosnia into 51 percent under the Muslim/Croat Federation of Bosnia and Herzegovina (largely Muslim and Croat) and 49 percent under the Republica Srpska (primarily Serb), with a weak central government in Sarajevo. The NATO Implementation Force (IFOR)—60,000 troops, including 20,000 Americans—took over from the ineffective UN force at the end of 1995. Some 20,000 NATO troops remained in Bosnia till the end of 2004, when they were replaced by a European Union-led contingent (EUFOR).[69]

Kosovo became an "autonomous" Albanian-majority province of Serbia after World War II. After Tito's death the Kosovar Albanians agitated for full republic status. Milosevic revoked the autonomous status of Kosovo and began to fire Albanians from government jobs. When peaceful protests led by nationalist leader Ibrahim Rugova were unavailing, some Kosovar Albanians formed the Kosovo Liberation Army (KLA) and demanded independence. In late 1998, Milosevic unleashed a brutal police and military campaign against the KLA, including atrocities against civilians. Large numbers of ethnic Albanians were displaced or killed. The Security Council requested the Yugoslav government to cease mistreatment of the civilian population, but both China and Russia threatened to veto to block any action, when Belgrade did not comply. Instead the Serbian ethnic cleansing campaign provoked a 1999 military response from NATO, under U.S. leadership. After 79 days of aerial bombing, Milosevic capitulated. International forces known as KFOR under NATO command, initially including 7,000 Americans, moved into Kosovo. The United Nations got back into action only after Milosevic's surrender, when it established the UN Mission in Kosovo (UNMIK).[70] KFOR worked closely with UNMIK in an attempt to ensure protection for all of Kosovo's communities, especially the now isolated Serbian minority.

After a slow start, the Clinton administration found its footing in the Balkans. Concluding in this instance that the United Nations was an ineffective instrument for ending the violence, it turned to NATO, which became peace enforcer and then peacekeeper, working in tandem with the United Nations. Washington thereby endowed NATO with a post–Cold War role, a momentous precedent for Afghanistan after 9/11.[71]

5. Liberia. The new found peace-building activism of the Clinton administration extended in more modest fashion to Liberia, where Charles Taylor's forces and the ECOMOG peacekeeping force dispatched in 1990 by Economic Community of West African States (ECOWAS) were stalemated. In 1995, under Congressional pressure, the White House named a Special Presidential Envoy for Liberia.[72] One new approach might have been to seek UN involvement, either to supplant or reinforce ECOMOG. At that point, the United Nations was simply providing military observers to monitor ECOMOG and try to keep it neutral. With arrears to the UN rising and Congressional support for the institution at historic lows, the strategy chosen was instead to strengthen U.S. backing for the leadership role of West African leaders in finding a settlement. Supported by American diplomacy, Ghanaian President (and ECOWAS chairman) Jerry Rawlings forged a bargain between rebel leader Charles Taylor and Nigerian military dictator Sani Abacha, whose troops formed the bulk of ECOMOG. The 1995 Abuja Agreement temporarily ended the Liberian civil war and created a reasonably fair electoral process which made Taylor President of Liberia in 1997. It was a pyrrhic victory for peace-building. Once in office, Taylor sought to destroy his political opponents, divert Liberia's resources to his personal accounts, and expand his regional influence by supporting rebellion in Sierra Leone. Armed resistance to Taylor revived. U.S. diplomacy continued, eventually moving toward sanctions, but had little effect.

George W. Bush: War on Terror and the Peace-Building Enterprise

In his 2000 campaign George W. Bush decried an activist, interventionist foreign policy and indicated he would be more selective than Clinton in assuming foreign commitments.[73] He was critical not only of Clinton's Somalia intervention but also of the use of U.S. troops in the Balkans. His early pronouncements as President asserted a desire to avoid being drawn into "endless" negotiations in which neither party seemed willing to compromise. The main referent was Israel and Palestine, but his statements hinted that his administration would not take an active peace-builder role.

The September 11, 2001 attacks on the World Trade Center and the Pentagon produced a 180 degree shift on foreign policy activism, while bringing to the surface basic orientations and reflexes toward national security hitherto partly obscured. The "global war on terror" (GWOT), as applied first to Afghanistan and then to Iraq, provides the major—but hardly the entire—context for studying the approach taken by the George W. Bush administration to peace-building and the deployment of U.S. government agencies for that purpose.

1. Afghanistan. When the Taliban regime in Afghanistan failed to respond positively to the U.S. ultimatum to hand over bin Laden and al-Qa'ida, Bush confirmed the U.S. objective as regime change. The strategy adopted was intervention in a civil war. Following the withdrawal of the Soviet Union in 1989, Afghanistan plunged into an anarchy of political violence and warlordism. Eventually, the Taliban, ethnically largely Pashtun, emerged to gain control of Kabul and most of the rest of the country. Resistance continued from the Northern Alliance, led by Tajiks, Uzbeks, and Hazaras, but largely confined to northern mountain fastnesses.[74] Instead of a full-scale American military assault followed by occupation, CIA operatives and about 300 Special Forces provided critical support for the Northern Alliance and other sympathetic warlords. They succeeded in overthrowing the Taliban regime within two months. The UN Security Council backed U.S. action as a legitimate act of self-defense under the Charter.

2. Iraq. The Bush administration's Iraq project, launched within the Defense Department in 2001 and gathering steam internationally by the first anniversary of 9/11, also aimed at regime change. The arguments presented relied partly on Iraq's violation of Security Council resolutions in the dozen years since the Gulf War but more centrally on Iraq's putative link to global terrorism. The link, subsequently revealed to be nonexistent, was presented as twofold: (a) the threat stemming from weapons of mass destruction being manufactured and stored by the Saddam regime—and thus potentially available to international terrorism—and (b) a tie between the Saddam regime and al-Qa'ida—and, by implication, the 9/11 attacks. At the insistence of British Prime Minister Tony Blair, the United States reluctantly sought Security Council sanction for the use of force. It obtained an initial resolution

under Chapter VII threatening "serious consequences" if Iraq did not comply with an intrusive inspection regime for weapons of mass destruction, but dropped the effort to secure a second resolution more explicitly sanctioning force, when France announced it would veto.[75] In the end, the administration took the position that Iraq's violation of previous Council resolutions, coupled with the first resolution, provided Washington with ample authority for the use of force. Unlike in the case of Afghanistan, planning for Iraq envisaged from the beginning an overwhelming air and ground assault.[76]

The administration did very little planning for post-conflict reconstruction in either Afghanistan or Iraq. In Afghanistan, the Defense Department wanted to concentrate on capturing or killing al-Qa'ida members and quick redeployment to new centers of the terrorism struggle as necessary. The NATO force (International Security Assistance Force, ISAF) which deployed to Afghanistan in support of the United States was confined to Kabul for more than a year rather than providing security around the country. In Iraq it was assumed that the overthrow of Saddam would prompt an "open arms" response to American forces, obviating the need for a large occupying army. Police and bureaucrats would go right back to work. A large injection of post-reconstruction funds would not be necessary because Iraq's oil revenues would finance reconstruction.[77]

As insurgency expanded in both theaters, there was belated recognition that effective R&S were vital to American success. That recognition launched a scramble to develop new formulas and interagency mechanisms for peace-building under increasingly difficult circumstances. Tied down in Iraq and Afghanistan, the George W. Bush administration found itself employing more traditional tools of peace-building in other conflicts engaging U.S. interests.

3. Sudan. The one conflict on which the Bush administration took the peace-building initiative was Sudan. During the 2000 campaign the Bush team was pressured by conservative evangelicals to play a more active role in ending the Sudan civil war and the ordeal of Southern Sudanese Christians.[78] Just before September 11, Bush appointed former Republican Sen. John Danforth as Special Envoy for Sudan. Danforth persuaded the Bush administration to back a regional and international approach. Mediation over a three-year period by the Horn of Africa regional organization IGAD (the Intergovernmental Authority on Development), backed by intense American diplomacy with the parties, led to the 2005 Comprehensive Peace Agreement (CPA). The outbreak of conflict in Darfur in 2003 placed obstacles in the way of improved U.S.-Sudan relations and distracted the international community from assisting both sides in implementing the complex CPA. Protecting the civilian population in Darfur and seeking to arrange an effective negotiation process for its diverse warring parties eventually became the major U.S. peace-building focus in Sudan.

4. Liberia. When unruly armed factions converged on Monrovia in mid-2003, as the Taylor regime crumbled, new pressures mounted on Washington to intervene. The interagency debate was intense. Eventually the

administration deployed a small force of marines for 90 days in coordination with a new West African peacekeeping contingent as a bridge to a full-fledged UN peace force of 15,000. Washington arranged exile for Taylor and worked behind the scenes to help produce a peace settlement brokered by ECOWAS. The United States also mobilized a major international assistance package for post-conflict reconstruction, including fair elections.

5. Haiti. The Bush administration reluctantly became drawn into dealing with escalating political conflict and violence between President Aristide and the opposition. The United States initially attempted to resolve the crisis through the OAS. By 2004 a violent rebellion was moving toward Port-au-Prince. Aristide executed a letter of resignation, which he later claimed was signed under American duress, and departed for Africa. A Multilateral Interim Force led by the United States set up a transitional government pending elections but phased out quickly in favor a UN peacekeeping mission (MINUSTAH) led by Brazil. The Bush administration has resisted significant involvement with MINUSTAH.

The last three cases demonstrate that, despite disdain expressed for the United Nations before and after the attack on Iraq, the Bush administration worked closely with both the United Nations and regional organizations on peace-building. Such collaboration is apparent in the mobilization of peacekeeping forces for Haiti, Liberia, and Sudan—conflicts affecting U.S. interests, but engaging briefly only small numbers of U.S. forces, if any. In Afghanistan and Iraq, the United States did not support UN peacekeeping, but somewhat belatedly, especially in Iraq, backed a UN post-conflict reconstruction role which has not been particularly successful.

* * *

An American vocation for peace-building began with the Monroe Doctrine, motivated by expansionism, the desire to forestall European meddling in the New World, and the sense of American exceptionalism.[79] The vocation became significant only with the emergence of the United States as a world power, when occupation became a tool for dealing with internal crises in the Caribbean states and when American services were sought for the first time to mediate interstate crises outside the Hemisphere. Woodrow Wilson, America's most ambitious peace-builder President, viewed the Covenant of the League of Nations as globalizing the best aspects of the Monroe Doctrine—defense of the independence of fragile states. Important aspects of Wilson's vision were carried forward into the UN Charter in the more tough-minded concepts of Franklin Roosevelt and the detailed proposals of American planners. Although the Cold War deflected the hopes of UN founders for management of serious conflict through peace enforcement, the United States successfully used the UN machinery to protect the independence of South Korea and to maintain the territorial integrity of the Congo, the first civil war challenge of the postwar period. While very selective in its involvement, the United States became the leading world mediator of conflict.

As civil wars became the predominant form of international conflict, Chapters VI, VII, and VIII of the Charter proved surprisingly adaptable to the challenge. The immediate post–Cold War period saw a proliferation of these conflicts, particularly in Africa, and a greatly expanded international effort, centered on the United Nations, to cope with them. The George H. W. Bush administration, triumphant in the Gulf War, supported the United Nations but resisted being drawn into major civil conflicts. The Clinton administration was more experimental, applying lessons learned from failure in Somalia and Rwanda which proved useful in Haiti and the Balkans. The George W. Bush administration, initially rejecting the Clinton approach as "social work," dismantled what machinery its predecessor had put in place. The consequences of failure to recognize the imperative of R&S in Iraq and Afghanistan, however, brought about a broad reappraisal of the peace-building process by 2004.

The last two administrations—and in particular, the second Bush administration after the initial debacle of stabilization in Iraq—devoted considerable energy and attention to designing an interagency approach for dealing with conflict and to implementing effective programs of post-conflict reconstruction. These efforts engaged the key U.S. international affairs agencies and generated numerous new institutions and offices charged with specific aspects of peace-building.

This study examines the peace-building role of these agencies as it has evolved over the past two decades. At the beginning of the period the President—and his National Security Advisor (NSA)—looked to the leadership of the State and Defense Departments. The Secretary of State in turn relied for staffing and the day-to-day diplomacy of conflict resolution on the geographic bureau concerned. The Secretary of Defense relied on his international security bureaucracy on the policy side and the relevant geographic combatant command on the operational side. By the end of the period, an Interagency Management System (IMS) had been formally created, with the Secretary of State in the lead, staffed by and working through a Coordinator for Reconstruction and Stabilization. In the Defense Department, a key player in the IMS, stabilization had been elevated in importance—on paper at least—to the level of combat operations. Responsibilities for stability operations were widely distributed among different offices and commands. The United States Agency for International Development (USAID), for the first time since the Vietnam War, was playing an important role in conflict resolution. The National Security Council (NSC) was the driver in designing the interagency process and in pressuring the agencies to make it work. The U.S. Institute of Peace (USIP), at the beginning of the 1990s a sleepy independent government think tank, became a "think and do tank," providing intellectual capital on conflict management and testing operational programs on the ground in an extensive list of conflicts.

Evaluation of the peace-building work of the individual agencies and of their coordination is an important task. The American government will continue to face challenging questions for national security stemming from internal conflict in fragile or failed states—including strife linked to international terrorism. Policymakers need to assess on the basis of past experience how best to harness the expertise and operational skills of the range of relevant government agencies and offices and how to yoke them together in an effective global effort.

CHAPTER 2

THE INTEGRATION OF PEACE-BUILDING AND NATIONAL SECURITY: THE NATIONAL SECURITY COUNCIL

> Truly the committee in charge of running the world, the White House leadership of the American foreign policy establishment, is a world within a world and a world unto itself.
>
> —David J. Rothkopf[1]

The U.S. Constitution makes the President commander-in-chief and allocates to the chief executive the power to formulate, initiate, and implement foreign policy.[2] These authorities place the presidency at the center of the national security policy process—and by implication make the President the "decider" on matters of war and peace-building. We therefore begin our study of the peace-building process with the White House and specifically that part of the White House office which supports the President on national security.

The NSC was created by the National Security Act of 1947.[3] It was called a Council because it was envisioned as a cabinet-level advisory body on national security issues, over which the President himself would preside. By law the Council includes the President, Vice President, Secretary of State, and Secretary of Defense. The Secretaries and Under Secretaries of other executive departments may be included at the "pleasure" of the President. Under the Act, the function of the Council is to coordinate more effectively the policies and functions of those agencies concerned with national security. NSC duties are laid down in very general and flexible terms—to assess U.S. "objectives, commitments, and risks" relative to its military power; to consider policies on matters of common interest to the national security agencies; and to make recommendations to the President. It is also charged with doing anything else directed by the President related to its coordination function.

The NSC is not just a council. It is also a permanent staff, housed in the White House West Wing and next door in the Old Executive Office Building. Under the law the Council staff is headed by an executive secretary. However, since the 1950s the staff has been directed by the Assistant to the President for National Security Affairs, also known as the National Security Advisor. That position is not referred to in the legislation but over time the incumbent has achieved virtual Cabinet status.[4] By contrast, the executive secretary has become the administrative manager of the staff and the pivot for moving national security information to and from the Oval Office. Since the Kennedy administration the NSC professional staff has been recruited specially for each administration.[5] Although it includes career officials drawn from the major foreign affairs agencies, it also includes political appointees selected for their expertise and ties with the administration. In recent years the staff has fluctuated at around 200 persons.

POST–COLD WAR ORGANIZATION OF THE NSC

Since the end of the Cold War the NSC has played a central role in U.S. government peace-building activity, but with varying success. It was during the George H. W. Bush administration that the NSC took on a shape that has survived for two decades. It was also during that administration that peace-building in the Global South began to gain particular policy salience.

Foreign affairs observers often point to the NSC under the first Bush presidency as the gold standard for the effectiveness of that institution. Its efficacy was rooted in the remarkable bond between George H. W. Bush and Gen. Brent Scowcroft. Bush arrived at the White House with a particularly impressive international resume: equivalent of Ambassador to China, U.S. Permanent Representative to the United Nations, and CIA Director. As vice president, he had been a member of the NSC and had chaired a crisis management committee called the National Security Planning Group, which drew on NSC personnel and expertise.[6] Scowcroft had been deputy NSC director to Kissinger and National Security Advisor (NSA) to President Ford. He had also served on the Tower Commission, which made recommendations on the operation of the NSC in the wake of the Iran Contra scandal.[7]

Bush and Scowcroft created what they believed would be the appropriate support structure for a president playing a "hands-on" role in foreign policy. They established two key formal subgroups and a less formal one:

- The Principals Committee consisted of the Secretary of State, the Secretary of Defense, the CIA Director, the Chairman of the Joint Chiefs, and the White House Chief of Staff. It was chaired by the NSA. Other cabinet secretaries would be asked to join as needed.

- Deputies Committee. A less elevated group to provide more intense scrutiny of issues and recommendations, the Deputies Committee was basically made up of the second-in-command at the participant agencies and chaired by the Deputy

National Security Advisor (DNSA). However, it was not entirely formalized, and the representatives from State and Defense were often the third-ranking officers at the under secretary level, who sometimes had closer relationships with the secretaries than did the deputy secretaries.

- An informal crisis group. In times of crisis a more informal group emerged as the key deliberative body around the President.

Although each new president had previously tended to re-create the NSC on arrival at the White House, since Bush 41 the basic formal structure has been retained. As David Rothkopf has written, "the principals and deputies committee structure is at the center of the foreign policy formation process in the U.S. Government today."[8] All succeeding presidents and NSAs saw the merits of the structure and have stayed with it with only slight variations. At the outset of the Bush 43 administration, the Secretary of the Treasury was made a member of the Council by executive order. The Director of National Intelligence, created in 2004 in response to a 9/11 Commission recommendation, has replaced the CIA director as the intelligence advisor to the Council.

PRESIDENTIAL USE OF THE COUNCIL

Even if the structure has remained largely the same since 1989, NSC operations continue strongly to reflect the *modus operandi* of the President. George H. W. Bush, an activist in foreign policy, infrequently convened the Council as a whole, preferring to rely on the deputies committee as the "engine of the policy process." However, in crises, particularly during the Gulf War, he relied on a less formal group—the Gang of Eight, consisting of the vice president, State and Defense secretaries, the deputy secretary of state, the chairman of the Joint Chiefs, the NSA and DNSA and White House chief of staff.[9] Bill Clinton entered the presidency with a limited interest in foreign affairs, largely focused on economics. He did not normally attend meetings of the Council but expected his NSA to structure the discussion of issues so that he could decide. Until 1995, in the absence of presidential engagement, there was a sometimes haphazard approach to issues and a degree of policy paralysis on policy questions on which the agencies disagreed.[10] The Council did not convene either on the Somalia crisis or on genocide in Rwanda and could not initially agree on Bosnia. By the second term, the President and his foreign policy team had learned from earlier mistakes and developed an NSC-led approach to international crises.

George W. Bush, by contrast, made extraordinary use of the formal mechanisms of the Council after 9/11, as the President and his senior national security team struggled to come up with a timely and effective response to al-Qa'ida. According to the careful documentation of Bob Woodward, Bush met with the Council on Afghanistan—with CIA Director George Tenet playing a major role—no fewer than 45 times between September 11 and November 13, when Kabul fell to the Northern Alliance and southern warlord groups.

By contrast the Principals Committee, chaired by NSA Condoleezza Rice, appears to have met only a dozen times on Afghanistan, and the deputies committee on only a handful of occasions.[11] The President, both personally in these meetings and behind the scenes through Rice, pushed the members of the Council hard to come up with a plan.

Bush handled Iraq quite differently. Although he was in continuous touch with his NSA, the Council was an irregular player, spending much of the time on the bench or in the clubhouse. Before September 11, 2001, there were several NSC Principals Committee meetings to review Iraq policy.[12] Iraq emerged as a possible target during considerations of the initial response to the al-Qa'ida attacks, but that option was ruled out by the President. After the fall of Kabul, however, Bush asked Secretary of Defense Rumsfeld to review existing military planning for Iraq, launching an intensive close-hold exercise within the Pentagon involving Rumsfeld, CENTCOM Commander Gen. Tommy Franks, and a small group of planners. This process was carried on entirely outside the NSC. The Council was not formally briefed until early February 2002, and even then remained on the policy sidelines.[13] Beginning in August 2002, the President met periodically with the Council for vigorous debate on key issues: renewal of weapons inspections, obtaining Congressional resolutions in support of military action, seeking Security Council resolutions of support, evidence of Iraqi possession of weapons of mass destruction, and, very belatedly, post-conflict reconstruction. Once the war began in March 2003, the President again dealt primarily with Rumsfeld, Cheney, Rice, and, after his appointment in April as head of the Coalition Provisional Authority, with L. Paul Bremer.[14] The NSC remained a nonplayer until fall 2003, when the President began using a "war cabinet" made up of Cheney, Rumsfeld, Powell, Rice, and Tenet—the NSC principals—to deliberate key issues.

NATIONAL SECURITY ADVISOR ROLE

Although each of the NSAs since 1990 has accepted the basic structure of the Council, the NSA's personality and conception of his/her role has had an important impact on the operations of the NSC. Scowcroft made use of his close relationship with George H. W. Bush to ensure that his president's wishes were implemented by the Council members but deferred to Secretary of State James Baker as the administration's spokesperson on foreign policy. He was the self-effacing "Mr. Inside," working to ensure that all the principals were well informed and to minimize personal suspicions. He abhorred the idea of an operational role in foreign policy.[15]

Anthony Lake intended to follow Scowcroft's example of being an honest broker among the cabinet chiefs, while eschewing an operational role. Lake did not have a close relationship with Bill Clinton and was hampered by Clinton's part-time engagement with foreign policy. Reaching interagency agreement on clear policies became difficult. In 1995 as paralysis over Bosnia policy unleashed severe criticism, Lake formulated and sold Clinton on a coercive diplomacy approach and became the prime actor in selling the policy to the Europeans, before handing it back to State Department for implementation.[16] His successor, Sandy Berger, had a closer relationship with Clinton, and, while avoiding an operational role, was more aggressive in pushing the principals to decisions and in overseeing their implementation. He also emerged as more of a foreign policy spokesperson than Lake, even though he had an amicable relationship with Secretary of State Madeleine Albright.

Condoleezza Rice, a protégé of Scowcroft during her tour as an NSC official under Bush 41, planned to model herself on her former boss.[17] She agreed with George W. Bush that policymaking should be left to the cabinet departments and expected to be less prominent in the media than Berger. She saw her role as NSC leader as dual: ensuring the coordination of the activities of Defense, State, CIA, and other agencies so that the president's orders were carried out, and serving as Bush's primary counselor on foreign policy and national security.[18] However, she faced a situation far different from that of Scowcroft. The NSC principals—Cheney, Rumsfeld, and Powell—were powerful figures with vast national security experience—far greater than the president's and greater than hers. Cheney and Rumsfeld, friends for decades, were closely aligned, and Powell was the odd man out. Bush lacked confidence in Powell's complete loyalty, in contrast to Bush 41's view of Baker. Rice concluded that it would not be her role to "referee intramural squabbles."[19] Equally important, Bush 43, unlike his father, had little experience in foreign policy and intended to focus on domestic and military affairs. Rice had become his tutor in foreign policy and, in the word of Glenn Kessler, his "confidante."[20] She saw herself as translating the new president's foreign policy views and instincts into policy. Rice's gifts as a concise and disciplined articulator of policy, coupled with her pioneering role as the first African-American NSC chief and stylish appearance, drew quick media attention and soon made her more of a spokesperson than she had probably anticipated.

The looting, collapse of civil order and the emergency of insurgency in Iraq in the months after U.S. troops entered Baghdad set off a firestorm of criticism. From an institutional perspective, critics were asking why the NSC was not forcing Defense and State to work together on an effective plan for R&S.[21] There were also questions about CPA chief Bremer's projection of a three-year transition to Iraqi sovereignty. During the summer of 2003 Rice decided that the NSC would have to become more operational to ensure that Iraq policy was responsive to the White House. She asked Robert D. Blackwill, at one time her boss in the Bush 41 NSC, to become Deputy National Security Advisor for Strategy and Senior Director for Iraq. Blackwill traveled to Iraq to work through with Bremer the political dilemmas facing the administration in Iraq.[22] Rice began almost daily telephone conversations with Bremer and by the end of 2003, in effect placed him under her supervision. Under her leadership the administration foreshortened the CPA's rule to a single year. Rice also succeeded in bringing the United Nations back into Iraq to aid with the political transition after the end of the CPA and by May 2004 persuaded Bush to reposition Iraq policy—as opposed to military strategy—in the State Department.[23]

VICE PRESIDENT

A number of observers have argued that the major factor in NSC failures in coordinating R&S was not the weakness of the NSA but the special role of Vice President Dick Cheney. David Rothkopf has described Cheney's influence as the "thumb on the scales."[24] The decades-long relationship between Cheney, Secretary of Defense in the Bush 41 administration, and Donald Rumsfeld, Bush 43's Secretary of Defense, overshadowed the counsel of Colin Powell as Secretary of State. The Vice President had up to 15 of his own staffers working on national security matters, and former associates were strategically located in the NSC (Deputy National Security Advisors Stephen Hadley and Elliott Abrams) and the Defense Department (Douglas Feith, Under Secretary of Defense for Policy). Moreover, I. Lewis (Scooter) Libby was both the Vice President's chief of staff and his NSA. Libby had the title of DNSA, and in that role was authorized—like the senior DNSA (Hadley)— to attend meetings of the NSC principals, both those with the President and those chaired by the NSA.[25] These circumstances, it is argued, along with the Cheney-Rumsfeld alliance, forestalled Condoleezza Rice in her responsibility to make sure that State Department views were fully registered.[26] From this perspective, her public disclaimer that it was not her job to "referee intramural squabbles" could be considered a bow to necessity, at least until the second half of 2003, when the shortcomings of the Rumsfeld-Cheney approach to Iraq became manifest.

The exceptional role of the vice president in Iraq policy, the most important national security decision of George W. Bush's first term, should be viewed not as an aberration, but rather as emblematic of a key development in presidential government since 1977—the rising importance of the vice president in national security matters. John Nance Garner's aphorism that the vice president's job is not worth "a bucket of warm spit" no longer applies.[27] The new trend began with the Carter administration, when Walter Mondale was brought into the policy process—and presidential trust—far more than his predecessors. Although Reagan and his vice president were not close, George H. W. Bush played a significant role on the NSC. Even Dan Quayle, often caricatured as a vice presidential lightweight, was regularly involved in informal crisis group meetings under NSC auspices. Not only did Al Gore play an important role in the Clinton national security process, but Leon Fuerth, Gore's chief foreign policy aide, became a DNSA within the NSC staff, a model for the role played later by I. Lewis Libby.[28] Viewed from this perspective, the powerful trend toward expanded vice presidential involvement reached its apogee in Cheney, who drew on his special ties with George W. Bush, his previous experience as White House Chief of Staff and Defense Secretary, and a vastly expanded personal staff to play an outsized role in national security issues after 9/11. Cheney's role declined during the second term, when Rice moved over to the State Department, rebalancing the State Department's influence at the White House relative to Defense. The resignation in 2005 of Libby, Cheney's most powerful aide and member of the Deputies Committee, and the departure of Cheney's ally Rumsfeld after the 2006 election reinforced the perception that the Vice President had lost influence over the national security process.[29]

THE NSC STAFF

In daily parlance the "NSC" usually refers to the NSC staff. It operates essentially as the foreign policy and national security staff of the president. It carries out three major functions. Daalder and Destler have stated that the critical mission of the NSC staff is "coordinating the policy process so that, simultaneously, agencies get a full and fair hearing and the president can make clear foreign policy choices in a timely manner." In their view, the critical NSC tasks are

- Managing the President's foreign policy actions, including foreign trips, communication with foreign leaders, and foreign policy speeches;
- Coordinating the policymaking process by ensuring that all important official stakeholders are involved and that all reasonable options have been analyzed and considered;
- Driving the policy process toward real and timely decisions; and
- Monitoring implementation of presidential decisions.[30]

The staff is organized hierarchically, but its structure is flatter and leaner than that of the departments and agencies. Historically, the DNSA, like the Advisor, bearing the rank of Assistant to the President, functions as the alter ego to the NSA. The DNSA slot has often been the stepping stone to the NSA position, as happened with Colin Powell in the Reagan administration, Sandy Berger in the Clinton administration, and Stephen Hadley in the second term of George W. Bush.

In recent years, the NSC has created additional positions at the level of DNSA, some of them related to conflict. The Clinton administration promoted a senior director to DNSA in 1997 to enhance his authority in dealing with the Pentagon on Balkan issues.[31] The Bush 43 administration named DNSAs to manage the GWOT (Gen. Wayne Downing) and Iraq and Afghanistan (Blackwill, Meghan O'Sullivan, and LTG Douglas Lute).[32]

Below the level of the NSA and DNSAs are senior directors, who head directorates, both geographic and functional. The Bush 43 NSC, after 2005, had directorates for Europe, Africa, Western Hemisphere, East Asia, South and

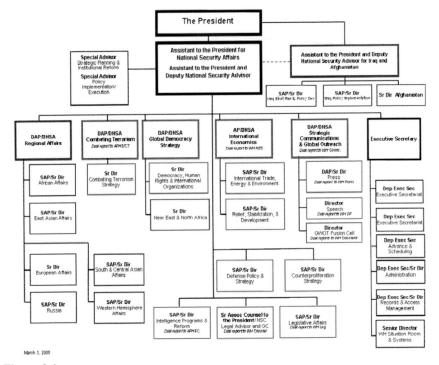

Figure 2.1
National Security Council Organizational Chart (2008).

Central Asia, and Near East and North Africa. In addition, there were single-country directorates, headed by senior directors, for Iraq, Afghanistan, and Russia. There were also functional directorates: democracy, human rights, and international organizations; terrorism strategy; international trade, energy, and environment; defense policy and strategy; relief, stabilization, and development; counter-proliferation strategy; intelligence programs and reform; legal affairs; legislative affairs; and press. Senior directors are considered as roughly equivalent to assistant secretaries of the departments, and lateral movement from those positions to assistant secretary positions at the State and Defense Departments is common. The senior directors normally have two to four more junior staffers, called "directors," often young people, selected as promising academics or "comers" from State or Defense or CIA, working under them.

The multiplicity of international crises since the end of the Cold War has required the creation of interagency mechanisms—centering on the NSC—for dealing with problems at the subregional or country level. The Clinton administration created a system of interagency working groups (IWGs—pronounced "eye-wigs") to draw together the information needed by the deputies and principals to sort through the range of realistic policy options and to monitor implementation of decisions made. Depending on the issue, the IWGs were supposed to be chaired by assistant secretaries at State or Defense, perhaps with an NSC senior director serving as cochair, as designated by the Deputies Committee. In practice, particularly after Sandy Berger assumed charge of the NSC in the second term, NSC staffers chaired the vast majority of IWGs.[33]

The Bush 43 administration immediately abolished the IWGs, but put in their place six geographic Policy Coordination Committees (PCCs), corresponding with the NSC geographic directorates, and eleven functional PCCs. Because the Bush administration intended to give greater primacy to the cabinet departments, the PCCs were chaired at the assistant secretary or under secretary level in the key agency concerned, with the NSC senior director or director exercising an executive secretary function.[34]

THE NATIONAL SECURITY STRATEGY

In 1986 the Congress mandated that the President should submit to the Congress an annual statement of national security policy. The Reagan, Bush 41, and Clinton administrations generally complied with this requirement. Generally speaking, the statements were an articulation of existing policy and tended to take on the quality of "boilerplate." That practice changed with the Bush 43 administration. Diplomatic historian John Lewis Gaddis has written that George W. Bush "has presided over the most sweeping redesign of U.S. grand strategy since the presidency of Franklin D. Roosevelt."[35] In part to indicate its intention to break with the past, the Bush 43 administration decided to carry out a major strategic review, leading to the issuance in September 2002 of a National Security Strategy, posted on the White House Web site. Its architect was Condoleezza Rice.[36] Its purpose was to convey to the Congress and the American people the broad national security objectives of the administration. As such, it became a foundational document for the NSC, as well as for the State and Defense Departments and USAID. While heavily focused on winning the GWOT, it provided a degree of guidance on the peace-building thinking of the Bush 43 administration.

The strategy overview emphasized that because of its unprecedented strength and influence, American power "must be used to promote a balance of power that favors freedom" in a new world in which the United States "is now threatened less by conquering states than ... by failing ones."[37] Almost all the "tasks" are related to the goal of peace, some indirectly:[38]

1. "Champion aspirations for human dignity"
    The task was to be implemented largely through public diplomacy and foreign assistance. Promotion of democracy and human rights—at the heart of this task—is a major element in post-conflict reconstruction programs.
2. "Strengthen alliances to defeat global terrorism and work to prevent attacks against us and our friends"

While the preponderance of the task was to combat terrorist organizations with "global reach," other elements included stabilization elements, such as supporting "moderate and modern" governments and "diminish[ing] the underlying conditions which spawn terrorism."

3. "Work with others to defuse regional conflicts"
This task included the Israel-Palestine and India-Pakistan conflicts but focused heavily on violent internal conflicts in Africa and Latin America.

4. "Prevent our enemies from threatening us, our allies, and our friends, with weapons of mass destruction"
That task became a major element in the justification for regime change and democratization in Iraq.

5. "Ignite a new era of global economic growth through free markets and free trade"
The task was primarily promoted through economic policy, but one aim of stabilization was to promote a free market approach in a state emerging from conflict.

6. "Expand the circle of development by opening societies and building the infrastructure of democracy"
Post-conflict reconstruction aimed to build the "infrastructure of democracy."

7. "Develop agendas for cooperative action with other main centers of global power"
The task embraced strengthening NATO and other alliances, which might be available for peacekeeping and post-conflict reconstruction. Cooperation with strategic competitors like Russia, India, and China could potentially include collaboration in finding peaceful solutions in specific countries.

8. "Transform America's national security institutions to meet the challenges and opportunities of the twenty-first century"
The task spoke explicitly of enabling American diplomats to help build police forces and court structures, as well as electoral and governance systems, in countries emerging from civil war. It also stood behind subsequent administration creation of a special apparatus to deal with R&S.

In 2006 the White House published a revised National Security Strategy. The revised document was drafted by Special Advisor for Strategic Planning and Institutional Reform Peter Feaver and his associate William Inboden, Senior Director for Strategic Planning, closely supervised by NSA Stephen Hadley. President Bush spent several hours with the draft doing his own line edits. The new document highlighted the theme of democratization, foreign policy *leitmotif* of the second Bush term. It emphasized a long-term effort to create "a world of democratic, well-governed states that can meet the needs of their citizens and conduct themselves responsibly in the international system." The tasks of the Strategy remained unchanged from 2002, with one addition: "The United States must engage the opportunities and confront the challenges of globalization."

A striking aspect of the revised document was the attention it devoted to conflict. Under "defusing regional conflicts," the Strategy, rather than cataloging the conflicts to be worked on, as in 2002, went into causality and modes of engagement. It noted that regional conflicts may arise from multiple causes, including ethnic or religious hatreds, internal revolt and competing claims, poor governance and external aggression. If these conditions are ignored, failed states, humanitarian catastrophes, and ungoverned areas turned refuges for terrorists may be the result. The Strategy envisioned three "levels of engagement":

1. Conflict prevention and resolution. Promotion of democracy was underlined as the most effective long-term approach to conflict resolution. In the short-term, however, working with key regional actors was the primary approach. The United States might also make a timely offer of "good offices"—"when appropriate." The regional approach was cited as having potential application to Israel-Palestine, the Great Lakes conflict in Africa, and Nepal's internal strife. At this level of engagement, peace-building diplomacy was the primary policy tool.

2. Conflict intervention—peacekeeping essentially—must be considered when a conflict "poses a grave threat to our broader interests and values." This segment focused on remedying an international shortage of "high quality military forces trained and capable of performing these peace operations," to be supported by the Global Peace Operations Initiative (GPOI; see Chapter 3), and further strengthening of UN peacekeeping missions. Backstopping for this level of engagement was envisaged as essentially diplomatic in nature.

3. Post-conflict reconstruction and stabilization. The Strategy recognized that long-term peace and stability can be expected after the intervention of peacekeepers, only if R&S are addressed. The Strategy linked this capability directly to the creation of State's new Office of the Coordinator for Reconstruction and Stabilization (S/CRS). (See Chapter 4.)

THE NSC ROLE IN PEACE-BUILDING

The NSC does not have a special apparatus for peace-building. There is no directorate by that name. However, the NSC has been at the center of efforts to achieve a government-wide approach to conflict and post-conflict reconstruction since the mid-1990s. The experience of the Clinton administration relating to Somalia, Rwanda, and Haiti was the stimulant. The outcome of the UN intervention in Somalia in 1993 (UNOSOM II), when U.S. Task Force Ranger lost two helicopters and 18 American troops, leading to the withdrawal of UN forces, inhibited a vigorous American response to genocide in Rwanda the following year. There was fierce criticism of both policy and process. U.S. intervention in Haiti in 1994, to restore the elected Aristide government to power in conformity with Security Council Resolution 940, was generally successful but demonstrated problems of civilian and military coordination and shortages of resources. In the run-up to the Haiti operation, the Chairman of the Joint Chiefs, Gen. John Shali-kashvili, briefed the President on the military plan, stating that it would take about a week. Clinton shot back, "What happens the second week?" When the general conceded that the question had not been closely studied, Clinton rejoined, "That's what I'm worried about."[39] In response, the Pentagon went to work on a planning document for Haiti, and the NSC asked the author of that document to draft what eventually became Presidential Decision Directive (PDD) 56 ("Managing Complex Contingency Operations"), issued in May 1997.[40]

The PDD remains classified, but a White Paper describes the basic outline. The Directive defined "complex contingency operations" to include peace operations and complicated humanitarian assistance operations. It excluded—"unless otherwise directed"—military operations to defend U.S. citizens, territory, or property, counterterrorism and hostage-rescue operations, and international armed conflict. It noted that the post–Cold War period had spawned civil wars, interethnic conflicts, and territorial disputes, requiring multidimensional operations with political/diplomatic, humanitarian, intelligence, economic development, and security components. When such a crisis arose, the Directive envisaged creation by the NSC Deputies Committee of an interagency Executive Committee (ExCom) to oversee day-to-day operations. The initial responsibility of the ExCom was to develop a political-military implementation plan ("pol-mil plan") to coordinate U.S. government actions. The components of the plan included assessment of the situation, a "mission statement," a desired "end state" and exit strategy, and a plan concept. A lead agency was to be designated, and different agency tasks spelled out. The objective: to enable "military and civilian agencies [to] operate in a synchronized manner ... [making] use of special mechanisms to coordinate agency efforts."

PDD 56 was not used in the Bosnia situation, since the interagency process and operational plan were well established by 1997. In fact, according to participants in the process, the Directive was never systematically applied. The NSC Directorate for Global Affairs, headed by Richard Clarke, became the locus for crisis response and the hub for generating about two dozen "pol-mil plans," using PDD 56 as guidance, if not as a template. To deal with a particular crisis or anticipated crisis, Leonard R. Hawley, Director for Multilateral Affairs under Clarke, put together an emergency planning team. The team drew together a director or senior director from the relevant regional directorate along with other NSC staff members working on humanitarian assistance, legislative and legal affairs, and public diplomacy. Most of the plans were actually written in the State Department's Political-Military Affairs Bureau. Contingency plans were prepared for conflicts ranging across the globe, including Kosovo, Georgia, Lebanon, West Bank-Gaza, North Korea, Liberia, Zaire, Ethiopia-Eritrea, and Haiti. If the plans were written at State, implementation was in the hands of the IWGs, normally chaired by the NSC. The driver—if not the implementer—of the process was the NSC.

The Bush administration did away with PDD 56 in its initial reorganization of the NSC. Chairmanship of the PCCs, which replaced the IWGs, was handed over to the departments. Crisis planning within the NSC was not eliminated, however, but retained in Clarke's former office, renamed the Democracy, Human Rights and International Organizations Directorate. Supported by the senior director and drawing on PDD 56 as background, Matthew McLean, Director for Planning and Contingency Operations, produced an updated and strengthened generic contingency plan to cover situations in which the United States was either in the lead or in a support role for the United Nations or another power. After interviewing 30 experts who had previously served in government, McLean collaborated with the State and Treasury Departments, the Joint Chiefs of Staff, and USAID to produce a document, which became known as National Security Presidential Directive (NSPD) XX. The new document found favor with the Joint Chiefs of Staff, who wished to promote the idea of forward planning and interagency cooperation. However, when Gen. Peter Pace, then Vice Chairman of the Joint Chiefs, brought the document to the Deputies Committee for action in 2003, Stephen Cambone, Deputy Secretary of Defense for Intelligence and a close associate of Donald Rumsfeld, insisted that the document be scratched from the agenda because it "usurped the national command authority of the Secretary of Defense."[41] That was the end of NSPD XX.[42]

Alarm over the faltering of R&S in Iraq was widespread in Washington by mid-2003. A variety of bills were introduced in the Congress. The most important emerged from the Senate Foreign Relations Committee (SFRC). Chairman Richard Lugar and Joe Biden, Ranking Minority, were appalled by the lack of coherent planning for post-combat Iraq. They organized a Policy Advisory Group, which concluded that the military needed "a well organized and strongly led" civilian partner at the State Department to work with the military on complex emergencies. They placed that conclusion in draft legislation.[43]

The NSC was moving in the same direction. J. Clint Williamson, an NSC staffer who had worked extensively on transitional justice issues in the Balkans, went to Iraq in early 2003 with the Defense Department's Office for Reconstruction and Humanitarian Affairs, which had initial responsibility for reconstruction. When he returned to the NSC in the summer, Rice asked him to prepare a memorandum proposing a R&S office. The focus was to be on providing transitional security and strengthening rule of law. As a result of interagency conversations, in which the State Department stressed the multi-faceted nature of post-conflict reconstruction and the Defense Department emphasized planning, the concept of the office evolved from being primarily a mobilizer of civilian operators to one of coordination.

A key question was where the office should be placed. A Center for Strategic and International Studies report had called for a separate agency, reporting to the NSC.[44] A Council on Foreign Relations Task Force proposed a new under secretary of state position. The NSC favored putting the office in the State Department, but there were reservations at State over

CLINT WILLIAMSON

John Clint Williamson, known as Clint, grew up in Louisiana. He did his undergraduate work at little-known Louisiana Tech University in Ruston and got a law degree from Tulane. After law school he went to work as an Assistant District Attorney in New Orleans and then served as a trial attorney in the Justice Department's Organized Crime Section. He was fascinated by the international arena and in 1994 jumped at the chance to work as trial attorney on the International Criminal Tribunal of Yugoslavia (ICTY) in The Hague. In 2001 the State Department asked him to take another assignment in the Balkans, which led to his appointment as director of the justice department of the UNMIK. His work on international crime issues attracted the attention of the NSC leadership.

He was interviewed by Stephen Hadley and Condoleezza Rice for the position of Director for Transnational Threats within the Directorate for Counter-Terrorism. He was surprised by their questions, focused on his Balkan experience, about how the United States could do better in post-conflict reconstruction, especially the rule of law. They asked him to look into that question when he came on board in January 2003. That inquiry was interrupted within three months by a temporary duty assignment to Baghdad in Gen. Jay Garner's Office of Reconstruction and Humanitarian Affairs (ORHA), as senior advisor to the Ministry of Justice. Back in the NSC by July 2003, Williamson, the only staffer who had actually worked in Baghdad, was reassigned to the Defense Policy Directorate, where most Iraq issues were then being handled. His title: Director for Stability Operations. Williamson's job was not to get involved in stabilization in particular countries. His task was strategic: How could the U.S. government do a better job of stabilization in the future?

Williamson forwarded a memorandum to Hadley in November proposing a high-level R&S office within the U.S. government. Hadley and Rice were impressed. Rice directed him to brief officials at the deputy secretary or under secretary level at State, Defense, Justice, and USAID. There was agreement at the NSC that the new office should be part of the State Department. Williamson held meetings in December and January with Douglas Feith, Under Secretary of Defense for Policy, Mark Grossman, Under Secretary for Political Affairs at the State Department, Adm. Walter (Skip) Sharp from the Joint Chiefs of Staff, and USAID Administrator Andrew Natsios. There was agreement to move forward. The Deputies Committee formally approved in March and the Principals Committee in April. Three months later the S/CRS was launched by Secretary Powell.

As the interagency briefings proceeded, partisans of the S/CRS concept made the case that the new approach required the formal imprimatur of the president.[45] Otherwise, the new office would lack heft in the interagency arena. Williamson spent much of the remainder of his White House tour trying to move forward an NSPD embodying State Department leadership of R&S. That took an additional 17 months, on top of the 8 months required to put S/CRS on its feet. Some of the delays came from the civilian leadership of the Defense Department, which was simultaneously working on its own internal directive on stability operations.[46] Defense had signed on to the concept of a State Department lead in R&S but quibbled over the fine points. After NSPD 44 appeared, Williamson moved over to the State Department to return to the field of international justice. His reward: appointment as Ambassador-at-Large for War Crimes Issues.

creation of a potential "unfunded mandate" and complications of establishing a new seventh-floor principal. The NSC Principals Committee, which included the Secretaries of State and Defense, approved the idea of a State Department office in April 2004. In July Secretary of State Colin Powell formally established the Office of the Coordinator for Reconstruction and Stabilization (S/CRS).

Conceptually, the new office was to be the point of the lance for a new State Department authority to lead and coordinate the elements of the U.S. government in carrying out post-conflict reconstruction. However, it lacked both legislative authority and a presidential imprimatur. Securing the latter was the primary responsibility of the NSC Director for Stabilization, working in tandem with the new Coordinator for Reconstruction and Stabilization. That proved to be a lengthy bureaucratic process, as the different agencies clashed over philosophies of executive authority and over language.

Finally, in December 2005, the White House issued NSPD 44 on "Management of Interagency Efforts Concerning Reconstruction and Stabilization" over President Bush's signature. NSPD 44 designated the Secretary of State to coordinate and lead *all* U.S. government agencies in R&S. It gave the Secretary of State responsibility, working through S/CRS, to develop programs and strategies and coordinate them among the agencies, and with the international community.[47] It then diluted that leadership authority by stating that "the Secretary of State shall coordinate such efforts with the Secretary of Defense to ensure harmonization with any planned or ongoing U.S. military operations." Other agencies were required to coordinate with State, but State and Defense "will integrate stabilization and reconstruction contingency plans with military contingency plans *when relevant and appropriate*."[48] The directive provided for the creation of an interagency PCC cochaired by the Coordinator and a designated member of the NSC. The committee was to be a "limited-time" grouping to focus on a country or region facing major R&S challenges. The NSPD therefore gave the Secretary of State substantial authority with respect to other civilian agencies, but left her to battle with the Defense Secretary over control of key elements. Aside from indicating that the Secretary would implement her new authority through S/CRS, the directive devoted very little attention to the new structure in the State Department.

The lack of urgency in pushing through NSPD 44, issued 17 months after the creation of S/CRS, reflected in part expectations for the new State Department-led stabilization process. It was not designed for use in the contemporary conflagrations of the Bush administration—Afghanistan and Iraq, at least at the outset. Rather it was seen as the mechanism for dealing with "the next Iraq." Nor was high priority for R&S apparent in the operations of the NSC. When Condoleezza Rice became Secretary of State and Stephen Hadley moved up to become NSA, the Council staff was reorganized to create a new directorate for Relief, Stabilization and Development. The Director for Stability Operations was pulled out of the Defense Directorate and placed in the new office. The rationale was that countries facing serious political and economic challenges are distributed along a continuum of need. Initially they may need humanitarian relief from a natural or man-made disaster. Once relief needs are met, they require a different type of assistance for R&S. If stabilization occurs, they require help in getting on the road to development. That justification, together with the promotion of John A. Simon, previously Director of Development and a former USAID official, as the new senior director, suggested that NSC leadership viewed stabilization as an essentially foreign assistance function—not one integrally linked to peace and security. It also indicated that the primary interagency interface was considered to be USAID, perhaps along with Treasury, Commerce, and the Agriculture Department, rather than Defense or State. That view was reinforced a year later, when Simon was replaced by Michael Magan, previously USAID Assistant Administrator for Latin America and the Caribbean.

A number of those involved in the creation of the new mechanism for R&S argued that a separate directorate should be created for stabilization to be the counterpart of the new high-level office in the State Department. That argument was deflected in early 2005. NSA Hadley took the position that since S/CRS was just getting launched and had limited capacity, it would be premature to create a full-fledged stabilization directorate at NSC.[49] There is no evidence that the argument was revisited during President Bush's second term. Given the uniqueness of their brief, Clint Williamson and his successor, Laura A. Hall, the two officers who served longest as directors for stability operations, operated relatively autonomously within the larger directorate, often dealing directly and informally with the ranking DNSA.

The central role of the Director for Stability Operations was to backstop and help "empower" S/CRS. The Director, who cochaired—with the State Department's Coordinator for Reconstruction and Stabilization—the R&S PCC, worked to ensure that interagency issues relating to the operation of NSPD 44 were addressed through the NSC process. In 2004 and 2005, the priority was obtaining agreement on the text of the NSPD. In 2006 and early 2007, the central task was securing approval of the IMS which would be triggered by a formal request from the President or Secretary of State for action on a foreign crisis. In 2007 much of the work centered on developing the "Civilian Stabilization Initiative" budget and legislative package, to put flesh on the bones of the Civilian Reserve Corps requested by the President in his 2007 State of the Union message. (See Chapter 4.) These three initiatives were recommended by the PCC and approved by the Deputies Committee. Within the NSC, the Director of Stability Operations worked in tandem with the Directorate for Defense on crisis response, because of the important interface with the Department of Defense (DOD), and with the Directorate for Democracy & International Organization Affairs, which handled UN peacekeeping responsibilities for the NSC. Other activities were budgetary, for example, emphasizing to the Office of Management and Budget (OMB) the President's support for the R&S budget, coordinating a common interagency line of support for the R&S budget with the Congress, and arranging calls as needed by senior NSC officials to key members of Congress.[50]

The Director of Stability Operations normally did not deal with specific cases of conflict, but did carve out a role on Lebanon the summer of 2006—decisively influencing the design of a humanitarian relief and reconstruction package amounting to $230 million. That was an aspect of the Lebanese crisis that the Near East Directorate was too overworked to deal with. In this instance the Director for Stability Operations was working as an integral part of the Relief, Stabilization and Development Directorate. NSC intervention shifted the approach from a rather standard USAID quasi-development package to budget support, couched within conditionality endorsed by the International Monetary Fund. Budget support, in the administration's view, more naturally supported U.S. political interests in Lebanon because of that country's financial fragility and high international debt levels.

THE GEOGRAPHIC DIRECTORATES

About half the professional staff of the NSC is assigned to regional directorates, each of which has three to five staff members. These small offices have a coverage which is a "mile wide and an inch deep" but play a major role in dealing with conflict within the interagency process. The directorates basically have the time and personnel to focus only on conflicts that are of personal interest to the President or, perhaps even more often, those conflict situations which could cause him potential political or public relations problems. In the Bush administration the NSC focused on the conflicts in Iraq and Afghanistan, of course, but also played a lead role on Haiti, Colombia, and Sudan. It played an important coordinate role on countries such as Liberia and Nepal. It left primarily to the State Department problems like Kosovo, Sri Lanka, and Zimbabwe.

With respect to their peace-building responsibilities, senior directors and directors are responsible for coordinating the interagency process—working through the PCCs—when important issues emerge for decision relating to countries in conflict. In spite of the NSPD and the creation of the position of Director of Stability Operations, the regional directors did not cede control of the PCC apparatus. Indeed the IMS structure provides for three cochairs, with the regional senior director cochairing for the NSC.

Iraq

Condoleezza Rice's move in the fall of 2003 to bring the Coalition Provisional Authority under NSC supervision helped crystallize and channel in new directions a policy debate raging in the key agencies—Defense and State—but also on the ground in Baghdad. During his intense Baghdad visits, Blackwill helped accelerate a change in perspective in the CPA. Bremer began to realize that he could not circumvent senior Shi'ite leader, Grand Ayatollah Ali al-Sistani, who had issued a *fatwa* (formal legal opinion) opposing adoption of an Iraqi constitution in advance of elections. When Bremer went back to Washington in November, he was carrying memoranda written by his staff suggesting that an interim constitution could be worked out with the Iraqis and recommending that sovereignty be transferred on June 30, 2004.[51] There was a convergence among Rice, Rumsfeld, and Bremer about limiting the CPA to a year.

In October 2003, as part of her move to bring the Coalition Provisional Authority under NSC supervision, Rice created the Iraq Stabilization Group. The NSC was dealing with Iraq through the prism of three directorates. Blackwill was in charge of the political arena. Frank Miller, Senior Director for Defense, watched over the military and reconstruction, and Reuben Jeffery, Senior Director for Economics, covered that sector. The Iraq Stabilization Group, cochaired by Blackwill and Miller, was supposed to integrate their activities and impose order on the policy process. It met daily for an hour, but tended to be tactical and operational rather than strategic. There were complaints that it did not effectively set up the issues for the principals to decide because there was no single person in charge. Meghan O'Sullivan, a veteran of both ORHA and the CPA, came back to Washington as Blackwill's deputy and eventually as his successor.

In 2005, as the new NSA, Stephen Hadley reorganized both the Iraq-related structure of the NSC and the interagency process. O'Sullivan was made DNSA and Senior Director for Iraq and Afghanistan in order to end the functional divide. In place of the Iraq Stabilization Group, Hadley created an Iraq Steering Group (ISG), chaired by her, which included the senior Iraq person in all the key agencies. The role of the ISG was to service both the Deputies Committee and the Principals. It met weekly for two hours and from the NSC perspective created a much more sound and thorough policy process. Some in the other agencies complained that the ISG tended to micromanage and focus on minutia. The ISG continued to operate after O'Sullivan resigned in mid-2007. She was replaced by LTG Douglas E. Lute. Lute inherited her DNSA title but got the enhanced rank of Assistant to the President to reinforce his position, touted in the media, as "war czar."[52]

The Iraq Directorate played an important role in briefing and in framing the administration's response to the Iraq Study Group, headed by former Secretary of State James Baker and former Congressman Lee Hamilton, which made 73 recommendations in December 2006 for a change of course. The White House responded that it was already implementing several of the proposals and would accept others. It demurred on the recommendations that by early 2008 all combat brigades not necessary for force protection should be out of Iraq and that it engage in direct diplomacy with Iran and Syria.[53]

The Directorate was by that time engaged in a significant way in the formulation of the "surge" policy announced by the President on January 10, 2007. O'Sullivan led an internal NSC review, with extensive participation

MEGHAN O'SULLIVAN

Meghan O'Sullivan grew up in Lexington, Massachusetts. Academic distinction at Georgetown University led the slender, striking redhead to Oxford, where she obtained a master's degree in economics and a D.Phil. in politics. She joined the Brookings Institution, where her supervisor was Richard N. Haass. He took O'Sullivan with him when he became Director of the State Department's Policy Planning Staff in 2001. With Haass also serving as Special Envoy for Northern Ireland, she worked on that conflict and hot spots like Kashmir and Iran.

In February 2003 O'Sullivan volunteered to go to Iraq as a civilian and was designated for Gen. Jay Garner's ORHA. She was initially rejected, in part because her pre-9/11 writings at Brookings recommended against using force against Saddam Hussein. Powell intervened directly with Defense Secretary Rumsfeld to secure her place. She went to Baghdad with Garner after Saddam fled and survived the transition from ORHA to the Coalition Provisional Authority. She became a close advisor to L. Paul Bremer. She coauthored a memo to him urging an accelerated transfer of sovereignty to the Iraqis by mid-2004.

When Bremer left Baghdad in June 2004, O'Sullivan was brought to the NSC as Senior Director for Southwest Asia, working under Deputy National Security Advisor Robert Blackwill. She was 34. The NSC was now in the lead on Iraq policy, but authority was divided among three NSC offices covering security, politics, and economics. In 2005, after Blackwill left, Iraq and Afghanistan were placed entirely under O'Sullivan, who was promoted to DNSA the following year. She chaired the ISG. Some participants remember ISG meetings as "micromanagement" and often a waste of time, but O'Sullivan was given credit for asking strategic questions and keeping the dialogue civil.

O'Sullivan played an important role in the development of the "surge" strategy of 2007. Beginning in October 2006, she led an internal NSC review, which, with advice from a small group of military and civilian experts, came up with a plan for additional troops, civilian protection, and a secure Baghdad. She had frequent conversations with the President during this period. From November until Bush's January 10, 2007 announcement of "a new way forward" in Iraq, her office backstopped almost daily meetings of the Deputies Committee and a number of full NSC meetings with the President.

She resigned after the new strategy was announced but agreed to stay until a successor was named. That took four months. George W. Bush had one more assignment. At the request of Gen. Petraeus and Ambassador Ryan Crocker, Bush sent her to Baghdad in June to assist with the surge and the complementary effort to conceptualize a long-term U.S.-Iraq relationship. Only in September 2007 was she able to take up Harvard's offer of a fellowship at the Institute for Politics. A year later, when she was ensconced as a Kennedy School faculty member, Crocker and Gen. Odierno, Petraeus's successor, persuaded her to return to Baghdad to work on the Status of Forces Agreement, finalized at the end of 2008.

by David Satterfield, Secretary Rice's Senior Advisor on Iraq and Coordinator for Iraq. She also met informally with the President, who was encouraged by her advocacy of the surge. The review provided the basic documents for the consideration of the Deputies and Principals Committees, which met frequently between October and December. According to Fred Barnes, the President was leaning toward a surge as early as June and probably committed to it by October, but he consulted many different military advisors informally, and even went to the Pentagon in a move to win over military opposition. The extensiveness of the formal process, supported by O'Sullivan and her staff, helped to secure "buy-in" by the military and others who were originally opposed to the surge.[54]

In step with planning for the military surge came NSC recognition of the need for increased civilian response capacity on the part of the State Department and USAID. The civilian surge in Iraq doubled Provincial Reconstruction Teams (PRTs) in 2007. But O'Sullivan also saw the relevance of S/CRS and its plans for a standing civilian response capacity. Working with Stability Operations Director Laura Hall, she successfully pressed for inclusion in the President's 2007 State of the Union message a call for enactment of the S/CRS-led civilian stabilization initiative.[55]

Western Hemisphere

From the beginning of the Bush administration, the NSC played a lead role in the formulation and execution of policy toward Latin America. George Bush came into the White House with experience as governor of a state bordering Mexico. Bush cared about relations with Mexico and wanted his policy toward the Western Hemisphere to appeal to the Hispanic voters which the Republican Party was wooing. Moreover, a Summit of the Americas, bringing together the democratically elected leaders of the Hemisphere and focusing on a Latin American Free Trade Area, loomed in April. NSA Rice turned to a Foreign Service veteran to head the Western Hemisphere Directorate. John Maisto, who had served as ambassador in Venezuela and Honduras, was favorably known to Republican foreign policy mavens for his work on the Philippines during the Reagan administration and on Central America during Bush 41.

The key conflicts for the directorate were Colombia and Haiti. For Colombia the key question was whether to continue to support Plan Colombia. The Plan was proposed in 1999 by President Andrés Pastrana to end decades of civil war, to eradicate coca through aerial spraying, and to bring about economic and social renewal. The Colombian government pledged to contribute $4 billion toward a total package of $7.5 billion and requested the balance from the international community. The Clinton administration endorsed Plan Colombia and secured $1.3 billion from Congress for the U.S. share.[56] In early 2001 the Western Hemisphere Directorate undertook an accelerated review of Plan Colombia, consulting the U.S. government agencies concerned and key Congressional committees. It recommended that U.S. support be continued, and the President agreed. Following the President's endorsement, there was no interagency conflict over Colombia. The accession in 2002 of a more hard-line president on security issues, Alvaro Uribe, who enjoyed early success in reducing violence against civilians, confirmed the Bush decision.

The Bush White House faced a trickier situation in Haiti. The Clinton administration's 1994 decision to intervene to restore the democratically elected Aristide regime to power, as mandated by the Security Council, was criticized vociferously by Republican members of Congress and foreign policy spokespersons. Aristide, facing a term limit, stepped aside for the 1995 elections in favor of his former prime minister, René Préval. He subsequently broke with Préval, created a new party and secured his own election in an early 2001 presidential poll of dubious validity. By then international peace-keeping forces had phased out. Violence and gridlock reemerged quickly, as the opposition refused to accept Aristide's election.

According to John Maisto, U.S. policy, orchestrated from the White House, was to manage the Haiti problem by "multilateralizing" it. Initially, the U.S. government looked to the OAS for the lead. The OAS passed a resolution urging on the Haitian government a series of steps leading to a new round of elections in 2003. The OAS set up a mechanism for monitoring the Haiti situation. These efforts made little headway. A violent rebellion got underway, which spread from town to town. The efforts of OAS Special Envoy, Ambassador Terence Todman, a retired American diplomat of Caribbean origin, came to naught. As the rebellion threatened to reach Port-au-Prince, the White House concluded, says Maisto, that the Haitian president would be killed by the mobs, if he did not leave office. The NSC pushed through an interagency decision: offer U.S.-assisted departure and exile to Aristide and his family; if he refused, he would be left to his fate. Secretary of State Powell announced that the United States was no longer interested in providing security for Aristide, and in a coordinated step, French Foreign Minister Dominique de Villepin called on Aristide to resign. On February 28, 2004, Aristide signed a letter of resignation, drove to the airport in the company of U.S. Deputy Chief of Mission Luis Moreno, and flew off on a U.S.-chartered aircraft to the Central African Republic. Aristide subsequently claimed that he signed his resignation letter under duress and was kidnapped by the United States.[57] Colin Powell denied the charge, saying that Aristide had asked the U.S. ambassador for advice and, after consulting his wife, had agreed that resignation was the best course of action. The United States had simply facilitated his departure. A U.S.-led Multilateral Interim Force, which also included substantial numbers of troops from Canada, France, and Chile, landed in Haiti to provide security until the arrival of a UN peacekeeping force.

With U.S. and French leadership, the Security Council passed a resolution creating MINUSTAH (UN Stabilization Mission in Haiti), which assumed the responsibilities of the Interim Force during the summer of 2004. The commanders of MINUSTAH have been Brazilian—with the exception of an interim Chilean commander—and the force has been largely composed of

Brazilian, Argentine, Peruvian, Uruguayan, and Chilean troops. Only a handful of Americans have been involved in the military and police forces. Likewise the UN Secretary-General's Special Representative for Haiti and his senior staff have been largely Latin Americans. Despite the continuation of disorder in Haiti, including serious problems of gang violence, the Bush administration was generally satisfied with management of the Haiti problem, taking special satisfaction that no major wave of Haitian boat people had materialized off the U.S. coast since the departure of Aristide.[58]

Africa

Under Bush 43 the Directorate for Africa was made up of a Senior Director and a more junior Director for Africa, plus a staff aide and an administrative assistant. During the first term of Bush 43, the directorate played an assertive role on Africa policy. Senior Director Jendayi Frazer, a Stanford PhD who had a brief stint in the African Directorate during the Bush 41 administration, was specially selected for the position by Condoleezza Rice, her academic mentor. When Frazer became Ambassador to South Africa in 2004, she was succeeded by Cindy Courville, a PhD from the University of Denver, who came to the job from a senior position in the Defense Intelligence Agency, following a tour as NSC Director for Africa. Frazer became Assistant Secretary of State for African Affairs after a year as ambassador in Pretoria. Courville became the first U.S. Ambassador to the African Union at the end of 2006.

From the beginning of the Bush administration, the White House played a leading role in shaping an activist policy toward Sudan, spurred by domestic U.S. politics. The Clinton administration, by contrast, had a hostile relationship with Khartoum and did not get involved in efforts to resolve the civil war.[59] The Sudan civil war became an issue in the 2000 presidential campaign. The Rev. Franklin Graham, whose organization, Samaritan's Purse, operated a clinic in Southern Sudan repeatedly bombed by Khartoum, told candidate Bush a few days before the election, "Governor, if you become president, I hope you put Sudan on your radar." Shortly after Bush took office, a group of evangelicals, plus Catholic and Jewish activists, met with senior presidential advisor Karl Rove and urged the White House to intercede in the war in Sudan and halt the oppression of Southern Sudanese Christians.[60] NSA Rice told Jendayi Frazer that the President wanted to do something about Sudan.

Meanwhile, at the State Department, Walter Kansteiner, the new Assistant Secretary for Africa, persuaded Colin Powell that policy toward Sudan should be changed. Powell authorized a meeting in Kenya in which the Sudanese were told that (a) if they cut their ties with terror networks, (b) stopped interfering with their neighbors, and (c) made a good faith effort to end the civil war, the United States would take Sudan off the terrorist list and send an ambassador to Khartoum. The Sudanese government replied positively a few days later.

The White House became alarmed. Rice chaired a Principals Committee meeting and announced that the President wanted a senior person to work on Sudan. Powell was willing to accept a special envoy, provided he could make the choice. A list of possibilities was vetted between the NSC and the White House. Just before September 11, Bush announced the appointment of former Republican senator John Danforth as Special Envoy for Peace in Sudan, a striking exception to his "no-envoys" approach.[61] Danforth, an Episcopalian clergyman with a degree from Yale Divinity School, was not warmly welcomed by the evangelicals but was acceptable to them.

The new envoy's relationship with the State Department got off to a rocky start. Danforth wanted an aircraft for his visits to the region to demonstrate to the parties that he had status and clout with the White House. The Africa Bureau had some trouble arranging the logistics, heightening Danforth's suspicion that he was being obstructed. After he secured the services of veteran diplomat Robert B. Oakley, who had worked in the NSC and as Special Envoy to Somalia, most of the problems in the interagency relationship were worked out, and Danforth collaborated closely with both the NSC Directorate for Africa and the Africa Bureau.[62]

Danforth accepted the informal State Department accord with Khartoum and set about exploring a basic framework for negotiations. He had an early success in securing a cease-fire in the Nuba Mountain region of south central Sudan, which permitted the resumption of food shipments to the devastated area. That confidence-building measure helped him to gain trust from both sides. After talks with the two parties and broad consultations in the region and in Europe, he reported to President Bush at the beginning of 2002 that the United States could not bring about peace by itself and that a workable peace process would have to be multilateral in nature. Danforth recommended that the United States support the IGAD (which grouped the countries of the Horn) as the mediator between Khartoum and the Sudan People's Liberation Army. He argued that the process should have balanced support from Kenya and Egypt, representing Africa and the Arab world, and should be monitored and encouraged by three extra-regional powers: the United States, the United Kingdom, and Norway. Bush agreed. The parties accepted this 2+2+3 formula and began talks under IGAD auspices, with Kenyan General Lazarus Sumbeiywo as mediator. That led rather quickly to the Machakos Protocol of July 2002, which incorporated basic principles of peace: priority to the unity of Sudan, but a six-year interim period leading to a referendum in which the South would choose whether or not to remain part of the Sudanese state.[63]

Despite the relatively quick agreement on basic principles, it took an additional 30 months to reach the CPA of 2005, requiring laborious negotiation of agreements and protocols on power-sharing, wealth-sharing, security arrangements, and contested areas lying on the fault line between North and South. Part of the reason for the protracted talks was the lack of trust between both sides and the conviction that the details were important.

A second reason was Khartoum's increasing preoccupation with the rebellion which broke out in Darfur, Sudan's vast western region, in 2003.[64] However, part of the delay stemmed from Sen. Danforth's intermittent engagement with the negotiation process. Even though the formal negotiations were carried out under Kenyan auspices, the U.S. government was heavily engaged behind the scenes in pressuring the parties to move forward. Danforth initially believed he could wrap up the assignment within six months or a year at most. The envoy continued his law practice and many of his other commitments and therefore "parachuted" into the region periodically, during openings in his schedule, to move the negotiations along or deal with specific problems. The timing of his visits did not necessarily always coincide with the exigencies of the Sudan peace process. Moreover, by mid-2004 he became U.S. Permanent Representative to the United Nations. At that point the NSC permitted the position of Special Envoy for Sudan to lapse.

Backstopping the day-to-day North-South negotiations was left to State's Africa Bureau, especially Deputy Assistant Secretary of State Charles Snyder and the Sudan Programs Group, led by Senior Representative for Sudan Michael Ranneberger and Coordinator for Sudan Affairs Jeff Millington. Ranneberger and Millington spent much of their time in Kenya, making suggestions and cajoling and pressuring both sides. Colin Powell made periodic phone calls to Sudan People's Liberation Movement (SPLM) leader John Garang and to Ali Osman Taha, the chief Sudanese negotiator. Powell visited Kenya, site of the talks, in October 2003, to push them along and returned for the signing ceremony in Nairobi in January 2005.

In 2006, the White House resumed the lead on Sudan because of a crescendo of criticism from a coalition of nongovernmental organizations (NGOs) that the Bush administration was not serious about stopping genocide in Sudan's western Darfur region. By that time it had become clear that the Darfur Peace Agreement, signed in 2005 after intense involvement by Deputy Secretary of State Robert Zoellick, had failed to bring the conflict to an end. (See Chapter 3.) President Bush was frustrated, and Hadley asked Peter Feaver, his Special Advisor for Strategic Planning and Institutional Reform, to come up with some new options. Working with the Director for Stabilization and the Africa Directorate, Feaver proposed new sanctions and appointment of a new Special Envoy for Sudan. Jendayi Frazer, who had become Assistant Secretary of State for Africa, and her replacement as NSC Senior Director for Africa, Cindy L. Courville, allied in strenuous resistance to another special envoy. Feaver favored selection of Michael Gerson, the presidential speech writer and assistant for policy and strategic planning who had become involved in deliberations about Darfur. However, President Bush announced in September 2006 the appointment of former USAID Administrator Andrew Natsios as Special Envoy for Sudan. Natsios clashed repeatedly with Assistant Secretary Frazer over policy leadership on Sudan. Interagency coordination did not proceed smoothly. Nevertheless, during

Natsios's tenure the United States succeeded in obtaining passage of a Security Council resolution approving a UN/AU force of 26,000, including police (UNAMID, African Union/United Nations Hybrid operation in Darfur).[65] Natsios also devoted much time to holding together the CPA, as disagreements over the border area of Abyei, a major oil center, threatened to explode into violence.

Natsios resigned at the end of 2007 and was replaced almost immediately by Richard S. Williamson, a Chicago attorney who had worked in previous administrations on UN business. The hope was that under Williamson Sudan would "not cause [the administration] so much difficulty internationally and internally."[66] The relationship with the Africa Bureau remained strained but became less tempestuous. However, Williamson worked largely out of Chicago, while continuing his law practice and relying on a junior staff in Washington. That approach complicated information sharing and interagency coordination. Williamson concentrated on moving UNAMID toward full deployment. He also helped broker agreement on a "road map" to resolve the standoff over Abyei. Khartoum's exploitation of the fragmentation of the Darfur rebel groups kept an effective Darfur peace accord out of reach.

The Sudan experience suggests there is a place for a high-level special envoy when there is significant international and domestic pressure on Washington to move a foreign conflict toward a negotiated solution. The envoy should have access to the President to be perceived as speaking on his behalf to both sides. Ideally the envoy should work at the task full time, rather than devoting half-time to another job. (That requirement would unfortunately probably reduce the pool of potential envoys.) For maximum effectiveness—and to reduce friction with the State Department geographic bureau concerned—the envoy should be staffed primarily by one or two relatively senior (office director/deputy director level) personnel from that bureau, as was the case with Senator Danforth.

Asia

During the Bush 43 administration, the Directorate for Asian Affairs covered the vast region from Pakistan to Japan and Oceania. It focused primarily on China, Japan, and the North Korean nuclear issue. On conflict issues the NSC played an important role on Nepal. Its modest role on the Philippines is delineated in Chapter 7.

After 1990, Nepal, a constitutional monarchy, experienced both fitful movement toward democracy and an indigenous Maoist insurrection, launched in 1996. In early 2001 the country was destabilized by a deadly royal family quarrel in which the Crown Prince shot to death the King and other family members before committing suicide. The King's surviving brother Gyanendra succeeded him. After peace talks with the Maoists failed in 2001, the insurgency resumed. Gyanendra dissolved the parliament and in 2002 assumed executive power, canceling parliamentary elections. When three successive appointed prime ministers failed to resolve the crisis, the king reconstituted a new cabinet in early 2005 under his direct authority, proclaimed a state of emergency, and suspended fundamental rights. A year later the political parties joined the Maoists in countrywide demonstrations which forced him to relinquish power and reinstate parliament. In 2006 a comprehensive peace agreement was negotiated between Maoists and a Seven Party Alliance led by the Nepalese Congress Party. The enactment of an interim constitution in 2007, which stripped the monarch of both real and ceremonial powers, set the stage for elections to a constituent assembly for a new constitution. The elections were twice delayed but took place in April 2008. No party won a majority, but the Maoists (now the Communist Party of Nepal) won the most seats, and their leader became prime minister four months later.

The Bush administration became alarmed over the advance of the Maoists, particularly after reports surfaced that they were seeking to establish a link with al-Qa'ida operatives in Bangladesh. India was the major arms supplier to the Royal Nepalese Army, but the United States was providing some training. To improve army effectiveness, New Delhi and Washington worked out an agreement under which American M-16 rifles were provided to the army. Gyanendra's dissolution of parliament and cancellation of elections set off a major internal debate in Washington. The State Department advocated halting the supply of weapons to promote a political settlement, while continuing training. Defense opposed suspending the flow of arms. To resolve the issue, the NSC Directorate for Asia placed the issue before the South Asia Policy Coordination Committee, chaired by Christina Rocca, Assistant Secretary of State for South and Central Asia. Although both the Defense and the Democracy Directorates had some interest in the issue, they deferred to the Asia Directorate. In the end the PCC reached consensus to halt the arms sales and continue training—the approach advocated by NSC and State—while pursuing a joint effort with India and Britain to persuade the king to come to agreement with the parties. Defense agreed to the approach following a phone conversation between DNSA Stephen Hadley and Deputy Secretary of Defense Wolfowitz.[67] The decision was reinforced by the Congress, which enacted an amendment to the foreign assistance appropriation bill in November 2005 cutting off new military assistance until the Secretary of State could certify that the Government of Nepal had restored civil liberties and had set down a clear timetable to restore democracy.[68] The United States, despite misgivings about the Maoists, supported the peace agreement and the democratic process, and the restriction on military assistance was lifted.

FUTURE PEACE-BUILDING ISSUES FOR THE NSC

The Bush 43 administration retained the basic NSC structural model bequeathed by the Bush 41 and Clinton teams, but operated differently in practice. Bush largely sidelined the NSC deputies and principals in the decision to attack Iraq. In part for that reason and because of the influence of the Vice President Cheney, NSA Condoleezza Rice failed to broker the division between the Secretaries of State and Defense with lamentable results for R&S. Bush did use the NSC mechanism to good effect in deciding on the mode of intervention in Afghanistan in 2001 and in deciding on the 2007 "surge." The experience of Bush 43 tends to confirm the wisdom of the Bush-Scowcroft structural model.

The Clinton administration's approach to complex emergencies contained in PDD 56 was neither fully developed nor applied in detail. Nevertheless, by jettisoning it at the outset, the President and NSC were empty handed when confronted by the challenge of R&S in Afghanistan and Iraq. With Defense in charge of both military strategy and "post-conflict" reconstruction, the NSC did not recapture a decisive role on Iraq until late 2003, and, arguably, an interagency approach to stabilization was applied too late to be fully successful. The debacle in Iraq did lead to the NSC initiative, under Congressional pressure, to create a new formal mechanism for R&S. The Secretary of State gained the interagency lead, working through a bureau-sized office, S/CRS, created in 2004. Other agency roles were prescribed by NSPD 44, mandating a "whole of government" approach, at the end of 2005. The new mechanism was not applied to Afghanistan and Iraq, however, although coordination among State, Defense, USAID, and the NSC improved in both war theaters.

For the future, the White House should learn the lessons of the early Bush 43 administration and build on its painfully constructed legacy. In particular, the NSC must play a central role in securing a whole-of-government approach to peace-building, stabilization, and reconstruction. The Obama administration should decide whether coordination of R&S—or more precisely the roles of coordinating contingency planning guidance and crisis response—will remain at the Department of State or be attached to the NSC. This study suggests that the NSC should not become operational except under extraordinary circumstances and then only temporarily, as for example in Anthony Lake's role in moving forward the Clinton administration's strategy on Bosnia. Even if S/CRS remains sited in the State Department, it cannot work effectively unless empowered by the NSC. The NSC must ensure that S/CRS is adequately funded in the administration's Function 150 budget requests. It must also lean on other agencies, especially Defense, but also Justice, Treasury, and others, if adequate cooperation with S/CRS is not forthcoming.

To carry out that empowering function, the NSC should position carefully those within its walls bearing the peace-building function. The current position of the Director for Stability Operations is anomalous. Although the experience in Iraq and Afghanistan was the reason for the new embrace of R&S, the Director has not been involved in Iraq or Afghanistan, even though more work in R&S has been done there than anywhere else. The position was taken out of the Defense Directorate in 2005 but mistakenly placed in the Directorate of Relief, Stabilization and Development, which positioned it under the DNSA for International Economics, who is primarily focused on trade and financial systems. The Director of Stability Operations, whose core relationship is with S/CRS, was able to operate rather autonomously, but did not have the advantage of the full bureaucratic weight of the NSC as a back-stop. Returning the position to the Defense Policy Directorate would be inadvisable; that directorate is too preoccupied with the concerns of the Defense Department. One possible alternative would be to modify the position of DNSA for Combating Terrorism into a DNSA for Combating Terrorism and Building Peace, placing under that official the existing Senior Director for Combating Terrorism and a Senior Director for Peace-Building, Stabilization and Reconstruction. To place stabilization in that cluster would be to tie it in more closely to Defense, State, and the intelligence community, as well as to collaboration with allies. Even the best organizational arrangement will work properly only if the DNSA and the Senior Director are included from the outset on all issues relating to U.S. military intervention abroad.

Apart from Iraq and Afghanistan, where large numbers of U.S. troops are deployed, peace-building and post-conflict reconstruction tended to follow traditional modes in the Bush 43 White House. The NSC, with the regional directorates in chief action roles, took the lead on conflicts of special significance to the President, with heavy emphasis on a broad multilateral approach in Latin America, Asia, and Africa. This approach often featured a vanguard role by regional organizations and the United Nations. Although this pattern worked reasonably well, it would be desirable to ensure the involvement from the beginning of those NSC elements concerned with R&S.[69] The purpose would not be to divide policy responsibility between the geographic directorates and the peace-building function. The geographic directorates should retain the policy lead. It would rather be to ensure that considerations relating to the strategy and techniques of R&S are factored into policy and its implementation.

CHAPTER 3

THE DIPLOMACY OF PEACE-BUILDING: THE DEPARTMENT OF STATE

Diplomats are the counselors of statesmen in the arts of peace.
—Chas. W. Freeman, Jr.[1]

THE ROLE OF DIPLOMACY IN PEACE-BUILDING

The State Department is the nerve center of diplomacy in the U.S. government. Diplomatic activity does take place in the White House, particularly from the President and the NSC. It takes place exceptionally at the policy levels of the Pentagon and USAID, as well as other agencies. But State is in charge of the diplomatic function.

Diplomacy today consists of three basic elements:

- Communicating with foreign governments and international organizations,
- Planning and implementing foreign policy, and
- Foreign operations.

Communication is the traditional task of diplomacy: talking and listening to foreign officials, reporting back home the interaction and the local context, and negotiating with other governments. American diplomats do not normally make high-level policy, but they do advise on policy, carry out policy, and engage in policy planning. In recent decades, American diplomats have increasingly been involved in operations, that is, running systems, programs, and projects.[2]

Diplomatic communication is a key ingredient in official peace-building. At the outset, it is normally the *only* ingredient. As soon as the U.S. government takes cognizance of a foreign conflict, diplomacy begins. The United States conveys its concern about the impact of the violence to the government where the conflict is taking place. It may seek additional information about that government's approach and usually urges a peaceful solution. Diplomatic communication is normally undertaken by a U.S. embassy under instructions from the Secretary of State or senior State Department officials to whom the Secretary has delegated that responsibility.

As peace-building gains momentum in a particular case, diplomacy has three basic functions:

1. To create—and maintain—a consensus on the approach to peace-building in any given case. Does the government of the country in which the conflict is taking place accept outside counsel and support or does it insist on treating the conflict as a matter solely of domestic jurisdiction? Are other governments in the region concerned about the violence? What do they propose to do? Is there interest in action in the UN General Assembly or the Security Council? Which government or governments should take the lead? How should the approach be adjusted to changes on the ground? Consensus is usually forged through diplomatic conversations between Washington and the capitals concerned.

2. To plan the vehicle for peace-building. It was diplomatic planning which put together NATO's role in Bosnia and Kosovo. It was diplomatic planning which fashioned a "coalition of the willing" to intervene in Iraq, when the idea of a second Security Council resolution was dropped in March 2003. Diplomatic planning set in motion sponsorship of negotiations between Khartoum and the SPLM by the IGAD.

3. To operate a program of post-conflict (sometimes mid-conflict) R&S. Multiple projects may be created, ranging from reintegration of former combatants into their communities to repair of local infrastructure and preparations for elections. The process normally requires careful diplomatic coordination with host country officials, international organizations, and other governments involved.

STATE'S PEACE-BUILDING ROLE IN THE NATIONAL SECURITY STRATEGY AND ITS OWN PLANNING

As discussed in Chapter 2, the White House published a National Security Strategy in 2002. The Strategy set forth a set of "strategic tasks," of which "working with others to defuse regional conflicts" was most directly related to peace-building diplomacy. The importance of "defusing regional conflicts" stems from the danger that regional crises will strain alliances and reignite major power rivalries. "Where violence erupts and states falter, the U.S. will work with friends and partners to alleviate suffering and restore stability." The strategic principle guiding the U.S. approach was the need to invest in "building the international relationships and institutions that can manage local crises when they emerge."

In a follow-up to the President's National Security Strategy, State and USAID published jointly a 2004–2009 Strategic Plan. In line with the Strategy, the Plan's first strategic objective, "achieve peace and security," emphasized the strategic priority of regional stability.[3] Internal conflicts slated for priority attention included Afghanistan, Israel-Palestine, Sudan,

Nepal, and Sri Lanka.[4] In Africa, the Plan projected coordination with European allies and international institutions "to strengthen fragile states, provide peace operations, and to attempt to address the underlying socio-economic factors feeding conflict, especially in the Great Lakes Region, Horn of Africa, and West Africa." The Plan was unexceptional as a State Department document. It was "policy planning," setting forth priorities but not tying them to detailed operational plans or to budgets and human resource requirements.

The updated Strategy published by the White House in 2006 devoted considerable attention to State Department modes of engagement in the strategic task of "defusing regional conflicts." Diplomacy was cited as the major tool for conflict resolution through engaging regional partners and advancing selective offers of U.S. mediation. Diplomacy, including cooperation with NATO and promotion of UN reform—and not the provision of U.S. troops—was to buttress an expansion of international peacekeeping capability. State's new Office of the Coordinator for Reconstruction and Stabilization was expected to plan and manage post-conflict R&S. The 2006 version, while noting challenges, avoided singling out for attention specific regional conflicts.

The next year State and USAID issued a revised joint Strategic Plan for the 2007–2012 period. Although the White House Strategy was referred to here and there in the Plan, the two documents were not closely integrated.[5] Indeed the Strategic Plan marked a sharp break with previous strategy documents both in the greater sophistication of its treatment of conflict and in its explicit linking of strategic objectives to budgetary objectives. The latter change reflected Secretary of State Rice's 2006 decision to integrate the State-USAID budget under a Deputy Secretary of State who would also serve as USAID Administrator and "Director of Foreign Assistance." (See Chapter 6.)

The strategic objective of peace and security dropped "regional stability" as a strategic priority in favor of "conflict prevention, mitigation and response" and "security cooperation and security sector reform."[6] Both are key elements in dealing with violent conflict. Under prevention/mitigation/response, the strategy pledged "diplomatic and development activities . . . [to] reduce the threat or impact of violent conflict through early warning, crisis response planning and management, and rapid response capability." State would "lead and coordinate whole-of-government efforts to prepare . . . and conduct stabilization and reconstruction operations." It would work with key international partners to improve efforts to prevent and respond to conflict and post-conflict situations. Recognizing the precarious legitimacy of post-conflict states, State and USAID would provide assistance to help secure justice.

The final point underlines a complication in the Plan schema. Several of the strategic goals listed alongside "achieving peace and security," such as "governing justly and democratically," "promoting economic growth and prosperity," and humanitarian assistance, often feed into conflict prevention or post-conflict reconstruction, even though they have applications broader than peace-building. Just and democratic governing embraces rule of law, good governance, political competition, and civil society. Economic growth promotion embraces fostering private markets and agriculture. That complexity was acknowledged in the Plan under "multilateral action in pursuit of peace and security." "Post-conflict peacebuilding [is considered] to promote democratic values, respect for human dignity, [and] respect for rule of law" and to create an environment for development.

The revised strategic plan outlined regional priorities:

- Iraq, for assistance in economic and political reconstruction, as well as in creating a capable security force;
- Afghanistan, to enhance government effectiveness and build the capacity of the army and national police;
- Sri Lanka and Nepal, where the United States is prepared, when appropriate, to provide reconciliation and mediation expertise, as well as post-conflict support for disarmament and demobilization;
- Sudan, top priority in Africa, to support implementation of the CPA between North and South, and negotiate introduction of a credible peacekeeping force into Darfur;
- Support for post-conflict reconstruction in Liberia and the Democratic Republic of the Congo; and
- For the Western Hemisphere, a focus not on peace-building but "protecting the democratic state." (There is no reference to specific countries, not even Colombia or Haiti.)[7]

THE SECRETARY OF STATE: LOCUS OF AUTHORITY IN PEACE-BUILDING DIPLOMACY

The center of power in the State Department is the seventh floor, where the Secretary, Deputy Secretaries, Under Secretaries, and the Operations Center of the Department are located. The Secretary of State is the chief diplomat of the United States but has multiple additional roles, including senior foreign policy advisor of the President, CEO of the State Department, and chief defender of administration foreign policy before the Congress. As chief diplomat the Secretary is constantly in communication with heads of government and foreign ministers of states with which the United States has relations, often dealing with questions of peace and conflict.

The Secretary's active involvement in peace-building activities is intermittent and highly selective. Involvement often reflects the interests of the President. After 9/11 Bush assigned to Secretary of State Colin Powell the diplomatic tasks required for an effective response to al-Qa'ida's attack. For Powell that meant mounting immediate diplomatic pressures on Pakistani President (and Army Chief of Staff) Parvez Musharraf to side with the United States against al-Qa'ida and the Taliban. Bush telephoned Musharraf, but it was Powell who talked soldier-to-soldier to the Pakistani leader to solidify the antiterrorist alliance and work out the *quid pro quo* in military and economic assistance.

Iraq was, of course, at the top of Powell's list of priorities from 2002 on, because of the President's determination to act, but the Secretary was a "reluctant warrior." As the war plan was being developed in the Defense Department and briefed to the Security Council principals by CENTCOM commander, General Tommy Franks, Powell perceived himself to be "in the refrigerator"—frozen out of the deliberations over Iraq. Meeting with President Bush and NSA Rice over a White House dinner in August 2002, Powell laid out considerations he believed the President had not taken into account: In taking down Saddam, Bush would become the "owner of 25 million people"; war could destabilize Egypt, Saudi Arabia, and Jordan; the intervention would not be "a walk in the woods" and could not be prosecuted successfully without a coalition; Bush would have to run for reelection on the war. Powell urged an approach to the United Nations or at least forging a broad coalition to topple Saddam Hussein. He did not, however, recommend against going to war.[8] The following month Powell called for resumption of UN arms inspections. He debated the issue with Vice President Cheney within the full NSC and won the argument to go for a UN Security Council resolution, probably because British Prime Minister Tony Blair—the indispensable "coalition" partner—insisted on it. With Powell leading the diplomacy, the UN Security Council unanimously passed Resolution 1441 in November, warning Saddam that if Iraq continued to violate its disarmament obligations, it would "face serious consequences." After Bush made the final decision to attack Iraq, he asked Powell, not whether he agreed, but "are you with me?" Powell said he would support the President. It was the Secretary of State who made the case, at a dramatic Security Council session, that Iraq's possession of weapons of mass destruction and failure to disclose them made military intervention essential to protect the American people.[9]

White House interest in Sudan also accounted for the periodic active engagement of Secretaries Powell and Rice. The President's intense desire to find a solution to the Darfur crisis was a factor in Colin Powell's unprecedented statement to the Congress that genocide was taking place after he visited Darfur in 2004.[10] Condoleezza Rice's visit to Sudan in 2005 reflected the President's interest more than personal commitment.[11]

High-level peace-building actions also often reflect the special concerns of the Secretary. Secretary Albright pushed Kosovo to the top of the U.S. diplomatic agenda in 1997. Secretary Rice seized the Israel-Palestine issue upon shifting from the NSC to the State Department. The Middle East peace process has traditionally taken a major portion of the Secretary's time, usually at the behest of the President. However, Rice has indicated to her biographers that when Bush asked her to become Secretary of State, she asked whether he would support creation of a Palestinian state and received an affirmative reply. In the wake of the Iraq imbroglio she wanted to help put the Middle East "back together in a different configuration . . . that lays a foundation [for peace]."[12] Before she could get talks started between the Palestinian Authority and Israel, however, Israel became enmeshed in war with the Hezbollah militia, ally of Syria and Iran, in a divided Lebanon. Rice became the chief negotiator in this crisis, traveling to Beirut and then Israel. She delayed endorsement of the cease-fire demanded by the Lebanese Prime Minister, European and other Arab governments in the hope that Israel would defeat or at least greatly weaken Hezbollah. When Israel failed to do so, she eventually backed a cease-fire. She negotiated personally the final Security Council resolution for a UN peacekeeping force acceptable to both Lebanon and Israel.[13] At the beginning of 2007, Rice launched her effort to bring about an Israeli agreement with the Palestinians on the formal creation of a Palestinian state. She did so even though the project was seriously compromised by the Hamas election victory of January 2006, the administration's decision to quarantine the Hamas prime minister, and the drift of Palestine toward civil war between Hamas and Fatah. She made seven trips to the region in 2007 and was the central figure in arranging the Annapolis Conference of November 2007, hosted by President Bush. It brought together Prime Ministers Abbas and Olmert to launch formal but unsuccessful talks aimed at a peace treaty.[14]

Often the Secretary is able to hand off high-profile peace-building tasks to the Deputy Secretary or Under Secretary for Political Affairs—or to a special envoy. In 2005 Rice passed the Sudan portfolio to Deputy Secretary Robert Zoellick. For a year Zoellick became, in effect, special envoy for Darfur and played an important personal role in the signature of the Darfur Peace Agreement (DPA) of May 2006.[15] Even though the Bush administration attempted to do away with special presidential envoys in its initial presidential directive, the possibility of a special envoy under the Secretary of State was left open. As described in Chapter 2, the decision to designate envoys for Sudan was a presidential action. The activities of special envoys for such tasks as Middle East Security (James Jones) and Gaza Disengagement (James Wolfensohn), Kosovo (Frank Wisner), Somalia (John Yates), and Northern Ireland (Richard Haass, Mitchell Reiss, and Paula Dobriansky) were more associated with the Secretary of State than with the White House.

MULTI-BUREAU ENGAGEMENTS IN STABILIZATION AND RECONSTRUCTION

Decisions by the President to commit the armed forces of the United States to regime change and/or intervention in a civil conflict in another state generate State Department involvement at many levels.

Afghanistan

The Bush administration's strategic response to 9/11—to intervene in the stalemated civil war in Afghanistan on the side of the Northern Alliance and dissident Pashtun leaders—immediately spawned a range of diplomatic tasks for the State Department. Among the first was securing international support through the United Nations, the function of the Bureau of International Organization Affairs. On September 12, at America's behest, the Council passed a resolution condemning the terrorist attacks, affirming the U.S. right of self-defense and calling on all states to bring to justice the perpetrators. A second Council resolution at the end of the month, invoking Chapter 7, termed the attacks a threat to international peace and called on all states to prevent the funding and harboring of terrorist groups. A third condemned the Taliban for harboring bin Laden and al-Qa'ida and expressed "support [for] the efforts of the Afghan people to replace the Taliban regime," in effect endorsing U.S. armed intervention in the civil war.[16] With U.S. support, Secretary-General Kofi Annan appointed Lakhdar Brahimi as his Special Representative for Afghanistan.

A second task was concluding arrangements with neighboring countries to facilitate U.S. military logistics in the theater. A. Elizabeth Jones, Assistant Secretary for European and Eurasian Affairs, led teams to Tajikistan and Kyrgyzstan which negotiated memoranda of understanding to set up support facilities, including temporary basing and force stationing rights in return for rent and additional assistance. "Gas and go" agreements were signed with Turkmenistan and Azerbaijan to permit refueling of aircraft. Overflight agreements were signed with Russia and Kazakhstan.[17]

A third task was centralizing the management of the diplomacy of intervention, stabilization, and reconstruction within the State Department. In October 2001 Secretary Powell appointed veteran diplomat James Dobbins, who had served the previous administration as special envoy for Somalia, Haiti, and the Balkans, as "Envoy to the Afghan Opposition." His mandate was to "corral the Afghan opposition and herd them into the government" and to work with concerned governments on issues related to the future of Afghanistan.[18] Dobbins and Brahimi convened the Northern Alliance and other opposition elements in Bonn in late November, where they created an interim authority and administration. Hamid Karzai, leader of the siege of Kandahar, became chairman. The "Bonn Agreement," signed December 5, also called for an international stabilization mission to help the Afghans establish security until they could do so on their own.[19] In late December 2002 the Security Council authorized an ISAF to reestablish a government and help reconstruct the economy.[20] Dobbins enjoyed considerable autonomy in his diplomatic role but laments that he was unable to influence the Defense Department on post-conflict reconstruction. The result was that ISAF was restricted to Kabul and could not play a wider peacekeeping role. A broad R&S program was stymied. Dobbins was able neither to obtain significant funding for reconstruction from the State Department budget nor to influence the use of narcotics and refugee funding, which was part of the State Department budget.[21] In the face of Defense Department resistance to a broad-gauged reconstruction program, Dobbins and U.S. military commanders struggled to come up with alternative approaches. The approach finally adopted was deployment after mid-2002 of Provincial Reconstruction Teams (PRTs) of up to 80 persons, basically made up of military personnel with a small Army civil affairs section and a handful of State and USAID officials. (See Chapter 5.) According to Dobbins, the military-dominated PRTs were an admission of failure to achieve post-conflict security and a "second-best approach" to R&S.[22]

In January 2002, Dobbins, retitled as Special Advisor to the Secretary of State on Afghanistan, shifted the site of his operations to Kabul and reopened the U.S. Embassy. Three months later Foreign Service Officer Robert P. J. Finn became Ambassador to Afghanistan and Dobbins stepped down. Finn was succeeded in November 2003 by Zalmay Khalilzad, an Afghan-American serving as Senior Director for Afghanistan at the NSC. The posting of a politically well-connected ambassador and administration preoccupation with Iraq shifted the weight of policymaking on Afghanistan somewhat away from Washington toward the embassy in Kabul. Khalilzad played a very active role, for example, in shepherding the Afghan electoral process through the presidential polls of October 2004, which elected Karzai as President.

The position of a special advisor for Afghanistan with international responsibilities lapsed with the departure of Dobbins. Instead, a Coordinator for Afghanistan, sited in the Bureau of South and Central Asian Affairs (SCA), was appointed to work the interagency process for the State Department, somewhat on the order of the Coordinator for Sudan Programs. (See Chapter 2.) Five senior officials served in that position 2002–2007, the last with the rank of Deputy Assistant Secretary of State.[23] The Coordinators for Afghanistan did not view themselves as managers or arbiters of the policy process, but instead as the day-to-day coordinators and integrators of the various elements of policy and resources among the agencies, with particular attention to the priorities of the State Department and the Ambassador in Kabul.

Critics in the State Department have charged that Afghanistan did not receive serious and sustained direction from the Secretary of State during the Bush administration and that there was no unified civilian command structure on Afghanistan. Some decisions were taken by the Secretary of State, others by the NSA. The absence of sustained leadership complicated the task of the Coordinators, who were constrained by being placed in a State Department geographic bureau. From that location the Coordinators had limited leverage to muscle their agenda through other State Department bureaus or other agencies such as USAID.

Iraq

From 2002 to 2008 the State Department struggled for influence on Iraq. NSPD 24 of January 20, 2003 gave responsibility for post-conflict Iraq not to the State Department but to Defense. Powell did not contest the decision, noting that it followed the model of postwar Germany and Japan.

He reasoned that only Defense would have the people and funds to carry it out. However, he did envisage an important role for the State Department —and particularly the Bureau of Near Eastern Affairs (NEA) with its expertise on the Arab world. He sent to the Pentagon State's Future of Iraq study, along with the names of some 75 State Department Middle East experts who could help with R&S.[24] The study, launched a few weeks after 9/11, assembled for nine months more than 200 Iraqi exiles into 17 working groups to strategize on reconstruction topics ranging from humanitarian assistance and economic revival to democracy and governance.[25] The voluminous report provided myriad useful details and identified key potential problems of stabilization. However, it was not crafted into the kind of operational plan dear to military planners and was largely ignored by the Defense Department.

The Pentagon's treatment of the roster of experts proposed by State for the reconstruction team also created friction. Rumsfeld personally rejected two heading the list: Thomas Warrick, who had led the Future of Iraq project, and Meghan O'Sullivan, a highly regarded member of State's Policy Planning Staff. Vice President Cheney's staff uncovered statements and writings attributed to Warrick critical of the administration's approach to Iraq. O'Sullivan's writings at the Brookings Institution before 9/11 had opposed military intervention against Saddam Hussein. Rumsfeld's office also rejected seven more State representatives Powell had asked to be assigned to the ORHA, the DOD unit assigned responsibility for post-conflict reconstruction. The rebuff led to a bitter dispute between the two cabinet secretaries. Ultimately, O'Sullivan (but not Warrick) was permitted to join the ORHA team, along with five of the other seven on Powell's list.[26] Actually senior positions in ORHA were fairly evenly divided among State (Humanitarian Affairs), USAID (Reconstruction), and Defense (civil affairs and governance).[27] Other State Department officers were assigned as senior advisors to the Iraqi Foreign Ministry, Ministry of Trade, Ministry of Minerals and Industry, and Ministry of Cultural Affairs, or as coordinators of specific sectors of the country.[28] ORHA soon disappeared and was replaced by the Coalition Provisional Authority (CPA).[29]

The U.S. administrator of Iraq and CPA chief from May 2003 to June 2004, Ambassador L. Paul (Jerry) Bremer, had spent a career in the Foreign Service, including an assignment as Ambassador to the Netherlands, but he did not get the job through the recommendation of the State Department. On his retirement from the Foreign Service, he became managing director of Kissinger Associates and developed ties with the conservative Heritage Foundation. He was CEO of Marsh Crisis Consulting, a risk and insurance services subsidiary of Marsh & McLennan Companies, when he was contacted by Deputy Defense Secretary Wolfowitz and Vice Presidential Chief of Staff I. Lewis (Scooter) Libby. The CPA was created and funded as a division of the U.S. DOD. Formally speaking, Bremer reported to the DOD and the White House and not to the State Department. In fact, he discovered after two months that his reports, which he had assumed were being forwarded by the Pentagon to other agencies, were being bottled up in the Pentagon.

He then insisted that his own separate diplomatic communication channel be established.[30] Bremer's first hires were two retired ambassadors, including Hume Horan, the leading Foreign Service Arabist of his generation. Senior CPA staff were largely from State, USAID, and the Treasury Department.[31] Nevertheless, numerous Bush administration loyalists were recruited for the CPA out of an office in the Pentagon, some almost completely lacking international experience. Perhaps the most controversial was former New York police commissioner Bernard Kerik, who took charge of police training for a few months before departing abruptly.[32]

In November 2003 the administration decided to end the CPA after one year. The CPA and the Iraqi Governing Council signed an agreement establishing June 2004 as the transfer of authority date. Secretary Powell asked Ambassador Francis Ricciardone, Jr., to become the State Department Iraq Transition Coordinator, working in tandem with a Defense Department Coordinator. A multi-sector transition team was created under the two coordinators.[33] When Bremer left Baghdad in June, the State Department assumed the lead role in representing and managing U.S. interests in Iraq, working through its embassy, reopened under the leadership of Ambassador John Negroponte. The embassy, unlike the modest unit closed down by Washington in 1990 after Saddam's invasion of Kuwait, was relocated in the highly fortified Green Zone and became the largest American diplomatic post in the world.

In March 2005, Secretary Rice, newly arrived at State, appointed Richard Jones, former Ambassador to Kuwait and briefly a deputy to Bremer, as Senior Advisor to the Secretary and Coordinator for Iraq (S/I). Jones's mandate was "to develop, coordinate and lead implementation of policy on Iraq," chairing an interagency steering group on Iraq policy. The appointment was aimed at ratcheting up the State Department's capacity to influence policy and its implementation. Two other Coordinators followed Jones—James Jeffrey, who then moved to the second position at the NSC, and David Satterfield. The Coordinator had a small office, ranging from three to five persons, formally part of the Office of the Secretary of State. The work of the office and the division of labor with the Office of Iraqi Affairs in the Bureau of Near Eastern Affairs (NEA/I) was *ad hoc*. In early 2008, for example, the Coordinator focused on the internal politics of Iraq. His deputy focused on the civilian budget for Iraq and the work of the PRTs, first used in Afghanistan and then imported into Iraq in 2005. A third officer worked on other politico-military issues. NEA/I was divided into three "pillars"—political, politico-military, and economic. The Coordinator had the closest relationship with the ambassador in Baghdad.[34] NEA/I was closest to the political section at Embassy Baghdad. The S/I relationship with NEA/I was carefully managed under a kind of "board of directors" comprising the Coordinator, the NEA deputy assistant secretary charged with Iraq, and the NEA/I director.

In 2007 the Coordinator's office was heavily engaged in moving forward the civilian "surge," accompanying the dispatch of five additional military brigades to Iraq. The President's speech presenting a "new way forward" in Iraq called for doubling the PRTs so that they might really influence R&S at the local level. Secretary Rice insisted on State leadership of the effort, and S/I chaired the PRT working group, which included representatives from Defense and Commerce and the Office of Provincial Affairs at the embassy in Baghdad. The working group in turn ran separate working groups on recruiting, training, funding, and logistics. State took pride in recruiting 300 officers for new PRTs during that year.[35]

GEOGRAPHIC BUREAUS: LINCHPINS OF PEACE-BUILDING DIPLOMACY

In the normal course of events, the Secretary's involvement in peace-building arises from decisions generated from lower levels of the State Department. The Secretary's engagement and ratification of such decisions stem less from her role as chief diplomat than from being State Department CEO, presiding over its numerous geographic and functional bureaus.

Headed by assistant secretaries of state, the geographic bureaus—Africa, East Asia and the Pacific, Europe and Eurasia, Near East, South and Central Asia, and Western Hemisphere—are the engines of most U.S. peace-building diplomacy. This traditional role is based essentially on geographical expertise.[36] Information on a particular country is centralized within these bureaus, organized into offices that group a number of countries as "desks."[37] In the case of small countries, one desk officer may be responsible for two or three countries. The desk is the focal reception point for reporting from the U.S. embassy in that country—including information about conflict—and draws the attention of the assistant secretary and relevant deputy assistant secretaries to events that may have policy significance. If civil conflict breaks out overseas, the U.S. embassy reports developments to relevant agencies in Washington, nearby U.S. embassies, and the concerned military combatant command. However, it is a small group of State Department officers, likely including the desk officer, the country director, and "policy level" individuals in the assistant secretary's office who decide how the State Department and the embassy should react. These officials normally take into account the recommendations of the U.S. ambassador, who is on site and therefore hopefully well placed to understand the developing crisis.

The following cases illustrate various modes in which the geographic bureaus deal with internal conflict overseas.

Bureau of African Affairs (AF): Liberia and the Democratic Republic of the Congo

In 2003 a new crisis in Liberia seized the attention of U.S. policymakers. The international community considers that the United States bears special responsibility for Liberia's peace and security in the international arena, but

U.S. leadership in dealing with the Liberian civil war, which began in 1989, had been uneven and limited. The first Bush administration declined to intervene when the rebel forces of Charles Taylor threatened to overrun Monrovia in mid-1989. Instead it supported diplomatically the decision by the ECOWAS to send a military blocking force. In the 1995–97 period, the Clinton administration facilitated an agreement between Nigeria and Taylor leading to a cease-fire and an election won by Taylor. Neither administration supported U.S. military intervention nor even a UN peacekeeping force. Taylor's repressive actions as President of Liberia revived the civil war, dormant since his election in 1997. His blatant intervention on behalf of the bloody Revolutionary United Front insurgency in Sierra Leone generated sanctions by the United States and the United Nations and an indictment by the Special Court for Sierra Leone.

In July 2003, when the leading Liberian insurgent opposition group (LURD) reached the outskirts of Monrovia, the Bush administration came under pressure to intervene militarily.[38] The Africa bureau favored intervention and won the support of Secretary Powell. The NSC Africa Directorate advocated intervention and was quietly working with the European command to develop the case. The issue was debated at several meetings of the NSC Principals, including the President. Powell made the case for intervention, but Secretary of Defense Rumsfeld argued that Liberia was not important to the United States, which should keep its focus on Iraq and Afghanistan. The Vice President backed Rumsfeld. Since President Bush was scheduled to leave soon for his first African trip, inaction on Liberia threatened to put him in an unfavorable light.[39] There was indecision for critical weeks until Colin Powell met one-on-one with the President, arguing that the dispatch of a small military force could quickly stabilize the situation, which could then be handed over to the United Nations.[40] Rumsfeld had a private meeting with the President counseling against intervention. NSA Rice had the final word with the President, advocating limited military action.[41] Bush finally agreed but instructed the Defense Department to keep "boots on the ground" to a minimum. Joint Task Force—Liberia, incorporating 2,000 marines, stood off Liberia for 90 days, but only about 200 rotated on shore any given day.[42] U.S. harrier jets buzzed the LURD forces menacingly to keep them in line. The U.S. naval force operated in tandem with deployment of a new ECOWAS force, a bridge to a larger UN peacekeeping force of 15,000 which arrived at year-end. Diplomatically, the State Department and U.S. diplomats in the field backed and facilitated the agreement reached by West African leaders and Liberian insurgents in Accra, Ghana in mid-August setting up a transitional government.[43] The United States also persuaded Nigerian President Obasanjo to offer asylum to Taylor, thus extracting him from the war zone and facilitating the transition to the successful democratic elections of 2005.

In the Congo, insurgent leader Laurent Kabila came to power in 1997 with the support of the Tutsi-led Rwandan government, after the fall of longtime president Mobutu Sese-Seko. The Tutsis had taken power in Rwanda when they broke the back of the 1994 genocide campaign. They wanted to keep under control the Interahamwe Hutu militia which had fled Rwanda into the Congo. After a year Kabila ordered his backers to leave. That precipitated a regional donnybrook when Rwanda and Uganda attacked Kabila, and Zimbabwe and Angola defended him. In 2001 Kabila was assassinated and replaced by his son Joseph. The change in leadership led to several years of negotiations under African auspices and a spate of signed agreements, but war continued, along with blatant exploitation of the Congo's mineral wealth by its neighbors. An important destabilizing element was poisonous relations among Kinshasa, Kigali, and Kampala. The United Nations deployed a peacekeeping force (UN Mission in the Congo—MONUC) beginning in 1999, but it was not very effective. An estimated 4 million died in the eastern Congo alone between 1998 and 2003, the vast majority from combat-related malnutrition and disease.

The Bush administration did not play an active diplomatic role. Washington quietly supported South African diplomatic leadership to bring the Congolese factions to a peaceful settlement and confined itself to dispatching humanitarian aid.[44]

In late 2003 a new deputy assistant secretary of state in the African Bureau, Donald Yamamoto, visited the region and received requests from Kabila, Rwandan President Paul Kagame, and Ugandan President Yoweri Museveni for U.S. assistance in ending the Congo crisis. Yamamoto recommended that the United States host a meeting of the three. The idea initially had little support from skeptical Foreign Service Officers but found favor at the Africa Directorate of the NSC, which had been advocating a more active U.S. policy. Defense was neutral because no military resources were at stake. Eventually, Secretary of State Powell approved support for convening what came to be known as the Tripartite Joint Commission, linking the three governments. It met for the first time in May 2004 at the ministerial level. The tension and animosity which marked the initial meetings gradually dissipated.[45] In 2005 Burundi joined the group, retitled as the Tripartite Plus Joint Commission. In addition to diplomatic support, the United States funded the creation of and training for an "analysis fusion cell" bringing together intelligence officers from the four countries to exchange information on "negative forces"—the various militia groups roiling the eastern Congo.[46] The Commission process reduced considerably but did not entirely eliminate the threat of a new Rwandan intervention in the eastern Congo.

UN operations strengthened, including MONUC, as the international community gained confidence from the Tripartite process.[47] The quieting of cross-border tensions and massive UN electoral assistance set the stage for the generally successful elections held in July 2006. After the elections the Commission continued its work.[48] In December 2007, Museveni, Kagame, Burundian President Nkurunziza, and the Congolese Minister of State for the Interior, representing Kabila, met with Secretary of State Rice

DONALD Y. YAMAMOTO

In 2003 Donald Y. Yamamoto became Deputy Assistant Secretary of State in the Bureau of African Affairs. Yamamoto, son of Japanese immigrants and a native of Seattle, grew up in New York and graduated from Columbia University, where he did graduate work in international relations. When he entered the Foreign Service in 1980, he focused on Asia, taking advantage of his Japanese language skills. An early tour in Beijing coincided with the Tiananmen Square massacres. He subsequently became principal officer at the U.S. consulate in Fukuoka, Japan. Thereafter he shifted to Africa, where his effectiveness as permanent chargé d'affaires at the U.S. Embassy in Asmara, Eritrea, attracted the attention of the Africa Bureau leadership. He was brought back to AF as deputy director for East Africa before being dispatched as Ambassador to tiny Djibouti. A slight and affable man, Yamamoto is a ferocious worker and very persistent.

Selected as Deputy Assistant Secretary of State, Yamamoto found himself with responsibility for a general peace-building portfolio for Central and East Africa. The Cameroon-Nigeria dispute had been arbitrated in favor of Cameroon in 2002 by the International Court of Justice. Yamamoto led a renewal of discussions on the Ethiopia-Eritrea conflict, unresolved by the 2002 Algiers Agreement, but he focused on the Congo. He encountered widespread cynicism in Washington about the prospects for peace in the Great Lakes region.

Yamamoto traveled to the region and held talks with Kabila, Rwandan President Kagame, and Ugandan President Museveni. To his surprise, all three said they needed U.S. assistance to resolve the conflict. Back in Washington, Yamamoto proposed that the United States underwrite a tripartite meeting, arguing that continuous outside intervention in the eastern Congo undermined the entire region. Initial interagency discussions and a couple of U.S. ambassadors in the field opposed the idea. Some colleagues questioned Yamamoto's sanity. Yamamoto found an ally in Alan W. Eastham, Jr., Country Director for Central Africa, however, and early in 2004 secured the critical backing of Jendayi Frazer, Senior Director for Africa at the Africa Directorate at the NSC, for the idea of a Tripartite Joint Commission. The Africa Bureau was in transition between assistant secretaries during the first half of 2003. Acting Assistant Secretary Charles Snyder shared the widespread skepticism about a commission but decided to back Yamamoto. Secretary of State Powell and National Security Advisor Rice supported the idea. Powell had one question: Did AF really believe a commission could work? When the bureau responded affirmatively, Powell commented that the approach was "high risk but innovative" and signed off on a proposal for interagency support for the peace process.

The Bush administration hosted meetings of the three parties at the ministerial level in May, July, August, and September 2004. Colin Powell opened the first meeting in Washington and Condoleezza Rice the second. Yamamoto and the NSC's Cindy L. Courville (initially deputy to Frazer at the NSC and then her replacement) presided over the substantive parts of the meetings. The first two were disagreeable. Yamamoto recalls that the Congolese were deeply resentful of the Rwandan delegation, and the Rwandans scornful of the Congolese. Later the tension began to ease. At a fifth meeting in Kigali in October 2004 the foreign ministers formally agreed to create the tripartite commission so that existing agreements would be honored and incidents threatening a new regional crisis could be sorted out. The addition of Burundi in September 2005 further defused sensitive feelings. Hostility gradually diminished between Congo and Rwanda. At the end of 2006 Don Yamamoto was confirmed by the Senate as U.S. Ambassador to Ethiopia and moved on to Addis Ababa, but the Tripartite Plus Joint Commission continued to meet. As of 2008 there had been more than 20 meetings, both at the ministerial and at the summit level.

in Addis Ababa. The meeting reinforced the Commission's commitment to implement existing agreements. Just as importantly, it confirmed high-level U.S. engagement with the Congo peace process, an engagement forged by the geographic bureau in alliance with its NSC counterpart.

Bureau of East Asian and Pacific Affairs (EAP): Philippines

The phasing out of U.S. military bases in the early 1990s did not end extensive military cooperation between the two countries. The State Department negotiated successfully the 1998 Visiting Forces Agreement, updating the Mutual Defense Treaty of 1952 and providing the basis for military collaboration with the Philippines in dealing with internal conflict. The most important violence has involved insurgent Muslim groups seeking an independent state on the southern island of Mindanao and the Sulu Peninsula: the Moro Islamic Liberation Front (MILF) and the Abu Sayyaf Group (ASG).[49]

After 9/11 the United States and the Philippines worked together in different ways to contain separatist insurgent terrorism. The State Department, operating through EAP, took the policy lead. State designated ASG, but not the MILF, as a foreign terrorist organization under the Immigration and Nationality Act and secured Philippine ratification of all international antiterrorist treaties. EAP viewed the MILF and ASG problems differently from Manila. The Philippine government was anxious to draw U.S. military forces into suppressing the MILF rebellion. The State Department, supported generally by the Defense Department, resisted, arguing that Manila had not made a good faith effort to deal with Muslim grievances, permitting its military to play a predatory role against the population. It also insisted that there were responsible Muslim leaders within the MILF.[50] The State Department deferred to regional and Islamic modes for negotiating peace. Since March 2001, Malaysia, an ASEAN partner of the Philippines, had been in the lead. Kuala Lumpur operated under the auspices of the Organization of the Islamic Conference (OIC), which became involved in mediating demands for Muslim separatism in the 1970s. In 2003, in the context of Malaysian mediation, the MILF issued a statement rejecting terrorism and denying ties to terrorist organizations. The statement set the stage for a limited Philippine military withdrawal and a cease-fire. Monitors from the OIC were stationed in the southern Philippines helping to keep the cease-fire in effect.[51]

The State Department did intervene with Manila to secure a role for the USIP in peace-building in Mindanao. USIP, headed by former Assistant Secretary for East Asia and the Pacific Richard Solomon, had received a grant to promote dialogue between Muslims and Christians in Mindanao but found the government in Manila unresponsive to its efforts to launch.[52] Suspicions voiced in the Philippine military that the project might work to the advantage of Jaamiyah Islamiyah, al-Qa'ida's Indonesian affiliate, may have made Manila's political leadership hesitate. EAP was anxious to demonstrate a united front in the U.S. government in favor of the USIP role. With the assistance of the NSC staff, it orchestrated a meeting of the East Asia Policy Coordination Committee, which endorsed the project. USIP was an important presence in Mindanao for the next four years.[53] (See Chapter 7.)

By contrast, the United States quietly supported a primarily security assistance approach to combating the ASG, which it considered an ally of al-Qa'ida and a group of ransom-seeking thugs.[54] In 2001 ASG seized a number of American hostages, beheading one, while two others died in a rescue attempt, creating a Congressional outcry and pressure for action. The State Department fended off demands for direct U.S. military action.[55] Instead, interagency consensus was reached that U.S. Special Forces troops should train, advise, and provide intelligence to Philippine forces without engaging in combat operations. The most dramatic American involvement was on Basilan Island, where during the first half of 2002 about 1,000 U.S. military personnel were involved in the mission, led by the 1st Special Forces Group in Okinawa.[56] Thereafter, the U.S. presence dropped to about 100. With U.S. support, the Philippine Army carried out a successful offensive against ASG in 2002 and again 2006 and 2007, killing several of the group's senior leaders.

Bureau of European and Eurasian Affairs (EUR): Nagorno-Karabakh

The collapse of the Soviet Union left the successor states with a group of territorial conflicts: Transnistria, Abkhazia, South Ossetia, and Nagorno-Karabakh. Transnistria, a strip of land populated by Russian speakers but falling within Moldova, declared its independence in 1990 with the objective of joining Russia. Abkhazia and South Ossetia are separatist regions of Georgia; the latter became the theater of the brief Russia-Georgia war of 2008. Nagorno-Karabakh is a former Soviet *oblast* (province) of Armenian speakers which voted in 1988 to secede from Azerbaijan and to join Armenia. The resulting war between Armenia and Azerbaijan, which lasted until 1994, was the bloodiest conflict emerging from the collapse of the Soviet Union. The Organization for Security and Cooperation in Europe (OSCE) attempted to deal with these disputes, sometimes called "frozen conflicts," because of their intractability. For the United States, Nagorno-Karabakh took priority among the conflicts because of a strong domestic Armenian lobby and the interest of U.S. oil companies in gaining access to Azerbaijani oil and, more generally, to the vast oil reserves of the Caspian Basin. The United States became cochair, along with France and Russia, of the OSCE's Minsk Group, set up in 1992 to deal with the crisis.

In 1997 the Clinton administration organized itself to play a more active role. It announced a policy to promote political and economic reform and reduce regional conflicts, while reinforcing energy security and exploiting U.S. commercial opportunities. It appointed both a Negotiator for Nagorno-Karabakh and Newly Independent States Regional Problems and a separate Senior Advisor for Caspian Energy Diplomacy. Both had ambassadorial rank, reported respectively to EUR and the Bureau of Economic, Energy, and Business Affairs (EEB) but worked in tandem.[57]

The Bush administration inherited a set of negotiations under the auspices of the Minsk Group which brought the Presidents of Armenia and Azerbaijan to Key West, Florida, in early 2001. Secretary Powell chaired the meeting, and President Bush met with the two leaders. Although American officials characterized the talks as making progress, there was little actual movement. Later in 2001, the Bush administration appointed its own Negotiator for Nagorno-Karabakh and Eurasian Conflicts (Rudolf Perina) and Senior Advisor for Caspian Basin Energy Diplomacy (Steven R. Mann). In 2004 the two positions were combined in Mann, and EUR became responsible for both issues. The major responsibility of the Negotiator has been to cochair meetings of the Minsk Group. Mann and the other OSCE negotiators brought the parties nearly to agreement in 2006 in a meeting chaired by French President Chirac. Peace-building efforts for Nagorno-Karabakh (and for Transnistria) remained an exclusively State Department concern and, with the exception of limited EEB involvement, a monopoly of EUR.[58]

Bureau of South and Central Asian Affairs (SCA): Sri Lanka

The United States was not involved in a major way in peace-building in Sri Lanka. Disaffection on the part of the minority Tamil population, concentrated in the northern Jaffna Peninsula closest to India, led to an outbreak of violence in the 1980s. India attempted unsuccessfully to play a peace-building and peacekeeping role, but withdrew its forces by 1990. U.S. policy was to support the territorial integrity of Sri Lanka and a negotiated settlement. Washington did not adopt a position of neutrality between the government and the insurgents. It designated the Liberation Tigers of Tamil Eelam (LTTE), perhaps the first insurgent group in the world to employ suicide bombings against civilians, as a "foreign terrorist organization" under the Immigration and Nationality Act.

The military struggle shifted back and forth during the 1990s. A permanent cease-fire was negotiated in 2002 under the mediation of Norway. Oslo became mediator basically because Norway had become a haven for Tamils seeking asylum. U.S. officials attributed the cease-fire to a tactical shift by LTTE leader Vellupillai Prabhakaran in response to the U.S. declaration of a GWOT. Although the LTTE soon dropped out of the talks, violence remained at a relatively low level, until a hard-line pro-Sinhalese government triumphed in the elections of 2005. In 2006 there was a complete breakdown of the 2003 cease-fire accords and an escalation of violence.

The United States supported Norwegian diplomacy, but with limited expectations of success. Although Deputy Secretary Armitage took an interest in the conflict in 2002, and Under Secretary Burns in 2006 and 2007, Sri Lanka policy was managed almost entirely by SCA. There were arguments within the State Department between SCA and the Bureau of Democracy, Human Rights, and Labor over whether sales of coastal radars and small arms for the Sri Lankan navy constituted "offensive" weapons and thus should be avoided. Since there were no significant pressures on Washington to adopt a more active peace-building role, the U.S. government was content to leave the matter to SCA.

Bureau of Western Hemisphere Affairs (WHA): Colombia

As described in Chapter 2, the Bush administration made a strategic early decision to continue the Clinton policy of support for Plan Colombia. The Plan was the Colombian government partnership with donors, primarily the United States, to combat insurgency and the local narcotics industry, while strengthening democracy and the economy. In the end the Bush administration committed $1.3 billion to Plan Colombia.[59] The decision at the presidential level provided the State Department and other U.S. government agencies with their marching orders, and there was relatively little debate within the administration. After that decision the State Department assumed the policy lead. In 2002, the administration sought and secured Congressional approval for enhanced authority to use U.S. counternarcotics funds for an integrated campaign to fight both drug trafficking and terrorist organizations.[60] The Revolutionary Armed Forces of Colombia (FARC) and the National Liberation Army (ELN) appeared on State's original Foreign Terrorist Organization list in 1997; the United Self-Defense Forces of Colombia (AUC) was added in 2001.

Colombia's civil conflict has in recent years involved both terrorism and massive production of and trade in narcotics. The State Department has a separate bureau to deal with narcotics (see below) and a Coordinator for Counter-Terrorism. However, WHA exercised overall policy leadership, integrating the different objectives involved in U.S. relations with Colombia. When Alvaro Uribe won the presidency of Colombia in 2002, promising an aggressive fight against insurgent terrorist groups, WHA offered help with Uribe's proposed national security strategy. It invited the Naval Post-Graduate School (NPS) to lead an advisory effort involving all the relevant Colombian civilian ministries and the country's military forces, thus integrating civilian with military considerations. The NPS team leaders met with Uribe to discuss the outline of the strategy and then, coordinating with the U.S. Embassy, conducted a series of high-level seminars for civilian and military leaders.[61] The plan, as finalized, established training programs, particularly for those being demobilized from insurgent groups. It also established a program of psychological counseling to assist ex-combatants reintegrate with their home communities and with the formal national economy. The State Department also got involved in the development of *Plan Patriotica*, Uribe's military campaign to recapture guerrilla-controlled territory. Designed as a civil-military strategy, *Plan Patriotica* envisaged a major role for the National Planning Ministry, after military clearance of a given area, in reestablishing basic services, health centers, and schools. WHA asked the Center for Hemispheric Defense Studies, one of a cluster of institutions under the National Defense University, to assume a role in training civilians for these post-conflict reconstruction tasks.

Although State's geographic bureaus are naturally equipped to take the lead in peace-building diplomacy, they do not always do so effectively. The diplomacy of peace-building is a necessarily imperfect art, but artistry can be improved by training. Officers in geographic bureaus working on conflict rarely receive training in conflict assessment or management, unless they have a personal interest. Likewise, senior officers selected as ambassadors, deputy chiefs of mission, or special envoys working on conflicts do not normally go through any kind of formal training on conflict management. They are usually picked for their expertise on the country or region and possibly for previous success in negotiation. The situation reflects the propensity of the Department of State for "on-the-job" training for its political officers. Secretary of State Powell has been quoted to the effect that Foreign Service Officers are better educated than military officers at the beginning of their careers, but military officers are better educated at retirement. The Diplomatic Readiness Initiative to expand the Foreign Service by more than 1,000 did increase training by 25 percent between 2000 and 2004, but did not focus particularly on political training and even less on conflict.[62] It was not until the creation of S/CRS in 2004 that a set of courses was developed at the Foreign Service Institute (FSI) on conflict assessment and management. Even then, those enrolled were largely representatives of that office and the Active and Standby Response Components that emerged from it.[63]

FUNCTIONAL BUREAUS: INTERAGENCY COORDINATION AND OPERATIONS

In addition to the geographic bureaus, the State Department has functional bureaus that carry out a variety of specialized tasks in peace-building. We look briefly at three.[64]

Bureau of International Organization Affairs (IO): United Nations Liaison

The Bureau of International Organization Affairs has basic responsibility for the diplomacy of the United States with the United Nations and its specialized agencies. IO's position relative to the UN organizations in New York, Geneva, Vienna, and elsewhere is analogous to a geographic bureau's relationship with the capitals in its region. IO provides instructions to and backstops U.S. missions in those cities, but the bureau has an anomalous power relationship with its New York office because the U.S. Permanent Representative to the United Nations is usually more prominent politically and better known than the IO Assistant Secretary. Since the end of the Cold War, the Permanent Representative position has been filled by such persons as Madeleine Albright, Former Energy Secretary Bill Richardson, Richard Holbrooke, architect of the Dayton Accords, former Senator John Danforth, and the controversial "recess" appointee John Bolton.[65] Unlike other U.S. ambassadors, the "PermRep," as he/she is known, maintains an office in the State Department. During the Clinton administration, the Permanent Representative was an official member of the NSC, a membership immediately terminated by the Bush administration.

IO gets drawn into peace-building diplomacy in the articulation of U.S. positions on a given international conflict in the General Assembly and the Security Council. If the United States decides to take a lead role in shaping the international response to the conflict, it will seek the agreement of other member states and the UN Secretariat for a proposed course of action. Measures short of the dispatch of peacekeeping forces usually involve consultations with the UN Department of Political Affairs, and often the Secretary-General, to work out agreement on a general course of action. The United States might promote, for example, the appointment of a Special Representative of the Secretary-General or a visit to the country by the Under Secretary for Political Affairs or even the Secretary-General himself. There will likewise be consultations in New York with major allies like the United Kingdom, France, Germany, Canada, and Australia (particularly if the conflict is in Asia). Such consultations often include officers from State Department geographic bureaus, but protocol requires that such conversations be arranged and monitored by IO. If the regional bureaus consistently bypass the IO, turf battles between the bureaus may slow down or obstruct effective U.S. diplomacy with the United Nations.

When the issue becomes of sufficient moment for consideration of a UN peacekeeping mission, consultations intensify with the leading countries of the affected region and the major UN funders. Within the UN Secretariat, the locus shifts to the Department of Peacekeeping. In this situation the IO becomes a kind of gatekeeper for U.S. peacekeeping funds. IO is primarily responsible for justifying and defending the peacekeeping portion of the U.S. international affairs account. Since the United States provides 27 percent of funding for authorized UN peacekeeping operations, it is up to IO to raise questions about whether a new peacekeeping mission would be cost-effective relative to U.S. interests. Washington lobbied other governments for a UN force in Liberia and Sudan, but initially opposed the dispatch of a force to Cote d'Ivoire, a high priority for France. When American personnel are involved as peacekeeping forces or observers—modest numbers in recent years—IO works closely with the Political-Military Affairs Bureau and with the Defense Department to work out the numbers and logistics.[66] IO also monitors whether peacekeeping operations meet the terms set out in Security Council resolutions. It gets involved in debates over whether such missions should be extended when their mandates (normally six months or one year) run out.[67]

Bureau of Political-Military Affairs (PM): Liaison with the Defense Department

The Bureau of Political-Military Affairs carries out the diplomatic tasks that arise out of its coordination role with the DOD.[68] These tasks include

- Negotiating and oversight of implementation of military agreements between the U.S. and other governments;
- Control and monitoring of arms transfers and trades and the proliferation of conventional weapon systems;
- Aggregating and providing general oversight for the security assistance budget (International Military Education and Training—IMET—and Foreign Military Financing—FMF);
- Securing agreements with other governments to join U.S.-led military coalitions; and
- Coordinating with military commands on overflight and landing requests, clearances for military visits, and overseas noncombatant evacuation operations (NEOs) of U.S. officials and American citizens, when their lives are threatened by political disorder abroad.

PM also gets involved in peace-building and stabilization, when U.S. armed forces are involved, including securing agreements with other governments to join U.S.-led military coalitions. PM took on an important peace-building role during the Clinton administration, when it became the center for State Department planning for complex emergencies under procedures summarized in PDD 56 (see Chapter 2). The Bureau created an Office of Contingency Planning and Peacekeeping. When a complex emergency arose or seemed likely, the NSC's Global Affairs Directorate would task the different agencies for responses, including a political-military plan, drafted in the first instance in the new PM office. During Clinton's second term more than 20 such plans were written.[69] Some of the plans provided useful benchmarks for gauging progress in particular cases.

When the Bush administration came into office, Secretary Powell picked Lincoln Bloomfield, a former Deputy Assistant Secretary of Defense (DASD) and close friend of Deputy Secretary Richard Armitage, as PM Assistant Secretary. Powell and Armitage wanted in the post a trusted individual who "knew the Pentagon and how it worked." After 9/11, Bloomfield set up a separate PM operations center, staffed by a Pol-Mil Action Team (PMAT), to secure a running flow of data from the combatant commands for the retired general who was Secretary of State. Bloomfield also became part of the team, heavily staffed by EUR, which negotiated agreements with the Central Asian republics. He headed the group that secured Uzbekistan's accord for contingency pilot rescue operations in that country. In the run-up to the Iraq war, Bloomfield was charged with heading the diplomacy required to pull together the "coalition of the willing" which eventually became the Multi-National Force—Iraq. His PM team sent messages to U.S. embassies in the capitals of potential coalition governments to determine interest, set up military liaison with CENTCOM for those responding positively, maintained a definitive tally of coalition member contributions, and kept their Washington ambassadors informed through weekly meetings at the State Department.[70]

Under the Bush administration, PM did not play the same planning role as during the second Clinton term.[71] The planning function was entrusted to S/CRS, when it was created in 2004 (Chapter 4). Instead, PM's role was essentially *ad hoc*, depending on the circumstances and the "bureaucratic space" available to the bureau. As Secretary Powell pushed for U.S. military intervention in Liberia during the summer of 2003, he dispatched Bloomfield to discuss possible intervention with the European Command. The assistant secretary and a group from the U.S. European Command were at a conference in Senegal with West African defense and foreign ministers, when the Liberian crisis exploded. During the conference, after discussions with Bloomfield, ECOWAS authorized entry into Liberia of a Nigerian-led battalion phasing out of UN operations in Sierra Leone. With UN Secretary-General Kofi Annan's support, UN forces in Sierra Leone facilitated Nigerian action.[72]

PM's Office of Plans, Policy and Analysis (previously Contingency Planning and Peacekeeping) did manage the Global Peace Operations Initiative (GPOI). GPOI was proposed by the Bush administration and adopted by the G-8 meeting at Sea Island, Georgia, in June 2004. The rapid expansion of peacekeeping operations during the previous decade created a worldwide shortage of trained peacekeepers and police with military skills.[73] The U.S.

government had been attempting to address the problem as an essentially African issue since 1996, primarily because the largest UN peacekeeping operations were taking place in Africa. Under the Clinton administration the African Crisis Response Initiative (ACRI) launched a training program under the "voluntary peacekeeping account" of the State Department.[74] The Bush administration expanded the program beginning in 2001, renaming it African Contingency Operations Training and Assistance (ACOTA). Under ACRI/ACOTA, the United States trained 16,000 troops from 10 African nations between 1996 and 2004.[75]

Beginning in 2002 the G-8 powers as a group had begun to focus on Africa. At the meeting that year in Canada, the powers agreed to a broad action plan for the continent, including conflict resolution and peace-building objectives. The following year in France a "Plan to Enhance African Capabilities to Undertake Peace Support Operations" was presented. Since the United States was hosting the 2004 meeting, Washington devoted special attention to the issue, with the objective of building on existing U.S. programs. Defense officials saw an opportunity to attract new donor countries to peacekeeping—and thereby potentially increase support for U.S. global interests—by making peacekeeping training available on a larger scale. Their objective was to improve the ACOTA program but also to expand the program out of Africa. Keeping in mind that the United States had launched the program in Africa, Secretary of Defense Rumsfeld proposed that the United States take the leadership of a broader peace operations initiative, focused on training and equipment.[76] Since the funding came out of the international affairs budget, rather than that of Defense, management was vested in PM. A committee comprising representatives of PM, the DASD for Partnership Strategy, and the Stability Operations and Security Assistance Division of the Joint Chiefs of Staff coordinated the program.

In 2005 the U.S. government began expanding its geographical scope, first to Central America and Europe, and then to Asia and the Pacific. By 2006 it included more than 40 countries, including 4 in Latin America, 9 in Asia, 8 in Eastern Europe, and 1 (Jordan) in the Middle East. Africa remained the largest element of the program with 19 partners. As of early 2007, almost 29,000 additional peacekeepers had been trained at a cost of $278 million, 94 percent of them from Africa.[77] The program was scheduled to end in 2009 but was extended by the Obama administration.

Bureau of International Narcotics and Law Enforcement Affairs (INL): Policing

State's Bureau of International Narcotics and Law Enforcement Affairs—known informally as "drugs & thugs"—has responsibility for organizing and managing the police function within R&S. Unlike the other two functional bureaus described above, INL has taken on operational responsibilities. Over the past two decades INL has developed a reputation for aggressiveness within State and the interagency process in its pursuit of antinarcotics and law enforcement programs, positions often bolstered by strong advocacy from members of key Congressional subcommittees.

Since 1994, when Washington recruited 50 police officers for the International Police Monitor mission in Haiti, international civilian police operations—or CIVPOL—have become an integral part of the American approach to peace-building. CIVPOL missions may perform a variety of functions within the R&S framework. Where the local police function has broken down, international officers occasionally patrol or investigate. More often they are responsible for restructuring, monitoring, and/or advising local police who are making the transition to democratic policing. Usually, they are directly involved in training.

There has been considerable bureaucratic conflict and confusion over the division of labor among federal agencies. The Department of Justice provides the basic interface between the federal government and police at the state and local level. Since 1986 it has maintained the International Criminal Investigative Training Assistance Program (ICITAP) to respond to requests for overseas police training. USAID is the major funder and implementer of U.S. foreign assistance programs, but during much of the past 30 years has been prohibited from doing police projects.[78] State has a leadership role in the allocation of military and security assistance and has assumed authority over policy implementation on the civilian police aspect of most post-conflict reconstruction programs. There has been deep-seated rivalry between State and Justice on police issues over the past decade. Since 2001, in the unique environments of Afghanistan and Iraq, the Defense Department has played a major role in shaping the policing aspect of stabilization.

A second complication for managing civilian policing in conflict is institutional, related to the federal system and American policing traditions. Unlike Italy or France, the United States does not have a federal police force from which to draw candidates for police operational and training roles overseas. It has therefore relied on recruitment by private sector contractors. Most recruits are mid-career state and local police officers, who take a leave of absence, or recently retired persons. Obtaining high-quality recruits is difficult, because state and local police forces are often severely constrained by budget stringencies and personnel ceilings. Cumbersome recruitment processes lead to delays in deployment.

A third problem is budgetary. Congress has not created clear authorities for funding an international police assistance program within the framework of peacekeeping. There is no line item for it in the international affairs budget, meaning that it is usually funded through various State Department regional bureaus and the State Department's Peacekeeping account.

In 2000, after lengthy interagency debate, the Clinton administration issued PDD 71 ("Strengthening Criminal Justice Systems in Support of Peace Operations and Other Complex Contingencies"). The bureaucratic goal of the Directive was to resolve the issue of interagency leadership. Responding to the tug of war between State and Justice, PDD 71 designated the State Department as the lead agency, presiding over an IWG which included Justice and USAID. It instructed State and Justice to prepare a plan to enhance assistance to foreign police in support of peace operations. That plan was to include strengthening the capacity of Justice's ICITAP program. PDD 71 also aimed at an interagency partnership on rapid delivery of assistance for judicial, penal, and legal code development for post-conflict areas. The Directive also enunciated the objectives of improved recruitment, training, and delivery of CIVPOL to field operations, but without specific guidelines.

The Directive was not implemented by the Clinton administration in large part because of interagency wrangling and the failure of the NSC to give sufficient priority to policing. There was much discussion between State and Justice about the future role of ICITAP, but it remained at Justice. PDD 71 lapsed with other Clinton administration directives on peace-building, although the Bush administration followed some of its provisions. Notably, it endorsed continued State Department leadership on transitional justice. The relationship between INL and ICITAP remained tense. INL's Web page made no reference to ICITAP.

INL manages the contracts for recruitment, training, and support of CIVPOL personnel. Until 2004 contracting was exclusively with DynCorp, a northern Virginia corporation. The process began to open up in 2002, when INL signed contracts with DynCorp and two other firms to develop rosters of qualified police officers to be drawn on for CIVPOL operations. After 2004 the three companies competed for CIVPOL contracts, but DynCorp, despite criticism by auditors and inspectors, continued to be responsible for the bulk of CIVPOL recruitment and training.[79]

Under the Bush administration, policing was a contentious issue both in Afghanistan and in Iraq. Under the 2001 Bonn Agreement on Afghanistan, the German government had responsibility for policing. However, by late 2003, the Bush administration was extremely dissatisfied by the energy and resources the Germans were devoting to the task, most of which centered on reviving the National Police Academy in Kabul, and was trying to move into the gap. INL was directed to have 20,000 Afghanistan police trained and in place by mid-2004 to help assure the smooth passage of the October 2004 presidential elections. It set up a central police training center in Kabul and seven regional training centers and by 2008 had trained about 60,000 Afghan police.[80] Likewise, in Iraq there was demand for a rapid expansion of trained police. The energetic INL Assistant Secretary, Robert C. Charles (see sidebar), rushed into place an off-site police training facility in Jordan which had 500 trainees enrolled by the end of 2004.

Differing INL and U.S. Central Command (CENTCOM) approaches to stabilization law enforcement became a significant interagency issue in 2004 and 2005. In Iraq the State Department believed it had the lead and funds

BOBBY CHARLES

Robert C. (Bobby) Charles grew up in rural Maine in a family with three siblings and a single mother, who stamped on him values of hard work and service. He won a scholarship to Dartmouth, then to Oxford, and got a law degree from Columbia. Charles served 1995–99 as Staff Director and Chief Counsel for the National Security, International Affairs, and Criminal Justice Subcommittee of the House Committee on Government Reform and Oversight. The subcommittee was headed by Rep. Dennis Hastert (R-IL), later Speaker of the House.

In October 2003, Bobby Charles became Assistant Secretary of State for International Narcotics and Law Enforcement. He insisted on the diversification of police training contracting, with three firms providing police trainers and other overseas personnel by 2004. He imposed fines of $20,000 per day on contractors for failure of timely delivery. He instructed his staff to scour bureau records for unliquidated police program funds. When he found $60 million lying unused, he gave the embassies two weeks to spend the money and deobligated most of it.

Charles believed he had a mandate to make dramatic changes in the law enforcement approach to Iraq and Afghanistan. He was in a particular hurry in Iraq. In less than two months a new police training school for Iraqis was created in Jordan, and 500 trainees were flown in for initial training. The number of trainees eventually rose to 3,000; Shi'ites, Sunnis, and Kurds all trained together. A police training facility was also set up in Baghdad. Charles insisted on post-training mentoring as key to a successful police operation and thought he had $250 million to implement it. He quickly collided with the Defense Department. The Pentagon demanded that the $250 million be used instead to create a group of specialized Iraqi units and to provide military police rather than civilian mentors. He was utterly dismayed about military police mentors, which violated what he viewed as a basic principle of policing in stabilization operations—"military to military and cop to cop." He enlisted Deputy Secretary of State Armitage to remonstrate against DOD's position, but says the NSC refused to confront the Pentagon on the issue. Charles says many of the DOD-favored specialized police units were suspected of evolving into sectarian militias.

The administration wanted 20,000 police in Afghanistan by mid-2004 to lay the foundation for peaceful parliamentary elections in October. Under hard-driving Bobby Charles, INL managed to get seven training locations up and running in Kabul, Gardez, Kandahar, Helmand, Badakhshan, Kunduz, and Nangarhar, producing 19,500 police by the deadline. Law enforcement in Afghanistan was complicated by the rapid spread of poppy acreage. Afghanistan opium production was already the highest in the world and since 2002 had soared higher than under the Taliban.[81] Since narcotics trafficking is the bedrock issue for INL, the high priority Charles placed on eradication is not surprising. However, it brought the bureau into conflict both with the Pentagon and key elements of the State Department. Charles argued that U.S. experience, especially in Colombia, demonstrated "you can't win against terrorism funded by an indigenous drug trade" and that "heroin was the fuel running the engine of Taliban terrorism." Charles advocated that U.S. combat units should destroy narcotics labs where they found them and that aerial eradication should be undertaken, even on an experimental basis. Charles claims U.S. Ambassador Khalilzad denied him permission to visit Afghanistan to brief President Karzai on eradication, even though he had the support of State Department principals and had already spoken to Karzai on the importance of counter-narcotics efforts in blocking funding to the Taliban.

After the departure of Colin Powell, Charles quickly ran into difficulties with Condoleezza Rice. She had opposed his position on policing in Iraq as NSA. As Secretary of State she disagreed with him on the priority to be given to eradication and military interdiction. Rice was also reportedly uneasy about Charles's habit of direct communication with members of Congress, including Speaker Hastert. Charles responded that most of the phone calls were at the initiative of the members and that their confidence in him was a plus for the administration. When Charles offered his resignation in March 2005, Rice accepted it.

---

to develop a civilian training program involving civilian American mentors with new police trainees emerging from the facility in Jordan. The military wanted to create special police units, rather than a single nonsectarian police force. It also wanted the mentors to be military police. Defense prevailed. Advocates of the State Department position argue that, as a result, the Iraq police remained a corrupt and sectarian force, unlike the Iraqi army which gradually improved its reputation for professionalism.

In Afghanistan, both INL and ISAF ran police training operations, with the U.S. military working on such programs outnumbering INL contractors by roughly four to one and European Union trainers, mainly German, by ten to one. Nevertheless, dissatisfaction with police performance—hampered by "corruption, insufficient training and equipment, and absenteeism," in the words of one analyst—remained pervasive.[82] INL advocated greater priority to antinarcotics programs in Afghanistan, including vastly expanded eradication programs and intervention by U.S. and ISAF forces to destroy narcotics labs when they came across them. INL encountered opposition from military commanders but also skepticism from U.S. chiefs of mission in Kabul, concerned about the negative impact of expanded eradication on Afghan hearts and minds. In late 2008 NATO defense ministers agreed to a U.S. proposal that ISAF act against narcotics labs and traffickers "supporting the insurgency," if requested by the Afghan government.[83]

Where U.S. military forces were not present, the interagency process was less conflicted for INL. In Colombia, a third major case of INL law enforcement activity in an internal conflict, antinarcotics activity was at the top of the U.S. agenda under the Plan Colombia partnership between Bogota and Washington. Relations between INL and WHA were harmonious.[84] The U.S. government consensus that the FARC, Colombia's largest and best equipped insurgent group—and one of three Colombian insurgent groups on the U.S. terrorist list—had become an essentially a narco-terrorist criminal organization facilitated closer integration of INL's antinarcotics agenda with counterterrorism activities aimed at R&S. With the agreement of Congress, helicopters and other aircraft supplied for the antidrug campaign were also used for antiterrorism objectives, including anti-kidnapping measures. In 2007 the State Department reported six consecutive years of record aerial eradication of coca production and an end to the "exponential" increase in the coca production of the late 1990s.

INL contributed to a number of other important CIVPOL missions, often operating within the framework of the United Nations. In Liberia, after the transition to the elected government of President Ellen Johnson Sirleaf, the United States contributed as many as 75 uniformed police officers to the UN Mission in Liberia (UNMIL). In Sudan following the 2005 CPA, INL provided a contingent of 15 police, judicial, and corrections officers to the UN Mission in Sudan to assist the Government of Southern Sudan to develop a criminal justice capacity. In Haiti INL funded 50 U.S. police officers and 3 U.S. corrections officers to MINUSTAH.[85]

PEACE-BUILDING ISSUES FOR THE STATE DEPARTMENT

The State Department carries out most of the routine peace-building activity of the U.S. government. Whether action is taken at the behest of the President, represents an initiative of the Secretary of State, or emerges from lower levels of the bureaucracy, State's geographic bureaus are the engines of peace-building diplomacy. In most situations of internal conflict abroad, the United States becomes engaged through diplomacy. If a peace agreement is secured, diplomacy continues through the processes of R&S. (IO's diplomacy within the United Nations, coordinated with the geographic bureaus, is a variant of this geographic-centered diplomacy.) The Department's special geographic expertise and practical experience dealing with individual foreign governments are essential components of the U.S. government's capacity to manage overseas conflict.

The first requirement for improving the practice of peace-building diplomacy is systematic training of political cone officers and those from other cones who serve as desk officers or office directors in regions facing conflict. State should cease relying on "on-the-job" training for those with peace-building responsibilities. Training in conflict management and experience in conflict situations should become a requirement for advancement by political officers into the Senior Foreign Service and should be taken into account in selection of deputy chiefs of missions and office directors.

The diplomatic communications function may be distinguished from both planning and operational functions in peace-building. The Politico-Military Bureau acquired a rudimentary peace-building planning role under the Clinton administration, because of its interface with the Defense Department, but that function lapsed under Bush. INL took on an important operational role through its policy lead on civilian policing and its management of police programs in major conflicts. Aside from that—and refugee programs managed by the Bureau of Population, Refugees and Migration—the State Department did not have general authority to operate peace-building programs until 2004. Then the State Department assumed by statute and executive order major new planning and operational responsibilities in peace-building vested in the Coordinator for Reconstruction and Stabilization. The second requirement for improving the peace-building work of the State Department is strengthened cooperation between the geographic bureaus and the new mechanism for a whole-of-government approach to peace-building operations. The nature of the new operational function in peace-building and the implications for the rest of the State Department and other concerned agencies are explored in Chapter 4.

CHAPTER 4

A NEW APPROACH TO PEACE-BUILDING: THE COORDINATOR FOR RECONSTRUCTION AND STABILIZATION

> The civilian foreign affairs agencies should be better organized for overseas crisis response, and the Secretary of State should play a lead role in this effort.... The agencies must be capable and flexible enough to provide a robust partner to the military when necessary or to lead a crisis response effort when appropriate.
>
> —Sen. Richard Lugar[1]

In 2004 the Bush administration decided to supplement—if not supplant—the traditional approach to peace-building diplomacy and complex emergencies. The traditional approach has been (1) high-level attention, including interagency coordination, for the most serious conflicts and (2) geographic bureau-led initiatives for conflicts of lower priority. The new project was the Office of the Coordinator for Reconstruction and Stabilization (S/CRS). As noted in Chapter 2, the NSC Principals Committee decided to place the office in the State Department as the key implementing instrument to correspond with the Secretary of State's new mandate to lead the interagency process for post-conflict reconstruction, formalized under NSPD 44. The Coordinator's office was attached to the Secretary of State. Colin Powell appointed as the first Coordinator Ambassador Carlos Pascual.[2]

The creation of S/CRS marked a major change in the peace-building function of the State Department. Rather than concerning itself almost exclusively with the foreign policy and diplomatic communications of peace-building and specialized operational functions such as police training, State vested in the Coordinator responsibility for strategic planning for R&S and for mobilizing and coordinating the civilian operations to carry it out. Under the Clinton administration, PM had acquired responsibility for drafting political-military plans for dealing with complex emergencies, working in close coordination with the NSC's Global Affairs Directorate. That responsibility lapsed with the arrival of the Bush administration. The operational role of the State Department in R&S had hitherto been limited to the INL, which had seized responsibility for police training and operations in post-conflict situations, and the Bureau of Population, Refugees and Migration, which manages refugee programs.[3] In short, the expectation was that S/CRS would play both a planning and an operational role in coordinating the interagency response to foreign crises.

LAUNCH AND EVOLUTION

Not unexpectedly, S/CRS encountered serious growing pains during its first two years. The new staff initially focused on conflict prevention, formulating a framework for R&S, and developing a capacity to plan for it, drawing in both the civilian agencies and the military. Making progress required ongoing negotiations with State Department bureaus and other agencies skeptical of the new office and jealous of turf. Initially, prevention focused on an "early warning" process involving the intelligence community and State Department geographic bureaus. Pascual arranged for the National Intelligence Council to prepare a watch list, which was to be reviewed periodically by him and the geographic assistant secretaries of state. However, the watch list soon became so large that it covered half the countries with which the United States had diplomatic relations; it lacked focus and priority. Moreover, there was a squabble about whether the list should be unclassified, a position advocated by conflict managers in USAID seeking to develop assistance programs and opposed by ambassadors—and some USAID directors—worried that the inclusion of their countries on a watch list would anger presidents and prime ministers.[4]

Developing a planning mechanism brought sometimes contentious relations with USAID, as well as other bureaus within State. USAID Administrator Andrew Natsios was unhappy about the creation of S/CRS because he had devoted considerable attention to building a conflict management capacity in USAID, centered on the new Office of Conflict Management and Mitigation (CMM) in the Bureau of Democracy, Conflict and Humanitarian Assistance (DCHA). (See Chapter 6.) The Office of Foreign Disaster Assistance in the same bureau feared its Disaster Assistance Response Teams (DARTs) would be commandeered by S/CRS. The geographic bureaus in particular did not welcome a new player which might threaten their control over policy toward a conflicted state. INL did not wish S/CRS to intrude into its operational control of police training. PM tried to reassert its earlier ownership of complex contingency planning and claimed a new responsibility for State Department-related aspects of counterinsurgency, a specific type of conflict response. The NSC—particularly Director for Stability Operations

J. Clint Williamson, midwife of the new office—weighed in to help it move forward. Nevertheless, S/CRS made little progress in securing interagency agreement on a formal framework and process to trigger a major R&S program.

S/CRS did make headway on conflict assessment methodology. It established a relationship with the Joint Forces Command (JFCOM), which in the wake of the Iraq conflict aggressively expanded its concept of "jointness" to encompass not only the different military services and commands but also cooperation with civilian agencies. In 2005 S/CRS and JFCOM issued a draft "Planning Framework for Stabilization, Reconstruction and Conflict Transformation."[5] That document found its way into the curricula of a number of military training schools.[6] A complementary document, the "Essential Tasks Matrix," also issued in 2005, became available to U.S. embassies and to the regional combatant commands as a guide to action.[7] In 2006 a third piece of the documentary toolkit emerged: "Metrics for Interagency Planning for Conflict Transformation," providing guidance on standards of measuring accomplishment of an essential task.[8]

Pascual gave particular attention to the development of a capacity to "move rapidly to help countries in the aftermath of conflicts."[9] In addition to the Washington-based staff of 80 he envisaged, Pascual wanted a swiftly deployable vanguard of 100 who could do crisis diplomacy or at least augment U.S. embassy staffs in an emergency. This "active response corps" would in turn be supplemented by active duty officers from State and other agencies, who could go out to do specialized tasks in law enforcement or economic reconstruction on temporary duty assignments. He also wanted to create a roster of specialists from the private sector with skills mostly unavailable in the federal government. To finance this expeditionary activity, the Coordinator proposed a "conflict response fund" of $100 million. The fund was promoted as a means to "jump-start" key R&S programs requiring immediate resources, while alternative funding was identified to sustain them.

S/CRS quickly encountered budget realities. At the end of 2004, the NSC staff arranged meetings aimed at providing additional funding for S/CRS. The Deputies Committee recommended as much as $350 million, to include the Conflict Response Fund, but the NSC Principals failed to agree. OMB chopped the request down to $100 million for the Fund and no more than $25 million for S/CRS. Although the Coordinator's Office continued to enjoy the support of the Senate Foreign Relations Committee (SFRC), the House Appropriations Subcommittee on Foreign Operations was unimpressed with the arguments for an active and supplementary expeditionary capacity. The $100 million request for the conflict response fund was "zeroed out" by the appropriators in the FY 2006 budget. Fears were expressed that approval of new staff would become a pretext for intervention in additional parts of the world. Opinion on the right fretted that the military would be dragged into peacemaking and policing and on the left that aid was being militarized. The conflict response money was dismissed as a slush fund.[10]

CARLOS PASCUAL, FIRST COORDINATOR FOR RECONSTRUCTION AND STABILIZATION

Carlos Pascual was born in Cuba in 1959. His parents fled in 1962, when his father, an accountant, was briefly detained for handing out leaflets at a political meeting. The family managed to catch one of the last commercial flights to the United States before diplomatic relations were severed. After five years on the east coast, they settled down in El Monte, California, a working-class and largely Hispanic suburb east of Los Angeles. He graduated from Stanford in 1980 with a major in international relations. He moved on to Harvard, where he earned a master's degree at the Kennedy School of Government, and then to USAID, where he worked on Africa and the former Soviet Union. In 1996 he was brought to the NSC by Coit D. Blacker, one of Pascual's mentors at Stanford, who had become NSC Senior Director for Russia in the Clinton administration.[11] At the end of his tour in the White House in 2000, Pascual was named U.S. Ambassador to Ukraine. In 2003, he returned to Washington D.C. to take the job of Coordinator for assistance to Eastern Europe and the former Soviet Union, a position which placed him in a key role to determine the allocation and use of about $1 billion.

Pascual faced an enormous challenge in activating his new shop. First, he had to secure a budget and the personnel capable of carrying out the planning and operational functions. He did a lot of strategizing with Robert Pearson, Director-General of the Foreign Service, and with Under Secretary for Political Affairs Marc Grossman, but his chief ally in getting started was Richard Armitage, Deputy Secretary of State, who ensured his access to Secretary Powell and helped with the budget. Pascal began with a contingent of five people, which grew to about 65 by the time he departed. Lacking analytic horsepower initially, Pascual forged an alliance with the U.S. Institute of Peace (USIP), which helped S/CRS reach conclusions about the lessons from Iraq and to think about indicators for determining progress in R&S.

A second equally important—and related problem—was to insert S/CRS effectively into the arena previously occupied by the geographic bureaus and INL, which managed the police function. The geographic bureaus were unenthusiastic about ceding a place at the table to a brand new coordinator whose staff lacked expertise about their particular conflict problems. Moreover, without an operational budget, S/CRS could not offer the bureaus the incentive of additional funds to deal with those problems. In early 2005, Pascual was instructed by the seventh floor to get involved in Sudan, where the outbreak of violence in Darfur threatened to undermine the Bush administration's triumph in securing the peace agreement between North and South. A planning group was set up for Sudan, cochaired by S/CRS, but the Bureau attempted to keep the Coordinator away from the policy issues by an endless series of meetings. Nonetheless, according to Pascual, the group produced the first comprehensive interagency strategy to deal with the conflict and contributed to a major increase in funding for post-conflict reconstruction.[12]

Pascual was an eloquent and passionate spokesman for his new office, skillful in selling others on the importance of a civilian-led mission to transform conflict in a positive direction. He threw himself into launching a series of activities to put S/CRS on the map. On the prevention side he arranged for the National Intelligence Council to put out a list of countries at risk of instability to be reviewed by him and the regional assistant secretaries. This eventually led to a simulation of election scenarios in the Congo and exercises at the U.S. embassies in Nepal and the Central African Republic. On the planning side, S/CRS became involved in a large project looking at contingencies relating to political instability and migration patterns in post-Castro Cuba with WHA and the Southern Command. On the operational side, S/CRS was able to get started with actual R&S activities in Darfur and Haiti. A former staffer credits Pascual's success in launching the Coordinator's office to the "sheer force of his personality" and the "hunger of the military" for an operational entity which would relieve it of post-conflict responsibilities which it neither desires nor excels at.[13]

After an exciting and frustrating 18 months in the job, Carlos Pascual happily accepted an offer from Strobe Talbott, President of the Brookings Institution, to become vice president and director of foreign policy at the Washington think tank.

The Condoleezza Rice era at the State Department initially proved problematic for the new office. The departure of Deputy Secretary Richard Armitage meant the loss of an important S/CRS champion in the budgetary wars and inter-bureau conflict. No other seventh-floor principal picked up the portfolio. The NSC was preoccupied with securing interagency agreement on the directive regulating interagency R&S management—NSPD 44 issued at the end of 2005. With Condoleezza Rice now at the helm, the NSC expected the Department to exercise the authority vested in it. The office made some headway. It continued to amass staff and to refine its own planning process. A partial and temporary solution to the budget impasse was developed, Sec. 1207 transfer authority, in collaboration with the Defense Department. Secretary of Defense Rumsfeld requested and Congress approved authority to transfer up to $100 million in Defense funds in FY 2006 "to assist the State Department [with] immediate reconstruction, security, or stabilization assistance to a foreign country."[14] In a speech at Georgetown University in January 2006, on her trademark vision of "transformational diplomacy," Rice included a paragraph on S/CRS. She said, "We have an expansive vision for this new office, and let there be no doubt, we are committed to realizing it."[15]

The resignation of Carlos Pascual at the end of 2005 led to turbulence and uncertainty. His position remained open for five months. The long transition, according to S/CRS staffers, provoked an effort by a group of senior State Department officials, led by the Director of Policy Planning and the Assistant Secretary for Politico-Military Affairs, to put the office out of business. The effort was joined, at least to some degree, by Randall Tobias, whom Rice had named to the new post of Director of Foreign Assistance. The new position combined the role of Administrator of USAID with a new Deputy Secretary of State position.[16] In particular, Tobias, as czar of the foreign operations budget, wanted to make sure that any budget for R&S came under his jurisdiction.[17] Pascual had tried unsuccessfully to persuade the Secretary of State that he should have command authority over that budget. The effort to eliminate S/CRS failed, but some believe that it was only the explicitness of Rice's pledge at Georgetown that kept it alive.

John E. Herbst became Coordinator in May 2006. His basic guidance from Secretary Rice was to get more S/CRS staff working on actual conflicts (i.e., that his office should become more operational). That guidance posed a dilemma. Should S/CRS focus its efforts on individual cases—a micro approach? If so, it faced the obstacle that the geographic bureaus did not want to involve S/CRS in their major conflagrations. That could leave S/CRS doing "boutique crises," as permitted by the geographic bureaus or dictated by the seventh floor. Herbst decided that it was essential that S/CRS remain involved on the macro planning side—shaping the overall government decision-making and planning process for dealing with R&S crises of varying magnitudes. At the same time, the office needed to build capacity to engage operationally in conflicts, both emerging and full-blown. Accordingly, Herbst defined two essential tasks for his office: to ensure a "whole of government" approach to R&S and to build a civilian surge capacity to meet specific U.S. government needs in that area.[18]

Herbst faced two serious challenges early in his tenure. The first was the Lebanon crisis, which erupted in July 2006, only two months after his arrival. Would the State Department turn to S/CRS to help coordinate the civilian agency response? Herbst's effort to insert S/CRS into the process was blocked not only by the Bureau of Near Eastern Affairs (NEA) but also by Deputy Secretary Tobias, the new budget czar. Rice, at the center of crisis diplomacy, did not look to S/CRS. The result was not very pretty from the point of view of mobilizing resources to deal with the crisis. Coordination among the agencies was haphazard. Afterward, Tobias told others that S/CRS should have had a lead role on resources for Lebanon.

The second challenge was securing an expanded budget. How could Herbst shepherd his budget request through F, the major new budget shop of Randall Tobias? F, launched only in March 2006, was trying to master and integrate the international affairs budget process, while at the same time drafting a proposed FY 2008 budget for presentation to the OMB within a few months. Herbst had little success. No money was placed in the budget for the Civilian Reserve Corps and only $25 million for the Conflict Response Fund. In desperation Herbst persuaded Tobias to make him a deputy in F, thereby giving him an inside track for the next budget exercise.[19]

INTERAGENCY MANAGEMENT SYSTEM

In 2007 S/CRS moved forward on the process and operational side, as well as in its visibility. Key operational procedures for a "whole of government" IMS were agreed upon by the NSC Deputies Committee in March. At the direction of the President, Secretary of State, or Secretary of Defense, a Country Reconstruction and Stabilization Group (CRSG), operating at the assistant secretary level, might be established to deal with an actual or a potential crisis. It could also be created by a decision of the relevant PCC, the regional NSC grouping reporting to the Deputies Committee. The CRSG would be cochaired by the relevant State regional assistant secretary, the S/CRS Coordinator, and the NSC Senior Director for the region. S/CRS would be the CRSG secretariat. An Integrated Planning Cell (IPC) would deploy to the headquarters of the regional combatant command concerned to work toward cohesive civilian-military planning. An interagency Advance Civilian Team (ACT), coordinated by S/CRS, would be dispatched to the country in crisis to implement whatever strategic plan the CRSG agreed upon. For example, if an ACT were sent to deal with instability in Kyrgyzstan, an IPC would be dispatched to the Tampa, Florida, headquarters of CENTCOM. The ACT, supported by Field ACTs to extend R&S activities beyond the capital, would operate under the authority of the American Chief of Mission. In the absence of a functioning embassy, the ACT would serve as the embassy.[20]

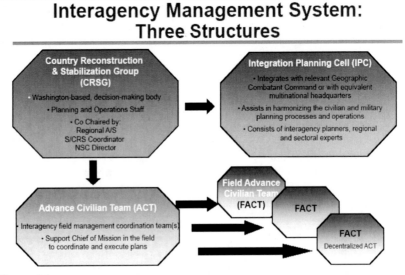

Figure 4.1
Reconstruction and Stabilization Interagency Management System (IMS).
Courtesy S/CRS.

No CRSG has been called into being and no ACT dispatched since approval of the IMS.[21] In August 2008, however, on the outbreak of the Georgia-Russia conflict, the State Department set up an interagency task force. It was disbanded after two weeks in favor of a S/CRS-run staff on the model of a CRSG secretariat. The S/CRS planning chief led a team to Tbilisi for two months, but it was not formally constituted as an ACT.[22] Several military exercises using the IMS and drawing on other agencies have taken place.

Questions were raised about the type of crisis the IMS would be applied to. In testimony before the Congress, Herbst stated that the IMS provided "coordinated, interagency policy and program management for highly complex crises and operations." The features of such crises would be that they

- Are national or security priorities,
- Involve widespread instability,
- May require military operations, and
- Engage multiple U.S. agencies in the policy and programmatic response.

He added that the IMS was not designed to deal with political and humanitarian crises normally handled by means of existing organizations and systems.[23] Still, the issue of the circumstances triggering the IMS remained subject to debate. The effort to define the circumstances precisely seems doomed to failure, since policymakers normally wish to exercise discretion in ambiguous situations.

ADVANCES ON THE BUDGET

S/CRS also gained traction in the budget process, despite the abrupt resignation in April 2007 of Randall Tobias. Somewhat unexpectedly, President Bush in his 2007 State of the Union message called for Congressional enactment of a Civilian Reserve Corps. Although the proposal had nothing behind it in the FY 2008 budget, it placed a White House imprimatur on building it into the next budget. A year later, in February 2008 the President's budget message for FY 2009 gave prominence to a "Civilian Response Capability, [requesting] $249 million to enhance the capability of civilian Government agencies to respond to crises and to create a rapidly deployable civilian reserve corps." The budget proposal gave substance to the civilian reserve proposal originally developed by Carlos Pascual.

ORGANIZATION

By the end of 2008, S/CRS staff had risen to 105, making it the equivalent of a small State Department bureau. After experimenting with different tables of organization, S/CRS divided itself into two major components—conflict transformation and conflict prevention, each headed by a deputy coordinator. Both divisions were heavily engaged in R&S operations.

The Principal Deputy Coordinator supervised two substantive offices—Planning and Strategic Communications.[24]

Planning

The Planning Office considered itself responsible for building the interagency capacity to do reconstruction, stabilization, and conflict transformation.[25] Although the IMS provided a macro-framework for dealing with major crises, the framework was adaptable to a range of reconstruction/stabilization situations: U.S. government civilian interventions with little or no military support, combined civil-military operations, and U.S. contributions to UN or multilateral operations. Triggers for planning would usually be the request of a regional assistant secretary of state to S/CRS for planning for a particular country or region. In that case, the planning process would proceed under the auspices of the regional Policy Coordination Committee of the NSC. A request for planning might come from another office in the State Department. S/CRS responded to a request from the Office of the Director of Foreign Assistance (F) to develop a set of improved measurements of effectiveness of PRTs in Afghanistan. Alternatively, the request might be made by a Defense Department geographic combatant command through the Secretary of Defense. In that case, planning would normally proceed under the auspices of the combatant command itself. If, as envisaged by the IMS, a CRSG were created, its activation, formally generated by the Secretary of State, might originate with the Coordinator.

Full-blown planning within the CRSG framework would operate in three sequences. S/CRS would pull together an interagency strategic planning team consisting of conflict transformation specialists and regional and country experts. The team would assess the situation and develop a policy guidance memo articulating an overarching policy goal—something on the order of "locally led nascent peace"—stated in terms relevant to the specific country situation—to be achieved within a two- to three-year time frame. It would then develop "major mission elements" (MMEs), "narrowly tailored" objectives necessary for the achievement of the overall goal with attention to phasing. Normally, several options would be examined under individual planning templates. This policy formulation document, including supporting narrative, diagrams of the different elements of the plan, and unresolved policy or resources issues for decision, would be sent to the NSC Principals Committee or Deputies Committee for action.

A second sequence would involve strategy development, to be done by an "MME planning team," further developing the MMEs to include measures of success and resource requirements.[26] The MME planning team would include key players from the different agencies involved and might even be multilateral (i.e., "coordinated" with host country officials or allied governments). The OMB would likely be involved at that stage to secure the necessary funding. The MME team would attach essential tasks to each MME and assign agency leadership for each. Other donor contributions, if any, would be plugged in at this point. The essential tasks would cover a broad range of the "tools" operable in international relations:

- Diplomacy, including persuasion, inducements, and coercion
- Public diplomacy
- Intelligence
- Military capability and deterrence
- Economic relations
- Assistance programs
- Law enforcement, including security reform and collaboration on terrorism and apprehension of persons for criminal acts
- Consular policy, especially visa policy targeting individual obstructionists

This strategic planning package would be submitted for approval to the CRSG—or alternatively to the interagency Policy Coordination Committee (PCC) concerned.

The third sequence would move the process on to individual agencies for implementation of programs normally falling to them. An example might be USAID's implementation of disaster relief or emergency food aid. The S/CRS role in this tertiary sequence would not be supervisory, but rather coordinating and monitoring, in particular identifying gaps in implementation planning so that individual agency responsibility might be determined to fill the gaps. S/CRS would work with the MME team to help the agency for which implementation performance is problematic.[27] The U.S. chief of mission in the country concerned would also have an opportunity to approve or seek to adjust the implementation plans.[28]

In line with John Herbst's emphasis on becoming operational, the Planning Office shifted its focus from the overall planning framework to coordinating the development of country- and region-specific plans. The revised focus was an effort to get away from the highly abstract quality of the planning framework to draft specific plans using approaches and measurements based on concrete experience. In carrying out specific planning, the Planning Office worked with other State Department bureaus, with USAID offices, and with the military, particularly the geographic combatant commands. The JFCOM continued to be a major facilitator and collaborator, providing experts, space, and some financing for planning exercises. S/CRS considered its most important planning to have been applied to Sudan, Haiti, and Kosovo, for which both strategic and MME planning exercises were completed. In 2007 S/CRS supported EUR in a medium-term strategic planning exercise for a four-year period following Kosovo's anticipated declaration of independence. In 2008, following that declaration, the Office launched a "whole of government" contingency and transition planning process for the first 90 days. It deployed staff to meet gaps at the new U.S. Embassy in

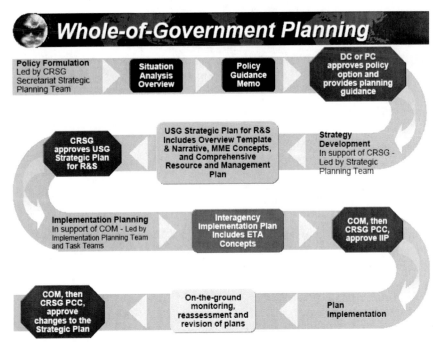

Figure 4.2
Interagency Management System Planning Process. Courtesy S/CRS.

Pristina and to assist the European Union's International Civilian Office in Kosovo.[29]

Becoming more operational did not extend to assuming a significant role in Afghanistan and Iraq. When S/CRS was established in 2004, Colin Powell warned it to stay away from both countries, fearing it would be swamped and founder. Instead it was charged with learning the right lessons for the next big crisis. The warning was not repeated by Secretary Rice. It is important to ask why S/CRS within three or four years of its founding did not try to demonstrate its value in the two countries where the Bush administration, after a poor start, made its heaviest investment in R&S. The State Department role in reconstruction was heavily focused on the PRTs, for which the civilian staff came mostly from State and USAID. (See Chapters 3 and 5.) In 2007, the Director of Foreign Assistance, with the concurrence of the SCA, asked S/CRS to look at the PRT planning process in Afghanistan. The Planning Office sent a team to Kabul, which interviewed all U.S.-led PRTs. It found that there was no formal planning process and worked with the embassy and ISAF to develop one. S/CRS wrote plans for the teams operating in the Eastern Regional Command, about half the total in country.

That useful, if quite limited, role in Afghanistan was not replicated in Iraq. Some S/CRS staff claimed that the NEA was too preoccupied with Iraq to ask for help.[30] That view is disputed by a former Deputy Iraq Coordinator. She reported that after it was decided to double PRTs in Iraq as part of the 2007 civilian surge, she and a policy level official in NEA, with seventh-floor encouragement, tried unsuccessfully to bring S/CRS into the planning process.[31] Under the Bush administration, S/CRS activity was basically limited to 30 end-of-tour interviews of Iraq PRT members. S/CRS was involved in developing training courses at the FSI for persons serving on PRTs in Iraq. In sum, the offices of the Coordinators for Afghanistan and Iraq (along with NEA's Office of Iraqi Affairs) provided civilian leadership for the civilian reconstruction in Afghanistan. In the Bush administration S/CRS played a minor part.[32]

Generally the U.S. military has been critical of the capacity of civilian government agencies, especially the State Department, to perform detailed operational planning—as opposed to policy planning. S/CRS leadership concluded it had achieved a "decent" operational planning capacity. DOD observers conceded that significant progress had been made, but noted that the degree of detail normally included in a military plan was still lacking. The Office of Stability Operations Capabilities in the Pentagon provided military planners to S/CRS to strengthen further operational planning.[33]

The Office of Planning also covered sectoral expertise and best practices, handled by a separate division until late 2008. Good planning must take into account experience in various aspects of R&S and lessons learned. S/CRS attempted with limited success to assemble a range of expertise in the sectors relevant to conflict management—security, law and order, infrastructure, economic reform, and governance—but became strongest in transitional security. For the other sectors, the office had one or two experts for each, most on contract. Because of a shortage of available experts in the U.S. government, S/CRS lacked "a deep bench," to cite the office director.[34] To synthesize lessons learned, S/CRS set up a working group for specific best practices, drawing in the relevant State regional and functional bureaus. For example, S/CRS (not INL) headed the working group on "stability policing," at the request of the NSC Deputies Committee.

In an assessment requested by the U.S. Congress, the Government Accountability Office (GAO) noted that the State Department had taken steps toward better interagency coordination of R&S activities but criticized it for inconsistency in the planning process. It claimed that there was ambiguity between NSPD 44 and the IMS framework on one side and the Foreign Affairs Manual, which governs State Department operations, on the other. While the latter gives to the geographical assistant secretary the authority to direct, coordinate, and supervise U.S. activities in countries in the region, GAO said S/CRS was claiming under NSPD 44 the authority to lead, plan, and coordinate R&S, thus undermining the assistant secretary's authority.[35] In rejoinder, it can be argued that the regional assistant secretary's cochairmanship of the CRSG permitted him/her to exercise those authorities and to provide general policy guidance on the country or region concerned, while the Coordinator, as second cochair, was enabled to provide leadership for the more specialized R&S planning function.[36] S/CRS also pointed out that in the clearance process for the IMS, all the geographic bureaus indicated their approval of the division of labor. In practice, of course, policy leadership may vie with planning leadership to shape the R&S strategy used. Whether the process gets mired down in a turf battle or makes decisions efficiently depends on the flexibility of both cochairs and their commitment to finding practical solutions to differences that may emerge. It is up to the Secretary of State to sort out persisting differences of view at the assistant secretary level.

Communication and Outreach

The Office of Strategic Communications, also reporting to the Principal Deputy Coordinator, was given responsibility for publicizing the work of S/CRS—including outreach to the academic and NGO sectors. It was also charged with building partnerships with other countries interested in the peace-building function and the numerous international organizations engaged in such work. Most of its attention focused on public affairs and diplomatic strategy. The major partners of S/CRS are its counterparts in Britain and Canada, set up at roughly the same time. Britain's Stabilisation Unit (previously called the Post-Conflict Response Unit) is a joint venture of the Department for International Development (DFID), the Foreign & Commonwealth Office, and the Defense Department. Canada's Stabilization and Reconstruction Task Force (START) is a permanent interagency group located within the Department of Foreign Affairs and International Trade. S/CRS interacted frequently with these two structures.[37] It also stayed in touch with the UN's Peace-Building Commission. S/CRS forged links with NATO, the OSCE, which has had heavy responsibilities for the Balkans, and the African Union, deeply enmeshed in the Darfur crisis.

Strategic Communications also had responsibility for developing a legislative strategy. That function was slow to come together. Until 2008, there was no one in S/CRS formally designated for Congressional liaison, although several staffers spent much of their time working with the Congress. The lack of consistent attention to Congressional liaison during the first few years handicapped S/CRS in making the case to Congress for the resources it needed.

Expeditionary Capacity

The Office of Civilian Readiness and Response and the Office of Conflict Prevention reported to the second Deputy Coordinator. Civilian Readiness and Response was the operational heart of S/CRS. It was responsible for developing and deploying U.S. resources in support of R&S. In particular, the office was charged with developing "civilian-military operational models" for an immediate surge response, to be followed by the insertion of more traditional support mechanisms to address longer-term needs.[38] S/CRS was supposed to coordinate the efforts of the relevant government agencies to mobilize their capabilities and to fill in the gaps.

The civilian expeditionary surge capacity was premised on a three-tiered structure. By 2006 S/CRS had created an Active Component of the Civilian Response Corps (CRC-A) consisting of civilian generalists and specialists drawn basically from the State Department and USAID.[39] It still numbered only 10 persons in 2008 but was projected to rise rapidly to 110 in 2009 and 250 by 2010, depending on Congressional funding. If one or more CRSGs were activated and ACTs dispatched, the demand for CRC-A services would increase rapidly. As of 2008, all CRC-A members were State Department employees, but USAID officers were expected to join the component as it expanded. The primary responsibility of Active Component members was to deploy quickly for up to six months to countries with stabilization crises, usually to augment the embassy staff. Approximately 75 percent of them were to be available to deploy within 48 hours of being called up. They were to retain employment in their home agencies and have other assignments when not in the field. They were expected to train up to eight weeks a year, including participation in joint civilian-military exercises.

Even in the absence of IMS activation, the CRC-A dispatched representatives to Lebanon, Kosovo, Haiti, Afghanistan, Liberia, Chad, Sudan, and Iraq. Their assignment to Sudan's troubled Darfur province, an early test of S/CRS expeditionary capacity, was designed to support Deputy Secretary of State Robert Zoellick in the negotiation of the 2006 DPA. (See Chapter 3.) Creating an embassy field presence for the first time in the remote far west of Sudan, CRC-A personnel established a peace secretariat for the DPA and served as observers for the African Union Cease-Fire Commission. Zoellick, in fact, gave credit to an Active Component staffer for the signature of the accord by SLA military leader Minni Minawi, the only rebel signatory.[40] Since the DPA almost immediately broke down, the ongoing responsibility of Active Component officers was primarily political reporting, based on extensive liaison with the parties to the conflict, the African Union forces (AMIS) and the United Nations.[41] The presence of a total of nine CRC-A members in Darfur until mid-2008 improved U.S. Embassy—and general U.S. government—understanding of the dynamics and evolution of the struggle.

The Active Response Component was augmented by a Standby Response Component (CRC-S) of people bringing relevant skills from the civilian agencies[42]—volunteers and "reservists" holding day jobs in different government agencies. In 2008, S/CRS also had 150 Foreign Service retirees on its roster. CRC-S members were to be available on 30 days' notice. In a crisis they would deploy at a rate of up to 25 percent within 30–60 days of a call-up. Duration of deployment would be 90–180 days. As of the end of 2008, there were about 500 CRC-S enrolled, including retirees. The hope was to expand the component to 2,000 by 2010, including representatives of other agencies and federal retirees. CRC-S members were slated for basic training at FSI and expected to hone their skills by follow-up courses. S/CRS targeted people with experience in overseas assistance, security, democratization, and business development—at a GS-09 or FS-4 level (early mid-career). Only a handful of CRC-S had been deployed by the end of 2008—in Darfur, Chad, Iraq, and Afghanistan—but additional numbers had been trained.[43] They might be mobilized by a CSRG or, less formally, within the State Department by agreement between the geographic bureau concerned and the S/CRS Coordinator. Standby Component members, when deployed, could form part of an ACT or Field Action Civilian Team (FACT) assembled under the authority of the ambassador.[44]

The third tier proposed was the Reserve Component (CRC-R), highlighted in President Bush's 2007 State of the Union message and his 2008 budget message (for FY 2009). Bush said the CRC-R "would ease the burden on the Armed Forces by allowing us to hire civilians with critical skills to serve on missions abroad when America needs them." The Reserve would consist of experts from state and local government, as well as the NGO community and the private sector, who have skills lacking in sufficient numbers in the U.S. government. Such specialists would include police trainers, persons able to set up court systems, correctional officers, city managers, lawyers, engineers, and agricultural specialists. Members would make a four-year commitment, and agree to deploy for up to one year. Reservists would receive several weeks of orientation, annual and mission-specific training prior to deployment.

Creation of the Reserve—unlike the CRC-A and CRC-S—requires Congressional authorization. Its activation, to be limited to major U.S. stabilization engagements, would require a presidential determination and would emerge from a CRSG-developed implementation plan. CRC-R members would become U.S. government employees, when mobilized for training and deployment. Approximately 25 percent of the Reserve would be available to deploy at any one time.

In mid-2008 the Congress made a supplemental appropriation of $55 million to enable S/CRS to expand the Active and Standby components of the civilian response capacity to 100 and 500, respectively, but left funding for the Civilian Reserve Component to the next administration and the 111th Congress.[45]

Both the Civilian Readiness and Response and Conflict Prevention offices were responsible for ensuring that S/CRS personnel and those selected for civilian expeditionary work received adequate training. FSI, located at the National Foreign Affairs Training Center in Arlington, Virginia, is the primary training site. A week-long introductory course, mandatory for CRC-A and CRC-S members, covered the IMS and the use of conflict assessment tools, particularly the S/CRS Essential Tasks Matrix. Students who had the five-day course were supposed to get further training annually, but that rule has not been strictly enforced. Active and Standby Components also took a course on failed states and could enroll in an offering on advanced planning.[46] The Office collaborated with the Bureau of Diplomatic Security, USAID, the military, and the USIP to put together about a dozen FSI courses. S/CRS staff are asked periodically to lecture at military training schools, including the Center for Army Lessons Learned (CALL) at Fort Leavenworth, Kansas, and the Peacekeeping and Stability Operations Institute (PKSOI) at the Army War College.

Prevention

Under the first Coordinator, the Office of Conflict Prevention gave considerable priority to early warning—periodic review by S/CRS and the geographic bureaus of a watch list of countries potentially afflicted with conflict. However, this early exercise came to be viewed as somewhat duplicative of existing government-wide intelligence efforts and lacking in operational usefulness. Under John Herbst, it was de-emphasized in favor of a more operational approach, centering on assessment.

At the invitation of a State geographic bureau, S/CRS would assemble an interagency team to do an in-country assessment of an incipient conflict situation and draw up recommendations for preventive action. The receptivity of the geographic bureaus to such S/CRS involvement was limited. Traditionally, the bureaus have tended to resist efforts of outside offices to insert themselves into crisis situations, including potential ones. S/CRS explored different approaches to improve the attractiveness and relevance of its prevention services. Rather than developing an assessment from scratch, Conflict Prevention drew on existing strategic planning such as the Mission Strategic Plan (MSP), done by all embassies, or the Operations Plan for each country, developed for the Office of the Director of Foreign Assistance. S/CRS found it useful to collaborate with State geographic bureaus on "scenario-based planning." A good example was cohosting with State's African Bureau a policy exercise to strengthen planning for the 2006 election in the Congo. It drew in both the U.S. interagency R&S community and participants from the European Union and the United Nations.[47] It helped expatriate agencies and personnel work through the planning implications for coping with 25 million voters over an area half as large as the United States.

Conflict Prevention also used roundtables to assess the nature of a situation which could explode into or revert to civil war. The Zimbabwe roundtable brought together the U.S. ambassador, previous ambassadors, and other experts to consider how the U.S. government and international community might proceed in the event of complete state collapse or transition to a post–Robert Mugabe situation. S/CRS viewed the exercise as scenario-based planning which could lead to a broader interagency strategic planning process. A similar roundtable was done for Kosovo to examine the implications of the impasse in negotiations between Kosovar Albanians and Serbia and of the expected Kosovar declaration of independence, which took place in 2008.

This variegated and somewhat *ad hoc* approach to assessment became more formalized in the last year of the Bush administration. In mid-2008 the NSC approved the Interagency Conflict Assessment Framework (ICAF) put together by a group cochaired by S/CRS and USAID's CMM. It is a planning tool used to assist interagency members reach consensus on a particular country's conflict dynamics and potential entry points for U.S. conflict management efforts.[48] The ICAF drew heavily on the Conflict Assessment Framework (CAF) developed by USAID. It feeds into the situation analysis and policy formulation aspects of the planning process in the Planning Framework for Stabilization, Reconstruction and Conflict Transformation described above.[49] It could be used for planning for a project under Section 1207. The new tool was applied to Tajikistan, the Democratic Republic of the Congo, and in an earlier iteration to Sri Lanka.

The Office of Conflict Prevention managed funds transferred by the Defense Department—Sec. 1207 grants—to support R&S activities. Although the DOD had authority to transfer up to $100 million in FY 2006, S/CRS received only $15 million for a project in Lebanon to train and equip police and remove unexploded ordnance. The bottleneck developed partly from the insistence of the Defense Department on approving each individual project and partly from the transformed State/USAID budget process under F, which also interposed its clearance requirement on each request. In FY 2007, however, funds eventually totaling $100 million began to flow faster with new leadership at the Defense Department and more streamlined F procedures. An initial $20 million grant for Haiti, focused on security, rule of law, and development projects to stabilize Cité Soleil, Port-au-Prince's most unruly neighborhood, came early in the fiscal year. A cluster of projects were approved before year-end, including two regional projects, for the Trans-Sahel Counter-Terrorism Initiative and Southeast Asia, as shown in Table 4.1.

In 2008 an additional $100 million was slated to go to nine different countries, but half the money was channeled to Georgia after its confrontation with Russia to meet the needs of displaced persons and rebuild the police force. Most of the remainder went to Afghanistan, Lebanon, the Congo, Tajikistan, and Sri Lanka.[50]

The prescribed role of Conflict Prevention was "to coordinate interagency processes to identify states at risk ..., lead interagency planning to prevent or mitigate conflict, develop detailed contingency plans [for integrated R&S], and coordinate preventative strategies with other governments, international organizations and NGOs."[51] Measured against its mission, the office, by the end of 2008, had not yet established itself as the U.S. government's lead entity in preventing conflict. It managed one of the most important

Table 4.1
FY 2007 Sec. 1207 Projects

Country/Region	Amount ($ million)	Purpose
Haiti	20.0	Cité Soleil
Somalia	25.0	Stabilize Kenya border region
Niger, Mali, Mauritania	18.8	Security and civilian development presence
Philippines, Malaysia, Indonesia	12.0	Infrastructure, maritime security, local law enforcement capacity
Yemen	10.0	Youth services and employment
Nepal	10.0	District level governance
Colombia	4.0	Areas liberated from insurgents
Total	99.8	

R&S programs—Section 1207 grants, but those grants were not strictly limited to preventive action, as demonstrated by their use in conflict-ridden countries like Haiti, Nepal, and Georgia after Russian intervention. Conflict Prevention had a formal but not actual lead in early warning, on which the National Intelligence Council held the major role on classified assessment and USAID's CMM on unclassified lists. Its major conflict prevention assessment tool, the ICAF, approved in 2008, is built on frameworks developed not in S/CRS, but in CMM. (See Chapter 6.) It is difficult to avoid the conclusion that the Office of Conflict Prevention at the end of the Bush administration was something of a hodgepodge, an assembly of divisions designed to pick up residual responsibilities not clearly related to crisis planning (Office of Planning) and expeditionary capacity (Civilian Readiness and Response).

VULNERABILITIES

Advocates of S/CRS suggest that it was extraordinary for a major new office in the U.S. government to move from drawing board to launch creation within a year and then to operations with a staff of 70 within 18 months of its creation. The federal budget process, which begins two years in advance of the budget year, makes it extraordinarily difficult to mobilize funding and people for a new office within a short period. S/CRS made considerable progress on both the planning and the operational side. Nevertheless, there is broad consensus that the prospects of this much heralded instrument of civilian conflict transformation were constrained by the reluctance of the Congress during the Bush administration to provide it with a strong mandate

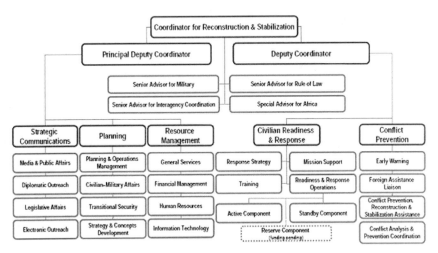

Figure 4.3
S/CRS Organizational Chart. February 2009, courtesy S/CRS.

and the budgetary resources required for it to play its projected role. A second, and closely related vulnerability, was the absence of a powerful champion within the administration.

Although the SFRC gave major bipartisan support for the office from the beginning, there was not much carryover to other elements of the Congress. The Lugar-Biden bill authorizing S/CRS passed the Senate unanimously in 2006 but died in the House Committee on Foreign Affairs (CFA). The Foreign Operations Subcommittee of the House Appropriations Committee showed little interest in the proposed civilian reserve and significant permanent funding. House staffers criticized the State Department's initial proposal as lacking "coherence." They voiced suspicions that the proposed Civilian Reserve Corps might become a tool for unwarranted international intervention and the Conflict Response account a potential "slush" fund.[52] Some feared S/CRS would weaken USAID. The Iraq and Afghanistan supplemental legislation passed in May 2007 did appropriate up to $50 million for the civilian reserve, subject to authorization. When Biden and Lugar requested passage of the authorizing bill by unanimous consent, Sen. Coburn (R-OK) imposed a hold, which was not circumvented until late 2008.[53] The resource picture would have been truly bleak had it not been for the support of the Defense Department and its Congressional appropriators. As noted above, Sec. 1207 transfers to S/CRS reached $99 million in FY 2007 and $100 million in FY 2008.

Despite reservations and inertia in the 109th Congress, there was not determined opposition to a well-funded civilian-led R&S capacity. Failure to secure adequate Congressional support stemmed more from the absence of strong administration support, in particular that of Secretary of State Rice. As NSA, Condoleezza Rice was part of the interagency decision process that resulted in the creation of S/CRS. And, as noted above, in her Georgetown University speech of 2006, she made a State Department-centered civilian reconstruction capacity, an integral part of her signature reform—"transformational diplomacy."

Even with this ringing endorsement, Rice did not prove to be a champion of S/CRS with the Congress. In the fall of 2006, Rice did not respond to suggestions that she lobby the House for approval of the Senate-passed Foreign Relations Authorization bill for 2006 and 2007, which contained specific authorization for S/CRS. Of course, the appointment of Roland Tobias as Director of Foreign Assistance made him the administration's arbiter and chief spokesperson on the international affairs budget. In the FY 2008 budget process the Coordinator found it necessary to persuade this major new actor of the importance of the S/CRS function. Rice was apparently not actively involved in the budget decisions for S/CRS and acquiesced in the number which went forward to OMB. There is likewise little evidence of a serious effort by Secretary Rice in 2007 to lobby Sen. Coburn to remove his hold on the authorization which would have made available $50 million for civilian reserve under the Iraq/Afghanistan supplemental.

Criticism of Rice's reticence on the S/CRS budget was typical of a more general assessment of her approach to mobilizing resources for the Department of State and international affairs. Whereas Colin Powell was viewed as successful in increasing the Department's budget and personnel levels, the Congress declined to approve requests for additional personnel after 2004, a situation attributed by many in the career service to lack of effort on Rice's part. In late 2007 a survey by the American Foreign Service Association included the question "How would you rate the job that Secretary . . . Rice is doing in resources for the department and its people?" Only 14 percent gave her "good" or "very good" marks, while 31 percent and 18 percent rated her as "poor" and "very poor," respectively.[54]

Perhaps responding to the criticism, Rice is reported to have made a concerted effort to secure the resources needed by S/CRS in the FY 2009 budget. When the OMB "passback" on the FY 2009 did not include all the funds the Department had requested, she successfully appealed, helping to secure the $249 million figure which went forward to the Congress. Both she and the leadership of the NSC pledged full engagement with the Congress in the budget fight. In a presidential election year when the "lame-duck" President generally lacks clout with the Congress, however, the Bush administration was not in a position to push through the FY 2009 budget request. Congress did authorize the Response Readiness Corps (active and standby components) and appropriated a total of $55 million to expand both components.[55]

JOHN E. HERBST

John Herbst grew up in New York State and acquired a classical Foreign Service education. Upon graduation from Georgetown University's School of Foreign Service, he took a master's degree from the Fletcher School of Law and Diplomacy. Entering the Foreign Service in 1979, Herbst alternated between Eastern Europe and the Middle East. As a political officer, he rose quickly and distinguished himself in challenging political assignments in Riyadh and Moscow, before becoming Consul General in Jerusalem. Appointed Ambassador to Uzbekistan in 2000, Herbst played an important role in the creation of an American base to support Operation Enduring Freedom in Afghanistan. By the time the Uzbeks evicted the United States from that base in 2005, Herbst had moved on to Ukraine, where he replaced Carlos Pascual as ambassador, when Pascual took the helm of the nascent S/CRS. In Kiev Herbst concentrated on channeling U.S. support to fair elections and witnessed firsthand the "orange" revolution which brought President Viktor Yuschenko to power.

In 2006 John Herbst was named Coordinator of S/CRS, replacing Carlos Pascual after a hiatus of almost five months. He inherited an office in a "holding pattern" with diminishing visibility. Secretary of State Rice wanted him to get more people into the field, in support of her "transformational diplomacy." Like his predecessor, Herbst soon ran into trouble with the leadership of some of the geographic bureaus, who did not want a new office interfering in their big crises. In the case of Darfur, however, the chargé d'affaires in Khartoum had asked for help, and S/CRS Active Response Component personnel were able to provide valued support to Deputy Secretary of State Zoellick, as he hammered out the ill-fated Darfur Peace Agreement with Nigerian President Obasanjo.

A more serious problem was acquiring a budget which would permit an active role. Herbst arrived at S/CRS only a few months after Randall Tobias had become Director of Foreign Assistance. There was a brand new budget process underway, and the new Coordinator was on the outside looking in. Herbst could not secure any money for the Civilian Response Corps and only $25 million for the Conflict Response Fund. Recognizing that an ally on the budgeting side was essential to the fiscal viability of his office, Herbst made a deal to become a deputy to Tobias, reporting to him, while retaining—formally speaking—a direct reporting role with the Secretary of State.[56] Without this alliance with F, Herbst believes his later efforts to increase staff and budget would probably have been fruitless.

Prospects brightened for John Herbst and S/CRS in 2007. In January President Bush proposed the Civilian Response Corps in his State of the Union message. In March the NSC approved the IMS to which he had devoted so much effort. To make good on the President's message, $249 million was placed in the FY 2009 budget proposal for the Civilization Stabilization Initiative. In 2007 and 2008 S/CRS received a total of $200 million in transfers from the Defense Department (Sec. 1207) for projects in 14 countries. The geographic bureaus were now coming to him for money and services. By the end of 2008 Herbst was receiving unaccustomed accolades from Defense Department colleagues for the important progress of his organization. Said one, "John Herbst is an amazing leader." In recognition of his accomplishments Herbst was promoted to Career Minister rank, second highest in the Foreign Service.

FUTURE PEACE-BUILDING ISSUES FOR STATE AND S/CRS

S/CRS was the single most important institutional creation for peace-building of the Bush administration. Its creation was an assertion that the State Department could take the lead in civilian R&S operations, in the face of critics who argued that State's bureaucratic culture is inimical to operational effectiveness. Such criticism ignored that fact that State already had substantial operational functions, as opposed to diplomatic and representational ones. They include consular operations and diplomatic security and—in the R&S arena—civilian police operations, refugee programs, and some democracy projects. S/CRS did not, during the Bush administration, demonstrate its capacity to run R&S operations for the civilian side of the government. Its failure to phase into a cutting-edge role in Afghanistan and Iraq, the administration's most important R&S efforts, left it with problems of credibility to be addressed by the Obama administration. S/CRS was ignored during the 2006 war in Lebanon. Despite approval of the IMS, S/CRS was kept on the sidelines in the Somalia crisis of 2007. Moreover, since the IMS was not activated, it is not possible to assess its value as a working model. The clout of State's geographic bureaus remains strong. Without a clear commitment by the Secretary of State to the Coordinator's designated role, when crises arise in which the White House, the Secretary of Defense, and the Secretary of State are deeply invested, S/CRS will be elbowed aside. It will be restricted to "boutique crises," where the stakes for the United States are limited. Although it has made a significant contribution in smaller crises, it may not survive in such a modest role.

One straightforward way to strengthen the operational capacity and credibility of S/CRS would be to make it a truly integrated State/USAID entity. After 2006 the Coordinator reported not only to the Secretary of State but also to the Director of Foreign Assistance. The first Coordinator, Carlos Pascual, came out of USAID, and the second Deputy Coordinator has been a USAID officer. However, surprisingly, no other USAID personnel appeared on the staff list at the end of 2008. In the future, filling up to a third of S/CRS positions with USAID officers, drawing to the extent possible on those with experience managing assistance projects in conflict areas, would inject operational depth into the Coordinator's Office. It would also convey a message that the leadership of the State Department is committed to strengthening its operational capability. In the context of making S/CRS an integrated State/USAID operation, the administration should examine the juxtaposition of S/CRS and USAID's CMM, which has seized the interagency lead in conflict prevention, and its Office of Transition Initiatives (OTI), already a proven expeditionary force for reconstruction. Those offices are analyzed in detail in Chapter 6.

The Obama administration will also need to consider the optimum mode of staffing to achieve an effective operational role in R&S. The proposed size of the Civilian Response Corps and the Civilian Reserve Corps, totaling

4,500, is modest by comparison to proposals to enlarge the U.S. military, but, in a period of increased budget scrutiny, will likely be weighed alongside proposals in Congress and elsewhere to expand the size of the Foreign Service, both State and USAID.[57]

CHAPTER 5

A Belated Embrace
of Stability Operations:
The Department of Defense

> Stability operations are a core U.S. military mission that . . . shall be given
> priority comparable to combat operations.
>
> —Directive 3000.05

Nowhere in the U.S. government has peace-building gone through as many abrupt course changes in the past 15 years as in the DOD. During the Bush 41 administration the Pentagon did not pay much attention to post-conflict reconstruction. The international community, led by the United States, offered little in the way of postwar reconstruction assistance to a devastated Afghanistan after the Soviet pullout in 1989. In its wake came warlordism and the rise of the Taliban. In the Gulf War, U.S. forces halted after Saddam's capitulation and soon withdrew from the part of Iraq they held, allowing Saddam's Republican Guards to massacre Shi'ites in the south and Kurds in the north who sought to overthrow him. "No-fly" zones eventually established in both areas were a belated response to the international outcry. In the north, Saddam's troops were expelled, permitting creation of a security zone in which the Kurds themselves were able to carry out some reconstruction.

The Clinton administration proved more willing to experiment with military peace-building, particularly in the Balkans. The push came not from inside the Pentagon, but from the NSC and, after 1997, from Foggy Bottom, when Madeleine Albright became Secretary of State. The Clinton administration created the Office of Peacekeeping and Humanitarian Assistance (PK&HA) under the wing of the Under Secretary of Defense for Policy and the Assistant Secretary for Special Operations/Low-Intensity Conflict (SO/LIC), but that office was not close to the center of policymaking on the Balkans. The key Defense Department decision-makers in the Balkans crisis were Secretaries William Perry and William Cohen and Under Secretary for Policy Walter Slocum, who set up task forces of 30–40 people for Bosnia and then Kosovo, outside the formal jurisdiction of the assistant secretaries. Coercive diplomacy featuring air strikes persuaded Serbian leader Slobodan Milosevic to sign peace agreements on Bosnia in 1995 and Kosovo in 1999. Then came NATO peacekeeping forces, including thousands of U.S. troops, and post-conflict reconstruction activities under UN leadership. Eventually the Clinton administration codified its experience from Somalia to Bosnia in PDD 56 for complex contingency operations.[1]

ASSAULT ON NATION-BUILDING

There was much opposition to U.S. military intervention in the Balkans. Critics argued that vital American interests were not at stake and that the United States should leave those problems to Europe. Proponents countered that it was the failure of the Europeans to make headway on Bosnia that pushed the United States ultimately into a leadership role. The verbal attacks on "nation-building," as post-conflict reconstruction activities were called at the time, became fierce. For its opponents, "nation-building" implied "mission creep" or overreach by the military into areas that did not concern it.[2] The Republican attack on Clinton administration nation-building in Somalia, Haiti, and the Balkans included the charge that it was "military social work." A focus on nation-building was viewed as deleterious to American forces. Distracted from their primary "war-fighting" function, U.S. troops were said to lose their combat edge and become less effective in fighting the nation's wars.

In the presidential campaign of 2000, George W. Bush said of his predecessor's peace-building efforts in Somalia:

I don't think our troops ought to be used for what's called nation building. I think our troops ought to be used to fight and win war. I think our troops ought to be used to help overthrow a dictator when it's in our best interests. But in this case, it was a nation-building exercise.[3]

The candidate's senior foreign policy advisor, Condoleezza Rice, said, "We don't need to have the 82nd Airborne escorting kids to kindergarten."[4]

Such criticism tended to ignore the fact that since World War II U.S. armed forces have engaged extensively in a variety of activities which do not fit the category of "war-fighting."[5] They include:

- Humanitarian relief, particularly for natural disasters. The post-Christmas tsunami of 2004 generated a huge military airlift of relief supplies to victims in the Indian Ocean nations. The Kashmiri earthquake of 2005 stimulated a large-scale diversion of U.S. military helicopters, including some of those assigned to Afghanistan, to bring in supplies and evacuate the wounded from remote mountain fastnesses.

- Military training, including joint military exercises. As Walter Russell Mead has noted, "The U.S. military has created a historically unique network of military-to-military [training] ties embracing almost every country in the world. . . . American standards of training are often considered a kind of gold standard in militaries all over the world."[6] In FY 2008 the U.S. government allocated training assistance estimated at $85.1 million for more than 125 countries.[7] Although training funds are appropriated to the Department of State, which determines its allocation, training is overseen by the Defense Security Cooperation Agency (DSCA) and carried out in dozens of institutions under Defense Department authority. Joint exercises overseas, particularly with countries in the Global South, are a form of training for both U.S. and local forces. These military activities are aimed at alliance building or maintenance.[8]

- Military assistance. Chas. Freeman, Jr., points out that "military assistance provides tangible evidence of an interest in the security of allies and friends and their ability to defend themselves."[9] It also provides U.S. access to military leaders and sometimes enables the United States to influence their military decisions. In FY 2008 Foreign Military Funding was estimated at $4.6 billion, of which $3.7 billion went to Israel and Egypt and the rest to 50 other countries.[10] The assistance is allocated by the Department of State and is not part of the defense budget, but the military is heavily involved in the transfer process.

- Shows of force, including temporary deployments, conspicuous military exercises, and naval visits, are designed to "call [U.S.] military capabilities to the attention of adversaries."[11] The dispatch of two aircraft-carrier task forces to the Persian Gulf in early 2007 had exactly this intention with respect to Iran. Large-scale military exercises conducted with South Korea in 2005 were aimed at North Korea. Both exercises were closer to public diplomacy than to war fighting. Naval visits are usually part shows of force, part alliance building and maintenance.

- Counter-narcotics operations, including assistance to other governments to prevent production and trafficking, as well as halting flows across U.S. borders.

- Peacekeeping. In addition to their deployment for peace enforcement roles in Somalia, Haiti, and the Balkans, U.S. forces have formed part of the Multinational Force in the Sinai Peninsula since the 1979 Treaty between Israel and Egypt. That force serves to enforce and verify the implementation of an international agreement, another non-war-fighting role of the military.

The U.S. Army has grouped these noncombat—or "non-kinetic"—missions generally as "military operations other than war" (MOOTW), or more recently as "range of military operations" (ROMO).[12]

THE DEFENSE DEPARTMENT AND PEACE-BUILDING: RUMSFELD BLOWS COLD THEN HOT

Initial Downgrading of Peacekeeping and Stabilization

When the second Bush administration took over the Pentagon, it moved to deinstitutionalize nation-building. The 2001 Quadrennial Defense Review, reflecting the views of Defense Secretary Donald Rumsfeld, became the *de facto* defense strategy for the administration. It deliberately set aside the question of stabilization. One of the inputs to the debate preceding the drafting of the QDR was a proposal by a bipartisan panel calling for the creation of a constabulary capacity, to be vested largely in the Army and the Marine Corps and "additive to other force structure requirements."[13] The proposal was soundly rejected. Rumsfeld's strategy required the military to "defend the United States; deter aggression and coercion forward in critical regions; swiftly defeat aggression in overlapping major conflicts while preserving for the President the option to call for a decisive victory in one of those conflicts—including the possibility of regime change or occupation; and conduct a limited number of smaller-scale contingency operations." With a force configured to defend the homeland, to carry out forward deterrence and warfighting missions, and to conduct smaller-scale contingency operations, DOD would be in a position to better address other "high demand, low density" requirements, including deployments like peacekeeping operations in the Balkans. The QDR was actually published three weeks after 9/11, requiring hasty reediting to place the GWOT at the center of the document, but without significantly altering Rumsfeld's strategy.

Senior officials in the Office of the Secretary of Defense (OSD) wanted to dissolve the PK&HA and phase U.S. forces out of existing peacekeeping missions, especially in Kosovo. They also wished to place all humanitarian assistance under the State Department. Implementation proved problematic. Under Secretary for Policy Douglas Feith made a strong pitch to pull U.S. troops out of the Sinai peacekeeping mission but was forced to back away because of loud objections from Israel and Egypt. Feith did eventually get U.S. forces out of SFOR, the NATO peacekeeping force in Bosnia, but not until 2004. Humanitarian assistance dispensed by the military had its staunch defenders on key committees on Capitol Hill. Moreover, PK&HA soon proved its mettle. The new DASD in charge of the office, Joseph R. Collins, was convinced that low-intensity conflict was a key military arena for the future and that the U.S. military could not "take a pass on peace-keeping."[14]

More controversial were moves against the Peacekeeping Institute at the Army War College. In 2001 rumors circulated that it would be closed as part of a general realignment exercise. Despite a letter of protest from 40 senators to the Secretary of the Army, the army staff recommended by mid-2002 "consolidation" of the function under the Center for Army Lessons Learned (CALL) at Fort Leavenworth. When the director of the Institute made a visit to CALL in early 2003 to lay the groundwork for closing his institution and securing a smooth transition, he was told that no one with peacekeeping expertise could be found on the CALL staff. Consolidation was a euphemism for abolition. However, word of the decision created a strong backlash in the press, which linked it to stabilization problems already apparent in Iraq. In July Rumsfeld gave the Institute a reprieve. It was renamed the Peacekeeping and Stability Operations Institute.[15]

JOSEPH R. COLLINS

Colonel (Ret.) Joseph R. Collins, a native of Long Island, joined the Army in 1970 and became an infantry officer, moving through command and staff positions. He also showed an intellectual bent, teaching at West Point and the National War College, and a knack for writing, serving for a time as chief speechwriter for the Chairman of the Joint Chiefs. Along the way he earned a PhD with a dissertation on Soviet policy on Afghanistan. Toward the end of the Clinton administration, he put in his retirement papers and started work at the Center for Strategic and International Studies. During the transition to the Bush administration he accepted a job at the National Defense University. However, Paul Wolfowitz, who had been designated Deputy Secretary of Defense, asked Collins to become his special assistant, basically to help him through confirmation hearings.

Happy with Collins's services, Wolfowitz asked him which Deputy Assistant Secretary position he would like. To his chief's surprise, Collins asked for Peacekeeping and Humanitarian Assistance, which he took over in July. It was hardly a prestigious seat in those early days of the administration. A senior Defense official wrote on one table of organization, "I thought we had done away with that." Principal Deputy Under Secretary for Policy Steven Cambone liked to refer to PK&HA as the "junk drawer" of the Defense Department policy shop. Collins decided to take on that moniker as a banner.[16] Under him the office seized responsibility for miscellaneous tasks, including noncombatant evacuations, humanitarian mine action, and civil-military relations, as well as peacekeeping and humanitarian assistance. Having received no guidance from his superiors about priorities, the new DASD immediately set about inserting his office into the policy arena to the extent possible.

The 9/11 attacks brought him increased prominence. Because of his doctoral studies, Collins was one of the few U.S. military experts on Afghanistan. He used this expertise to carve out a position for his office, first on the issue of humanitarian assistance but subsequently on policing and other peacekeeping issues.[17] He also forged relationships with American and international NGOs which quickly reestablished themselves in Afghanistan, when the Taliban fell.

In January 2003, PK&HA was renamed "Stability Operations," the opening tremor in a seismic shift in Pentagon views on R&S resulting from the Afghanistan and Iraq experience. By that time, Joe Collins was moving on to the National Defense University, where he became professor of strategy. He has said, reflecting on his experience, "The businesses we're in—humanitarian assistance, peacekeeping, post-conflict reconstruction—these are all part and parcel of the business of national security."[18]

9/11 and the Afghanistan Campaign

The military plan for Afghanistan, forged in the immediate aftermath of 9/11, played down R&S. The objectives were to seize, arrest, or kill the al-Qa'ida leadership and to overthrow the Taliban and secondarily to provide humanitarian assistance and some help with rebuilding infrastructure.[19]

The de-emphasis on R&S reflected two basic considerations beyond a general allergy to "nation-building." First, the Pentagon leadership doubted that a general peacekeeping or stabilization force could operate in Afghanistan. The country was legendary for its xenophobia and fierce resistance to foreign "invaders," a lesson imposed on the Soviets a decade before. No one was certain what the Afghan response to peacekeepers would be.[20] Rumsfeld was interested in leaving a small foreign "footprint" and staying out of internal Afghan politics.[21] Second, Pentagon leaders saw the primary U.S. interest as winning the war on terror, a global war. They did not want to tie down significant U.S. forces in Afghanistan, when they might need to be redeployed quickly elsewhere. Rumsfeld wanted strictly to limit reconstruction tasks in Afghanistan and to hand over as many as possible to U.S. allies, the United Nations, and to the Afghans themselves. Already, some policymakers had Iraq in their sights and viewed Afghanistan as a distraction.

The United States assembled for Operation Enduring Freedom a coalition force which eventually reached 8,000. That force was sanctioned by the Security Council as exercising the right of collective self-defense to carry out counterterrorist operations against al-Qa'ida and the Taliban.[22] In December the Security Council authorized the creation of a separate ISAF, also including U.S. troops, to assist in the maintenance of security.[23] The task of reconstruction was basically left to the United Nations, but under tight constraints.

Reconstruction and stabilization in Afghanistan were extremely weak, especially for the first two years. At U.S. insistence, the ISAF was initially restricted to Kabul. In the absence of security, reconstruction of schools, health clinics, and infrastructure outside the capital could not move forward quickly. Initially the approach of the military was to deploy Special Forces and Civil Affairs teams—all military—in cities like Herat, Mazar-e-Sharif, and Kandahar to carry out small-scale reconstruction projects in order to build local goodwill.[24] However, the cumulative effects were not great.

Ground commanders began looking at a different model: joint military and civilian teams. By mid-2002 the first PRT was deployed in Gardez.[25] Basically the PRTs in Afghanistan constituted a military force of about 80 (a security force of about 50 troops and civic affairs officers), commanded by a lieutenant colonel, conjoined with a group of about 5 civilians—typically State and USAID officers, a U.S. Department of Agriculture specialist, and representatives of the Army Corps of Engineers. The PRT commander reported through military channels, while the State representative reported to the PRT office in the U.S. Embassy in Kabul. PRT objectives were to promote a more secure environment in the provinces, stimulate development, and strengthen the influence of the central government. Typically they built roads and schools, created agricultural cooperatives, and set up training centers for basic skills like construction. When the initial PRTs showed some effectiveness, it was decided to expand them to the entire country over a phased period. In mid-2003, when ISAF was permitted to deploy outside of Kabul and its command was turned over to NATO, it began running PRTs as well. At the beginning of 2008, there were 12 American and 14 European-led PRTs in Afghanistan.[26]

The PRTs had limited effectiveness during the Bush administration. Seeing their own security as depending on the local situation, the PRTs tended to avoid taking action which might offend warlords, thereby perpetuating the weakness of the central government. The PRTs were an interesting experiment in stability operations under very difficult security conditions, but seemed unsuited to long-term stabilization operations. During the Bush administration the U.S. teams in Afghanistan varied in composition, but most of them were 5–10 percent civilian, largely State and USAID officers; their military composition included civic affairs personnel, but a majority were "shooters." Force protection was a major priority for these groups, and command clearly resided with the military.[27] Given their composition, PRTs were unable to address the full range of R&S tasks, which included institution building, rule of law, and facilitating a return to economic normalcy. Long-term stabilization requires an integrated national reconstruction approach developed in close cooperation with the local government.

Iraq Prompts a New Look at Stabilization

The military attack on Iraq was brief, decisive, and took less time than the Pentagon anticipated.[28] None of the nightmare combat scenarios anticipated materialized—use of chemical weapons against U.S. troops, house-to-house urban warfare with the Republican Guards, and oil well fires. But the stability operations part of the scenario went badly almost from the beginning: looting, the absence of law and order, collapse of the Iraqi state, and the gradual rise of insurgency.

President Bush made a critical decision at the outset to back Cheney and Rumsfeld's insistence that the Defense Department keep control of the post-conflict process, once the Iraqi military was defeated and Saddam overthrown. That decision was enshrined in NSPD 24 of January 20, 2003, less than two months before the war began. The basic planning was carried out in the secretive Office of Special Plans, created by Under Secretary Feith.

The Office of Special Plans created within the Pentagon—and made sure it was explicitly mentioned in NSPD 24—a vehicle for stabilization, the Office of Reconstruction and Humanitarian Assistance (ORHA), headed by LTG Jay Garner (Ret.). It was to carry out humanitarian relief, reconstruction, and civil administration.[29] It began work in Washington in January 2003, but it was entirely excluded from war planning. Garner and his core team flew to Kuwait at the beginning of the war but were not permitted to enter Iraq until April 21, 12 days after the fall of Saddam. Garner viewed ORHA's primary task as managing a large-scale but short-term humanitarian crisis in a defeated state, where most of the government bureaucracy would continue to function. He expected his team to be in Iraq 90 days, when the government would be turned over to the Iraqis.

Looting and disorder and the beginning of insurgency, plus scathing press reports on the chaos of postwar operations, quickly doomed ORHA. On May 6 Bush announced that retired ambassador L. Paul (Jerry) Bremer would become Administrator of the Coalition Provisional Authority (CPA). Garner was asked to stay on under the CPA but declined to remain longer than to overlap with Bremer. ORHA was dissolved. Bremer had about ten days to prepare for his responsibilities.

Although the Pentagon had nominal control over stability operations, there were serious differences within the administration on how to proceed. State sought to internationalize participation in postwar reconstruction, but had little initial influence on policy or operations. At the NSC, Condoleezza Rice had become disillusioned with the Pentagon's Office of Special Plans and had handed postwar planning to Frank Miller, NSC Senior Director for Defense. Miller was pushing two lines of policy: de-Baathification would apply to only the top 1 percent of party members, and the Iraqi army would be reduced, but not disbanded.[30] The civilian leaders of the Pentagon were leaning toward thoroughgoing transformation of Iraq into a democratic government and a free market economy. They had in mind the successful military-led reconstruction of Germany and Japan.[31] These competing policy differences were never brought to the President for resolution. Bremer, who considered that he reported only to Rumsfeld and the President, decided that de-Baathification would be broadly applied and the army disbanded. His decisions led to tension with the military command and contributed to the rise of an insurgency which intensified during the final months of 2003.

In the absence of a carefully planned R&S program, commanders on the ground looked for instruments to serve those purposes. The most important financial instrument became the Commander's Emergency Response Program (CERP). Commanders on the ground were initially given authority to use huge amounts of Baathist cash assets for reconstruction purposes. When the CPA was set up, Bremer had control of those funds but redelegated some of his authority to the commander of coalition forces "to operate a Commanders' Emergency Response Program ... [to carry] out programs that will immediately assist the Iraqi people and support the reconstruction of Iraq."[32] The seized cash ran out at the end of 2003, but Congress appropriated funds for the same purpose. CERP was to be used for urgent humanitarian relief and reconstruction requirements within the area of the commander's responsibility, but not for development or infrastructure construction projects typically funded by the State Department and USAID.[33] (See Chapter 8.) Eventually, the concept of PRTs was appropriated from the Afghanistan experience, but the first Iraq PRT was not in place until 2005. The PRTs drew on CERP for a considerable part of their funding.[34]

Already by late 2003 there was considerable restiveness in the Defense Department about the course in Iraq, including unhappiness over the contentious relationship between Bremer and Gen. Ricardo Sanchez, commander of the Multi-National Force—Iraq. A variety of proposals were circulating in the Pentagon to shorten Bremer's three-year timetable for turning over sovereignty to an Iraqi government. The driver of change in the fall of 2003 was the NSC, not the Defense Department, but a process had been set in motion, which eventually resulted in a dramatic change at the Pentagon. In parallel with the changes that created S/CRS at the State Department, the Pentagon in 2004 renamed its Office of Peacekeeping as the Office of Stability Operations and gave the deputy assistant secretary the same title. As work began on NSPD 44, "Management of Interagency Efforts Concerning Reconstruction and Stabilization," DOD began work on a revolutionary directive.[35]

STABILITY OPERATIONS BECOMES DOCTRINE

Directive 3000.05

In November 2005, Defense Department Directive 3000.05 on "Military Support for Stability, Security, Transition, and Reconstruction Operations" (SSTRO) was published. It announced that "stability operations are a core U.S. military mission that the Department of Defense shall be prepared to conduct and support. They shall be given priority comparable to combat operations." The announcement reflected a "Damascus Road conversion" at the apex of the Department. According to a senior OSD official, the words "comparable to combat operations" came from the mouth of Secretary Rumsfeld.[36] A catalyst was a Summer 2004 briefing of the Defense secretary by Craig Fields, former Director of the Defense Advanced Research Projects Agency (DARPA), who was cochairing the Defense Science Board. Fields presented Rumsfeld with results of his study on "Transition to and from Hostilities." It called for an effective whole-of-government process for managing stability and reconstruction, for enhancing DOD capabilities in that area, and for empowering the State Department.[37] Rumsfeld, stung by the criticism of Defense's performance in Iraq, ordered that the recommendations for his department be incorporated into a Defense Department directive within 90 days. It took more than a year. Responsibility for the directive was handed to the renamed Stability Operations (SO) office. The services were resistant, and SO found itself laboring office by office to move the project forward. Part of the delay resulted from a difference of approach. During the 2003–2005 period, the Joint Forces Command (JFCOM), under Adm. Edmund Giambastiani, had already been working on projects stressing the importance of applying all elements of national power, including civilian agencies, to the pursuit of national strategic objectives.[38] JFCOM and SO disagreed on the extent of involvement of the armed forces in stability operations, the former arguing for an earlier hand-off of responsibility to civilian partners. In August 2005, Giambastiani moved up to Vice Chairman of the Joint Chiefs, and a compromise was worked out, leading to issuance of the directive.

Three particularly striking points stand out:

- Breadth of goal: "Stability operations are conducted to help establish order. . . . The immediate goal . . . is to provide the local populace with security, restore essential services, and meet humanitarian needs. The long-term goal is to help develop indigenous capacity for securing essential services, a viable market economy, rule of law, democratic institutions, and a robust civil society." The language was a throwback to Clintonian "nation-building" at its most comprehensive.
- Mainstreaming throughout the military structure: "[S]tability operations shall be explicitly . . . integrated across all DOD activities including doctrine, organizations, training, education, exercises, materiel, leadership, personnel, facilities, and planning."
- Interagency cooperation: "[W]hether conducting or supporting stability operations, the Department of Defense shall . . . work closely with U.S. agencies, foreign governments and security forces, international organizations, NGOs, and the private sector."[39] However, the default position falls to the military. Although "many stability operations tasks are best performed by indigenous, foreign or U.S. civilian professionals, . . . [n]onetheless, U.S. military forces shall be prepared to perform *all tasks necessary to establish or maintain order when civilians cannot do so.*"

Disdain for nation-building 2001–2004 thus gave way to an acknowledgment of the importance of stability operations—"priority comparable to combat operations." At that point the challenge became how to ensure that the Directive was incorporated into military doctrine and operations.

JFCOM: Joint Operating Concept for Stabilization and Reconstruction

JFCOM was created by the Goldwater-Nichols Act of 1986, which imposed "jointness" on a military riven by interservice rivalries. JFCOM's current mission is to "support the development and integration of joint, interagency, and multinational capabilities to meet present and future operational needs."[40] It is responsible for developing "jointness" in concept, training, experimentation, and doctrine.[41] In 2005, at the time of publication of Directive 3000, stability operations was not yet a candidate to become "joint doctrine." It did not yet have the compilation of "best practices" in the "joint" arena considered to be the foundation for doctrine. However, JFCOM was already working on a "joint operating concept" (JOpsC) on support for security, stabilization, transition, and reconstruction, and wrote into the Directive a lead role for itself in completing the JOpsC exercise.[42] A JOpsC represented a kind of halfway house to doctrine.

The Capstone Concept for Joint Operations, approved by the Secretary of Defense in August 2005, a few months before the Directive, characterizes JOpsCs as descriptions of broad joint force operations. A JOpsC provides a detailed description of how future operations may be conducted and a conceptual base for joint experimentation and assessment. The emphasis is on integrating joint force actions with those of interagency partners and even multinational partners, thereby contributing to broader national objectives.[43] The Capstone Concept identified stability operations as an integrated operation which the joint force must be able to conduct "prior to, during, and after combat operations, or as a stand-alone mission."[44] JOpsCs are integrated into existing doctrines, and the purpose of the Directive assignment to JFCOM was to ensure that stability operations would be given equivalent weight to combat operations. To implement that task, JFCOM set up an integrated process team of 50–80 experts from inside the command, from other commands, and from the civilian sector.[45]

In 2006 the Secretary of Defense approved an SSTRO Joint Operating Concept drafted by JFCOM.[46] The Concept used a narrower definition of stability operations than Directive 3000. The latter defined military support to SSTRO as "DOD activities that support U.S. Government plans for stabilization, security, reconstruction, and transition operations, which lead to sustainable peace while advancing U.S. interests." The Concept limited itself, however, to the following "subset" of stability operations:

[T]hose activities that the Joint Force might conduct in foreign countries across the continuum from peace to crisis and conflict in order to assist a state or region that is under severe stress or has collapsed due to either a natural or man-made disaster. Additionally, military support to SSTR operations includes a variety of theater security cooperation activities that play a direct role in setting the conditions for SSTR operations. These activities include building partner capacity to conduct SSTR operations and/or assisting states in the efforts to cope with internal instability challenges.[47]

The Concept envisaged a varying combination of "lines of operation" to stabilize the situation and strengthen the capacities of the host government:

- creating a secure environment
- providing humanitarian assistance
- reconstructing infrastructure and resuming vital services
- getting the economy going again
- creating representative and effective governance and the rule of law

It added that "strategic communication" with the local populace, the host government, coalition partners, and the American people undergirds all the foregoing individual mission elements.

A critical distinction is the role of the military in high-end and low-end situations.

- High-end: Operations associated with a U.S.-imposed regime change or collapse of a government from internal failure or military defeat. The military task is to establish a safe, secure environment, including force protection for itself and civilian agencies, and simultaneously work with interagency, coalition, multinational, and host nation partners to support a new domestic order. The most critical determinant of success will be convincing the local populace to recognize the legitimacy of the existing or new government and actively support the government's efforts to build a "new domestic order."

- Low-end: The U.S. military will coordinate its reconstruction efforts with those of USAID and S/CRS, as well as with the host nation and multinational relief organizations. In some cases, only security assistance and disaster aid may be required, if the government is stable.

The document was not highly specific in guidance about concrete situations. It did emphasize, however, the importance of keeping combat operations and stability operations in balance, probably reflecting experience in Iraq.

[W]ithin a joint campaign, . . . campaign planners, and even individual units, must continually balance their activities. . . . For example, during [major combat operations], the [campaign] should refrain from tasking friendly forces to destroy critical infrastructure needed to maintain security and provide essential services for the general populace, unless its destruction is absolutely necessary to achieve campaign objectives and desired effects. Similarly, care should be taken to actively protect key administrative facilities . . . from destructive attack and from looting, if feasible, because these key assets could be critical for successful SSTR operations by the new host nation government.[48]

It noted the difficulty created in the battle space by the involvement of non-USG actors—NGOs, private companies, news organizations, and commercial security companies—which dramatically increase the complexity of trying to figure out "who is supportive of U.S. efforts, who is neutral, and who is the enemy."[49]

The JOpsC hinted that in high-end operations, particularly counterinsurgency could be less emphasis on interagency coordination. That implication was reinforced by the assertion that "even if civilian capabilities to support SSTR operations double in the next 10–15 years, there will still be a capability gap that the military [using its own resources] will be called upon to fill, even in a secure environment."[50]

The operating concept cited risks to the success of stability operations. The American people may be unwilling to accept or sustain high-end stability operations. Civilian agencies may fail to develop the required capabilities for long-term stabilization operations viewed as "high risk." The military may be unable to recruit and retain personnel for extended, "manpower-intensive" stabilization operations.

Stability Operations as Army Doctrine: Field Manual 3.07

The caution of JFCOM about writing a doctrine of stability operations was not shared by the Army, which considered that it could draw on "lessons learned" for stability operations dating back to the American colonies.[51] For the Army brass, the publication of Directive 3000.05 was a mandate to proceed. The task fell to the Army's Combined Arms Center (CAC). CAC, at Fort Leavenworth, Kansas, is a major part of the U.S. Army Training and Doctrine Command (TRADOC) and likes to call itself the "intellectual center of the Army." The work did not get underway until October 2007. Before stability operations in the doctrine production line came the manual on counterinsurgency, produced under the leadership of Gen. David Petraeus before he took command in Iraq, and a new version of the Army Field Manual on Operations, which appeared in February 2008. The Operations manual incorporated stability operations into its survey of "full-spectrum operations."[56]

LTC Steven Leonard, who had also written the Operations manual, was put in charge of the exercise. He and his bosses were convinced that it was necessary to be as inclusive as possible, bringing in the other services, the civilian agencies, and NGOs with experience in conflict areas. The writing team worked with the doctrine and concepts offices of the different services and with the Joint Warfighting School at the JFCOM. It collaborated particularly closely with the PKSOI at the Army War College and with the OSD Office of Stability Operations Capabilities. On the civilian side the main collaborators were from the S/CRS Planning Office and the Center for Post-Conflict Peace and Stability Operations (PCP&SO) at the U.S. Institute of Peace (USIP) and a handful of experts from USAID.

In October 2008 the new Army Field Manual 3.07, entirely devoted to Stability Operations, was unveiled. It set the context as follows:

[T]he greatest threat to our national security comes not in the form of terrorism or ambitious powers, but from fragile states either unable or unwilling to provide for the most basic needs of their people. As the Nation continues into this era of uncertainty and persistent conflict, ... military success alone will not be sufficient to prevail in this environment. To confront the challenges before us, we must strengthen the capacity of the other elements of national power, leveraging the full potential of our interagency partners.

The manual did not project the need for stability operations into new Iraqs. Building on a speech by Secretary of Defense Robert Gates, the doctrine states flatly that "America's future abroad is unlikely to resemble Afghanistan or Iraq."[52]

Instead, we will work ... with the community of nations to defeat insurgency, assist fragile states, and provide vital humanitarian aid to the suffering. Achieving victory will assume new dimensions as we strengthen our ability to generate "soft" power to promote participation in government, spur economic development, and address the root causes of conflict. ... At the heart of this effort is a comprehensive approach to stability operations that integrates the tools of statecraft with our military forces, international partners, humanitarian organizations, and the private sector.

The manual acknowledges that national policy charges the Department of State to coordinate and lead integrated U.S. government efforts and activities in stability operations, working through S/CRS, which "leads, coordinates and institutionalizes" U.S. civilian capacity for R&S. Generally, the division of labor is as follows: the military role is in security and stabilization aspects of SSTR, while State focuses generally on the reconstruction side and USAID supports through its projects the governance, conflict mitigation, and rule of law agenda.[53]

In spite of this nod to broad interagency responsibility, the Manual enumerates a far-reaching list of potential military security and stabilization tasks. The military's basic role in security and stabilization is to create security, establish civil control, and restore essential services, while supporting governance, economic revival, and infrastructure rehabilitation. However, the list also includes identifying legal professionals, facilitating assessment of the central bank, supporting agricultural development, establishing and verifying voter registration, and developing ethical standards for civil servants.[54] Asked about this expansive list, the author of 3.07 responded that although the military focuses on security and the civilians on reconstruction, there is a large gray area which includes tasks that both military forces and civilians must be prepared to do. The split of responsibilities will be different in each particular case, depending on the situation on the ground and the resources in funding and people which the different American elements can bring to bear. The argument comes back in the end to resources, with the implication that the military will have to be prepared to undertake those tasks which under-resourced civilian agencies cannot accomplish.[55]

AFM 3.07 represents Army doctrine. It is not Joint Doctrine. However, JFCOM has begun the process of creating a joint manual on stability operations. Since the Army manual has been well received and makes few references to the Army in its pages, it appears likely that, after vetting its substance with the different services and commands, the JFCOM will basically edit the existing manual and place a new cover on it. The process was scheduled for completion in 2010.

INSTITUTIONALIZING MILITARY SUPPORT FOR SSTR

Directive 3000.05 called for the integration of stability operations across all DOD organizations.

Office of the Secretary of Defense

The DASD for Stability Operations, Jeffrey M. (Jeb) Nadaner, became the counterpart to the State Department's Coordinator for Reconstruction and Stabilization. He initially presided over two divisions: U.S. Government Policy and Capability and International Policy and Capabilities. The former was given explicit responsibility both for implementing Directive 3000 within the military and for "building interagency capacity," as guided by NSPD 44. It was therefore dealing with the Joint Chiefs and the unified combatant commands, on the military side, and other agencies, especially the State Department, on the civilian side. Its mandate was complicated by the addition of responsibilities for counterinsurgency and irregular warfare.

The International Capabilities division was mandated to work with foreign partners—NATO allies, the United Nations, and regional allies in the developing world, particularly those seeking U.S. assistance for stabilization and international organization. It was also encumbered with oversight of the residual functions of peacekeeping, emergency evacuation of U.S. civilians from foreign crisis zones (NEOs), and humanitarian assistance.

In late 2006 Eric S. Edelman, who had succeeded Douglas Feith as Under Secretary for Policy, decided to reorganize his office. Nadaner, concluding that his staff was being overwhelmed by two separate mandates, saw an opportunity to create different offices from the two divisions. His bosses agreed but decided to place them under different assistant secretaries. A new Assistant Secretary position for Global Security Affairs was created. Given his choice of staying put or moving, Nadaner joined the new cluster as Deputy Assistant Secretary for Partnership Strategy. He brought with him the International Policy and Capabilities Division, which morphed into the Office of International Capacity Building.[57]

Stability Operations—renamed Stability Operations Capabilities—remained under the Assistant Secretary for Special Operations/Low-Intensity Conflict and Interdependent Capabilities (SOLIC/IC), and a new DASD was eventually appointed. Under the new division of labor, however, Stability Operations Capabilities focused on the internal function within the Defense Department. It had lines out to the unified combatant commands and to the military training and doctrine centers. One division within the office continued to have the major responsibility for compiling and finalizing reports on the implementation of Directive 3000; a second covered implementation within the Defense Department of NSPD 44 and had the task of making sure that stability operations are adequately factored into military strategy documents, war plans, and planning scenarios.[58]

Responsibilities for supporting other agencies in stabilization—"strengthening other agency stabilization capacity," as one OSD official termed it—largely moved over to Partnership Strategy, which viewed itself somewhat patronizingly as "helping" S/CRS with planning and budgeting and "making USAID more interoperable."[59] Partnership Strategy became the key action office in Defense for transferring Department of Defense Sec. 1207 funds to S/CRS for reconstruction projects during 2007 and 2008. (See Chapter 4.) At USAID it worked primarily with DCHA.

With the 2006 reorganization the number of people working on stabilization in the OSD doubled, but the division of labor was somewhat confusing. In practice it proved difficult to divide cleanly liaison responsibilities between

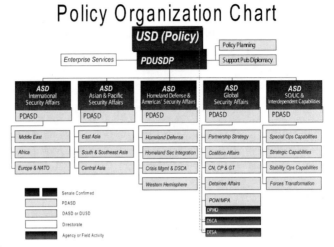

Figure 5.1
OSD—Organizational Chart for Stability Operations (2008). Courtesy DOD/ OSD/Office of Partnership Strategy.

internal Defense Department matters and interagency matters. Turf battles between the two offices, laboring under different ASDs and DASDs, were common, but the two DASDs tried to keep the lines clear through frequent meetings.[60]

Joint Chiefs of Staff

Directive 3000.05 handed major responsibilities to the Chairman of the Joint Chiefs. They included identifying stability operations capabilities within the military, developing joint doctrine, participating in government-wide stability operations planning, and ensuring that stability operations are integrated into training at military educational institutions. The JCS chairman designated the Director for Strategic Plans and Policy (J-5) as providing staff oversight for implementation of the Directive. The Deputy J-5 for Global Strategic Partnership (DDGSP) was named as the Joint Staff point of contact for coordinating with the OSD and with the interagency community, especially S/CRS and USAID, on plans and policy related to stability operations.[61] JCS created a Stability Operations division, further subdivided into Stability Operations and Capacity Building branches, roughly mirroring the divisions in OSD. The Navy captain heading the Stability Operations Division cochaired with his counterpart in OSD/Stability Operations the Defense Department's Stability Operations Working Group, which became the main vehicle for ensuring that the work mandated by 3000.05 was accomplished by the combatant commands. By 2008 that work was largely completed.

In 2007 JCS representatives described a "growing" relationship with State S/CRS, a tie as close as that with OSD. The JCS chairman's posture statement for that year focused on developing an "expeditionary capacity" in the State Department:

We need greater expeditionary capabilities in U.S. government civilian agencies for stabilization and reconstruction operations. Our civilian agencies are under-resourced to meet the requirements of the twenty-first century. Greater investment in these agencies is required if they are to be more effective in the Global War on Terrorism. To increase their *expeditionary* capability, ... [we strongly support] creation of a Civilian Reserve Corps for the State Department. ... Rewarding interagency education, interagency experiences, interagency collaboration, and interagency planning will facilitate better synergy between departments and better integrate our Nation's diplomatic, military, intelligence, information, and economic instruments to forestall and address crises.[62]

The relationship continued to expand, as S/CRS gained heft.

Geographic Combatant Commands

There are six geographic combatant commands.[63] The commanders, all four-star generals or admirals, report directly to the Secretary of Defense and through that official to the President. Directive 3000 assigns to the unified geographic combatant commands special responsibilities for stability operations in their areas of responsibility (AORs):

- incorporation into their planning, training, and exercises;
- interagency engagement—presumably including U.S. embassies and other civilian agencies involved in the region—in such planning, training, and exercising;
- coalition engagement in those activities, that is, foreign security forces in the AOR;
- intelligence collection on ethnic, cultural, religious, tribal, economic, and political relationships, infrastructure, health infrastructure, and border controls to support the planning process.[64]

Given the vast geographic and political diversity of the AORs, the geographic combatant commands have all dealt somewhat differently with stability operations, but at the initial stages of its integration into overall military operations, the organizational approach was similar.[65] The core effort centered in the plans directorate (J-5) of each. The Deputy Director of Plans (brigadier general or equivalent) was formally designated as the Joint Force Coordinating Authority for Stability Operations, a position prescribed by Directive 3000.[66]

The Joint Chiefs mandated that the unified combatant commands incorporate into their training the Essential Tasks Matrix for R&S, published by S/CRS as "a standardized tool for describing requirements for ... conducting ... joint and multinational training." That matrix was reflected in the evolving versions of both the Universal Joint Task List and the Mission Essential Task List published by JCS.[67]

CENTCOM was unique in its handling of stability operations because of its responsibilities for U.S. forces in Afghanistan, Iraq, and, from 2006 until 2008, the Horn of Africa. Its J-5 staff assigned to stability operations were all civil affairs specialists, a unique configuration among the combatant commands (COCOMs). They considered stability operations an integral part of all the command's plans and operations and critical to improving its operations in those theaters. CENTCOM's ongoing use of PRTs in both Afghanistan and Iraq provided a basis for deriving lessons learned and best practices. CENTCOM was also farthest advanced in its "engagement" of foreign forces. CENTCOM headquarters at MacDill Air Force Base in Tampa, Florida, hosted a Coalition Coordinating Center with representatives of more than 60 governments from Europe, the Americas, the Middle East, and the Pacific, either supporting military operations in Iraq and/or Afghanistan or generally siding with the United States in the GWOT. The purpose was primarily to share intelligence and to determine troop ratios and types from different coalition partners. It was not aimed at coordination of joint operations.[68]

Focused on current operations, CENTCOM was less engaged in more generalized planning for future stability operations. Its relationship with JFCOM was rather distant. Intensive combat operations in Iraq and Afghanistan constrained resources available to document experiments and lessons learned.[69] Its involvement in the interagency process has been driven by its ongoing requirements. Although the State Coordinator for Reconstruction and Stabilization visited CENTCOM, there was no ongoing, day-by-day relationship because S/CRS was not heavily engaged in Iraq or Afghanistan. CENTCOM found the S/CRS Essential Tasks Matrix a useful training tool for its forces for Afghanistan and Iraq, however.

The other geographic combatant commands proceeded at a somewhat more leisurely and systematic pace with integrating stability operations into their mission. The European Command, headquartered in Stuttgart, Germany, developed the concept of "Phase Zero." According to a National Defense University scholar, Phase Zero is

everything that can be done to prevent conflicts from developing in the first place. Executed properly, Phase Zero consists of *shaping* operations that are continuous and adaptive. Its ultimate goal is to promote stability and peace by building capacity in partner nations that enables them to be cooperative, trained, and prepared to help prevent or limit conflicts. For the United States, this approach is typically non-kinetic and places heavy emphasis on interagency support and coordination. In many instances, Phase Zero involves execution of a broad national strategy where the Department of Defense (DOD) is not the lead agency and its programs are only one part of the larger U.S. Government effort.[70]

EUCOM worked with S/CRS on a "shadow" IMS exercise at the time of the Georgia crisis. Further S/CRS exercises with EUCOM were placed on the drawing board.

Through 2008 the Southern Command gave little prominence to stability operations in its self-presentation. The Pacific Command, which at that point was only engaged in stability operations-related activity in the Philippines (see Chapter 3), also gave limited attention to integrating R&S into its operations. By contrast, the Africa Command, which entered into operation in 2008, signaled its intent to pay close attention to stability and reconstruction, given the multiplicity of conflicts and the limited prospects of a U.S. "kinetic" role in the region.

The Peacekeeping and Stability Operations Institute

PKSOI thrived after its 2003 reprieve from closure. The staff reached 40, spread over four divisions. One covered doctrine and concepts and focused on the insertion of stability operations concepts into training for the military, civilian agencies, NGOs, and foreign military forces. The operations division attempted to draw up stability operations lessons learned. The operational integration division promoted the insertion of stability operations concepts and lessons learned into military and interagency operations and exercises. The governance division concentrated on the political and economic side of R&S, including justice, political participation, restoration of essential services, and infrastructure rehabilitation.

Under Col. John Agoglia, who directed PKSOI during its rise to prominence, PKSOI developed a dense network of military and civilian relationships. It offered its assistance to S/CRS as soon as the office was created, and close ties developed between the two staffs. It operated in intimate partnership with the USIP's Center for Post-Conflict Peace and Stability Operations. The Army's CAC hailed PKSOI as a major partner in the production of Army Field Manual 3.07. Both State and USAID assigned a senior officer to PKSOI.

Three years into Directive 3000, Defense Department efforts to integrate the stability operations into all aspects of its operations had been notably comprehensive, given the scope of the objective and the vastness of the Pentagon and military bureaucracy. Even so, there was unevenness in implementation. The Army and Marines were understandably far more advanced in their application of stability operations doctrine than the Navy and Air Force, while the Pacific Command lagged the other geographic COCOMs in interest. Moreover, the 2007 GAO report on Stabilization and Reconstruction stated that, although combatant commanders were engaging in outreach to include non-DOD organizations in formulating military plans, results had been limited because of asymmetry in the planning capabilities of the other organizations involved and military inhibitions about information sharing. That analysis is accurate, but hard to remedy in

COL. JOHN F. AGOGLIA

John Agoglia was born in Brooklyn. He graduated from West Point and became an infantry officer. He also carved out a specialty in planning. When 9/11 dawned, he was Deputy Chief of Plans at CENTCOM. He was immediately drawn into the midst of crafting the blueprint for Operation Enduring Freedom. After that exercise he became Gen. Tommy Franks's chief war planner for Iraq. During preparations for Operation Iraqi Freedom, he was a member of the U.S. negotiating team which sought unsuccessfully to persuade Turkey to consent to invasion from that country into Iraq. Early in the war, he helped set up the first Interim Iraqi Governance meeting in Nassiriya, on the western edge of the Shi'ite marshlands ravaged by Saddam Hussein after the Gulf War, and a subsequent meeting in Baghdad.

Agoglia became the CENTCOM military liaison on the staff of L. Paul Bremer, who headed the Coalition Provisional Authority (CPA) 2003–2004. The outspoke military planner, who noted that reestablishing the Iraqi army was a key part of the post-conflict plan he wrote for CENTCOM, watched with dismay as Bremer ignored the advice of the military on the ground and issued CPA Order No. 2, formally disbanding the Iraqi army. "That was the day we snatched defeat from the jaws of victory and created an insurgency," he said.[71]

When the CPA was dissolved in 2004, he took the helm of the reprieved Peacekeeping Institute—awkwardly renamed the Peacekeeping and Stability Operations Institute—at the Army War College in Carlisle Barracks, Pennsylvania. Recognizing that stability operations had become a growth industry, Agoglia was determined to maneuver the Institute into a central role. A networking virtuoso, he took advantage of proximity to Washington to ensure that PKSOI was well and favorably known to the Pentagon's Office of Stability Operations, which described PKSOI as "our face for stability operations policy." PKSOI became a valued partner for the Army's CAC in drafting both the Counterinsurgency Manual associated with Gen. David Petraeus and the Manual on Stability Operations issued in 2008.

Agoglia was at least as aggressive in courting the civilian agencies. Upon arrival at Carlisle Barracks, he moved at once to create an alliance with Carlos Pascual, the new Coordinator for Reconstruction and Stabilization in the State Department, even participating in some of S/CRS's early staff meetings. Another close ally was the Post-Conflict Peace and Stability Operations Center at the USIP. Agoglia recruited Elena Brineman, former USAID Mission director in the Dominican Republic, and Roy Williams, a veteran of the International Rescue Committee and former Director of USAID's Office of Foreign Disaster Assistance, to provide PKSOI with the USAID and NGO perspective. Intense and profane, Agoglia projected an openness to new ideas and to collaboration outside military boundaries which expanded his clout.

After four years at PKSOI, Colonel Agoglia accepted an assignment to return to Afghanistan. Under his leadership the PKSOI staff had quadrupled. The Institute has become a much admired player in U.S. government peace-building operations. According to a former colleague, the Institute "would probably still be a backwater without the leadership of John Agoglia."

the absence of a massive shift of resources in budget and personnel toward the civilian agencies. State Department and USAID offices complained frequently that they were badgered by the military about not allocating sufficient personnel to interagency coordination, when they simply lacked the officer cadre to do so.[72]

Consortium for Complex Operations: "A Virtual University"

In 2008 the Defense Department, with support from S/CRS and USAID, created the Consortium for Complex Operations (CCO). Complex operations are defined as including stability operations, counterinsurgency, and irregular warfare. The initiative came from L. Celeste Ward, DASD for Stability Operations Capabilities. She had observed firsthand the convergence of these three problems and the difficulties of interagency coordination in Iraq, first as a senior member of the Coalition Provisional Authority and then as senior advisor to LTG Peter Chiarelli, Commander of the Multinational Force. Working out of an office near the Pentagon in nearby Crystal City, CCO became an information clearing house for complex operations, collecting lessons learned and best practices. Its password-protected Web site provided a compendium of information on complex operations events and problems. It also offered training drawn from courses provided by different government agencies or piloted by government-sponsored think tanks. As a kind of "virtual university," bringing together academics, educators, trainers, and practitioners, CCO aimed to promote patterns of whole-of-government thinking and collaboration.[73]

PENTAGON ATTITUDES TOWARD INTERAGENCY RECONSTRUCTION AND STABILIZATION

At the close of the Bush administration there was a range of views in the Defense Department about interagency capabilities. Among those civilian officials who served in the OSD associated with Jeffrey Nadaner, the Department's first DASD for Stability Operations, there is skepticism that the civilian agencies, particularly the Department of State, will acquire the resources and generate the capacity to function as a coequal partner with the military. First, there is keen awareness of the human resource mismatch between the State Department and USAID, on the one hand, and the Defense Department on the other. The total State Department Foreign Service cadre is 6,600 out of a total contingent of 19,000 American employees, while USAID officers total only about 1,300.[74] By contrast DOD has an active duty officer corps of about 225,000 out of active duty uniformed services numbering about 1.4 million and 700,000 civilian employees.[75] Therefore, without a quantum jump in civilian agency numbers, they point out, the civilian agencies are unlikely to be able to allocate sufficient numbers to stabilization. They note that thus far Congress has proved unwilling to expand significantly the civilian side. At the time of writing, S/CRS had not secured from Congress funding for contingencies and had only received in 2008 and 2009 about half the amount requested to launch the civilian stabilization initiative. Second, the skeptics view planning capacity in the State Department with disdain. One former official, who regards the civilian side as "pretty empty," observed that diplomats shy away from detailed planning as limiting flexibility, a key diplomatic virtue. What is required in R&S, in their view, is the detailed kind of operational planning done by the military. State and other civilian agencies are considered to do "policy planning," dismissed as little more than a "listing of good ideas." Third, some officials question the desirability of a full-blown civilian expeditionary capacity. One former official, who worked closely with Nadaner, notes that the most crucial recent R&S tasks have occurred, not in post-conflict situations, but in counterinsurgency, in which civilian officials working on reconstruction may be deliberately targeted for assassination. According to her, civilian agencies have never demonstrated they can do R&S under fire.[76]

These civilian officials insist they would like to see the civilian agencies succeed in developing R&S capacity "so that the military won't have to do it." However, they note that Directive 3000 states explicitly that "U.S. military forces shall be prepared to perform all tasks necessary to establish and maintain order when civilians cannot do so." There is a tendency to apply that sentence to the full range of R&S tasks, even though it is *prima facie* limited to the establishment of security and order. Some Bush administration policy officials began to think about how DOD should organize for the task over the long-term, using its own *civilian* capacity, particularly for R&S under fire, if the civilian agencies were unsuccessful.[77] Nadaner, who left the Defense Department in 2008, has said,

The military wants the civilian agencies to do the other things the military does not want to do, but the military often gets called in to do them. . . . If the civilian agencies are not there, DOD has to be ready to do them.[78]

Some of that thinking is evident among the military authors of Army Field Manual 3.07. LTG William Caldwell, who was in command of the Army's CAC and supervised production of the manual, has said, "The intention is to have a 'whole-of-government' approach. We have found in Iraq and Afghanistan that these responsibilities 'have defaulted on the military.' So we have to be sure we have the skills and capabilities."[79] However, AFM 3.07 indicates that the doctrine is not aimed primarily at "nation-building under fire," since "America's future is unlikely to resemble Afghanistan or Iraq." Gen. Caldwell's excellent relations with civilian agencies and his public remarks demonstrate strong support for an expanding "whole of government" approach, in which the military "fills in the gaps and holes."

By contrast, career military officers in stability operations assignments tend to be more sanguine about the interagency process than the Nadaner faction, if the Congressional appropriations are provided. They see growing acceptance within the military of long-term partnership with civilian agencies in doing R&S. A senior officer working on stability operations in the Joint Staff pointed to the references in the JCS Chairman's 2007 Posture Statement to the Congress which emphasized President Bush's proposal in the 2007 State of the Union message for a civilian reserve and "building partnership capacity" for stability operations. He termed himself "very optimistic" about the success of the interagency effort, if there is Congressional support. He dismissed the skepticism of those civilians associated with the OSD as "holdover thinking" from the days when the military was expected to do stabilization on its own. The key stability operations officer in a unified geographic combatant command also expressed confidence in the interagency, if resources are made available.

S/CRS will bring the interagency process to fruition, but it will take time. I am surprised that it doesn't have more champions in the interagency and Congress. Stability Operations are to the advantage of both political parties.

That view was also articulated by L. Celeste Ward, Nadaner's successor as DASD for Stability Operations Capacity, who found a lot of momentum both in Defense and in the civilian agencies and was impressed by the "heroic efforts" of S/CRS and the evolving "habits of cooperation."[80]

PEACE-BUILDING ISSUES FOR THE DEPARTMENT OF DEFENSE

Between 2001 and 2004 the DOD came full circle from seeking to excise Clintonian nation-building from military operations to embracing it warmly under the name of stability operations. The change of heart occurred in Secretary Rumsfeld himself and stemmed from experience in Iraq. It also derived from the desire of the military to see civilian agencies take over responsibility for post-conflict reconstruction tasks it would prefer not to perform.

Directive 3000.05, placing stability operations on a par with combat, was a revolutionary change in approach, at least in rhetoric. It mainstreamed stabilization into a broad range of Defense Department activities and established a far-reaching network of responsibility within the OSD, the Joint Chiefs of Staff, and the combatant commands. It pushed JFCOM into a broad exploration of the application of jointness to incorporate civilian agencies. The Army was first to reach the goal of translating the directive into doctrine, and a joint doctrine of stability operations will likely emerge in the near future. Although doctrine does not portray Afghanistan and Iraq as the model for future stability operations, much of the practice of interagency stability operations has emerged from the work of the PRTs in both countries.

The directive trumpeted an interagency approach to stability operations, provoking military sponsorship of a spate of interagency symposia and incorporation of civilian agencies into military training and exercises.

That experience has underscored for Defense and the civilian agencies the mismatch between the number of military personnel and the far smaller total of civilian personnel available for interagency coordination. That mismatch has prompted some cynicism at policy levels in the Defense Department about the capacity of State Department-led civilian agencies to meet the requirements of NSPD 44. Some have even suggested that the Defense Department may need to do most R&S tasks with its own civilian cadre.

The task of R&S requires political and economic development skills to promote the rule of law and good governance, reintegrate former combatants, and relaunch a democratic process, as well as the military skills needed to create a secure environment, establish civil control, and restore essential services. For the Pentagon to arrogate to itself political and development tasks—except in an exceptional "stop gap" mode—would push the military and military-led civilians into tasks they are unequipped to perform well. It would bespeak hubris about U.S. military capacity and would further advance perceptions abroad of the militarization of U.S. foreign policy. The view that the military must be able to do virtually everything in the portfolio of R&S tasks is unlikely to find much support in Congress, where many on the Armed Services Committees and the defense appropriation subcommittees believe the military is overstretched.

Chapter 6

Foreign Assistance for Peace: The U.S. Agency for International Development

> Among the most important things donors can do is develop a deeper context-specific understanding of what drives conflict. . . . Conflict management involves long-term interventions that strengthen the capacity of states and societies to manage sources of tension and strain.
>
> —*Foreign Aid in the National Interest* (2002)

For almost half a century USAID has been the principal U.S. government agency providing assistance to countries recovering from disaster or attempting to escape poverty. Since the end of the Cold War it has taken on additional functions, including promotion of human rights, democracy, and conflict management. USAID is an independent federal agency that receives overall foreign policy guidance from the Secretary of State. Over the decades its degree of independence from the State Department has fluctuated. However, since 1990 the pendulum has swung toward greater direction from and integration with State. The process was accelerated by Secretary of State Condoleezza Rice, who brought USAID even more formally under the State wing.

RECONSTRUCTION AND STABILIZATION IN THE U.S. FOREIGN ASSISTANCE STRATEGY

In describing its role to the public, USAID has pictured itself at the center of foreign policy implementation.

As stated in the President's National Security Strategy, USAID's work in development joins diplomacy and defense as one of three key pieces of the nation's foreign policy apparatus.[1]

Actually, nowhere in the Strategy document was development explicitly cited as one of the "three key pieces" along with defense and diplomacy. Nevertheless, both versions of the strategy indicated a significant role for USAID, essentially under two overlapping objectives. The first was to "expand the circle of development by opening societies and building the infrastructure of democracy."[2] The second was to "champion aspirations for human dignity." USAID was mandated to use foreign assistance to support the development of free and fair elections, rule of law, civil society, human rights, women's rights, free media, and religious freedom. Strikingly, these are all political rather than economic goals, related—but not explicitly—to peace-building. Neither version of the Strategy referred to USAID's role in peace-building and post-conflict reconstruction. Nonetheless, the agency construed its role under the National Security Strategy as pivotal to the American peace-building enterprise:

USAID *promotes peace and stability* by fostering economic growth, protecting human health, providing emergency humanitarian assistance, and enhancing democracy in developing countries.[3]

Andrew Natsios, George W. Bush's first USAID administrator, had a strong personal interest in conflict management. He brought considerable experience to the job. As Director of USAID's Office of Foreign Disaster Assistance and then Assistant Administrator of the Bureau of Food and Humanitarian Assistance during the Bush 41 administration, he was particularly concerned about timely delivery of assistance in crisis situations, including conflict situations. In a 1997 book Natsios deplored the failure of the agency to give adequate attention to conflict. Surveying the countries in which the agency was involved, he noted that two-thirds were unstable and argued that conflict often led to "de-development."[4] If the agency were to succeed at development, he concluded, USAID must deal frontally with conflict.

Natsios put a powerful stamp on USAID's approach. After White House publication of the Strategy, USAID issued *Foreign Aid in the National Interest*, asserting that "foreign assistance will be a key instrument of foreign policy in the coming decades." That report focused on six central issues of development assistance, including "mitigating conflict," along with democratic governance, economic growth, health, and humanitarian assistance.

The section on mitigating conflict placed great importance on understanding it in a holistic manner, examining not only ethnic and religious grievances, but how economic conditions can fuel conflict and channel resources to those who seek to exploit it. With Afghanistan in high profile, the report also emphasized the ability—or inability—of certain governments to manage or contain violence, identifying "weak" or "failed" states as a special category. It called for experimentation with new varieties of foreign assistance, more "political" than "developmental" in nature, such as intervention with critical groups like young men and victimized women, efforts to provide physical security and "transition assistance" for countries moving into or emerging from violence.[5] Many of these themes were reflected in USAID programming, particularly during the 2002–2005 period.

Subsequent USAID publications placed special emphasis on "failed" states, also a Natsios preoccupation. A January 2004 White Paper asserted, "Failed states and complex emergencies now occupy center screen among the nation's ... national security officials. ... Development is now as essential to U.S. national security as are diplomacy and defense." "Strengthening fragile states" was listed second among the core operational goals of U.S. foreign assistance.[6]

The White Paper set the stage for the unrolling in January 2005 of USAID's highly touted Fragile States Strategy. It noted that one-third of the world's population live in unstable or fragile areas and that 20 percent of U.S. foreign assistance targeted such countries in 2003. The strategy set an overall goal of guiding USAID's efforts to reverse decline in fragile states and advance their recovery "to a stage where transformational development progress is possible."[7] Mirroring organizational changes underway in the State and Defense Departments—particularly creation of the Coordinator for Reconstruction and Stabilization at State—the strategy stressed the importance of a "whole of government" approach to the failed state problem.

The strategy took a nuanced approach to fragile states, distinguishing between "vulnerable" states, where legitimacy and government effectiveness were weak, and states fallen into "crisis" or conflict. With the former, USAID would seek to enhance effectiveness and legitimacy, particularly in strengthening civil society and the private sector. Where conflict is raging, the emphasis would be on "stabilizing" the situation and promoting with key actors reform related to the causes of conflict, drawing on other elements of the U.S. government. USAID programming was to focus specifically on providing basic humanitarian assistance, supporting rapid job creation and income generation, and returning children to school. In post-conflict situations, USAID could implement concurrently a range of humanitarian, transitional, and development activities. The strategy called for the development of a new "business model" for USAID, emphasizing rapid response, quick and visible impact, shorter planning horizons, and budget flexibility. A Fragile States Council was created within the agency, chaired by the USAID Counselor, and Fragile States Quick Response Teams were on the drawing board.

In "Democracy and Governance Strategic Framework," which appeared at the end of the year, the USAID leadership linked its Failed States Strategy more closely to democracy and governance:

In fragile states—those vulnerable to or already in crisis—steady democratization can strengthen both the capability and legitimacy of government institutions. In countries emerging from conflict, democratic reforms offer a path for national dialogue and for shifting confrontations from the battlefield to the political arena.[8]

Elections were viewed as only one element in democratization. Elections can help achieve consensus and establish a base for the rule of law. With surprising caution, the strategy noted that election "may be an appropriate ingredient in post-conflict transitions." In fact, elections have been an essential element in all post-conflict situations involving the United States, ranging from Iraq to Nepal.[9] The strategy paid no explicit attention to the issue of the timing of elections, even though premature elections, undertaken before the groundwork is laid, may damage the long-term prospects of democracy, but the document recognized that democracy is "home grown" and thus must be tailored to local circumstances. The strategy recognized that assistance to democracy does not end with an election but in the postelection period is likely to involve USAID in training elected officials, strengthening democratic institutions, and promoting partnerships between state and society.[10]

The Policy Framework for Bilateral Aid, released at the beginning of 2006, purported to "[bring] together our work over the past five years in a single document and [inscribe] in policy USAID's change in strategic direction." The change in strategic direction was said to have derived from an expanded agenda for foreign aid to include transnational issues, the transition from communism, and "crisis, conflict and complex emergencies," as well as other specific concerns. Distinct frameworks were therefore required so that "budgetary resources are aligned with the goal they primarily support."[11] The new policy framework recrafted the goals mentioned in the 2002 "Foreign Aid in the National Interest," giving more attention to a typology of targeted recipients. Thus it substituted "strengthen[ing] fragile states" for "mitigating conflict" as one of five core strategic goals for foreign assistance.[12] It stated that in countries of instability and weak governance, the United States would support stabilization, capacity development, and reform, where U.S. assistance could make a difference. Decisions were to be made in consultation between State and USAID. In other countries beset by violence, natural disasters, and extreme poverty, presumably where other kinds of assistance were deemed unlikely "to make a difference," the United States would provide humanitarian assistance to save lives.

A NEW STATE-USAID BUDGET PROCESS

Andrew Natsios, the Bush administration's strategic visionary on foreign assistance in the post-9/11 world, resigned in January 2006. He was replaced by Randall Tobias, a former Eli Lilly executive, who had been serving as the President's Global AIDS Coordinator. Tobias's position was expanded to give him the title of "director of foreign assistance." As such he served both as Administrator of USAID and as a deputy secretary of state.[13] In his new position ("F" in State Department acronymic), Tobias took on the mandate to reorganize the foreign operations budget process to consolidate the various accounts managed by USAID and State. The task required a mammoth effort to bring together the different "spigots" operated by USAID and State, which constitute 75–80 percent of all foreign assistance funding under the international affairs account.

The new budget process, laid down hurriedly in 2007, created five major budget functions or objectives: peace and security, governing justly and democratically, investing in people, economic growth, and humanitarian assistance.

The budget functions were applied to five categories of recipients:

Rebuilding (countries in or emerging from conflict)

Developing (poor countries with modest economic and governance records)

Transforming (poor countries riding high on economic and democratic reform)

Sustaining (middle- or high-income countries with close U.S. relations)

Restrictive (countries with reprehensible human rights records)

Although the system was applied flexibly, assistance was expected to be allocated by objective to the different country groups as indicated in Table 6.1.

To build the FY 2008 budget, F coordinated a hierarchical process of review bringing together State and USAID offices in "core teams," covering more than 100 operational plans for countries and programs. Budgeting for R&S was largely subsumed under a major subcategory of the "Peace and Security" function called "stabilization operations and security sector

Table 6.1
Allocation of Funding by Objective among Recipient Countries

Strategic objectives\ Country categories	Rebuilding	Developing	Transforming	Partnership	Restrictive
Peace and security	*				
Governing justly and democratically	*	*	*		
Investing in people		*	*		
Economic growth		*	*	*	
Humanitarian assistance	*	*			*

reform." Some R&S elements were also included under governing justly and humanitarian assistance.

After a one-year effort to establish the new budget process, Tobias resigned abruptly in April 2007, when press accounts linked his name to the activities of the "Washington Madam," Deborah Jean Palfrey.

Those in the agency committed to the Failed States Strategy as a broad and coherent approach to dealing with conflict were disappointed with the new budget approach. They complained that the Failed States Strategy was shelved.[14] They pointed out that nowhere in the new budget functions was found the differentiated approach contained in the strategy, which portrayed fragile states as falling along a u-shaped spectrum of "vulnerable," "in crisis," or "emerging from conflict."[15] Instead, most fragile states were somewhat arbitrarily divided into the rebuilding or developing group. Although F originally agreed to examine "crosscutting" categories after the basic categories were created, it did not have the time—or perhaps inclination—to get into this further layer of complexity. As a result, it was argued, the F budget process returned to a "stovepiped" approach to country categories, abandoning the key axiom of the Fragile State Strategy that assistance should be applied to the basic impediments to resolving conflict, impediments varying from country to country.

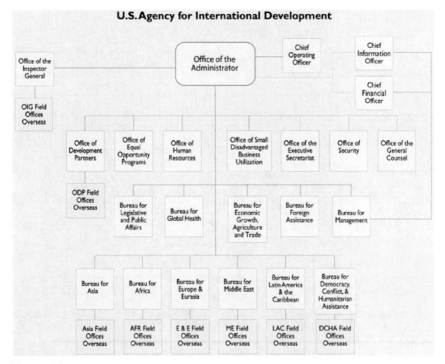

Figure 6.1
USAID Organizational Chart.

ORGANIZING FOR CONFLICT RESOLUTION

The following section describes, as of the end of 2008, the function and organization of the USAID functional and geographic bureaus primarily engaged in R&S, with emphasis on the offices concerned within the Bureau of Democracy, Conflict and Humanitarian Assistance (DCHA).

DCHA

The functional locus of peace-building in USAID is DCHA. Created in 1992 as the Bureau of Humanitarian Response, it originally housed the major offices involved in humanitarian assistance, in particular the Offices of Foreign Disaster Assistance (OFDA) and Food for Peace (FFP). During the Clinton administration it acquired a new function, "transition initiatives," which launched it into the field of conflict resolution. Under the Bush administration, the bureau took on its present name and inscribed conflict at the center of its agenda.[16]

Natsios, who had headed the bureau during a previous stint in the Bush 41 administration, saw DCHA as an important U.S. government spearhead for dealing with fragile states and conflict within the framework of foreign policy guidance from the Secretary of State. He was therefore not pleased when the NSC Principals created a Coordinator for Reconstruction and Stabilization in the State Department. Natsios did not go out of his way to put USAID firmly behind the new office.[17] He asked Michael Hess, his choice as DCHA assistant administrator, to reform the bureau and carve out an interagency role on conflict.

Office of Transition Initiatives (OTI)

Hess did not have to worry about reforming the OTI, which had acquired considerable bureaucratic renown over its first decade of existence. OTI was the brainchild of J. Brian Atwood, USAID Administrator under President Clinton. After his nomination Atwood consulted a variety of figures from the previous administration. Former Secretary of State Lawrence Eagleburger told him USAID needed a quick-acting mechanism, located on the spectrum between relief and development, to respond nimbly to political opportunities like the overthrow of a dictator. During his 1993 confirmation hearings, Atwood piqued the interest of several senators, when he mentioned his interest in improving U.S. government capacity to assist "countries in transition." Their interest prompted a pledge from the new administrator that he would establish an office to facilitate transitions.[18]

The transitions Atwood had in mind were those in Eastern Europe from communism to democracy. By the time the OTI was up and running in March 1994, those transitions had almost been accomplished—except in the Balkans, which was awash with violent political conflict. Under OTI's first director, Frederick D. Barton, the office was built around transitions to democracy and from conflict.[19] Its purpose is to "provide fast, flexible, short-term assistance

MICHAEL HESS

In 2005, as George W. Bush launched his second administration, USAID Administrator Andrew Natsios asked Michael E. Hess to take charge of DCHA. Hess was an unusual choice for a USAID executive: a retired U.S. Army colonel who had spent much of a 30-year career specializing in humanitarian operations, including stints in Turkey, Bosnia, Kosovo, and Northern Iraq, where he was involved in Operation Provide Comfort. As the second Iraq conflict loomed, Hess was called back to military duty to serve as deputy humanitarian coordinator in General Jay Garner's ill-starred ORHA. When ORHA was eliminated by the White House, Hess became Deputy Chief of Staff to Ambassador Paul Bremer in the Coalition Provisional Authority. He was doing risk analysis as a Citibank Vice President when USAID telephoned. Natsios told Hess, "Reform the operation so that it works like a bureau and not like a set of independent fiefdoms."[20]

Easier said than done. OFDA, FFP, and the Office of Democracy and Governance (DG) were well established, had their own constituencies and strong support in Congress. The new Office of Conflict Management and Mitigation was Natsios's love child. OTI was coming off a huge effort in Afghanistan and Iraq. So Hess focused on what he knew about—the military. By October 2005 the Office of Military Affairs (OMA) opened for business. Two months later, Andrew Natsios resigned, leaving Hess without a major backer at the head of the agency.

Although Randall Tobias, the new Director of Foreign Assistance, was preoccupied with reform of the foreign assistance budget, he was generally encouraging. OMA gained traction and brought USAID closer to the military commands and the senior civilian leadership at Defense. The 2007 military surge in Iraq provided new opportunities for DCHA. The doubling of PRTs in Iraq required urgent USAID staffing. Even more important, President Bush's blessing of a civilian response capability, coordinated by S/CRS, envisaged an important USAID component. The 2008 Congressional supplemental appropriation of $55 million for the active and standby components of the civilian response capability included $25 million for USAID. At the end of that year Hess inaugurated within DCHA a new Office of Civilian Response with an authorized staff of 36.

to take advantage of windows of opportunity to build democracy and peace." It sought to "lay the foundations for long-term development by promoting reconciliation, jumpstarting economies, supporting nascent independent media and fostering peace and democracy through innovative programming."

OTI takes pride in its innovative and non-bureaucratic setup and style, which it views as distinguishing it from most of the rest of USAID. It modeled itself on USAID's well-regarded OFDA, known for its speed of response and willingness to dispense with bureaucratic rules in the interest of delivering assistance. The OTI Web site claims it encourages "a culture of risk-taking, political orientation, and swift response among its staff and partners. This culture is reflected in a strategic approach that continually incorporates best practices and lessons learned."

A second distinguishing feature of the office has been its central attention to political issues. Frederick Barton told senior USAID officials at the outset that OTI would look at "the central political development issue in countries emerging from distress," in essence the distribution of power and the quality of leadership. OTI highlighted the sophistication of its political analysis.[21] Initially, OTI exercised discretion in choosing the countries with which it would engage. Engagement required affirmative responses to four basic questions: (1) is the country important to U.S. interests? (2) if so, "is there a window of opportunity?"—is the situation ripe internally for a successful transition? (3) if so, is OTI capable of having an impact? (4) Does the operating environment permit staff to travel outside of the capital to implement and monitor its activities?[22]

A third distinguishing feature of OTI is budgetary. Initially, OTI funding was carved out of the OFDA budget, an action that signaled the commitment of USAID leadership to the new office.[23] For FY 2001, however, the Clinton administration created a separate budget line. The "transition initiatives" budget account has special authorities that allow immediate spending where it is most needed. In bureaucratic parlance, OTI funds are "no year," that is the budget allocation does not have to be spent in that year but can carry over to the next. In addition, OTI has "notwithstanding" authority; it can spend notwithstanding other restrictions that might limit funding, such as "Buy America" or cumbersome contracting procedures.[24]

How has OTI construed "windows of opportunity" for peace? Admittedly, definition is difficult, since a country's ripeness for transformation is a judgment call. Typically, an opening is what OTI has called a "constitutive settlement," broadly defined as an agreement among political actors on how to move forward. It might be a peace agreement among warring factions. Alternatively, it might follow from the emergence of a government committed to fundamental reform and in control of most of the national territory, or it might be the ratification of a new constitution. In these situations, OTI has sought to strengthen the chances for success by identifying and addressing critical bottlenecks and by increasing civil society's involvement in the negotiation process.

OTI's typical mode of intervention has been to send members of its "bull pen," a roster of over 20 part-time specialists prepared to go anywhere in the world on short notice. Their mission is normally to carry out an assessment and to design a strategy for the target country emphasizing quick-impact activities. OTI then typically sends a couple of personal service contractors to the country to carry out the program. OTI's approach is community-based, aimed at working with local partners, including NGOs, local entrepreneurs, women and student groups. Activities might center on campaigns of mass communication, using soap operas to convey themes of reconciliation and resolving differences. Projects might include reintegration assistance for ex-combatants and other youth, backing local human rights groups, providing materials for small infrastructure repair projects, and getting communication equipment and computers to civil society organizations. OTI local staff provide grants of up to $100,000 in response to brief project applications, on which it collaborates with the applicant. Decisions are made within days. OTI has designed its country involvement for completion or handover to the regular USAID mission within two to three years, with expenditures averaging about $8 million. Transaction costs are low and a high percentage of funds spent go to local people.

During the Clinton administration OTI opened programs in 20 countries, rather evenly balanced among Africa, the Balkans, Latin America, and Asia. Haiti proved an important launching pad. Despite opposition to its involvement by the USAID mission in Port-au-Prince, OTI was able to deploy a team of veterans into the country in the wake of U.S. military intervention in 1994, which forced out the military government and reinstated the democratically elected regime of Jean-Bertrand Aristide. Between 1994 and 1997 OTI funded vocational training for about 5,000 former members of the armed forces, financed over 2,000 small infrastructure projects, and after local elections, trained 1,500 newly elected officials.[25]

Under the Bush administration, OTI launched programs in 12 new countries and restarted programs in Angola, Colombia, Congo, Liberia, and Sri Lanka. Interesting new starts included Sudan (focused on southern Sudan after the 2005 CPA), the West Bank and Gaza (after Israeli evacuation of settlements in Gaza and the West Bank in August 2005), and Somalia (for 10 months after the ouster by Ethiopia of the United Islamic Courts regime in early 2007).[26]

OTI's customary discretion about country involvement and modest program size was overridden by Bush administration priorities on Afghanistan and Iraq. Officers from OTI were operational in Afghanistan by January

---

OTI IN HAITI

In mid-1994, General Wesley Clark, then in charge of planning for the Joint Chiefs of Staff, phoned Deputy USAID Administrator Carol Lancaster to ask her about potential USAID assistance, if the United States were to help restore the Aristide government to power.[27] Lancaster referred Clark to OTI chief Frederick Barton, rather than to the Assistant Administrator for Latin America, Mark Schneider. Barton and staff quickly set about devising a quick impact program. The USAID Director in Port-au-Prince was alarmed, seeing OTI's involvement as a bid to create an USAID program independent of his authority. However, when he sought to enlist Schneider against OTI involvement, he was rebuffed. Schneider was anxious to mount a successful program and saw OTI involvement as a means of securing additional USAID money for Haiti. Offers of assistance from the USAID mission to the OTI team were scant. OTI was able to use its ties with the Joint Chiefs to bring some of its people into Haiti aboard military helicopters, as well as on chartered flights. The episode quickly gained OTI a reputation for aggressive resourcefulness but offended more traditional-minded USAID officers.

2002, and the program continued for three and a half years. Initially the activities focused on "rapid, highly visible support designed to establish governmental credibility and space for longer term development assistance." As time went on, OTI sought to build national, provincial, and local governance capacities by engaging rural communities in projects connecting them to their government. Three-quarters of the projects and almost two-thirds of the funding were devoted to strengthening central government capacity. Initially, OTI played a major role in the effort to create democratic government. Prospects for an emergency loya jirga assembly of tribal, military, and religious leaders and government officials were bleak, until OTI moved $3 million to a UNDP Trust Fund to fund it. In June 2002 that assembly set up the Transitional Administration and the drafting of a new constitution. OTI also helped fund the constitutional loya jirga of December 2003, focusing on public education, but by that time USAID's DG had assumed the major role. OTI worked to increase Afghan media capacity, financing 14 community radio stations and 3 independent radio stations. Overall, OTI funded over 700 projects in all 34 provinces totaling about $50 million.[28]

Afghanistan was OTI's first large program, but it was soon dwarfed by that in Iraq, where OTI made more than 5,200 individual grants totaling at least $337 million.[29] An OTI team arrived in Baghdad about the same time as the first U.S. troops. Unlike the military command, it demonstrated an exemplary awareness of the need for post-conflict reconstruction. It evolved four program objectives:

- enhance capacity of local/national governments
- increase citizen participation in social/political/economic life
- prevent, manage, mitigate, and resolve conflict
- encourage respect for human rights and enhance transitional justice

To help get the ministries up and running, OTI financed the "ministry in-a-box" program, providing key ministries with desks, computers, and other furnishings for the first 100 officials. The furniture was built by a local firm. However, only 12 percent of the grants went to help government. OTI quickly moved on to community and civil society groups.

About 62 percent of grants by number and more than 75 percent in funds went to deal with conflict. The bulk of these grants were made in close cooperation with U.S. army units (e.g., the First Cavalry Division and the Third Infantry Division working in unstable Baghdad neighborhoods and the 3rd Armored Cavalry Regiment in Tal Afar), often for neighborhood cleanup projects providing employment for local inhabitants.[30] Another 25 percent of the grants (but only about 10% of total funds) went to promote citizen participation in economic and political life. In 2005 OTI gave particular attention to the electoral process, providing funding for the election of the transitional government, then the referendum on the constitution, and finally the election of a permanent government. Slightly more than 2 percent of the grants went for human rights and transitional justice projects, often focused on the rights of women and minorities, handling of mass grave sites, and services for victims of the Saddam Hussein regime.

Average grant size in Iraq was $64,000, compared with $20,000–50,000 in other OTI programs. During its three years in Iraq, OTI officials initially came in under the Office of Disaster Assistance, but its dynamic performance quickly enabled it to assume leadership of the civilian assistance effort. As security became more and more difficult in late 2004, OTI restricted its officers to a supervisor in the Green Zone and sub-offices in Hilla and Basra. Later on, OTI contractors commuted into Iraq via helicopter from Kuwait or Jordan.

At the end of the Bush administration, OTI had a total staff of 86, including 10 local national staff at USAID missions overseas.[31] The Transition Initiatives (TI) budget for the office averaged about $50 million in 2003–2005 but dropped to $40 million in FY 2006 and 2007. (The figures for 2003–2005 do not include the bulk of the funds for grants in Iraq and Afghanistan, which came out of supplemental appropriations for those countries. In subsequent years, TI funds were also supplemented by other sources.) In FY 2008 $45 million was budgeted under TI, but actual expenditures reached $103 million with supplemental funding, up from $80.8 million in FY 2007. Total 1994–2008 OTI expenditures totaled $1.3 billion, of which $811 million fell into the 2004–2008 period.[32]

There has been no systematic evaluation of the office for the full 14 years of its existence. A 2005 Harvard study done on the occasion of OTI's 10th anniversary concluded

[O]verall, OTI has done very well, using a model of direct action and engagement that deserves to be more widely understood—even emulated. . . . OTI has been strongest at empowering stakeholders. It has managed across a wide range of projects to involve civil society at the grass roots as well as to engage civil society as a whole.[33]

Looking specifically at OTI's peace-building function, the study credited OTI for playing key roles in East Timor's transition to independence and Sierra Leone's transition to peace. It concluded, however, that OTI's small grant approach seems to work better for building civil society than for more broad-gauged peace-building activities. Curiously the Harvard study virtually ignored Serbia, a case which OTI alumni consider a major triumph, and its writers visited neither Afghanistan nor Iraq.[34]

USAID's outside evaluation of OTI in Afghanistan—"its first megaprogram"—gave credit for a coherent strategy combining "top-down government support to bottom-up community democratization . . . to connect community leaders with government representatives in the process of community infrastructure rehabilitation." The office was praised for raising government visibility, influence, and legitimacy, but not for its efforts to link local communities to the central government. Its support to the electoral process likewise had an important initial impact, particularly for the emergency loya jirga of June 2002, when quick OTI funding "save[d] the day," as the UNDP "found itself bureaucratically unable to deal with the organizational complexities and fast-unfolding timetable."[35] OTI was "least successful," according to the same evaluation, in its projects to raise the level of participatory democratic processes in local Afghan communities, where community consultation on its projects was minimal. The evaluation praised OTI's "wise" investment in media programs, which it termed "clearly the most successful avenue for OTI transitional funding." OTI was criticized for failing to review and adapt its objectives once the post-crisis situation had stabilized.[36]

Evaluations of OTI's role in Iraq have been solidly positive. An evaluation by a USAID contractor in 2006 credited OTI with having a "significant impact" in helping restore the government function in the early period and in helping create the legal forms and processes for the elections and referendum in 2005. Most significantly, the study asserted that OTI "clearly had a major impact on the U.S. military in Iraq, paving the way for future close civilian and military collaboration in Iraq and other countries."[37] That judgment is corroborated by the final report of the Special Inspector General for Iraq Reconstruction (SIGIR), which praised OTI's work with the 1st Cavalry Division in Baghdad's Sadr City for "quick results" in putting people to work in the neighborhood.[38] SIGIR cited that collaboration with the military as a model for the "Clear, Hold, and Build" strategy adopted by the White House in late 2005.[39]

OTI is probably more popular with the Defense and State Departments than within its own agency. In 1999 there was reportedly an effort to abolish the office, orchestrated by USAID's powerful Policy and Program Coordination Bureau, which subjected OTI to a series of evaluations. The move backfired when the assessments proved more positive than expected. Within USAID, OTI officers are sometimes known disparagingly as "cowboys," for the absence of a careful analytic approach, their willingness to flout normal agency rules, and their concern about short-term political impact. By contrast, admirers in USAID and other agencies refer to OTI as USAID's "Delta Force" because of its ability to allocate a few operatives and limited fund increments to small targets in a rapid and flexible manner.[40] At a major U.S. government conference on counterinsurgency in September 2006, Col. H. R. McMaster, Commander of the 3rd Armored Cavalry Regiment at Tal Afar, characterized OTI's capabilities as formidable.[41]

Office of Conflict Management and Mitigation (CMM)

When he took up his duties as Administrator in 2001, Andrew Natsios set up a task force to deliberate how the agency should organize to deal with conflict. There was a debate over where to put the conflict function. Natsios rejected the task force recommendation that it be housed within the

Democracy and Governance office or OTI. So it was created as a separate Office of Conflict Management and Mitigation in 2003.

With OTI already in place, an obvious question was the division of labor. The basic distinction was that OTI would be "operational" and CMM "analytical." OTI is hands-on, deploying teams to the field to smooth a particular "transition to peace." CMM, by contrast, would undertake the intellectual work of conflict assessment and assist USAID missions to apply the available assessment tools to conflict problems in their countries. It would also provide general training on conflict to USAID officers and local employees. CMM's ambitious long-term objective, blessed from the outset by Natsios, was to "mainstream" conflict resolution into all sectors of the agency's work. CMM's first director, Elisabeth Kvitashvili, wanted to develop a "bull pen" of specialists who could be dispatched to work on conflict analysis in the field, following the OTI model, but it was decided to keep the office lean. As of the end of 2008, personnel numbered 15, all in Washington.

From CAF to ICAF

CMM's main achievement in its initial years was development of a Conflict Assessment Framework (CAF) for use by USAID's overseas missions and other government entities. Since the Clinton administration, most USAID missions have been required to submit a regular conflict analysis report. The CAF provided an intellectually rigorous basis for those reports, designed to map out destabilizing patterns and trends in specific developing countries, while offering recommendations for restructuring development programs to address these patterns more effectively.

The CAF process has three parts. The first—and the one to which CMM devoted the bulk of its efforts—is an analysis of factors linked to violence. In the second, the USAID mission is expected to "map existing development programs against identified causes of conflict . . . to identify gaps and potential areas of intervention." The final step is to propose "new configurations of development assistance" calibrated to the various dimensions of conflict. The final product is expected to be a U.S. assistance program which copes effectively with conflict on the way to development.

The CAF document appends a detailed checklist of questions in three parts addressed to the causes and different dimensions of violence.[42] The first set is about incentives for violence—"grievance and greed." Through this duality CMM was able to embrace older theories of civil conflict based on grievances (ethnic, religious, economic) and theories emerging in the late 1990s pointing to greed as a motive for both leaders and followers of rebellion.[43]

The CAF then focuses on questions relating to "access to conflict resources." This dimension, which follows from increased theoretical emphasis on greed over grievance, is posited on the assumption that "elites foment . . . violence to gain, maintain or increase their hold on political or economic power."[44] For potentially violent elites to generate rebellion, they must have access to organizations—"dense, social networks"—which can be mobilized.

SHARON MORRIS

Sharon Morris got excited about conflict while studying for her doctorate at the University of Chicago. She then joined the John D. & Catherine T. MacArthur Foundation in Chicago, where she labored for four years on its program of global security and sustainability. She came to USAID in 2001 to work on conflict, even before CMM was established. As she talked with persons in USAID and State who had experience in conflict situations, she was struck by the absence of broad-gauged analyses. Robert D. Kaplan's *The Coming Anarchy*, published in 2000, had made a big impression on practitioners with his emphasis on atavistic ethnic and religious hatreds. In her view excessive emphasis was being placed on a single-factor analyses which did not take into account the growing body of academic research in the field, including studies of the economic roots of conflict emerging from the World Bank and the British Government.[45] There was likewise little focus on why grievances generate civil wars in some cases and not in others.

So Sharon decided to draw together the research results into a framework of analysis, which she hoped could be useful in deciding how to deal with individual conflicts. She started with an analysis of what drives violence—ethnicity, religion, natural resources, and bad governance. Then she moved on to how certain leaders or groups are able—or not—to mobilize followers for violence and then to whether governments are able to contain potential violence. She was particularly interested in the next step: how would a USAID mission rework its program to deal with the conflict situation it had dissected? The product impressed several key people inside and outside the Bureau of Humanitarian Response (soon to be renamed Democracy, Conflict and Humanitarian Assistance) and was brought to the attention of Andrew Natsios, who endorsed it. By the time CMM was up and running, it had the initial part of its toolkit—the CAF.

The plainspoken scholar-practitioner left CMM at the end of 2006 to go to Kabul, where she became Director of the Afghanistan PRT program. A year later she signed on as senior advisor for Darfur policy to Andrew Natsios, by then Special Envoy for Sudan. In 2008 she joined Mercy Corps as Director of its Conflict Management Group.

They must have access to financial resources, since war is expensive, and must be able to tap recruits, particularly aggrieved young men.

The third critical dimension, receiving almost as much attention as incentives, is institutional capacity. Some nations and societies are better equipped to deal with violence than others. Democracy and good governance are key aspects of government capacity to cope with civil violence.[46] However, the questions broaden to include economic governance, management of natural resources, and government's capacity to adapt to demographic shifts. The capacity of the security forces to deal with civil violence is also central—capacity ranging from nonviolent containment to ruthless repression.

The questionnaire gives brief attention to "regional and international factors." Those include not only "bad neighbors" but vulnerability to regional environmental degradation and global economic shocks.[47]

By the close of 2008 the CAF had been applied to about 40 countries in different parts of the world.[48] From conflict assessments have come significant changes in existing assistance programs. For example, in Nepal the U.S. Embassy initially resisted the CMM proposal for an Office of the High Commissioner for Human Rights, arguing it could undermine the authority of the king. In 2005 the king dismissed the parliament when a Maoist rebellion appeared to be gaining ground. The embassy eventually acquiesced in the proposed CMM approach. CMM partially funded the office, which reported on specific cases and general trends, while advising civil society representatives and local human rights activists. CMM provided ongoing support for conflict management programs in certain countries. Since the office lacked an "expeditionary" cadre like OTI, such support normally came through occasional temporary duty visits by CMM personnel. CMM claimed success in its work in Sri Lanka, Kosovo, and Uganda. In Sri Lanka a peace forum was introduced to promote communication among political parties, national civil society, and grassroots communities. The conflict assessment in Kosovo led to a project for improving interethnic communication using teams of paired Serbian and Albanian Kosovars, who wrote, filmed, and edited a full-length documentary and nine half-hour episodes representing the views of both communities. The Northern Uganda Peace Initiative fostered opportunities to get people talking in the region, ravaged by the Lord's Resistance Army rebellion, through a meeting of cultural leaders, a youth conference, and a peace-building camp for women. Although these programs can be deemed innovative approaches, it is difficult to claim success in conflict resolution in any of them at this point.

The CAF also gained the attention of the U.S. military. Collaboration between CMM and DCHA's new OMA led to the recasting of the CAF as a tactical document for use in a battle zone. The Tactical Conflict Assessment Framework (TCAF) was adapted for use by field-grade officers and PRTs in Afghanistan.[49] DCHA Assistant Administrator Mike Hess crowed that in Afghanistan the TCAF had been "downloaded on everyone's personal digital assistant."[50]

CMM took the lead at the end of 2007 in a new interagency phase of the use of the CAF, cochairing (with S/CRS) a group developing an interagency CAF—or ICAF. The ICAF represented a "shared understanding among [U.S. government] agencies about the sources of civil strife ... [and] a joint interagency process for conducting the assessment." It drew very heavily on the CAF. It was designed to be used in a range of assessments: country team assessments in U.S. missions abroad, Defense Department theater security cooperation planning, preparations for a conflict management (Sec. 1207) project by S/CRS, or a full-blown "whole of government" crisis response under the IMS. (See Chapter 4.) It provided for a direct "segue" into program planning.[51]

Toolkits

CMM also developed "toolkits," packages of technical assistance in areas shown to be contributing to conflict. Those published so far include youth and conflict, land and conflict, minerals and conflict, livelihoods and conflict, forests and conflict, and women and conflict. The toolkits are designed to provide USAID missions with practical program options, lessons learned, plus monitoring and evaluation tools for their conflict programs. CMM drew on academic experts, large-scale research organizations, some of them foreign-based, and prominent NGOs in putting the toolkits together.[52]

Early Warning

CMM was originally asked to work with State and CIA to develop a conflict Early Warning System to alert the U.S. government to countries that are at greatest risk for violence, thereby enabling the relevant agencies to focus their resources better.[53] CMM worked on an unclassified system, which could be made available to NGOs working on conflict. That approach quickly encountered problems with U.S. ambassadors overseas and some State and USAID officials, concerned that an "unstable" or "fragile" label would upset the host government, and with the CIA, which was unwilling to confine itself within an unclassified domain. As a result, CRS de-emphasized early warning. (See Chapter 4.) CMM persisted, however, and became the custodian of two related unclassified lists, though neither is distributed outside the U.S. government. The first is a forecast of countries deemed likely to experience significant conflict. The second is a rank ordering of "fragile states," which involves a weighted average of scores for effectiveness and legitimacy based on a set of political, security, economic, and social variables.[54]

Training

CMM considered training highly important to its overall success in "mainstreaming" conflict within USAID. The office sponsored a series of speakers at USAID offices. Sessions in 2007 included counterinsurgency and religion in conflict, looking particularly at Islam. CMM put together a "Conflict 101" course basically for USAID officials, a one-day course which included how to do a conflict assessment and relied heavily on case studies. A second iteration of the course (Conflict 102), a two-day offering, added program design and evaluation to the basic conflict analysis core. Offered 10 times in 2008, both in Washington and overseas, principally for a USAID audience but including military, State Department, and other agency personnel as well, Conflict 102 has been characterized by CMM as "enormously popular."

CMM inserted itself into the training program for PRTs headed for Afghanistan and Iraq, where it provided a condensed version of "Conflict 101." CMM training reached hundreds of military personnel. Courses have been held overseas for those assigned to Central Asia and the Horn of Africa. With the launching of the TCAF in Iraq in 2007, USAID's role in training the military expanded in the final years of the Bush administration, although CMM then handed off responsibility for such training to OMA (see below).[55]

In sum, in five years CMM made its mark. It has contended, credibly, that its leadership on the CAF/ICAF process, widely used toolkits, developed models for early warning, and expanding guidance on effective programming demonstrate that CMM—and not S/CRS—has secured the lead technical role on conflict prevention within the U.S. government.[56] In view of the short life of programming trends at USAID, however, it would be premature to conclude that CMM succeeded in making conflict a permanent part of the USAID mainstream. It does appear that CMM has had an impact on most of the USAID geographic bureaus and has touched through training a considerable portion of the total body of USAID officers. Arguably, it has had more impact on USAID bureaucratic culture than S/CRS has exerted on that of the State Department.

Office of Military Affairs (OMA)

The Afghanistan and Iraq conflicts brought USAID into its most intensive relationship with the U.S. military since the Vietnam War, when USAID was heavily invested in the Civil Operations Rural Development Support (CORDS) program. Administrator Natsios became concerned that the agency was being buffeted by a plethora of Defense Department demands, which, if not handled systematically, could deflect USAID from its development mission. A major reason he hired Col. Michael Hess as Assistant Administrator was to take advantage of his knowledge of the military to set up an OMA. Hess brought on another retired colonel he had worked with in Iraq, Thomas Baltazar, to head up the new office. Initially, Baltazar was primarily concerned with creating effective liaison with the regional COCOMs by assigning a development expert from OMA to each command and bringing a command representative into the OMA office in Washington. Generally the commands were enthusiastic, recognizing the desirability of having a development advisor on hand to counsel the commander, just as the commander had drawn for decades on the political and diplomatic advice of a senior Foreign Service Officer from the State Department (the political advisor or PolAd). By 2008 OMA had signed agreements with most of the COCOMs, and an OMA officer was assigned to each of the geographic combatant commands. Liaison officers from each of those commands, plus the Special Operations Command (SOCOM), were assigned to OMA, which numbered 23 persons.

OMA seized a role in the development of the PRTs—training. Baltazar was surprised to note that no training programs had been set up for the teams as a whole—only for individuals or civilians on the team—and began pressing the bureaucracy to remedy that shortcoming. Eventually a two-week course was established at Fort Bragg, beginning December 2006 for Afghanistan and March 2007 for Iraq. The course was equally divided between a week of training related to security and force protection and a week conveying how to implement and manage reconstruction. However, OMA had little initial impact on training for PRT personnel at the State Department's FSI. FSI insisted that trainees take area studies, while OMA urged that priority be given to management training for reconstruction programs. That debate appeared to camouflage a deeper interagency quarrel. FSI, a part of the State Department, naturally resisted the notion that a new USAID office, specializing in military affairs, should have a significant influence on its curriculum.

Office of Civilian Response

The 2007 military surge in Iraq provided new opportunities for DCHA. The doubling of PRTs in Iraq required urgent USAID staffing. Even more important, President Bush's blessing of a civilian response capability, coordinated by S/CRS, envisaged an important USAID component. The 2008 Congressional supplemental appropriation of $55 million for the active and standby components of the civilian response capability included $25 million for USAID.[57] At the end of 2008 a new Office of Civilian Response, with an authorized staff of 36, was inaugurated in DCHA.

Office of Democracy and Governance (DG)

DCHA's DG does not fit neatly into a study of U.S. government peace-building offices. Its objectives are much broader. The U.S. National Security Strategy of 2002, as revised in 2006, stated

The goal of our statecraft is to help create a world of democratic, well-governed states that can meet the needs of their citizens and conduct themselves responsibly in the international system. This is the best way to provide enduring security for the American people.[58]

DG's explicit goals are to strengthen rule of law and respect for human rights, promote fair elections and political processes, stimulate a politically active civil society, and improve governance.[59]

None of these goals explicitly mentions conflict, but the relationship between democracy and conflict is an important part of DG's mandate. At the most general level the Bush administration stated that promoting democracy is the primary engine of peace-building, a claim with deep roots in the Wilsonian vision of the international order.[60]

American administrations have long considered the construction of a democratic polity as a key component in post-conflict reconstruction. That was the case in U.S. occupation of Germany and Japan after World War II. The same view has been consistently applied to post-conflict reconstruction in societies ravaged by civil war. Along with disarmament, demobilization, and reintegration of combatants and the return of refugees and displaced persons, the United States has viewed postwar reconstruction, particularly since 1993, as including a timetable and preparations for democratic elections. That paradigm was applied by the Clinton administration to Bosnia and Kosovo and by the Bush administration to Afghanistan, Iraq, Liberia, Sudan, and Congo.

DCHA/DG emphasizes its mandate of promoting democracy without explicit reference to post-conflict reconstruction. The majority of its activity is carried on in countries where civil conflict is not an issue. A veteran of the DG office in both the Clinton and Bush administrations observed that Administrator Natsios encouraged the DCHA Bureau to give greater attention to countries on the "low end of the stability spectrum," but that the office continued to devote much of its attention to relatively stable countries like Ghana and Mongolia. DG looks askance at "exit strategies" since even seemingly stable democratic states sometimes encounter sharp reversals.[61] Although USAID has published numerous documents on the application of U.S. assistance to building democratic and well-governed states, it has not developed a theory about the relationship between conflict, democracy, and governance. The Democracy and Governance Strategy Framework cited above simply noted that "in countries emerging from conflict, democratic reforms offer a path for national dialogue and for shifting confrontations from the battlefield to the political arena."[62]

Even if it lacks an operative doctrine for conflict situations, the Democracy and Governance Office has been heavily engaged with post-conflict reconstruction. Its most consistent engagement has been with Africa—its "biggest client."[63] Working with USAID's Africa Bureau, particularly its democracy and conflict specialists, and with State Department desk officers, DCHA/DG has mounted major programs in Sudan, Congo, Liberia, and Burundi. According to a programmer, "DG shaped the democracy and governance program in Southern Sudan completely." The office was also heavily engaged in democratization activities in Liberia after the 2003 peace agreement, an electoral process which led to the internationally applauded election of Ellen Johnson Sirleaf as President. The DG office sent out numerous specialists to assist the USAID mission in Monrovia. Although the United Nations managed the costly 2006 elections in the Congo, DG was at the center of a democratization assistance program launched nearly a decade earlier, after the fall of President Mobutu. DG's work in the Western Hemisphere and Asia has been heavily concentrated in Haiti and Nepal. It has not worked on conflict in the Balkans and the countries of the former Soviet Union. That role was played by the Office of the Assistance Coordinator for Europe and Eurasia, based in State's Bureau for Europe and Eurasia.

DCHA/DG was not initially involved in democracy planning in either Afghanistan or Iraq, where USAID, like State, was sidelined at the outset. In Afghanistan, the United Nations was given charge of managing the constitutional and electoral processes under the 2002 Bonn Agreement. As described above, OTI initially did much of the funding for the emergency loya jirga. DG did work with the United Nations on staging the December 2003 constitutional loya jirga. With the adoption of a "whole of government" approach to R&S in both countries in 2004, USAID became more active, and DG took on a training role for the PRTs.

Among DG's activities—in both post-conflict and other states—are pre-election assessments, creation of systems for quick and accurate ballot counts, and training for election commissioners, poll watchers, and local and international observers. DG also supplies election equipment, including ballot boxes and portable voting booths, working through contractors like the International Foundation for Electoral Systems.[64] After the election DG may help train elected officials.

Offices of Foreign Disaster Assistance (OFDA) and Food for Peace (FFP)

A review of the offices concerned with peace-building would be incomplete without inclusion of humanitarian assistance programs. Created in 1964, the Office of Foreign Disaster Assistance provides humanitarian assistance of a nonfood nature to the victims of both natural and man-made disasters, including civil wars.[65] The latter situation, often characterized as a "complex emergency," has predominated since the 1990s. In complex disasters, as in natural ones, affected populations require potable water, emergency shelter, health care, relief supplies such as soap, cooking utensils, and blankets, and food security. Countries facing or emerging from political or economic instability also need help with local capacity building, protection for the displaced, particularly women, children, and the elderly, and coordination of the international humanitarian response. OFDA funding is highly flexible; like that of OTI, it is "no year" and has a "notwithstanding" waiver.

The heart of OFDA is its operations division, which deploys squadrons to the field, most notably its celebrated DARTs. The model for the OTI teams created in the 1990s, DART members vaunt their ability to deploy to disaster scenes in 24–48 hours. In complex operations a DART may be deployed with a logistical Ground Operations (GO) team, while a Response Management Team backstops the effort in Washington D.C. The first step of a DART, as conflict displaces large numbers of people and begins to inflict undue suffering on civilians, is to conduct an assessment of food, water, sanitation, shelter, and health care needs, plus protection requirements, and convey recommendations back to Washington. Funds are quickly made available to NGOs and UN agencies, most already registered with OFDA.[66] OFDA staff then focus on overcoming bottlenecks in distribution of relief materials—opening up relief corridors, arranging airlifts if necessary, negotiating with local officials or militia groups. OFDA works with the U.S. military, but not in direct combat situations. When U.S. military logistical support is necessary to get supplies to a disaster scene, OFDA activates special humanitarian assistance arrangements with the COCOMs through its own military Operations Liaison Unit. Such cooperation is applied to large-scale natural disasters like hurricanes in the Caribbean, the 2004 Asian tsunami, and the 2005 Kashmir earthquake.

In Iraq, in FY 2003, OFDA assistance reached $81.4 million.[67] The budget fell as low as $6 million but mushroomed once again after the bombing of the Samarra shrine in February 2006. OFDA works through dozens of NGOs but relies primarily on five big ones. These partners are not publicized for security reasons. The OFDA Director lamented that inability to publicize its achievements limited U.S. government ability to counter exaggerated reports of deteriorating conditions for Iraqi civilians.[68] Darfur became the largest OFDA program in 2006, with more than $104 million programmed to support shipments of cargo, flights for humanitarian workers, and information-sharing. In 2006 disaster assistance to the Congo reached $6.6 million, mostly to improve access to health care for 1.8 million in the eastern Congo—rehabilitating health facilities, training local health staff, and providing essential medicines. In Afghanistan OFDA aid to the complex emergency was only $1.5 million by 2006, basically to improve shelter for internally displaced persons in Kabul. It had fallen sharply from $114 million in 2002 and from about $10 million in 2004.

Providing food supplies in conflict-related emergencies is not the function of OFDA but of DCHA's FFP. The U.S. Department of Agriculture purchases hundreds of millions of dollars' worth of U.S. agricultural commodities and processed food products, such as wheat flour, refined soybean oil, and blended cereals. Many of the commodities are refined and processed domestically, and nearly all are shipped abroad on U.S.-flag carriers. The authority for emergency food shipments comes from Title II of the venerable Public Law 480.[69] As in the case of OFDA, emergency assistance is extended in food crises resulting from both natural disasters and complex emergencies. Both emergency and nonemergency aspects of Title II are administered in DCHA/FFP, rather than in the Agriculture Department. The food is distributed, however, through the UN's World Food Program (WFP) or through a number of NGOs. Most, but not all, are U.S.-based. Two dozen FFP Officers are permanently assigned overseas to USAID missions or regional offices, but FFP, unlike OFDA and OTI, does not make use of an "expeditionary" contingent.

In conflict situations FFP works closely with OFDA and overseas USAID missions to design an appropriate program with input from both USAID and State Department desk officers. The bulk of food for complex emergencies goes through the WFP, but a portion goes through NGOs.[70] Where governments are deemed likely to channel food aid in line with political rather than humanitarian criteria, FFP uses U.S. NGOs or ensures that WFP avoids government channels for distribution. After the outbreak of violence in Darfur in 2003, the emergency food program there became USAID's largest. In 2006

FFP channeled $370 million in emergency food aid through WFP to Darfur, complementing OFDA's emergency assistance of more than $100 million.[71] FFP also coordinated its program with OTI, which maintained the only USAID presence in the troubled Sudanese region from 2003 until the arrival of the S/CRS active response component representatives in 2006. Food aid programs were initiated in eastern Chad and the Central African Republic to assist refugees from Darfur. Other large FFP programs included Afghanistan, the Congo, and Somalia. About $60 million in commodities went to Afghanistan in 2006, also through WFP, and $39 million went to the Congo through WFP and Food for the Hungry International, a U.S. NGO.[72] Somalia, long-time recipient of U.S. emergency food assistance, received expanded assistance beginning in 2007 through new UN airlifts as well as traditional truck corridors from Kenya. FFP also coordinated its Somalia program with the Joint Task Force/Horn of Africa (initially under CENTCOM, but in 2008 transferred to AFRICOM).

Diplomats sometimes charge that high volumes of humanitarian assistance over an extended period can decrease the incentive of dissident groups to negotiate a political solution to violent conflict. OFDA Director Ky Luu reported that some working on Darfur had voiced such criticism. He acknowledged the argument but noted that by law OFDA has a mandate to channel assistance to the needy in emergency situations. In fact diplomats experienced in conflict are aware that the American public, and thus the U.S. Congress, insist on disaster assistance for civilians caught in conflict situations, whether or not it lengthens the conflict. State Department officials

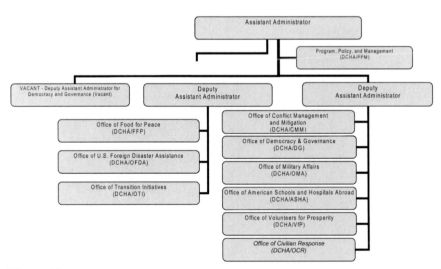

Figure 6.2
Organization: Bureau of Democracy, Conflict and Humanitarian Assistance (2008).

involved in negotiations must always keep in mind the obligation to pressure the warring parties to keep humanitarian assistance corridors open and must factor such assistance into their peace planning.[73]

When Randall Tobias replaced Natsios in 2006, DCHA lost its champion at the apex of the organization. Tobias, preoccupied with integrating USAID and State assistance budgets, had relatively little time or inclination to carry on Natsios's objective of making the DCHA the "tip of the spear" to create the conditions under which development assistance might work more effectively to support national security objectives like defusing regional conflicts and promoting democracy. Tobias's abrupt departure after a year left even more confused the debate—and institutional balance—between the traditional development proponents in USAID and those viewing the agency primarily as an important tool of U.S. foreign policy. Under Administrator Henrietta Fore, the agency got back on a more even keel for the remaining 21 months of Bush's second term, as the new budget process became more routine. DCHA was able to continue and deepen its role in conflict management. The change in administration in 2009, however, left room for doubt about the future nature of USAID's involvement in peace-building.

Geographic Bureaus

As with the State Department, the geographic bureaus of USAID are where country assistance programs are backstopped. However, USAID's geographic bureaus play a lesser role as conveyor of policy guidance. As a practical matter, a USAID director overseas reports to the Assistant Administrator of the relevant bureau and, on a day-to-day basis, works with the office directors for the subregion and desk officers for the country. The geographic bureau is responsible for attempting to assure that the country assistance program is coherent and that its component parts serve U.S. development interests for the country. For that reason, the geographic bureaus regularly get involved in conflict management and reconstruction programs at different phases and levels in the hierarchy.

USAID leadership in the Bush administration viewed DCHA as the lead for a country or region as a crisis erupted, whether natural or man-made. It chaired a working group for the crisis, while a representative of the regional bureau acted as deputy chair. When the crisis normalized, however, the chairs switched. The regional bureau took charge from there.[74]

During the Bush administration, the assistant administrators generally viewed conflict issues as requiring extensive personal engagement, each bringing a particular point of view. Kent Hill, who led the Europe and Eurasia Bureau from 2001 to 2005, had a particular interest in projects aimed at defusing religious hostility. Adolfo Franco, as Assistant Administrator for Latin America and the Caribbean, 2002–2007, saw his role as using assistance to "get at underlying issues"—particularly marginalization—in resolving conflict in Colombia, Haiti, and Bolivia. Constance Newman, Bureau of African Affairs 2001–2004, also sought to use development to ease conflict. In this regard Newman and Franco were comfortably aligned with the views expressed by Administrator Natsios. All considered their relationships with their State Department counterparts, geographic bureau assistant secretaries, as essential for success. (The unique ambassador-level role of the - Coordinator for Assistance to Eastern Europe in State's Bureau of Europe and Eurasian Affairs made that relationship more important for the USAID assistant administrator than his ties with the assistant secretary.) By contrast most of them were easily able to contain their enthusiasm for the role of the Coordinator for Reconstruction and Stabilization. Several expressed doubts that the position was justified.[75]

The geographic assistant administrators also valued their involvement in the interagency process formally orchestrated by the NSC. They attended key meetings on particular crises—Kosovo, Colombia, Haiti, and Liberia— backing up the USAID administrator or his deputy. For Assistant Administrator Newman, ongoing discussions with the NSC were important to keep pressure on the Defense Department to take a proactive stance on Liberia, an objective frustrated for a time in the summer of 2003, when there was resistance to calls for U.S. military intervention to ensure the departure of renegade president Charles Taylor. The assistant administrators had limited interaction with their Defense Department counterparts, mostly with the regional combatant commands. Two described their relations with the commands as better than with the Pentagon bureaucracy, particularly at higher levels of the OSD. One Africa Bureau chief expressed frustration that the Pentagon during Secretary Rumsfeld's tenure refused to give any consideration to "an African country costing DOD any money."[76]

Below the assistant administrator level, USAID's geographic bureaus allocate work on conflict among technical specialists and desk officers. Each geographic bureau has had a unit mandated to work on democracy and human rights, which usually doubles in conflict resolution. Specialists on conflict periodically travel to the field, often with counterparts from other offices or agencies, to do joint assessments of peace-building program needs. Typically an assessment identifies the problem, looks for windows or opportunity for engagement, and evaluates potential modes of intervention like strengthening local government or promoting dialogue among local NGOs.[77] In 2003 the Congress began appropriating funds for programming on behalf of peace-building, with much of the money divided among the geographic bureaus.

USAID's Africa Bureau (AFR) has been more active in conflict mitigation work than the other geographic bureaus, and its technical unit is the only one explicitly labeled "Conflict and Governance."[78] AFR has been particularly active in programming through the Africa Conflict & Peace-Building Fund, the Africa Bureau's share of the global amount appropriated for peace-keeping. It funded a variety of projects in different parts of the continent—

KENT R. HILL

In 2002 Kent Hill came to the position of Assistant Administrator for Europe and Eurasia from academia. He had a master's degree in Russian studies and a PhD in Russian history from the University of Washington. After teaching Russian and Eastern European History at Seattle Pacific University, he became President of Eastern Nazarene College (1992–2001). He came to Washington D.C. to head the Institute on Religion and Democracy, a conservative think tank. On its Web site IRD describes itself as

an alliance of mainline and other evangelical Protestants, Roman Catholics, and Eastern Orthodox Christians working together in common cause ... [to] reform their churches' social witness, in accord with biblical and historic teachings, thereby contributing to the renewal of democratic society at home and abroad.

During an exchange teaching assignment at Moscow State University in 1991–92, he found himself in the unusual position of defending the rights of atheists and Marxists to freedom of conscience, when the formerly persecuted Orthodox gained ascendancy after the collapse of the USSR. That experience shaped his interest in how religious people communicate with nonreligious persons.

At USAID, he promoted programs in the former Soviet Union and the Balkans which addressed religious and ethnic tension, seeking to foster values necessary to sustain democracy and encourage reconciliation. Administrator Natsios supported Hill's interest in finding ways to facilitate discussion of how democracy and human rights can be supported by the Qur'an. Hill contended in interagency councils that the United States should support moderate Islamic voices who advocate those objectives out of their own religious traditions, since they are far more convincing than secularists. Drawing on the work of Abdulaziz Sachedina, a Shi'ite scholar at the University of Virginia, Hill applied his insights to Albania, which had gone through serious instability and episodes of political violence in the 1997–2002 period. He encouraged USAID to facilitate dialogue between Muslims and Orthodox, who constitute roughly 70 and 20 percent of the population, respectively. Hill believes these projects contributed to Albania's democratic transition.[79]

reducing sexual violence in the Congo, protecting children in northern Uganda, and training Casamance rebels in Senegal how to negotiate with the central government. It helped fund the controversial GEMAP program in Liberia, which has sought to fight corruption and promote accountability by placing international experts with co-signing authority in a variety of government agencies.[80] In FY 2008 USAID proposed to spend $45 million on conflict management and reconciliation, half for Sudan and much of the rest for regional programs like the East African Regional Security Initiative. The Governance and Peace-Building unit in AFR works in general harmony with the geographic offices but in recent years has focused on regional projects, such as the Trans-Sahel Counter-Terrorism Partnership (TSCTP), leaving country programs to the desks. AFR officers believe they have drawn productively on CMM's CAF in completing their assessments and proposing new interventions. For Africa, in any case, the geographic bureau forged an effective partnership with the elements of DCHA in developing a broad-gauged approach to peace-building.

PEACE-BUILDING ISSUES FOR USAID

Veteran watchers of the agency may be excused for doubting the long-term commitment of USAID to peace-building. Over the past half century, development doctrines guiding the agency have changed rapidly with the intellectual and political currents sweeping through Washington. Technical assistance, infrastructure, and agriculture were mainstays of foreign aid in the 1950s and 1960s. The doctrine of "basic human needs" reigned during the Jimmy Carter years, as stimulating the private sector did during the Reagan era. More recently investment in education and health has held pride of place. It could be argued that USAID Administrator Atwood's emphasis on assisting transitions and Natsios's focus on conflict are only the latest development fashions, which will fade, as policymakers find new orthodoxies.

It would be rash to predict confidently that conflict will remain close to the center of USAID's attention in future administrations. However, a general bipartisan consensus exists today supporting use of the international affairs budget of the United States to buttress efforts to end conflict in states prone to political violence—especially those of particular interest to the United States. Although the Republicans were fierce critics of Clinton administration peace-building in the Balkans and the Democrats of the Bush administration's approach to Afghanistan and Iraq, there is general support for the idea that assistance can suitably be used for R&S purposes. This consensus was perhaps most apparent during the Bush administration in the SFRC, where successive chairmen of different parties—Senators Lugar and Biden—backed interagency efforts, under State Department leadership, to deal with conflict and post-conflict situations.[81] If this consensus holds, USAID, as the major civilian foreign assistance arm of the U.S. government, is likely to play an essential role.

The creation of a Director of Foreign Assistance, the integration of the USAID and State Department foreign operations budget under Function 150, and budgeting against strategic objectives were important, but incomplete, moves toward coherence in the foreign policy process. Within the F process, peace and security became a specific strategic objective, even though a somewhat amorphous one including stabilization, security reform, and post-conflict elections. Budgeting against other strategic objectives, such as governing justly and democratically and humanitarian assistance, also highlighted the broader conflict management agenda. However, Bush administration "presidential initiatives" in foreign assistance in HIV/AIDS (PEPFAR), malaria (PMI), and education (PEI) were excluded from the F, leaving the foreign assistance budget process unnecessarily fragmented. Moreover, since the Office of Management and Budget still budgets by agency, the transition to budgeting by strategic objectives for international affairs is still unrealized. These issues require the attention of the Obama administration.

There are voices calling for a reversal of the recent degree of integration of USAID into the State Department. They charge that it has distracted the U.S. government from dealing with the long-term needs of development in favor of short-term foreign policy fixes.[82] It is easy to sympathize with those who seek to shift the balance of resources somewhat more toward development and less toward security and the military. However, in the post-9/11 world, an appreciation for the security concerns of states in conflict will of necessity remain a concern, regardless of the party holding the White House. A reversal of the integration which has occurred on peace-building would be a mistake.

Consideration should be given to modest alterations in the architecture of USAID, as it relates to R&S. There are legitimate questions about the positions of CMM and OTI, given the creation of State's Coordinator for Reconstruction and Stabilization. This study has suggested in Chapter 4 that, if the basic concept of a Coordinator for Reconstruction and Stabilization is retained, S/CRS should be transformed into a truly interagency operation, largely composed of State and USAID officers. Under that scenario, does USAID really need an office of Conflict Management and Mitigation? CMM could logically be integrated into S/CRS, taking over the bulk of its conflict assessment, prevention, and at least part of its training functions. And, if an integrated S/CRS receives sufficient funding to create a permanent civilian expeditionary capacity, is there an independent role for OTI, USAID's existing expeditionary force in conflict situations? One option would be to make OTI the foundation of the Active Response Component of S/CRS's Civilian Response Corps. That would provide the Coordinator's Office with a seasoned and tested roster of specialists for deployment abroad on very short notice. The fit might be initially somewhat awkward. The CRC-A has exercised a primarily diplomatic liaison and reporting function, while OTI has taken on an "investment financing" role. However, a strengthened project initiation and management capacity would be desirable for S/CRS.

Otherwise, there appears little reason to tamper with the USAID architecture for the purposes of U.S. peacefare. DCHA's other offices can be left pretty much alone, since Democracy and Governance, Disaster Assistance, and Food for Peace function well within the current interagency process for dealing with conflict. USAID's geographic bureaus are cognizant of the importance of programming dealing with conflict situations and are already fully capable of effective interaction with the counterpart bureaus at State. If S/CRS becomes an integrated State/USAID office with the capacity for an expeditionary role, USAID's geographic bureaus will adapt to that reality, as circumstances dictate.

CHAPTER 7

BUILDING PEACE THROUGH KNOWLEDGE: THE U.S. INSTITUTE OF PEACE

> In recent years ... we have debated whether we should be a think tank or a "do tank". That is a false and dangerous choice.... We cannot, in my judgment, afford to make a choice between being a place of ideas, of research and education ... and a place with operational capacities to deliver programs and advisory services ... in conflict zones.
>
> —Chester A. Crocker[1]

It may seem curious to include the U.S. Institute of Peace (USIP) in this survey of U.S. government agencies involved in peace-building, stabilization, and reconstruction. It is not an agency of the executive branch of the federal government. It does not operate under the authority of a Cabinet officer or the President. It has by far the smallest budget. By law it is independent and nonpartisan. However, it is chartered by the U.S. Congress and responsible to it. It operates under an independent board of directors, most selected by the President. The vast majority of its budget is approved by Congress. It is also "national," incorporating "United States" in its title and designed to enhance federal government leadership "to expand and support the existing international peace and conflict resolution efforts of the nation."[2] Most casual observers of the institute probably consider it a U.S. government "think tank" for peace. That characterization is resisted by USIP staffers, who like to think of it as a "think and do tank" or even a "think, do, train and educate tank." In the mid-1990s, USIP moved decisively beyond being basically a repository and transmitter of knowledge to assume an increasingly large role in the U.S. government's approach to peace-building.

HISTORICAL BACKGROUND

The USIP grew out of the movement to create a federal peace agency, a time-honored objective of the American peace movement. During the late 1930s, as isolationism reached its height, Democratic Senator Matthew Neely of West Virginia introduced a bill to create a U.S. Department of Peace.[3] In the 1950s the nuclear balance of terror stimulated calls for alternative approaches and disarmament. A Joint Congressional Committee on a Just and Lasting Peace was created by the Democrats who ran Congress during that period, with some support from the Eisenhower administration. The Democrats in particular proposed creation of a U.S. peace agency. When Kennedy was elected, he attempted to respond to that proposal by creating the Arms Control and Disarmament Agency (ACDA). That was not really what the peace partisans had in mind, but Kennedy convinced them to go along. So ACDA was established in 1961, the third institutional foreign policy innovation of the Kennedy administration, alongside USAID and the Peace Corps. During the 36 years of its existence, ACDA played a foundational role in landmark agreements like the 1968 Nuclear Non-Proliferation Treaty, the 1972 Anti-Ballistic Missile Treaty, and the 1996 Comprehensive Test Ban Treaty, but many in the peace movement saw the agency as a hostage of the Departments of Defense and State.[4] ACDA was absorbed into the State Department in 1997.

The Vietnam War gave new impetus to the peace movement. In 1968 Sen. Vance Hartke (D-IN) cosponsored with Sen. Mark Hatfield (OR), a Republican moderate, a bill to create a Peace Department, which would incorporate USAID, ACDA, the Peace Corps, and a proposed International Peace Academy. The Nixon administration was unresponsive to the Congressional proposal, but President Carter was more sympathetic. The idea of a Peace Academy—rather than a new cabinet department—gained adherents.

The Congress created in 1978 a bipartisan Commission on Proposals for the National Academy of Peace and Conflict Resolution, chaired by Sen. Spark Matsunaga (D-HI). The Commission, which held hearings throughout the country, got behind the idea of "us[ing] both international and national peace-making and conflict resolution experiences in designing [the Academy's] education and training and information services programs." The Commission made the case that a government institution to study peace was needed to offset the war colleges, to legitimize peace studies, to increase American public awareness of that field, and to burnish the peaceable image of the United States.[5] A key question was how to assure the political independence of such a government agency. A basic compromise was reached: USIP would be independent but would have no policymaking role. In fact, it would not be in the business of policy advocacy. Moreover, it would be governed by a bipartisan board of directors: 12 members from outside the federal government appointed by the President and confirmed by the Senate, plus four *ex officio* members—the Secretary of State, the Secretary of Defense, the president of the National Defense University, and the USIP President (non-voting).[6] No more than 8, of a total of 15 voting members, could come from the same political party.

The Reagan administration opposed legislation to create the Academy, but the hard-driving and persistent Matsunaga managed to slip it into the 1984 Defense Authorization Bill, which President Reagan was reluctant to veto. In the final negotiations to eliminate the differences between the two Houses, the Congress agreed to drop the "academy" nomenclature in favor of "institute." Reagan, in the end, reportedly agreed with advisors who urged him to appoint strong members to the board and thus shape the new institution from the outset.[7] Even so, the Reagan administration signaled its displeasure by holding back $6 million of the $10 million initially appropriated.[8] The institute opened its doors in 1986.

SEEDING THE FIELD

The mandate of the institute, as provided by law, is to "support the development, transmission, and use of knowledge to promote peace and curb violent international conflict." In short, USIP builds "peace through knowledge."[9] Given the initial suspicion, if not hostility, of the Reagan administration, the institute initially interpreted its mandate cautiously, with a focus on expanding knowledge about promoting peace. The board's first project was "an intellectual map of the international peace studies field," completed in 1990.

More broadly, the institute gave priority to "seeding the field"—launching a fellowship program to stimulate research with an operational application, and publishing the product of scholars, both of those in academia and think tanks and then increasingly of those in-house. The Jennings Randolph Fellowship Program, rooted in the institute's charter, annually selects 10–12 scholars, policymakers, journalists, and other professionals for senior residential fellowships. There are no citizenship requirements. The selection committee focuses on "people with good ideas." A majority of the fellowships relate to current institute priorities. However, the selection of candidates with topics outside those priorities helps incubate new ideas which could generate future shifts in USIP priorities. Through its Peace Scholar program, USIP supports graduate students from U.S. universities writing dissertations in fields of special interest to the institute. Competition is stiff; only 5–7 percent of applicants receive an award. By means of its Web site and e-mail service, USIP offers government, NGOs, other think tanks, and the interested public a heavy schedule of speakers and symposia, presenting the findings and views of its fellows and other distinguished practitioners and scholars from around the world.

USIP's founding legislation requires it to use at least one quarter of its appropriated budget to make grants to nonprofits for applied research in peace and conflict resolution or to enhance education, including public education, in the field. The institute has made more than 1,750 grants since its inception. These are basically divided between "solicited" grants on subjects of current strong interest to USIP and "unsolicited" grants for especially good ideas that are not particularly topical. Since 2006 the institute has sharpened the focus of solicited grants on "top priority" countries for which new ideas and approaches are in great demand, such as Colombia, Iran, Nigeria, and Sudan.[10] In addition, USIP received $2 million during the 2006–2008 period from the State Department budget to fund solicited grants related to Iraq and Afghanistan.

The obverse of its fellowship and grant programs has been an increasingly ambitious program of publication of the work of its staff, fellows, and grantees. USIP has published about 150 books since 1990, including as many as 20 titles annually in recent years. Particularly prominent are the compendia of best writings in the peace and conflict resolution field—*Leashing the Dogs of War* (2007) or *Taming Intractable Conflicts: Mediation in the Hardest Cases.*[11] The compendia are both an effort to define the field and handbooks of best practices—what seems to work in conflict resolution. They are now widely used in university courses in conflict resolution and peace studies around the United States. The institute has produced three volumes of lessons learned from institute projects in its *Advances in Understanding International Peacemaking* series. Other major publishing tools for conveying knowledge of the field are the special report, 16–20 pages in length, published in hard copy but available on the Web site, and shorter peace briefings available only on the Web. The special report often details the results of a symposium of experts on a particular topic. Many of the reports focus on particular conflicts, especially the "priority" conflicts formally adopted by its major centers. There are also numerous reports on more general topics: peacemaking and peacekeeping, rule of law, religion and conflict, including many studies relating to Islam. USIP publishes the work of both practitioners and scholars, but tends to emphasize experience in the field, underlining its action orientation. This practical academic approach laid a solid and recognized academic foundation for its work.

By the beginning of the 1990s the USIP had largely overcome the reservations of Republican conservatives. Under the chairmanship (1985–93) of Professor John Norton Moore, one of America's leading authorities on international law, and the presidency (1987–93) of Samuel W. Lewis, U.S. Ambassador to Israel under the Carter and Reagan administrations and a former Assistant Secretary of State for International Organization Affairs, USIP gained credibility with the Congress. There was growing recognition on both sides of the aisle that the research done by the institute might provide some guidance for the uncertainties of the post–Cold War world, a world in which violent political conflict seemed to be springing up all over. USIP enjoyed stability and increased prominence under a second generation of leaders—Chester A. Crocker as Chair (1992–2004) and Richard H. Solomon as

President (1993–present). Through the end of the 1980s the Congressional appropriation for USIP remained $10 million a year but rose to $15 million for FY 1992. Nevertheless, there was concern in the organization during the mid-1990s that it might be targeted for elimination in the wake of the Contract with America adopted by Congressional Republicans for the 1994 Congressional elections. USIP was small and collegial, working in essentially "niche" areas. It maintained a low profile on Capitol Hill and in Washington in general.[12]

As it entered its third decade, USIP had become an important player in conflict management within the U.S. government. It had launched training and post-conflict activities in "zones of conflict" around the world, including those of major concern to the executive branch, first in the Balkans and then in Afghanistan and Iraq. Budget constraints eased further with expanded activity. The FY 2008 appropriation was $25 million. The institute's enhanced prestige was demonstrated dramatically in 2004, when Congress appropriated $100 million for a distinctive new building, scheduled to open in 2010 on one of the last available sites on the National Mall.

CURRENT MISSION AND GOALS

The current goals of USIP, reflecting its evolution over two decades, are framed more on behalf of an activist mode of conflict management and somewhat less for knowledge generation and transmission. The institute aims today to help the United States meet the challenge of managing conflict in a world of fragile states, ethnic and religious conflict, extremism, competition for scarce resources, and the proliferation of weapons of mass destruction. Specifically, its goals are "to help

1. Prevent and resolve violent international conflicts
2. Promote post-conflict stability and development
3. Increase conflict management capacity, tools, and intellectual capital worldwide."

At the end of 2005 USIP was reorganized to place primary emphasis on the work of three centers: Conflict Analysis & Prevention, Mediation and Conflict Resolution, and Post-Conflict Peace & Stability Operations. The concept behind the change was to concentrate on the three separate phases of the "conflict life-cycle"—pre-conflict, conflict, and post-conflict—so as to apply or adapt the tools at hand more precisely to the goals of those different phases. The reorganization was also policy-related. The institute considers a key element in its mission working actively to support policymakers by mobilizing the best talent from around the globe and by providing creative options to prevent, manage, and resolve international conflicts. It tries to create a bridge between policymakers and leading experts from academia and the private and nonprofit sectors. The reorganization left in place "cross-cutting programs," including grants and fellowships, education and training, and several "centers of innovation," loosely affiliated with the primary centers. The latter include the Religion and Peacemaking program, associated with the Center for Mediation and Conflict Resolution, and the Rule of Law program, associated with the Post-Conflict Center.[13]

Each of the three major centers has the lead role for a separate set of "priority conflicts"—a list which varies somewhat from year to year. The purpose of those assignments is to focus strategies and associated projects on the results being sought, while promoting a balanced investment across the three phases. USIP managers hope that such an allocation will avoid spreading resources too thin, by discouraging one or more centers from taking on too many conflicts.[14] However, recognizing that precise lines between the phases of conflict cannot be drawn, the center which takes the lead is charged with creating a team for each priority conflict, drawing on the other centers and divisions of USIP. For example, a team for Lebanon was led by the Center for Conflict Analysis and Prevention but included experts from other USIP centers, plus representatives of other government agencies, think tanks, universities, and Congressional staff. The team process is highly flexible; each team is *ad hoc* in its operation and its use of staff.

Because it is mainly through the work of the three major centers that USIP intersects with the U.S. government interagency process, most of the remainder of this chapter will be devoted to their work.

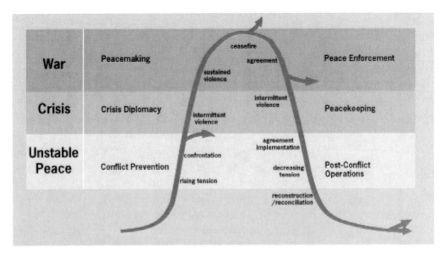

Figure 7.1
The Cycle of Violent Conflict—the USIP Paradigm. From *Preventing Violent Conflicts*, Copyright © 1996 by the endowment of the United States Institute of Peace. Reprinted with permission by the United States Institute of Peace, Washington D.C.

PROGRAMS

1. Center for Conflict Analysis and Prevention (CAP)

The Center for Conflict and Analysis was created from the Office of Research and Studies, led by Paul B. Stares, who had been Director for Research and Studies. Stares was an important advocate of the 2006 reorganization based on segments of the life cycle of conflict. However, the conversion of his research shop into a conflict prevention center proved problematic. How do you transform conflict analysts into prevention specialists? To avoid too wrenching a transformation, the Center incorporated the term "analysis" and added "prevention," seeking to create a synthesis between the research and conflict prevention functions. Stares hired a specialist in early warning and genocide to help marry general strategies for conflict prevention with the region-specific expertise of program officers.[15] Drawing on the expertise of the existing analysts, CAP selected areas of the world it wished to specialize in: South Asia, the Middle East, northeast Asia, and Africa.[16] In 2008, CAP's "Tier 1" conflicts were Iraq and its neighbors, Iran, Pakistan, and the Korean Peninsula. Lebanon and Zimbabwe constituted "Tier 2" conflicts.

The work of synthesizing regional expertise with strategies for conflict prevention had not advanced very far by 2008. The area specialists have tended to continue working on conflict analysis in their regions, rather than giving priority to conflict prevention as a USIP activity, although some have successfully reoriented their work toward more explicit prevention objectives.[17] Stares departed in 2007, and his replacement, Abiodun Williams, did not arrive until mid-2008. Williams, a former Director for Strategic Planning for UN Secretary-General Kofi Annan and a veteran of the UN's Preventive Deployment Force in Macedonia, secured approval of a strategic framework for conflict prevention to lay the groundwork for a more operational center.[18]

Much of CAP's policy-related work is carried out under special projects: the Muslim World Initiative (MWI), the Iraq and its Neighbors Project, and the Genocide Prevention Task Force.

The MWI was launched after September 11, 2001 to deal with the "vital foreign policy and national security challenges associated with the Muslim world." Its objectives were to enhance American engagement by informing policy and promoting public education, while promoting peace and stability in the Muslim world by "mobilizing the moderates" and "marginalizing the militants."[19] The MWI spawned working groups on Syria, Lebanon, and Iran, all of which produced written reports. Those on democracy and Islam have attracted particular attention, and those from the Syria Working Group have provided input for the U.S. policy process.[20] At the end of 2008, the MWI was focusing less attention on the moderate/militant split to aim more broadly at security and reform—how to promote democratic change without destabilizing those countries undertaking it.[21]

A subproject on Political Oppositions in the Arab World examined the reasons for opposition weakness and fragmentation in Egypt, Jordan, Morocco, and Yemen. The objective was to assess the efficacy of U.S. democracy promotion in those states where there are active, legal Islamist parties. That project in turn generated a series of dialogues in Cairo in 2008 for the *wasat* (middle) generation of younger Arab political leaders, generally more reform-minded than the traditional Islamist opposition. The dialogues included participants from State and USAID, plus the International Republican Institute and the National Democratic Institute—two U.S. government democracy-promotion organizations.[22]

An MWI Study Group on Reform and Security in the Muslim World, launched in early 2008, examined how the United States could support political reform in a group of key Muslim countries without compromising its security interests. The Study Group has produced a series of country memoranda on Pakistan, Palestine, Jordan, Egypt, the Gulf states, and the Maghreb with specific policy recommendations.

The work of the initiative was initially guided in part by an Advisory Committee on U.S.-Muslim World Relations. The Committee was made up of Muslims who are American citizens, most of whom originated in the Arab world, Iran, and South Asia. The group met with Secretary of State Rice and other senior policy officials, expressing their perspectives and concerns as Muslim Americans connected with their lands of origin. However, the Committee did not have the impact anticipated. Its original chair, Abdeslam M. Maghraoui, a Moroccan-American nonprofit leader and former professor at Princeton, had a more academic than policy orientation. After his departure in early 2007, the Committee quietly died. However, its shortcomings have not been a significant drag on MWI's busy agenda.

The "Iraq and its Neighbors Project" was an effort initiated in 2004, when USIP established a working group of experts. It was variously described as Track 2 diplomacy (unofficial private conversations) or "Track 1½"—signifying officials and nonofficials meeting in their private capacities. "Iraq and its Neighbors" was conceived as operating in parallel with a Track 1 series of Expanded Neighbors Conferences started in 2004. The Expanded Neighbors Conferences brought official representatives of Middle East governments together with Security Council Permanent Five/Group of 8 officials to promote Iraqi and regional stability.[23] The USIP project generated a series of individual reports on Iraqi bilateral relations with Turkey, Iran, Saudi Arabia, and Jordan. A major milestone was a meeting in Istanbul in March 2007, which USIP cohosted with a Turkish think tank, bringing together 50 high-level foreign policy and national security officials from seven countries.[24] On the basis of a wide-ranging nonofficial dialogue, the participants issued a declaration detailing some 29 recommendations on stabilizing the region. They included specific proposals to the United States: improve relations with Syria and Iran, "commit to a comprehensive strategy for a responsible withdrawal" from

Iraq, reiterate that it seeks no permanent military bases there, and keep future forces in country only if requested by Iraq.[25]

Another major policy-oriented Center activity in 2007–2008 was the Genocide Prevention Task Force, cosponsored with the Holocaust Museum in Washington D.C. and the Academy of Diplomacy. Chaired by former Secretary of State Madeleine Albright and former Defense Secretary William Cohen, the project involved extensive interviewing not only of current and previous U.S. officials but selected experts from different regions of the world.[26] The Task Force proposed an early warning system, a high-level interagency Atrocities Prevention Committee to prepare genocide prevention and response plans for high-risk situations, and a diplomatic initiative to create an international network for information sharing and coordinated action.[27]

Less successful was CAP's Iran Policy Forum begun in January 2007. The objective was to use USIP's convoking function to bring into being an off-record forum of policymakers and nongovernment experts in Iran with the hope of influencing the administration. Prof. Vali R. Nasr, an Iranian-born academic and expert on Shi'ite Islam, and Suzanne Maloney, then a member of the State Department's Policy Planning Staff and later at the Brookings Institution, were asked to cochair. After several positive meetings, the Forum experienced difficulty in attracting policymakers with heft. Nasr resigned and the Forum quietly waned, although it remained on the USIP Web site. An exchange program between U.S. and Iranian religious leaders was established in 2005 under the auspices of the program of Religion and Peacemaking (see below).

Thus far, CAP has exerted a modicum of influence on U.S. interagency policy, more through its particular projects than through its more general research on conflict prevention. Perhaps its most important structural interaction with the bureaucracy to this point was through the ICAF working group, cochaired by State S/CRS and USAID's Office of Conflict Management & Mitigation. (See Chapters 4 and 6.) CAP had two representatives on that working group, which also included representatives of the OSD, the Army Corps of Engineers, JFCOM, PKSOI at the Army War College, USAID's OFDA, and the National Intelligence Council. The framework document was approved by the NSC in 2008.

2. Center for Mediation and Conflict Resolution (CMCR)

CMCR, led by veteran USIP staffer and Vice President David Smock, is the smallest of the three major centers but has responsibility for the largest number of priority conflicts and has been growing steadily. Its mission is to address current conflicts—with particular attention to its "priority" conflicts—and extract lessons from them to be applied more generically to future conflicts that may arise. It also seeks to fit certain kinds of general practical initiatives to individual conflicts. For example, what are the steps required to set up a mediation requested by the parties? What measures are required to bring a cease-fire into effect? How do you establish a "friends of" group, a set of governments and international organizations which will take responsibility for pushing forward a peace process in a single country? CMCR is in the process of publishing a series of handbooks on each of these mechanisms, as a kind of "peacemaker's toolkit."[28]

CMCR projects come from a variety of external and internal sources. In 2008 the Center's Tier 1 conflicts were Nigeria, Darfur, Colombia, and Israel/Palestine, with Tier 2 embracing Kashmir, Nepal, Northern Uganda, and Sri Lanka. On Nigeria, CMCR has focused on the Niger Delta and conflict between Christians and Muslims. Initially David Smock viewed the Delta project as one in which USIP might advise and assist the oil companies active there to find ways to improve their footprint and thereby avoid exacerbating the high tension in the region. The project evolved into one of partnerships between Chevron Nigeria and eight clusters of Delta community organizations. State governments are signatory to memoranda of understanding with the clusters running for three years. A regional development council was established for each cluster to make decisions about spending the development funds provided to the communities by Chevron's joint venture with the Nigerian National Petroleum Company. Working with the Africa Center for Corporate Responsibility, a Nigerian NGO, USIP has provided funding, training, and general guidance in support of the process.

In the case of Sudan, USIP assigned CMCR lead responsibility for Darfur, where conflict is raging, while the Center for Post-Conflict Peace and Stability Operations (PCP&SO) works on the follow-up to the 2005 CPA between North and South. A 2008 project emerged from a request from the African Union, which in 2004 assumed responsibility for sponsoring negotiations between Khartoum and the Darfur rebels. A frustrating problem for the negotiators has been the increasing fragmentation of the Darfur rebellion and its leaders.[29] The AU requested that USIP convoke a conclave of different elements of the Darfur diaspora as an approach to arriving at a common rebel agenda for negotiations. The Conference brought to Washington in 2007 about 30 Darfurians resident in the United States and Canada. The project was a modest initial effort to contribute to the evolution of a common Darfur insurgent negotiating position.

On Kashmir, USIP pursued an approach to conflict resolution de-emphasizing the importance of borders, a flash point for war between Pakistan and India. Both governments were receptive to this idea, but dialogue about specific implementation steps had been lacking. USIP partners were the Pugwash Council, which sponsored a series of Track II conferences on Kashmir in the region, and the Institute for Peace & Conflict Studies, a New Delhi think tank. USIP enlisted the services of a prestigious former senior civil servant on both the Indian and the Pakistani sides to be the primary advocates with their governments. They authored a paper presented to both governments. The sensitivity of U.S. involvement in Kashmir induced USIP to downplay its role. By mutual agreement the version of the project report published in India by the Institute for Peace & Conflict Studies did not refer to USIP.[30]

Complications relating to the experts of individual staffers and their location within USIP can lead to organizational contortions in carrying out projects related to conflict priorities. For example, in 2008 USIP published Daniel Kurtzer and Scott Lasensky's *Negotiating Arab and Israel Peace*, a major analysis of Israeli-Palestinian negotiations since 1988, which offers lessons learned for the future. Scott Lasensky has been affiliated with the CAP, and the project has been largely funded by CAP. However, since Israel-Palestine is an ongoing conflict, the project fell under CMCR. The CMCR Director set the guidelines for the advisory board and provided suggestions on who should be interviewed for the project, in addition to making suggestions on the manuscript. Although CMCR has the leadership on Colombia, there are no experts on Latin America in the Center. So the Colombia team leader has been an expert whose primary assignment was with USIP's fellowship division.

RELIGION AND PEACEMAKING PROGRAM

Before the creation of CMCR, David Smock was in charge of the Religion and Peacemaking Program, now one of the "Centers of Innovation." Religion has been a significant concern of USIP from its inception, but most of the early analysis focused on the role of religion as a motivator for violence in "identity-based" conflicts. For example, the insistence by government leadership in Khartoum on Islam as a marker of Sudanese nationalism was a key factor in the Southern revolt, just as the Buddhist identity of the Sinhalese majority in Sri Lanka was a factor in the Tamil (Hindu) rebellion. Smock took a different approach, when he assumed charge of the program in 2000. Drawing in part on the work of Douglas Johnston and the International Council for Religion and Diplomacy, Smock shifted the focus to engaging religious leaders in promoting reconciliation between parties divided by religion. The program tries to make contact with local clergy and religious communities as the basis for organizing its work.[31]

There have been significant projects with Israel-Palestine and in Sudan, Nigeria, and Sri Lanka—all exercises in Track II diplomacy. When the Oslo process for peace between Israel and Palestine broke down, one lesson drawn was that religious leaders had not been included, did not view themselves as stakeholders in the process, and therefore did not support it. Some became spoilers. More than a dozen Jewish, Muslim, and Christian religious leaders from both Israel and Palestine were convened in Alexandria, Egypt in 2002 to discuss the conflict and try their hands at drawing up mutually agreeable texts, particularly on the issue of sacred space—the status of Jerusalem and shrines sacred to the three Abrahamic traditions. They issued a joint declaration pledging to work together for a just and lasting peace. The "Alexandria process" was supposed to mirror the political negotiations. A group of the clerics represented in the process came to the United States in late 2007 and met with Secretary of State Rice, then laboring to set up the negotiations initiated by the meeting of Prime Ministers Olmert and Abbas in Annapolis, Maryland. Nevertheless, the Alexandria group largely remained on the sidelines, although CMCR continued to support its efforts.[32] In Nigeria the program brought together a duo of former radicals—one Muslim, one Christian —previously in the forefront of religious violence, who together began mediating local religious disputes. In Sudan, the Religion and Peacemaking Program has collaborated with the World Council for Religions of Peace, headquartered at United Nations Plaza in New York, and with the Washington-based International Center for Religion and Diplomacy in creating and funding the Sudanese Inter-Religious Council (IRC) and its Committee to Protect Religious Freedom. The IRC has engaged Muslim and Christian leaders in support of the CPA between North and South and the Darfur peace effort.

CMCR has relatively little engagement with the U.S. interagency process. That is mainly because of its heavy involvement in Track II diplomacy. David Smock indicates that only about 5 percent of his time has been spent on working with State and USAID and virtually none with DOD. Work on Darfur has generated some sensitive Track I issues. The Darfur Diaspora Project, a Track II activity aimed ultimately at supporting the Track I negotiation between rebel leaders and Khartoum, led to a State Department request that a signatory to the DPA, now a government official, attend the meeting. USIP demurred because of the gathering's Track II nature but agreed to facilitate his meeting with diaspora representatives subsequently. When the AU later asked USIP to train Darfur rebel leaders, USIP was required to inform the State Department because it is legally required to obtain State Department blessing when it moves into the arena of Track I diplomacy.

The Center has had minimal collaboration with S/CRS. CMCR's responsibility for ongoing conflict does not naturally align it with S/CRS activity, which is organizationally divided between conflict prevention and post-conflict reconstruction. Alignment may be more comfortable with USAID, which sometimes gets involved in activities aimed at dampening ongoing conflicts.[33] USIP has approached USAID's Conflict Mitigation and Management office to explore coordination of projects in Nigeria's Niger Delta, but nothing had materialized as of mid-2008. USAID has been working there to strengthen the capacity of local organizations to mediate resource-based disputes and to introduce early warning and conflict prevention networks.[34]

USIP AS QUASI-GOVERNMENT AGENCY: THE PHILIPPINE FACILITATION PROJECT

An important exception to the institute's disengagement from the interagency process in ongoing conflicts was the Philippine Facilitation Project

WHITE HOUSE INTEREST IN RELIGION AND PEACEMAKING

After David R. Smock graduated from Oberlin College, he wanted to do grass-roots economic development in Africa. He completed a doctorate in anthropology at Cornell and spent 16 years working for the Ford Foundation in Ghana, Kenya, Nigeria, and Lebanon. In 1982 he enrolled at New York Theological Seminary, attending night classes. After graduation he was ordained in the United Church of Christ and worked three years as Executive Associate to the president of the United Church of Christ. When he joined USIP in 1990, his efficiency, quiet competence, and prolific writing soon moved him from program officer in the grants division to Director of the Grant Program and Coordinator for USIP's Africa program.[35] In 2000 he became director of the Religion and Peacemaking Program. In the 2006 reorganization, Smock retained that portfolio but became Vice President and Director of the CMCR.

On May 30, 2007, he was invited to the Oval Office with five other academics. Each was asked to speak for 10 minutes. Smock spoke about USIP's work in several zones of conflict encouraging "enemies" to talk to each other. President Bush asked him if the United States should be talking to Iraqi religious and militia leader Muqtada al-Sadr. Smock noted that although religious leaders can sometimes exacerbate conflict, his program's work in bringing together religious leaders in Israel and Palestine, Sudan, and Nigeria has helped promote reconciliation. Smock described Bush as "very engaged" in the conversation. Vice President Cheney took notes but did not speak.

(PFP; 2003–2007).[36] That was USIP's effort to contribute to a peaceful settlement between the Philippine government and Moro Islamic Liberation Front (MILF) dissidents on the island of Mindanao. In January 2003, MILF Chairman Salamat Hashim wrote to President Bush requesting U.S. assistance in resolving the conflict between the Philippine government and the Moro people. When Washington indicated a willingness to assist, if the MILF formally disavowed a connection with Islamic terrorism, the MILF issued a statement denouncing terrorism. The State Department, still unsure of the solidity of the MILF commitment, sought USIP involvement as a "facilitator" of the peace process. Since 2001 the Malaysian government had been the official mediator between Manila and the MILF, and in July 2003, under Kuala Lumpur's auspices, a cease-fire agreement was signed by Manila and the MILF as a step toward a more comprehensive accord. Since USIP is not an official executive branch agency, "facilitation" underlined that the United States was not becoming a mediator. Instead, USIP's role would be to support the Malaysian government. USIP was also asked to monitor the official negotiations closely in order to assist the U.S. government in determining whether to provide assistance during the implementation phase of any agreement reached. The Congress set aside $3 million to support USIP's administrative expenses.[37]

USIP responsibilities were set forth in a "scope of work" with the State Department. The USIP project leadership was to communicate with the representatives of the Philippine government and the MILF, coordinate directly with the Government of Malaysia, staff a secretariat for the negotiation process, and facilitate "unofficial meetings, negotiation training, and study trips." The PFP was to report to and coordinate with State's EAP bureau. If an agreement resulted, USIP would be available to assist in its implementation; if there was no meaningful progress, the institute would advise the U.S. government "when to withdraw its support of the process." In the scope of work, the State Department agreed to "delegate substantial discretion" to USIP in carrying out its tasks, in recognition of its expertise and independence.

USIP President Solomon, a former ambassador to Manila, hired G. Eugene Martin, a retired Foreign Service Officer who had been deputy chief of mission in Manila, to run the project. Solomon also convened an advisory committee of senior former diplomats.[38] An initial problem was the suspicion of the Philippine military, which in turn caused the political leadership in Manila to hesitate. USIP had trouble getting access to senior leaders to get the project launched. EAP concluded it was desirable to demonstrate White House support for the project. With the assistance of the NSC staff, it orchestrated a meeting of the Deputies Committee, which endorsed the project.[39] Project Director Martin then proceeded to Manila for meetings with President Macapagal-Arroyo, military and political leaders, and civil society, before going to Mindanao for meetings with the MILF leaders, local government officials, and local NGOs.

Project Director Martin initially enjoyed close and complementary working relationships with the embassy, particularly with Ambassador Francis J. Ricciardone, a strong backer of the project. In fact, since Martin was accompanied by the ambassador and embassy officers during initial calls in Manila, the impression was created among some Filipinos that USIP was part of the State Department. A similar confusion about the project's independence from the embassy was created in Mindanao. That early close tie was an advantage because the embassy encouraged the Philippine government to take the peace process seriously, but Martin found it expedient to distance the project somewhat from the embassy embrace as time passed. Project officials established good working ties with the initial Philippine negotiating team and with most Mindanao leaders. These relationships with Americans and with the parties helped the PFP weather a major problem, namely the unwillingness of the Malaysian government to permit PFP representatives observer status in the formal talks.

Ultimately, the PFP did not succeed in "facilitating" a final agreement between Manila and the MILF, although the cease-fire remained in place, at least until late 2008. The basic reasons lay with the parties to the conflict. The Philippine government, facing opposition from Roman Catholic groups and certain Mindanao landowners, failed to muster the political will to make the accommodations necessary for a political settlement. A 2006 offer of self-determination by Manila was not pursued to a conclusion. Moro leaders were ethnically divided and had difficulty arriving at a common agenda.

The project also suffered, however, because PFP lost embassy support when a new ambassador arrived. Complaints were voiced that PFP was not "part of the country team." Embassy officials started meeting with MILF representatives, and USAID began planning development activities in Mindanao directly with the semiofficial Bangsamoro Development Agency, controlled by the MILF. USIP therefore gradually lost its intermediary role with Moro leaders. The embassy intimated to Martin that the project did not offer "value added." One embassy officer told him that the formal peace process (USIP's focus) was not "the most critical element in future stability in Mindanao."[40] The new view in the embassy was that economic development leading to prosperity was the key to stability.

In June 2007, the project was terminated when the project exhausted its funding. USIP President Solomon and some on the PFP advisory committee spoke with senior officials in the State Department in an effort to get new money, but the panel concluded that if the administration was not solidly behind it, the project should not continue. The EAP front office had also turned over, and its new leadership indicated it would not contest the ambassador's view that the project was no longer necessary.[41]

USIP believes that the PFP was well managed and accomplished important peace-building tasks: on the issue of "ancestral domain," Moro demands for additional territory to constitute a homeland, USIP's workshops, which brought in participants from other "homeland" negotiations (e.g., Bougainville, Inuit, and Native American), provided concepts and approaches which could be useful eventually in resolving the question; PFP public education programs helped sensitize Christian Filipinos to issues of equity and nondiscrimination; the PFP helped to strengthen inter-Moro communication, especially through dialogues with young Moro leaders.[42] The final report also argued that PFP work emphasis on the historical and social basis for the conflict helped to counter public perceptions in Mindanao that the United States was solely concerned with counterterrorism and not with the legitimate grievances of the Muslim peoples of the southern Philippines.[43]

Despite its potential contributions to an eventual settlement, the unfinished PFP can be characterized as a missed opportunity. In 2008 the MILF and the Philippine government reached a draft agreement on ancestral domain.[44] Before the agreement could be signed, Mindanao Christian opponents of the agreement and their allies challenged its constitutionality. In response to a temporary restraining order, the Philippine government broke off negotiations. A Supreme Court finding of unconstitutionality led within a few months to an upsurge in the fighting.[45] Continued use by the U.S. government of the independent USIP to push forward the peace process with Manila in the intervening year would have been a modest investment with negligible downside risk that could have paid off in stabilizing an unstable area of the globe and in garnering for the United States some additional credit in the Muslim world.[46] The project was promoting a broad-based consultation of stakeholders, including Christian groups, which might have paid off in the meantime, but was halted with USIP departure. Moreover, the embassy's view that economic incentives could solve the Moro problem, festering since colonial times, appears shortsighted. Those involved in the project argue that the conflict is at base political, rather than economic, and requires a political solution. The body of knowledge assembled by USIP over the past two decades strongly suggests that best results in peace-building emerge from a comprehensive approach in which economic incentives are only one element.

3. Center for Post-Conflict Peace and Stability Operations (PCP&SO)

The largest of the centers, Post-Conflict Peace and Stability Operations is also the most integrated into the U.S. interagency process. That reflects both the recent emphasis in executive branch peace-building—the transformation from conflict to stability and reconstruction—and deliberate action on the part of the institute. Daniel Serwer, Vice President and Director of the Center, recalls that when he came to USIP to work on the Balkans, the institute was basically publishing books and doing education and training. Serwer believed that USIP should also become operational in conflict zones. Such work had already started on a small scale in the Balkans. Serwer became Director of USIP's Balkans Initiative and then Director of Peace & Stability Operations. Involvement in Afghanistan and Iraq followed. PCP&SO was formally created as a Center in 2005 and provided the "think and do tank" model for the reorganization of the same year. Despite its many activities in "zones of conflict," PCP&SO remains grounded in the concept of "peace through knowledge." A senior program officer described its mission:

To do cutting edge research, analysis and writing that helps establish the intellectual capital to improve performance in peace and stability operations, to bring that work to a wider audience, and help apply it on the ground.[47]

In 2008 the Center's priority conflicts were Iraq, Afghanistan, and Sudan (North-South conflict), while its Tier 2 conflicts included Kosovo/Serbia, Liberia, Haiti, and Congo-Kinshasa. That work kept busy seven program officers, three program specialists, four program assistants, and assorted contractors, plus graduate students doubling as research assistants.

The initial pattern for "zones of conflict" was established through USIP's Balkans Initiative, which began in Bosnia after the 1996 Dayton Accords and then expanded into Kosovo, Montenegro, Serbia, and Macedonia. USIP helped eight Bosnian political parties craft a new constitution, assisted with the creation of a Bosnian truth commission, and helped start an interreligious council of Orthodox, Catholic, and Muslim leaders. It provided a grant for a Serbian NGO called the Center for Free Election and Democracy, which has done workshops for political activists all over the country. It supported the Management Center in Belgrade, which offered training courses for judges, prosecutors, and police. USIP's operations in

Kosovo included training leaders on both sides of the failed final status talks, plus courses for professional organizations and municipal officials. USIP projects were part of a panoply of government, international organization, and NGO activities in the Balkans, which in the aggregate contributed significantly to R&S.

USIP surprisingly passed up an initial opportunity to work on peacebuilding in Afghanistan in late 2001.[48] However, in 2004 the institute put together an Afghanistan Working Group initially headed by Prof. Barnett Rubin, a leading American expert on the country. The Working Group, intended as the coordination place for government agencies and nongovernment elements involved in Afghanistan, has worked with both policymakers and members of Congress in promoting understanding of Afghanistan and how the task of peace-building might be promoted more effectively. USIP has concentrated on rule of law issues, with emphasis on schools and higher education. The Center has also completed for the State Department a comprehensive map of security assistance programs in Afghanistan, looking for

DANIEL SERWER PROPOSES A "DO TANK"

After completing a PhD at Princeton, Daniel Serwer did a stint at the United Nations and then joined the Foreign Service. He moved through the ranks in European affairs, eventually becoming deputy chief of mission at the U.S. Embassy in Rome. During that assignment he became fascinated with the Balkan crisis unfolding to the east. In 1994 Richard Holbrooke, Assistant Secretary of State for European Affairs and later chief architect of the Dayton Accords, appointed him Special Envoy and Coordinator for the Bosnian Federation 1994–96. His responsibility was mediating between Croats and Muslims. He notes sardonically that he went to Bosnia, the first place he ever heard shots fired in anger, without an iota of training in peace-building. He, nevertheless, played a key role in negotiating the first agreement reached at Dayton. In late 1997, he was approaching the time-in-class deadline for his minister-counselor rank.[49] He told the European Bureau he wanted to work on Kosovo, but the bureaucracy declined to find him a temporary slot before his retirement. He was told that putting a senior officer in such a position would draw too much attention to that conflict. At his request, he was seconded to USIP as a senior fellow.

Serwer became Director of USIP's Balkans Initiative and within two years a quarter of the institute's budget was devoted to the area. Drawing on his Balkans experience, Serwer suggested at a 1999 USIP staff retreat, along with several colleagues, that not only should USIP write about peace-building, it should start "doing" it. Serwer proposed that USIP create a "do tank," operating alongside the think tank. A year later the USIP Board endorsed the approach, calling for the organization to expand its operations outside the Balkans.[50] Serwer was promoted to Vice President for Peace and Stability Operations, and his office became the model for the 2005 reorganization which established three major "do" centers as the core of USIP.

threats, gaps, and redundancies. The document provided input for the incoming Obama administration.

USIP has been engaged in Iraq since 2004, focusing on building relationships among Iraqis across sectarian lines and strengthening the rule of law. It initially trained more than 30 "facilitators" who have since mediated local conflicts and established their own training programs. Concluding that the facilitators succeeded in reducing violence in some areas, USIP undertook to train an additional 100. Working in violence-torn Mahmoudiya District south of Baghdad, a mixed Sunni-Shi'ite area sometimes referred to as the "Triangle of Death," PCP&SO convened a facilitator-led conference of tribal sheikhs, who agreed on a set of goals to improve security and quality of life. One sign of progress was an announcement in 2008 that Sunni sheikhs had agreed to rebuild a Shi'ite mosque destroyed by violence. A special peacebuilding initiative was piloted in oil-rich and heavily contested Kirkuk District, bringing together Kurd, Arab, Turcoman, and Assyrian Christian leaders. The 36 participants, drawn from religion, business, politics, journalism, and civil society, decided on a variety of community projects now underway.

What is the impact of PCP&SO on the U.S. government's peace-building work?

State/USAID. Daniel Serwer claims the institute was "directly instrumental" in the creation of the S/CRS. One strand in the rope of causality that led to S/CRS was a USIP report on reestablishing the rule of law in conflict situations. The report recommended that a post-conflict office be created at the State Department, to include a civilian reserve for creating "rule of law operations" in the aftermath of an international military intervention.[51] S/CRS founding Coordinator Carlos Pascual came to USIP at the outset for help in putting together a strategic framework, and a close partnership was forged. USIP convened a meeting of former special representatives of the Secretary-General to draw up for the new State office a set of lessons for future post-conflict operations that would avoid the mistakes of Iraq.[52] PCP&SO assigned a senior program officer to be USIP's major link to the interagency process. She and a number of others spent much of their time working with senior S/CRS staff. The most intensive period came at the beginning, lasting until the promulgation in late 2005 by the White House of NSPD 44, which set forth the guidelines for interagency cooperation under State Department and S/CRS leadership.[53] Since that formative period, the relationship remains strong and cordial, if less intimate.

To carry out its work in "zones of conflict" the Post-Conflict Center has developed close relationships with several State Department geographic and functional bureaus. Collaboration on the Balkans continued with EUR. USIP was a mainstay in the creation and work of a parliamentary working group to design constitutional amendments to prepare Bosnia-Herzegovina for eventual membership in the European Union and possibly NATO. Opening an office in Kabul, the Center collaborated with SCA and INL to encourage the Afghanistan Ministry of Interior to develop professional standards and institutions to promote the rule of law. USIP's Iraq program drew on a special $10 million FY 2004 Congressional appropriation and $2.9 million in transfers from State to carry out a series of projects, including training for Iraqi national security officials and assistance to local NGOs and educational institutions in promoting respect for the rule of law.[54] From an office in Baghdad's Green Zone USIP worked closely with the U.S. Embassy, particularly the Iraq Reconstruction Management Office (IRMO), while PCP&SO coordinated in Washington with State's Iraq desk and Iraq Coordinator's office. Through its contacts with Africa Bureau Assistant Secretary Jendayi Frazer, USIP secured $1.2 million in State Department funds to work on strengthening rule of law and higher education in Southern Sudan.

In contrast to its alliance with S/CRS in the State Department, USIP's relationship with USAID's DCHA Bureau has been somewhat arm's length. The CMM, creation of USAID Administrator Andrew Natsios, was intent on establishing its intellectual and theoretical autonomy. PCP&SO has enjoyed a closer association with OTI—AID's "Special Forces"—sharing a common interest in strengthening NGOs relevant to peace-building in zones of conflict, such as Iraq and Afghanistan. There has been little relationship with USAID's geographical bureaus, which are represented from time to time at USIP's many colloquia. A senior USIP representative hinted that those bureaus tend to view USIP as an unwelcome competitor for USAID funds with their regular contractors, which include both NGOs and for-profit firms. PCP&SO representatives in zones of conflict like Afghanistan often find themselves working comfortably overseas with USAID missions, however.

Defense Department. Since 2004, when DOD rediscovered the importance of stability operations, USIP has developed an extensive relationship with the U.S. military. A major effort has involved "civilian doctrine." Military doctrine, a collection of "fundamental principles by which the military forces . . . guide their actions in support of national objectives," is a major preoccupation of the U.S. military. (See Chapter 5.) The "Peacefare Initiative" undertaken by PCP&SO developed a standard concept of operations. USIP convened a series of working groups to review various aspects of stability operations. Their conclusions were synthesized in a manual of *Guiding Principles for Stabilization and Reconstruction*, published in November 2009. Major military partners in this endeavor were JFCOM—in particular its Joint Concept Development and Experimentation Directorate (J-9)—and PKSOI. There has also been a partnership with JFCOM to produce sectoral handbooks on rule of law, governance, infrastructure reconstruction, and economics of conflict. JFCOM has actively sought USIP assistance in those areas of peace-building where the military lacks depth.

USIP also served as "convener" of a major dialogue between the humanitarian NGOs working in conflict zones and the military. The issue was joined in Afghanistan where the U.S. military launched humanitarian operations as part of a "winning hearts and minds" strategy. Initially, troops providing humanitarian aid dressed in civilian clothes and operated vehicles indistinguishable from those of the NGOs. The NGOs complained that the U.S. military was blurring the lines between military and humanitarian activities, jeopardizing the lives of their staff members.[55] Direct contacts between the NGOs and the Pentagon led to *ad hoc* arrangements. USIP responded to a request from S/CRS Coordinator Carlos Pascual to convene a civilian-military group to review the larger issue. The resultant dialogue provided comprehensive input to the military and influenced consideration of the topic in the 2008 Army Field Manual for Stability Operations.[56]

RULE OF LAW PROGRAM

USIP's Rule of Law program is a "Center of Innovation" active in conflict zones. The program is built on the premise that rule of law adherence, far transcending application of static rules and procedures, calls for "an evolutionary search for those institutions and processes that will best bring about authentic stability through justice." It organizes its projects around certain themes, including several relevant to work in conflict zones: tools for rebuilding the rule of law in post-conflict environments, transitional justice activities, and constitution writing. In Iraq USIP worked closely with those writing the 2005 constitution by sponsoring a roundtable and advising on particular issues. After the adoption of the constitution, USIP specialists followed up by encouraging use of the amendment process to remedy problems left unresolved, providing expert advice to the Iraqi parliamentary committee for constitutional review. In Afghanistan the program provided support for rule of law aspects of the November 2001 Conference on Rebuilding Afghanistan. The program embarked on a study of the non-state and traditional justice system to assess its applicability to future rule of law in the country, where the official judiciary is woefully weak. A similar study has been carried out in Liberia. In Nepal the program organized a series of roundtable discussions for politicians, civil society, and journalists on the applicability of the truth and reconciliation commission process for the victims of the decade-long armed conflict in the country.

IMPACT ON POLICY: THE IRAQ STUDY GROUP

USIP did not ignore questions relating to justification of the Iraq war during the run-up to the conflict. In December 2002, the institute organized a symposium in which four presenters were asked to answer the question, "Would an invasion of Iraq be a 'just war'?" Their different assessments were then published. One month before U.S. forces invaded Iraq, USIP circulated a 16-page report entitled "After Saddam Hussein, Winning a Peace if It Comes to War." It discussed a cluster of potential problems, including insurgency, the collapse of civil society, and a surge in terrorism. It offered suggestions for avoiding them and urged postwar planning for quick stabilization of the country. Referring to the latter report, USIP board chairman, J. Robinson West, said, "We were basically ignored."[57]

An opportunity of a different nature arose in 2006. Alarmed by the situation he found in Iraq, Rep. Frank Wolf (R-VA), then chairman of the House Appropriations subcommittee overseeing USIP, began sounding out members of Congress about a high-powered bipartisan group to examine U.S. policy. Finding support from more than two dozen members from both parties, he quietly forwarded a proposal to the White House.[58] Initially cool, the White House decided to accept the idea. Former Secretary of State James Baker and former Indiana Congressman Lee Hamilton (cochair of the 9/11 Commission and President of the Wilson International Center for Scholars) were named cochairs. They selected the other members, including retired Supreme Court Justice Sandra Day O'Connor, former White House chiefs of staff Leon Panetta and Edward Meese, former senators Alan Simpson and Charles Robb, former Secretary of Defense William Perry, and former CIA Director Robert Gates. Wolf asked the USIP to be a "facilitator" for the Study Group; PCP&SO became its secretariat.[59] USIP assembled expert working groups which provided briefing papers. It coordinated the Group's interviews with top U.S. and foreign officials.

Launching its work in March 2006, the Iraq Study Group examined the strategic environment in Iraq and the region, the security challenges, political and economic fundamentals, and reconstruction prospects. It made one visit to Iraq. In December 2006 it issued its report to the administration, the Congress, and the public with 79 recommendations. Most controversial were

- "Engage directly Iran and Syria in order to obtain their commitment to constructive policies toward Iraq and other regional issues";
- Make "a renewed and sustained commitment to an Arab-Israeli peace on all fronts";
- "Reduce its political, military or economic support for the Iraqi Government," if it does not meet a set of milestones for national reconciliation, security, and governance by early 2007; and
- Withdraw all combat brigades not needed for force protection by the first quarter of 2008, while giving priority to training, equipping, and advising Iraqi forces and to counterterrorism.

The administration rejected the phased withdrawal recommendation, and in its place enacted the "surge" strategy in 2007. It also rebuffed a direct dialogue with Syria and Iran, but did promote a regional dialogue of Iraq's neighbors to which both governments were invited. Although there were criticisms that the White House ignored the report, officials of the NSC contended they cooperated closely with the Study Group and followed a majority of its prescriptions. In this instance, USIP played an important role in facilitating high-level policy dialogue on the key foreign policy issue of the Bush administration, even while it was carrying out important activities on the ground in Iraq.[60] Richard Solomon notes that the Iraq Study Group points to a new function now being exercised by USIP, in addition to studies and operations in conflict zones—providing a "platform for consensus building."[61]

BUILDING THE "ACADEMY": TRAINING FOR THE INTERAGENCY PROCESS

The act creating USIP gave it a mandate "to develop programs to make international peace and conflict resolution education and training more available ... for practitioners, policymakers, policy implementers, [including] citizens and non-citizens." Since its founding the institute has trained thousands of government officials, military personnel, law enforcement officials, and humanitarian workers, while the education program has built relationships with universities, sponsored seminars for faculty members, held workshops for high school teachers, and run an essay contest for high school students. At times training and education have formed a single division, but at other times they have been separate, interacting, programs. Since the late 1990s USIP training has concentrated intensely on conveying useful skills to practitioners. It eschews long lectures and voluminous readings for a practice-oriented approach, relying heavily on short presentations and simulations.

In 1999 Richard Solomon requested then Board Chairman Crocker to recommend how the institute should structure itself to play an appropriate future role in training and education. The board adopted the concept of a training center which could eventually become a "national academy," echoing in some respects the 1981 Matsunaga Commission report. To enable the Washington staff to concentrate on making the expanded training center a reality, the 2006 USIP reorganization created an Education and Training Center/Domestic. (That left the new Education and Training Center/International staff free to continue aiding practitioners in "zones of conflict" to improve conflict resolution skills.) At about the same time the Department of the Navy decided, with Congressional blessing, to transfer to the institute two buildings on a site adjacent to the new USIP headquarters on the National Mall, as the Washington home of the Education and Training Center (ETC).[62]

USIP leaders hope to make the ETC the premier U.S. government training facility. Domestic training for practitioners has been undergoing rapid expansion. Sixteen core courses, running 40 hours each, have been designed and piloted, centered on the three major USIP centers. Core courses include

- Introduction to Conflict Prevention Strategies and Operations
- Introduction to Peacemaking Strategies and Operations
- Introduction to Post-Conflict Strategies and Operations

- Negotiations
- Third Party Intervention and Mediation
- Cultural Adaptability in Peace-building Operations

In addition there are specialized courses covering rule of law, governance, economics, and peace-building, and religious, ethnic, and minority engagement. ETC will experiment with the format in order to accommodate the different profiles of the various U.S. government agencies, as well as the NGOs and international organizations it will serve.

Plans for the ETC respond to a significant growth in interest within the U.S. government. The civilian foreign affairs agencies were previously not much interested in peace-building training, says Pamela R. Aall, Vice President of the Domestic Training and Education Center. "Since 9/11 they are riveted to it."[63] However, the training process within the government is highly fragmented. USIP has thus far trained only a fraction of government personnel involved in conflict management activities. The U.S. military has for decades forcefully integrated training into career development for military officers and enlistees and offers vast numbers of courses in the many service-run colleges and institutes. Since the 2005 DOD directive elevating stability operations to the level of combat operations, the military has injected courses on post-conflict activities into its training programs. The State Department, which runs a National Foreign Affairs Training Center in the Virginia suburbs, has added courses in "reconstruction and stabilization" to its offerings, largely designed by S/CRS, but has not placed major emphasis on building a program to impart peace-building skills. USAID's CMM has designed courses for USAID officers (and some other agency personnel) held at agency sites around Washington D.C. and at its overseas missions.

LITTLE CRITICISM OF USIP

The USIP has been largely immune from significant criticism, at least since its early days, when critics of the left charged that its board of directors was "a who's who of rightwing academia and government, [calling into question] . . . the institute's credentials as a nonpartisan and non-ideological organization."[64] A radical blog asserted in 2007, "Today the USIP is still busy promoting its militarily-sanctioned form of 'peace.'" It marveled, however, that it has "received next to no criticism from the progressive media."[65] A far-right spokesman claims, "USIP, one of Ronald Reagan's biggest mistakes, is subsidized by the American taxpayer to promote a variety of left-wing initiatives."[66] Controversy erupted for a time in 2003 when President Bush nominated the controversial Daniel Pipes to the USIP Board. When the Senate Health, Education, Labor and Pensions Committee tabled the nomination, after several Senators criticized statements by Pipes as indicating bigotry against American Muslim immigrants, he was given a recess appointment.

That appointment lapsed at the end of 2003, and the White House did not renominate him.[67]

Surprisingly, the USIP encountered little criticism from the political mainstream for its extensive involvement in post-conflict activity in Iraq and Afghanistan, in spite of the unpopularity of the Iraq war and heavy criticism of administration approaches in both theaters. Its emphasis on training, enhancing rule of law, and promoting dialogue among different tribal and religious groups have not been controversial and have thus far provoked little faultfinding. That the institute undertook similar activities in the Balkans under a Democratic administration may have provided some insulation. That USIP as an institution is enjoined under its legislative charter from policy advocacy has also provided some protection. The injunction against adopting a policy position does not preclude advice on improving existing programs or projects or advancing suggestions for potential alternative approaches. Institute representatives believe they have exercised a lot of freedom to speak out about what's gone wrong in both Afghanistan and Iraq. USIP gets around the limitation on policy advice by allowing its individual experts speak for themselves, rather than on behalf of the institute. So, roughly speaking, its experts may give policy advice, but USIP does not.

One mild challenge to USIP has come from the Congress. Rep. Dennis Kucinich (D-OH) has advanced since 2005 a proposal for a U.S. Department of Peace and Non-Violence, a bill which had at one point more than 50 House and 2 Senate cosponsors. The proposal harks back to the Hartke-Hatfield bill of 1968, which preceded the Matsunaga Commission, but would address domestic as well as international conflict. The purpose of the new department would be to balance the influence and budget of the Pentagon and place peace high on the national agenda. It would absorb the USIP, the Peace Corps, and the functions of the State Department's Under Secretary for Arms Control and International Security. It would also create an Academy of Peace, modeled after the military service academies. Kucinich and his colleagues have not been critical of USIP. Their proposal would in some respects transform the institute into a cabinet department. However, since the bill is generally considered to be coming from a small ultraliberal constituency within the Congress, it has no current prospect of passage.

FUTURE PEACE-BUILDING ISSUES FOR THE USIP

In the past decade, USIP has been transformed from a quiet think tank, "seeding the field" of conflict resolution and peace studies, to a significant actor on the interagency peace and security scene. The shift has happened in spite of its special role as an independent and nonpartisan body, separate from the executive branch. The transformation has occurred even though USIP has by far the smallest budget of the agencies surveyed in this study. Its 2006 reorganization to focus on the "life cycle of conflict" has positioned the institute to interact in a more coordinated manner with U.S. government agencies attempting to prevent conflict, to bring active conflicts to an end, and to ensure post-conflict stability. USIP involvement with the interagency process is far and away most comprehensive in the post-conflict arena, reflecting the emphasis of the executive branch. The preoccupations of the Clinton and Bush administrations with the Balkans, Afghanistan, and Iraq have enabled the institute to become a "do tank," specializing in strengthening rule of law, overcoming ethnic and religious divisions, and strengthening civil society, while working alongside other government agencies. The institute's special status also equips it for a unique role among U.S. government agencies as "convener" of dialogue, most notably thus far as the secretariat for the Iraq Study Group.

In particular, USIP's long experience and vast expertise in training have made it the flagship government educational institution in the field of conflict management. The fragmentation of current training programs among the State Department, USAID, and the military's many facilities warrants a careful look at the possibility of a USIP takeover of much of the U.S. government training function in peace-building, particularly on the civilian side. The current USIP plan for development of an expanded and centrally located ETC on the National Mall strengthens the argument.

The Obama administration should consider USIP an important resource as it develops its approach to international peace and security. The administration should use the dedication of the new USIP building, scheduled for 2010, as an occasion to underscore in a major way its commitment to a global program of conflict prevention, resolution, and postwar reconstruction.

At this point, USIP prestige is riding high, and the institute faces relatively few significant challenges. Two deserve brief mention. First, USIP should give attention and resources to strengthening the CAP so that it can play a future catalytic role on conflict prevention in the interagency process. At this stage, conflict prevention is the weak link in the official U.S. approach to conflict management. USIP should work itself into the position of providing much of the intellectual capital for policy-relevant conflict prevention programs to be mounted by State, USAID, and Defense. Second, there is a degree of opposition in Congress to expanding funding for USIP lest it "crowd out" the work of private think tanks in the peace-building field. Given the complex nature of international conflict and the plethora of problems stemming from it, there should be plenty of room for both private sector entities and a government "think and do tank" for conflict management. Congress would be wise to ensure the playing field remains open to both.

CHAPTER 8

FUNDING PEACE-BUILDING: THE BUDGET PROCESS AND CONGRESSIONAL APPROVAL

> Peace and Security (P&S): Programs funded under this objective help
> nations establish the conditions and capacity to achieve peace, security
> and stability and respond effectively to threats to national or international
> security and stability.[1]

The executive branch exercises a high degree of authority in determining the
organization of the peace-building function within the federal government.
The White House, acting through the NSC, determined in 2003 that the
DOD would have responsibility for the R&S of Iraq. It was also the NSC
which decided in 2004 to create S/CRS in the State Department and in
2005 to give the Secretary of State leadership in post-conflict reconstruction.

By contrast, overall funding levels for the peace-building function and their
general allocation are determined by an integrative process within the executive branch and then by a complex interplay between the executive branch and
Congress. In theory the executive branch formulates an annual budget which
is acted upon by the budget, authorizing, and appropriating committees in
both Congressional chambers. In practice there are variants upon the process
which depend on the relative strength of the President, the balance between
the parties in both chambers, the international situation, and budgetary constraints. Single appropriation bills for international affairs and national
defense are rarely the final result.

This chapter addresses three questions:

How is funding organized for peace-building?

How are decisions made about the magnitude and use of these funds?

How much money has the U.S. government been spending on the peace-building
function?[2]

DISTINGUISHING THE 150 ACCOUNT AND THE 050 ACCOUNT

Out of the 20 functions in the budget covering the entire range of federal government activities, two are applicable to peace-building: the international affairs account (Function 150) and a few elements of the national defense account (Function 050).[3] However, funding for peace-building is not subject to easy grouping as part of these two functions.

The international affairs budget—the 150 function—contains three major elements: the conduct of foreign affairs (the expenses for operating the State Department), international agricultural programs, and all other international programs not included in the Defense Department budget. The third element is called the foreign operations budget. "Foreign ops," as it is usually termed, includes development and humanitarian assistance, USAID operational expenses, funding for international financial institutions like the World Bank, international broadcasting, and other information programs. There are military components in the 150 account, comprising international security assistance, which are managed by the State Department rather than by Defense. The proposed FY 2009 international affairs budget of $3.9 billion constituted just 1.3 percent of the total federal budget request.

The national defense budget is known as the 050 function. The military activities—and military support and administrative expenses—of the Defense Department constitute more than 95 percent of that function, but 050 also includes the nuclear weapons-related activities of the Department of Energy and the National Nuclear Security Administration, some activities of the Coast Guard and the Federal Bureau of Investigation, and those of several other agencies. The proposed FY 2009 national defense budget of $517.4 billion constituted 17.6 percent of the total federal budget request.[4] Of total defense spending proposed for FY 2009 (including emergency amendments submitted in May 2008), about $8.5 billion was allocated to specific programs used in peace-building. The most important elements were funding to build Iraqi and Afghan security forces and the CERP, used in both Iraq and Afghanistan for reconstruction programs.

THE INTERNATIONAL AFFAIRS BUDGET

Until 2006, the budgets of the State Department and USAID were developed separately.[5]

In January 2006 came a major reform in the foreign operations budget process. Secretary of State Rice appointed Randall L. Tobias as Director of Foreign Assistance, a new position combining the role of Administrator of USAID with that of a Deputy Secretary of State. The major rationale for the new position was to amalgamate the separate State and USAID processes for the development of the foreign assistance budget. With the position came a new Office of the Director of Foreign Assistance, known as the F Bureau. At State the Resource Management Bureau retained responsibility only for developing the State Department operational budget, in coordination with F. USAID's Bureau of Policy Planning and Coordination, previously driver of the USAID budget process, was abolished, as its functions and many of its staff members were absorbed into F.

The F Bureau came up with a new standardized program structure dividing assistance into five strategic or program objectives:

Peace and security

Governing justly and democratically

Investing in people

Economic growth

Humanitarian assistance

It might seem logical to conclude that peace-building activities would fall entirely within the peace and security category. The bulk of them do, but some also fall into "governing justly and democratically" and humanitarian assistance.

ASSEMBLING THE INTERNATIONAL AFFAIRS BUDGET

Before getting into the nitty-gritty of the peace-building accounts, it is useful to review overall 150 budget construction, including the new procedures developed under F. The budget process is a never-ending one, tied to the fiscal year (October 1–September 30).[6] The White House Office of Management and Budget (OMB) issues informal guidance at the beginning of the calendar year and binding guidelines in July (Circular A-11), providing detailed directions to all the agencies. Budget-making starts within each agency early in the calendar year—at State and USAID in the overseas missions.

During the first quarter of the calendar year, each mission submits to its geographic bureau in State and USAID a Mission Strategic Plan (MSP). The MSP includes foreign assistance objectives and proposed funding levels based on the F functions, developed collaboratively between the embassy and the USAID mission (where there is one).[7] The geographic bureaus then formulate the proposals of all their overseas missions into a joint State/USAID bureau request.[8] This exercise requires the formation of geographic bureau teams representing State and USAID, cochaired by a deputy assistant secretary of state and a deputy assistant administrator of USAID. The bureaucratic struggle to finalize allocations to different countries is fought out within these teams, as deputy assistant secretaries and deputy assistant administrators vie to bulk up their favorite programs and engage in the necessary horse trading to come up with a near-final figure.[9] The joint State/USAID bureau requests, along with the functional bureau requests, are posted to the internal State and USAID Web sites to provide an opportunity for comment, including opinions from other agencies like Defense or Justice.

Under the Bush administration, major disagreements on program levels were taken to an assistance working group (AWG), convened by F only as required. There were AWGs for each geographic region. They included representatives of all offices affected by the decision and could draw in other agencies such as Defense, the NSC, or the OMB. They were cochaired by the geographic deputy assistant secretary and/or deputy assistant administrator concerned and by a senior F official. The meetings of the AWGs were to wrap up by early June, at which point the bureaus came back to F with a revised budget.

At the senior review, each geographic assistant secretary presented the regional budget to the Secretary and Deputy Secretary. Other agencies sat in at the assistant secretary level, if sufficiently concerned.[10] Then F would go back to the bureaus with the Secretary's priorities for final adjustment. The Secretary forwards the ultimate product—the foreign operations budget, as well as the State Department operations budget—to OMB by early September.[11]

The focus of action then shifts to OMB. It was not basically affected by the decision to create F and to budget for the foreign operations budget according to strategic objectives. Instead it continues to budget in the aggregate by agency. Its career staff clarifies technical and policy questions with the agencies as background to their recommendations to the OMB director. In November the formal director's review takes place, as the agencies gird up for the OMB "passback." The passback may simply specify the fund ceilings for major accounts—usually lower than the agency request—and give guidance on a few specific issues of interest to the White House. In some cases it may direct that certain items not be included. The arrival of the passback on Thanksgiving eve can ruin the holiday for the F staff, because a rapid decision must be made whether to appeal. F gets back quickly to the bureau teams and determines with them where the fit is least comfortable. State and USAID are forced to make cuts in some projected programs, and F decides the handful of issues on which it feels obliged to do battle with OMB.

The formal appeal process is over by December 1. After that there may be some further argument at the level of the Secretary of State, intervening with the President's senior aides in the West Wing. The Bush administration created a Budget Review Board, chaired by the Vice President, to adjudicate appeals. In theory, the Secretary could seek a meeting with the President on a budget issue she deemed essential.[12] Just before Christmas, OMB comes back with final numbers. State/USAID has two weeks to tweak the voluminous narrative presentations and tables which go into the formal International Affairs FY 2009 Budget Request. OMB does final adjustments, proofing, and validation. On the first Monday in February the proposed budget arrives at the Congress, and the President delivers the budget speech.[13] The budget is accompanied by draft appropriation legislation and possibly authorization language for certain of its elements.

PEACE-BUILDING ACCOUNTS WITHIN 150

Budget functions for peace-building are widely distributed within the international affairs budget. Only a few items are readily identifiable as peace-building in their entirety:

1. Contributions to International Peacekeeping Activities (CIPA). The formal U.S. share of the UN peacekeeping budget is 27 percent, but in most years since the mid-1990s, actual payments have been capped at 25 percent.[14] The large U.S. share gives Washington a major interest in debates within the Security Council about UN peacekeeping responsibilities and burdens. As a practical matter, a new peacekeeping force cannot be authorized without U.S. concurrence. The State Department's IO bureau is responsible for the CIPA account and institutionally biased in favor of keeping a cap on its magnitude. Once created, a peacekeeping mission remains in operation for an extensive period. The average duration is now 8–10 years.[15] A geographic bureau favoring creation of a new peacekeeping force must therefore overcome inertia or outright opposition from IO. In 2008 the United Nations was mounting 20 peacekeeping missions around the world. In FY 2007 U.S. expenditures for CIPA were $1.7 billion. In the FY 2009 budget the largest amount—$414 million or 28 percent—was allocated to the newest, UNAMID, authorized in 2007. CIPA was not subject to the F budget process because UN peacekeeping funding is a treaty obligation, even if Congress places ceilings on it.

2. Peacekeeping Operations (PKO). A separate account from CIPA and grouped with other forms of military assistance programmed by the State Department, PKO is used for "voluntary multi-national stabilization efforts" (i.e., those not authorized by the Security Council). It provides funds for the GPOI, which "enhances the ability of states to participate in peacekeeping and stability operations." (See Chapter 3.) In post-conflict situations, it purportedly "reforms military establishments into professional military forces [which] ... respect ... the rule of law."[16] Much of FY 2009 proposed funding was for creating professional armies in Liberia, Congo, Southern Sudan (ostensibly for integration into the Sudanese army), and for Somalia (forces loyal to the beleaguered Transitional Federal Government). It is also the account for the long-running Multilateral Force and Observers in the Sinai, first deployed in 1982.[17]

3. Civilian Stabilization Initiative. In 2004 and 2005 the State Department's Office of Reconstruction and Stabilization (S/CRS) faced the liability of most new bureaucratic entities—no standing in the budget process. Funds for the new office had to be squeezed from elsewhere in the Diplomatic and Consular Program account—the State Department operational budget. S/CRS managed to secure $7.8 million in the FY 2005 supplemental. However, Congress did not appropriate a specific number in FY 2006 and 2007, leaving the office to make do with about the level of 2005. The money used for its important operations in Darfur in 2006, in support of the diplomacy of Deputy Secretary of State Zoellick, including leasing a headquarters for the secretariat of the DPA, computers and satellite communications equipment, and supplies for Active Reserve personnel deployed to Darfur, came from other offices, including the budget of the Africa Bureau.

The new F budget process, launched in early 2006, dealt harshly with S/CRS and its new director, as noted in Chapter 4. There was no line item for the new office in the request that went to Congress before FY 2009. No money was put into the FY 2008 budget for operations, even though President Bush in his 2007 State of the Union message to Congress called for creation of a Civilian Reserve Corps to be operated by S/CRS. For the year it had only $7 million. As a result, S/CRS did not have any of its own funds to bring to the table as it attempted to broaden its role in conflict operations by the Department of State. In FY 2009 budget preparations, S/CRS was at last in a position to demand resources in its own right, based on the President's commitment to the Civilian Reserve. Four months of interagency discussions involving 15 different agencies, coordinated through the Readiness Policy Coordinating Committee of the NSC, and negotiation with OMB ultimately resulted in a $249 million figure to fund the Civilian Reserve Corps, the Active Response Corps, and the Standby Reserve Corps, as well as operational funds for S/CRS. Secretary Rice played an active role.

4. Transition Initiatives (TI). These funds are used by USAID's OTI. (See Chapter 6.) OTI also received additional funds from the Economic Support Fund (ESF; see below) for its activities in Afghanistan and Iraq. After it phased out major programs in both countries in 2005 and 2006, respectively, funding for OTI from the TI account stabilized at about $45 million. OTI's good reputation—and small budget—has assured it of favorable treatment both by OMB and by the Congress.

5. Since the USIP was created by the Congress as "independent" and "nonpartisan"— and therefore outside of the executive branch—its budget is not subject to the F process. It might thus be expected that the USIP budget would also not pass through OMB. However, ironically, when they presented their budget to the Congress, USIP leaders were asked, "What is the President's mark?" So USIP established a working relationship with OMB, which provides an initial budget number, subsequently negotiated with USIP.[18] It has become part of the President's budget request and is considered by the Appropriations Committee as part of the 150 account. The FY 2009 request was $33 million, a 50 percent increase over actual appropriations in FY 2007.

Other accounts are used partially for peace-building purposes. These include funds allocated to countries for which the primary assistance objective is peace and security. Such accounts include

1. Economic Support Fund (ESF) and similar funding for Eastern Europe and Eurasia. Traditionally ESF funding has been used in countries where the United States has important political and diplomatic interests. It is applied more flexibly than Development Assistance (DA) and Child Survival & Health Programs, the primary USAID instruments for long-term development. Although budgeting has been done by the State Department, USAID has usually been in charge of implementation on the ground. In a few instances, both ESF and DA have been used in the same countries. As a result of the State/USAID budget reform of 2006, ESF became the assistance instrument for "rebuilding" countries—"states in or emerging from and rebuilding after internal or external conflict"—and a few "restrictive" countries, that is, "states of concern where there are significant

governance issues."[19] ESF is presented to the Congress as "helping countries overcome short and long-term political, economic, and security hurdles" and supporting certain U.S. foreign policy goals. Support for R&S, particularly in Africa and South and Central Asia, constituted $3.6 billion or 70 percent of ESF in 2007 (including the supplemental appropriation) and 68 percent of the amended 2009 ESF budget request. Major proposed recipients for 2009 ESF funds relevant to peace-building were Afghanistan ($707 million), Iraq ($300 million), Sudan ($254 million), and Colombia ($142 million). Much of 150 account money used for funding the PRTs in Iraq and Afghanistan—and not provided by the defense budget—has come from ESF.

Other ESF-like funds have been allocated during the past two decades under the Support for Eastern Europe Democracy Act (SEED) and the Freedom Support Act (FSA—for countries in the former Soviet Union).[20] Although a number of states have been phased out of the programs, these funds have continued to be used for the conflict-ridden states of Bosnia-Herzegovina, Kosovo, Armenia, Azerbaijan, and Georgia. SEED and FSA money have also helped fund U.S. support for the OSCE focused on stabilization, reconstruction, and democratization.[21]

2. International Narcotics Control and Law Enforcement (INCLE). Overall, INCLE funds are used to fight transnational crime and terrorist networks involved in the illegal drug trade. However, a significant portion is used to support CIVPOL training programs needed for R&S, as well as criminal justice sector reform and capacity building in Iraq. CIVPOL programs are important in West Bank-Gaza, Liberia, Haiti, and Southern Sudan. INCLE funds also support the Center of Excellence for Stability Police Units (COESPU) in Vicenza, Italy under the GPOI. About 43 percent ($513 million) of the $1.2 billion FY 2009 request figure was designated for R&S.[22]

3. Development Assistance (DA). In spite of the 2007 assistance reforms, some long-term USAID DA continues to be allocated to countries falling into the "rebuilding" category, and therefore can be adjudged to support reconstruction. Some falls into the education sector, for example, in Liberia, where it funded projects under President Bush's International Education Initiative. Other states experiencing conflict but targeted for DA in FY 2009 included Haiti, Sri Lanka, Timor-Leste, Philippines, Chad, Guinea Bissau, and Uganda.[23]

4. Refugee Assistance. Most refugee funding assistance is allocated to support persons fleeing states afflicted by civil conflict. Refugee funds fall into two main categories. Migration and Refugee Assistance (MRA) is programmed to deal with ongoing refugee crises. The U.S. Emergency Refugee and Migration Assistance Fund (ERMA), roughly 10 percent the size of MRA, is a contingency fund for unforeseeable emergencies resulting from new refugee flows. Between 40 and 50 percent of MRA programming—allocated by region and not by country—has been devoted to Africa in recent years, much of it related to major conflicts in Liberia, Congo, Cote d'Ivoire, and Sudan. In FY 2007 the emergency fund (ERMA) was used to support refugees from conflict in Iraq, Sudan, and Sri Lanka. An approximate value of annual refugee funding devoted to support for peace-building and stabilization is $700 million.

5. Disaster and Emergency Food Assistance. These accounts are good examples of dual-use funding, since they are applied to both natural disasters and complex emergencies involving civil conflict. International Disaster Assistance (IDA)

cannot be programmed ahead of time, since it is allocated only following disaster declarations. It is budgeted on the basis of past history. However, proposed budget figures commonly fall well short of the final allocation—only 70 percent in FY 2008 for example. In FY 2006 IDA funding for complex emergencies in conflict countries reached $280 million, or 70 percent of the total; in 2007, $310 million or 84 percent.[24] In both years, Sudan accounted for 44 percent of funds for complex emergencies.

PL 480 Title II emergency assistance is partly programmed in advance on the assumption that emergency food needs will persist in conflict-ridden or generally food-insecure countries. New emergencies often require supplemental appropriations to keep up with needs. Title II is requested by the U.S. Department of Agriculture, since it involves purchases from U.S. food stocks, but is programmed and administered by USAID. This anomalous status means that it is part of Function 150, but the appropriation request is handled in Congress by agricultural subcommittees. Most emergency food is distributed through the UN's WFP, but some is allocated to NGOs like CARE, Catholic Relief Services, and World Vision.[25] Emergency food assistance for conflict countries exceeded $700 million in FY 2006 and 2007.

6. Other State-Programmed Military Assistance. FMF funds equipment for allies and friendly governments. Over 90 percent has gone to Israel, Egypt, Pakistan, and Jordan. In FY 2006 only 3.5 percent ($155 million) went to countries suffering from or recovering from conflict, mostly to Colombia and the Philippines. It more than doubled to 7.9 percent ($380 million) the following year when Lebanon got into the mix. Some funding has gone to support military allies assisting in Iraq and Afghanistan. IMET funds are spread among almost 150 countries. Only about two dozen get more than $1 million. In FY 2006 and 2007, 14–15 percent of the account ($14–15 million) went to about 24 conflict countries, including Iraq, Afghanistan, Lebanon, Colombia, and the Congo.

7. Democracy Funding. Democratic governance and elections are major U.S. objectives in a post-conflict situation. The bulk of funding for promotion of democracy is through country allocations for DA, overseen by USAID's Democracy and Governance Office, and for ESF—both covered separately above. Over the past two decades additional funds have come from the Human Rights and Democracy Fund (HRDF), administered by State's Bureau of Democracy, Human Rights, and Labor, and the appropriation for the National Endowment for Democracy (NED). However, NED's core appropriation is only one source of its funding, since it has also drawn on DA and ESF over the years.[26] In 2006, the last year for which a comprehensive project list is available, a large number of NED projects, including the majority in Iraq, Bosnia and Herzegovina, Kosovo, Liberia, and Somalia, were funded from ESF or DA.[27] In that year a substantial amount of core funding for both the NED and the HRDF, totaling $117 million, was also used for conflict countries.[28]

PEACE-BUILDING ELEMENTS OF THE DEFENSE BUDGET

As discussed in Chapter 5, the post-conflict experience in Afghanistan and Iraq led to the 2005 conversion of the Pentagon leadership to stability operations as a priority "comparable to combat operations." That conversion and the exigencies of R&S in both theaters resulted in the insertion of peace-building elements into the Defense budget—the 050 function. An analysis of the 050 budget process is beyond the scope of this study and not necessary to an analysis of the discrete elements used for peace-building. Almost all of these accounts are of recent vintage and therefore represent temporary rather than long-term authorities. Most either come out of stability operations improvisations in Iraq and Afghanistan or have evolved from closer DOD collaboration with the State Department, including S/CRS.

Afghanistan- and Iraq-related accounts are as follows:

1. Building security forces (ISFF and ASFF). In 2004 the Bush administration announced its "Accelerating Success in Afghanistan" strategy, which included training Afghan National Police and expanding training of Afghan Army troops. Its National Strategy for Victory in Iraq, published in 2005, advanced as a core assumption that "the training, equipping, and mentoring of Security Forces will produce an army and police force capable of independently providing security and maintaining public order."[29] Funds for that purpose were appropriated for the Afghanistan Security Forces Fund (ASFF) and the Iraq Security Forces Fund (ISFF) beginning in FY 2005. They covered training, equipment, infrastructure, and sustainment, but the breakdown has been difficult to ascertain.[30] They were implemented by the Combined Security Transition Command—Afghanistan (CSTC-Alpha) and the Multinational Security Transition Command—Iraq (MNSTC-I), commands created to assist the two governments to organize, train, and equip their military and police forces. Over time, and under pressure from Congress, infrastructure projects (such as bases) were virtually eliminated and equipment reduced in the Iraq program, but infrastructure remained significant in the ASFF.

    The budget numbers have been developed by the two commands in conjunction with ground commanders and forwarded to CENTCOM. From CENTCOM the proposed number passed to the Comptroller of the Pentagon and the J-8 (Resources) division of the Joint Chiefs of Staff, before submission to OMB. Like other funding for Afghanistan and Iraq, it appeared only in supplemental appropriation legislation. The process has not been systematic and orderly. According to an OMB veteran, "the Pentagon waits until the last minute and then jams us. There is no real budget scrub." If OMB cut back the number, the Pentagon sometimes went to the NSC to try to get the decision overridden.

2. The Commander's Emergency Response Program. CERP funds are provided "to enable local military commanders in Iraq and Afghanistan to respond to urgent humanitarian relief and reconstruction requirements ... by carrying out programs that will immediately assist the indigenous population."[31] The objective is to build trust and support at the grassroots level. CERP was launched by the Coalition Provisional Authority in 2003, drawing to a considerable extent on seized assets of the Saddam regime. Subsequently, funding was provided for the program from the Emergency Supplemental Appropriations Act of 2004 at a level not to exceed $180 million. CERP was initially viewed in part as an instrument of force protection, reducing danger to the troops from a hostile

population. Why the "Commander's Fund?" The Defense Department argued, revealingly, that commanders are "often the only U.S. government officials in daily contact with communities about local needs."[32]

Initially the projects were to be used for civic cleanup, education, electricity, food production, health care, irrigation, rule of law and governance, telecommunications, water, and sanitation. The majority of projects were expected to be in the $10,000 range, rising sometimes to $100,000.[33] Over time the average size of projects grew, sometimes to the level of $500,000 or even more than $1 million. The category of approved projects expanded to include repairs of battle damage, condolence payments to individuals for death or injury resulting from coalition operations or to family members of Iraqi military or police personnel killed in action.[34]

Like other funding for the wars in Afghanistan and Iraq, CERP has appeared only in supplemental appropriation bills. It is part of the massive category of Operations and Maintenance (O&M)—Army, which totaled more than $81 billion in 2007.[35] The supplemental budget process for CERP begins with the staff of the commanding general in each theater and then moves to the CENTCOM command. It then goes to the Office of the Under Secretary of Defense (Comptroller) to be included in the proposed supplemental package to be forwarded to OMB. During the Bush administration there does not appear to have been much debate over the numbers in the supplemental request, which tended to go forward to Congress without much adjustment.

The final appropriation for CERP is allocated to both Iraq and Afghanistan with a Congressional suggestion on the split. However, the Commander of the CENTCOM ultimately makes that decision. Then the ground commander in each theater decides which commanders get what amounts. Marine commanders get CERP through this process, but the Army is the "executive agent." In FY 2007 CERP levels reached $1 billion, about evenly split between Iraq and Afghanistan, and $1.7 billion was appropriated in 2008.[36]

3. Coalition Support Funds. Beginning in 2003, emergency supplemental appropriations acts authorized DOD to use Defense-wide O&M funds to reimburse coalition countries less capable of absorbing the costs of their logistical and military support to U.S. military operations in Iraq. This funding amounted to $274 million in 2004 and $246 million in 2005, before soaring to $900 million in 2006 and an estimated $1.2 billion in FY 2008. Coalition Support Funds are essentially a Defense Department counterpart to the ESF managed by the State Department.[37]

4. Factory Revitalization Program. An unusual element crept into the mix of Function 050 stabilization funding at the initiative of Paul A. Brinkley, Deputy Under Secretary of Defense for Business Transformation. Brinkley secured special funding for restarting state-owned factories in Iraq. These factories, fixtures of the Saddam Hussein regime, were shuttered by Coalition Provisional Authority Director Bremer in 2003, spiking unemployment. To provide new employment, DOD secured $50 million in the FY 2007 supplemental—as part of the massive and largely secret Iraq Freedom Fund—to restart the factories.[38] It asked for $100 million in the FY 2008 supplemental but again got $50 million along with language indicating that Congress wanted such a program paid for in the future by the Government of Iraq.

Outside Afghanistan and Iraq, stability operations funding is included in the regular annual defense budget under the category of O&M—Defense-wide. The Pentagon has viewed these programs as part of its recent emphasis on "building partnership capacity," a responsibility assigned in 2006 to the new DASD for Partnership Capacity. The programs break down into the following categories.

1. Global Train and Equip (Sec. 1206). The FY 2006 National Defense Authorization Act (Section 1206) provided the Secretary of Defense with authority to train and equip foreign military forces. Two purposes were indicated. One is to assist those forces to carry out counterterrorism operations. The other is to assist them to support military *and stability operations* in which U.S. armed forces participate. Virtually all Section 1206 assistance has been for counterterrorism, since, by mutual understanding between DOD and the Congress, the U.S. military does not use this authority for operations in Iraq and Afghanistan. In 2007 Congress rebuffed the administration's request to expand the authority to train and equip foreign police forces. Sec. 1206 authority is exercised by the Secretary of Defense with the "concurrence"—construed to mean the approval—of the Secretary of State. In practice that means that projects submitted by the geographic combatant commands are not considered unless they show approval of both the commander and the U.S. chief of mission.[39] Obligations in FY 2007 reached $289 million, and $500 million was requested for FY 2008 and 2009.[40] Although Sec. 1206 assistance falls formally within the category of "stability operations," a perusal of projects for 2006 and 2007 uncovered only a few which can be characterized as supportive of stability operations in a conflict situation, as opposed to counterterrorism. Most were to support maritime interdiction, cross-border security, or general counterterrorist preparations. Projects in Chad, Lebanon, and Sri Lanka appear to have had stabilization or dual-use applications.[41] Global Train and Equip is a counterpart to the State Department-managed FMF.

2. Security and Stabilization Assistance (Sec. 1207). As reported in Chapter 4, the National Defense Authorization Act of 2006 authorized up to $100 million to be transferred to the State Department (S/CRS) in the form of "defense articles, services, training or other support for reconstruction, stabilization, and security activities in foreign countries." Proposals for use of the funds come to S/CRS, usually from U.S. embassies. There are both selection and review committees with State and Defense participation, including Partnership Strategy in the OSD. There is a bit of horse trading; some projects more reflect Defense priorities and others State priorities. After formal Defense Department approval, the funds are transferred to the Coordinator's Office. They tend to bunch at the end of the fiscal year. In FY 2006 only $10 million was transferred, but $100 million in both FY 2007 and 2008.

 For FY 2009, $200 million in Sec. 1207 funds were requested in the Defense budget, even though $249 million was proposed for the Civilian Stabilization Initiative to be implemented by S/CRS. The bulk of the CSI funding would be for the three-tiered system for civilian surge capacity and the remainder operational funds for S/CRS. The continuing request for Sec. 1207 funding indicated administration hopes that S/CRS project funding would still be funded out of the Defense budget.

3. Combatant Commander's Initiative Fund (CCIF). The other geographic combatant commands became jealous of the CERP mechanism provided to CENTCOM. They also wanted to be able to deploy in a timely and flexible way significant levels of funds for R&S in their own regions. Deputy Secretary of Defense Paul Wolfowitz had initially pressed for CERP as a worldwide DOD funding mechanism, but the Pentagon had to settle for its limitation to Iraq and Afghanistan. DOD continued to press for a "global" CERP in the face of Congressional resistance. The FY 2007 National Defense Authorization Act transformed what had been a small account for priority projects for the Chairman of the Joint Chiefs of Staff into a somewhat larger Combatant Commander's Initiative Funding for Urgent Humanitarian Relief and Reconstruction, available to the COCOMs for use in their AORs.[42] In 2008, the first year of the new authority, $25 million was made available and $75 million was requested for FY 2009.

4. Overseas Humanitarian, Disaster Assistance and Civic Assistance (OHDACA). The humanitarian assistance program, created in 1986, has been expanded over the years to include foreign disaster relief, emergency response, and humanitarian demining. Humanitarian demining is clearly a peace-building activity in countries previously in conflict. Humanitarian assistance generally falls into the same category; it is designed "to help avert political and humanitarian crises, promote democratic development and regional stability, and enable countries to begin to recover from conflicts."[43] Emergency disaster relief, by contrast, is usually in response to natural disasters like the 2004 tsunami in Asia and not conflict situations. In 2007 demining and humanitarian assistance totaled $45 million, or 72 percent of the account.[44]

5. Lift and Sustain Funds. Although the O&M—Defense-wide account does not apply to Iraq, which has been largely covered by supplemental appropriations, regular annual defense appropriations bills have authorized the use of O&M since 2005 to provide supplies, services, air and sealift, and other logistical support to coalition forces for supporting military and stability operations in Iraq and Afghanistan. The difference between "coalition support" and "lift and sustain" is that the former is used to reimburse supporting countries for their expenses, while the latter reimburses U.S. military departments for services rendered to eligible countries. The largest beneficiaries of combined coalition support funds and lift and sustain funds have been Poland, Jordan, Georgia, and Ukraine.[45]

CONGRESSIONAL BUDGET BILL, AUTHORIZATION AND APPROPRIATION

There are three distinct elements of the Congressional budget process. The first is the Congressional budget resolution, which sets total new budget authority and outlay levels for the upcoming fiscal year and the four subsequent ones. A resolution rather than a law, it is the first response to the President's proposed budget. It allocates spending among the 20 functional categories—including 050 National Defense and 150 International Affairs—thereby providing ceilings to the committees which have jurisdiction over the spending. The appropriations committees in both chambers receive ceilings only for the approaching fiscal year, since appropriations are annual. The budget resolution is supposed to be passed by April 15. It is frequently delayed and in some years has not been passed at all. Delay or absence of the resolution does not halt the appropriation process but makes it more difficult because of a lack of consensus on ceilings. If no budget resolution is passed, a separate resolution must be voted to get around it.

The most basic distinction in the Congressional budget process is that between authorization and appropriation.

Authorization acts establish, continue, or modify agencies or programs, as, for example, establishing a legislative base for S/CRS at the State Department. An authorization act also provides authority for appropriations for individual agencies and programs, often in the form of spending ceilings.[46] Authorization is done by the committees which have policy oversight over the agencies concerned: the SFRC and the CFA for State and USAID, the Senate and House Armed Services Committees (SASC and HASC) for DOD.[47] Foreign affairs authorization has been frustrated in recent years, particularly on foreign assistance and the creation of a new peace-building function in the Department of State. The problem has not been the partisan divide, since both committees have generally exhibited cooperation across party lines, but rather a lack of consensus, particularly in the Senate, where objections from individual senators outside the Committee have stymied a final vote. As a result, the SFRC and CFA actually spend less time authorizing and more on oversight—holding hearings and pressuring the administration to follow their guidance. A subcommittee chairman may be given latitude by the committee chairman to hold hearings on certain issues relating to conflict; those in the media spotlight like Afghanistan, Kosovo, or Darfur are held at the level of the full committee. In both chambers, foreign assistance is handled before the full committee, but the regional subcommittees may hold hearings on assistance issues related to their regions —especially Middle East and South Asia.[48] In 2008 Secretary of State Rice testified on behalf of the FY 2009 international affairs budget to the full SFRC and the House Foreign Affairs Committee on the same day. Assistant secretaries and USAID assistant administrators may be called to testify before subcommittees.[49]

On the 050 side, SASC and HASC pass an authorization bill every year, in contrast to the SFRC and CFA. The armed services committees pay close attention to the Defense accounts applied to R&S and maintain relatively close and amicable relationships with the appropriations committees. In 2008 Secretary Rice appeared with Secretary of Defense Gates before the HASC to emphasize the partnership between State and Defense in what she described as the "continuum between war and peace." The appropriators tend to take into account the authorizers' views on defense policy as they mark up appropriation bills.[50]

When it comes to actually securing funds for programs, however, it is the appropriations process which is paramount. Members of Congress serving on appropriations committees tend to have a somewhat different perspective than the authorizers. They are usually more concerned about how their programs fit into the overall budget or parts of the budget—and therefore about spending and deficits—and somewhat less about foreign policy—or at least about "high policy." Their staffers tend to be more detail-oriented than their counterparts on the authorizing committees. Often they have been worked on the same programs for a number of years and may actually know more about them—or at least more about their histories—than the State Department, USAID, or DOD people advocating for them.

For the appropriations process, subcommittees are far more important than for the authorizing committees. Since 2007, the House and Senate Subcommittees on State, Foreign Operations and Related Programs review the 150 account, including USIP and the Peace Corps, but not international agricultural programs, which come under the subcommittee that handles agriculture.[51] In both chambers the Defense Subcommittee handles the defense budget.

The subcommittees hold hearings during the late winter and spring, inviting administration representatives to testify, along with selected representatives of concerned interest groups, including NGOs and academics. In 2008 Secretary Rice appeared before both House and Senate subcommittees covering Function 150. After the hearings—and usually following the passage of the budget resolution—the subcommittees "mark up" their bills, filling in numbers and altering, where they wish, the language submitted by the administration. The appropriations often have earmarks or "functional directives." Subcommittee chairs and ranking minorities have their own preferences among accounts, and those preferences often find their way into funding levels. When the subcommittees finish their work, the bill is then approved by the appropriations committee in each House and goes to the floor for a vote. If there are significant differences between House and Senate versions, the bill is "conferenced." In principle the House and the Senate leadership choose conferees, which would normally include the committee chairman, the relevant subcommittee chairman, and ranking minorities in both chambers. In recent years, however, the leadership of both Houses has increasingly assumed authority to sort out differences. The conference—formal or informal—adjusts the differences in numbers between the two bills, sometimes choosing a figure somewhere in between, but also horse-trading among accounts.

The appropriation process has become so labored, however, that in most years Congress does not approve all appropriations bills by the October 1 date marking the beginning of the fiscal year targeted. To avoid a shutdown of those particular functions, Congress passes continuing resolutions (CRs), extending funding, usually at the level of the previous year appropriation, for 30 days or 60 days.[52] There may be several CRs before the appropriation process is completed. In December 2007, Congress passed—and the President signed—a FY 2008 Omnibus Appropriations Bill consisting of

11 separate appropriations bills, including the international affairs budget, after four CRs had expired.

When regular appropriations for military operations or foreign operations become clearly insufficient for the task at hand—a frequent occurrence—the White House goes back to Congress for a "supplemental" appropriation. Supplemental requests generally contain much less detail than included in the annual budget requests. Such requests are always referred to the appropriations committees of both Houses, where they are quickly marked up, ordinarily without a preliminary hearing, and, if favorably reported, sent forward to the floor for discussion, amendment, and a vote. Traditionally, supplementals have not been undertaken lightly. Generally speaking, the appropriations committees dislike them as violating good budget order and vitiating budget discipline.[53] Supplementals have occurred most frequently in the military area. If the administration can make the case that, without a supplemental, U.S. forces deployed overseas will run short of equipment, the Congress does not want to be accused of failing to support the troops. A supplemental is less likely with the 150 function. However, after the bombings of the U.S. embassies in Nairobi and Dar es Salaam in 1998, the State Department was able to get a large supplemental to buttress security overseas. Supplementals also sometimes cover international disasters.

Since 9/11 the Bush administration has relied primarily on supplemental appropriations to fund the GWOT and the wars in Afghanistan and Iraq. These bills have usually included funding not only for the Defense Department but also for programs of State and USAID. As a result, much of recent funding legislation for peace-building activities is found in supplemental legislation. During the period 2001–2007, supplemental appropriations for operations in Iraq and the GWOT totaled $503 billion. Of that amount $34 billion, or about 7 percent, was for diplomatic operations and foreign aid.[54]

CONGRESSIONAL SHAPING OF FUNDING FOR PEACE-BUILDING: FUNCTION 150

Securing passage for authorizing legislation on foreign affairs has become very difficult—particularly for foreign assistance. There has, in fact, been no reauthorization of the Foreign Assistance Act of 1961 since 1985. Efforts were made on a couple of occasions, most importantly in 2003. However, a contentious extraneous issue (a change in the minimum wage) was grafted to the bill as an amendment, and during the two days allotted for debate, the amenders refused to yield, and the bill was ultimately pulled from the floor. Even much more limited authorizing legislation is difficult to pass as a separate measure. One obstacle in the upper House is the "hold." Any senator may interpose an objection to passage of a bill which has majority support in order to review the bill, negotiate changes in it, or kill it. The Congress employs different mechanisms to overcome such obstacles.

Authorizing legislation may be attached to another bill to improve prospects for passage. Alternatively, Congress may place authorizing language in an appropriation bill.

The SFRC has taken the lead in pushing forward the idea of an enhanced civilian capacity to carry out the various tasks of post-conflict reconstruction. It was the Advisory Panel formed by Chairman Lugar to study the issue which constituted a first step toward the creation of S/CRS.[55] Lugar and then ranking minority member Joe Biden introduced the Reconstruction & Stabilization Civilian Management Act (RSCMA) of 2004 (S. 2127). It did not go anywhere, but the following year, in the 109th Congress, it was incorporated into an authorization bill for foreign relations and the conduct of foreign affairs (S. 600). The RSCMA provisions proposed codifying the existence of S/CRS by amending the State Department Basic Authorities Act of 1956, making the Coordinator appointment subject to the advice and consent of the Senate. It proposed providing authority and funding for a Ready Response Corps to include both an active duty group along the lines of S/CRS's Active Component and two reserve groups along the lines of the Standby Component and the proposed Civilian Reserve. Finally, it proposed modifying the Foreign Assistance Act to give the President broad authority to furnish R&S assistance through U.S. civilian agencies or the Civilian Reserve. It backed the President's budget request for a $100 million Crisis Response Fund for R&S activities. Although the bill passed the Senate in 2006, it ultimately died in the House.[56]

In the 109th Congress, with the switch in party control, the basic RSCMA bill was reintroduced, once again on a bipartisan basis by Sen. Joe Biden, the new Foreign Relations Committee Chair, and now Ranking Member Sen. Lugar. Rep. Sam Farr (D-CA), a member of the House Appropriations Committee, became the champion of S/CRS in the second chamber, introducing companion bills in both 2006 and 2007. The authorization seemed on track to passage in 2007, particularly when the Iraq and Afghanistan supplemental legislation passed in May of that year included $50 million for the Civilian Reserve Corps—"subject to authorization." However, Sen. Tom Coburn (R-OK) imposed a "hold" when the authorization was presented by the Senate leadership for approval "by unanimous consent." The hold continued for more than a year, despite pleas to Coburn from senior State and Defense officials and key generals. Eventually, the National Defense Authorization Act 2009 circumvented the Coburn hold by authorizing S/CRS, a Response Readiness Corps, and the Civilian Response Corps.[57]

On the appropriation side, both Houses were resistant to funding for S/CRS and particularly dismissive of the proposal for a Conflict Management Fund. The subcommittees complained of inadequate documentation on how the funds would be used in "post-conflict contingencies."[58] It was not until the FY 2009 Civilian Stabilization Initiative request came in that sentiment began to shift. As noted in Chapter 4, in 2008 Congress appropriated

$55 million for expanding the Active and Standby Components of civilian response and the following year added $75 million. The appropriators declined to provide any funding for the Civilian Reserve, however.

Both Houses have been generally favorably disposed toward the other major 150 accounts used in peace-building since the beginning of the Iraq war, particularly those used exclusively for peacekeeping and post-conflict reconstruction. With respect to the CIPA account, both the House and the Senate Committees have done their best to minimize arrears on peace-keeping. In 2008 appropriations, including supplemental, reached $2.1 billion, larger than the administration requested. The second 2008 supplemental earmarked $333 million or 89 percent of total CIPA money for the UNAMID force in Darfur. There are currently no serious issues, although UN peacekeeping funding, given its large size, is always potentially subject to challenge.

The appropriations committees are likewise generally favorable to the PKO account but tend to deal with the numbers at the level of individual countries. There is sympathy for the focus on four African countries (Democratic Republic of Congo, Liberia, Sudan, and Somalia). Some concern has been expressed at State Department's alleged raiding of the GPOI for other purposes, but a second phase of the program for 2010–2014 appears likely to have Congressional funding support.

The Congress generally holds USAID's OTI in high regard. One Congressional staffer commented that "All USAID programs should meet the OTI standard" of specific objective and political relevancy.

USIP continues to benefit from the positive reputation gained in Congress from its work in the Balkans, Iraq, and Afghanistan. It is perceived as keeping its key Capitol Hill committees well informed.[59] Its $25 million appropriation in 2008, an increase of almost 9 percent over the previous year, was not controversial. Future increases are by no means certain, however. There is some sentiment in Congress that further growth in funding would give USIP an unfair advantage and that it should be obliged to compete with nongovernment think tanks for ESF or democracy money.

With the possible exception of INCLE, the appropriators are generally satisfied with other accounts in the 150 function contributing to peace-building. There is criticism that administrations tend to understate funding needs for disaster relief and refugees. At the present time, there is general bipartisan agreement with the distinction between DA, aimed at long-term development, and the ESF, the more flexible and U.S. diplomatic interest-based account. The "F process," which designates ESF for countries in the "peace and security" category—facing internal conflict—has garnered praise for providing greater intellectual rigor to assistance policy. There appears to have been no significant challenge to the categorizing of countries. Significantly, the appropriators added some funding to the ESF request for the Philippines and Sri Lanka in the second 2008 supplemental.

Although the bulk of the INCLE account goes to narcotics control—with the focus of recent debate on Mexico and Central America—there is concern that the State Department is not exercising adequate oversight over contractors, including those carrying out CIVPOL training. There was no special language on controls in the second supplement on INCLE, but the administration's request was slashed by almost 47 percent from $734 million to $390 million for the remainder of FY 2008 and by 12 percent in the bridge supplement for 2009. A total of up to $100 million was allocated to police training in the West Bank and Gaza for both years. The appropriations committees have regularly increased amounts requested for disaster assistance and refugees. At the staff level, there is a suspicion that administrations tend to "low ball" the request to create an impression of commitment to budget discipline, calculating that the Congress will increase these popular programs. The appropriators also added $76 million for the Democracy Fund for Iraq and Chad which the administration had not requested.[60]

The FFP appropriation is not handled by the State and Foreign Operations Subcommittee, but by the Agriculture Subcommittee. That subcommittee is highly "stovepiped"; it carries out its responsibilities in isolation from the other subcommittees. Its uniqueness does not translate into low levels of appropriation—quite the contrary, since a high appropriation increases U.S. farm revenues. However, the subcommittee, dominated by farm state representatives, has been resistant to the proposal to use some Title II funds for local food purchases overseas, which could give a stabilizing boost to rural income in conflict regions.[61]

CONGRESSIONAL DISQUIET OVER 050 ACCOUNTS FOR PEACE-BUILDING

Congress grew increasingly unhappy with the Bush administration pattern of funding war reconstruction activities through supplemental appropriations. There were precedents for initial funding of military actions like Korea, Vietnam, the Gulf War, and U.S. actions in the Balkans.[62] As the Afghanistan and Iraq conflicts entered their eighth and sixth years, respectively, both parties complained that the supplemental process was undermining budget discipline by adding large sources of "off-budget" expenditure and forestalling careful scrutiny of priorities and programs.

The appropriators grumbled over the ISFF.[63] While conceding that reasonably strong Iraqi security forces were necessary to U.S. withdrawal of combat troops, the appropriations subcommittees believed the Iraqi government should be meeting much more of the funding requirements for its security forces. ISFF originally contemplated training, equipment, infrastructure, and sustainment expenditures. The subcommittees were not happy with the reporting on ISFF projects and imposed a new reporting requirement in 2007. They pressed for the elimination of infrastructure funding and reduced the administration's request from $2 billion to $1 billion in FY 2009 bridge funding, while insisting that the Government of Iraq fund a third of the total. There has been greater support for ASFF because of the paucity of resources of the Afghan government and the basic absence of infrastructure in that country. ASFF funds have even been used to pay for some security forces salaries—a usage proscribed for Iraq—and for some funding for narcotics police. The bridge funding appropriation raised the administration request from $1.35 billion to $2 billion.

IMPORTANCE OF ANNUAL DEFENSE AUTHORIZATION

Both authorizing and appropriating committees have kept a close eye on CERP. Committee members from both parties have asserted that the Iraqi government should increasingly fund infrastructure repair and development, doubting the need for regular DOD involvement in such projects, which, at least in Iraq, gradually took on a greater "economic development" cast.[64] In fact, a program known as Iraq-CERP emerged, funded by the Iraqi government but implemented by the Multi-National Force—Iraq.[65] The bridge appropriation for 2009 in the May 2008 supplemental was slashed from $1.7 billion (for both Iraq and Afghanistan) to $1.2 billion. Surprisingly, the supplemental introduced the possibility of launching CERP in the troubled southern Philippines, but a third country program had not been authorized by the HASC and SASC as of 2008.

Congress has used the CCIF to accede to military requests to fund a global CERP, while keeping its scope very modest. The committees like the way the reformed CCIF places limited funds in the hands of local commanders on the ground, while restraining the size of the overall program. Recognizing that CCIF provided the only currently feasible vehicle for a worldwide authority to do reconstruction projects, the Defense Department formally rescinded its request for global CERP in early 2008.[66] CCIF was budgeted at a level of $75 million for FY 2009, compared with CERP levels for Afghanistan and Iraq of over $1 billion.

Congressional subcommittees have evinced some discomfort with other peace-building funding under O&M—Defense-wide. Sec. 1206, Sec. 1207, and Lift and Sustain funding began to figure in a general discussion on Capitol Hill about the need for a new consensus on the extent to which Defense or State should be responsible for military assistance. Critics see these Defense-wide accounts as evidence that the State Department has lost —or unwisely handed over to DOD—control over the recipients and allocation of U.S. military assistance. DOD, calling for permanent and expanded authority for "Global Train and Equip" (Sec. 1206), has argued that a "dual-key" approach, requiring agreement in the field between Chief of Mission and combatant commander" for specific projects under Sec. 1206 and between S/CRS and the Pentagon under Sec. 1207, provides a new model for State-DOD cooperation. However, Congressional committees have been reluctant to underwrite permanent authority for these programs. They have considered the balance between State and DOD on military assistance as an important issue for future resolution.[67] In the interim, the authorizing committees have confined themselves to a temporary extension of both Sec. 1206 and 1207 authorities. As for the latter, some on the authorization side have complained that Defense seems to erect "bureaucratic obstacles" to what they believe should be virtually automatic approval of S/CRS-proposed projects.[68] At the close of 2008, the appropriateness of requesting an increase in 2009 Sec. 1207 funding to $200 million under the 050 function while seeking $249 million for the Civilian Stabilization Initiative under Function 150 had not come into focus, apparently reflecting the absence of dialogue on this question between authorizers and appropriators on both sides of the divide between the 050 and the 150 functions. Funding for Lift and Sustain exceeded $200 million 2004–2006, but there was no line item appropriation in FY 2007 and 2008.[69]

The military's glowing reputation for humanitarian relief during the 2005 Asian tsunami and the 2006 Pakistan earthquake have solidified support for the OHDACA account at a level of about $100 million per year, keeping at only about 20 percent of the level of expenditures for the IDA account under Function 150.

To sum up, there is strong support on Capitol Hill for those elements of the international affairs function supporting peace-building. Congress has been highly accommodating to Defense Department requests for related funding but particularly impatient about reconstruction funding for Iraq. It has resisted providing permanent and global authority for the CERP funding which has played such a forward role in Iraq and Afghanistan, while supporting modest funding for humanitarian assistance and reconstruction projects undertaken at the initiative of local commanders. It has also signaled that the issue of expanded DOD authority over funds used for military assistance to foreign governments—train and equip, security and stabilization assistance, and "lift and sustain"—is ripe for major review and possible rebalancing. In that regard, they are in agreement with authorizers and appropriators overseeing State and USAID that the civilian agencies involved in peace-building require strengthening both in funding and in personnel levels.

TOTAL U.S. FUNDING FOR PEACE-BUILDING

What is the overall magnitude of U.S. government expenditures for peace-building?

The reform of the State/USAID budget function for FY 2008, aligning certain types of expenditures under the "peace and security" program objective, makes it relatively simple to derive total expenditures for that broader objective under Function 150: $8.6 billion in FY 2007. However, the peace and security objective includes a much broader set of activities—counterterrorism, combating weapons of mass destruction, and transnational crime, which this study has chosen to place outside the framework of peace-building. It is also possible to extract from "peace and security" the totals for the subcategories of "stabilization operations and security sector reform" and "conflict management and mitigation." That figure was $7 billion in FY 2007.

However, two significant problems remain. First, that assistance total includes aid to a significant number of countries which fall outside the category chosen by this study, that is, those suffering from or emerging from civil war. Countries receiving ESF, an account particularly targeted to "rebuilding" and "restrictive" countries, include Ghana, Namibia, South Africa, China, Egypt, Jordan, Tunisia, the Dominican Republic, and Ecuador—none of which have experienced large-scale political violence since the early 1990s.[70] Second, the total derived by F does not include CIPA, estimated at $2.3 billion in 2008.

For purposes of this study, therefore, it is preferable to try to aggregate the various accounts used in peace-building. That approach also has its drawbacks. Because of the "dual-use" nature of many of the accounts in the 150 function—e.g., INCLE, which combines narcotics control with civilian police training, and MRA, which provides aid for refugees who may not be fleeing civil war—it is not possible to come up with a precise measurement of total U.S. government funding for peace-building. Moreover, the enormity of expenditures related to Iraq and Afghanistan since the outset of the

Table 8.1
Peace-Building Funding by Program Objective

Achieving peace and security ($ million)	FY 2007 actual[a]	FY 2008 estimate	FY 2009 request
Stabilization operations and security sector reform	6,668.6	6,782.4	7,693.6
Conflict mitigation and reconciliation	346.6	235.9	255.0
Subtotal	**7,015.2**	**7,018.3**	**7,948.6**
Counterterrorism	242.1	170.5	191.7
Combating weapons of mass destruction	228.0	240.2	231.5
Counter-narcotics	1,148.1	897.7	1,385.4
Total	8,633.4	8,326.7	9,757.2

[a] Figures unavailable for FY 2006.
Source: Congressional Budget Justification, Foreign Operations, Fiscal Year 2009, 740, available at http://www.usaid.gov/policy/budget/cbj2009/101368.pdf.

GWOT runs the numbers far higher than they would likely be during "peacetime" for the United States.

For the 150 function, the figure for FY 2007 is $9.8 billion (including supplementals).

Table 8.2
Peace-Building in the 150 Function

Peace-building account ($ million)[a]	FY 2006 actual	FY 2007 actual	FY 2008 estimate	FY 2009 request
S/CRS from Diplomatic and Consular Programs[b]	7.8	6.9	7.0	–
Civilian Stabilization Initiative	–	–	–	248.6
Contributions to International Peacekeeping Activities (CIPA)	1,141.6	1,729.3	1,691.0	1,497.3
National Endowment for Democracy (NED)[c]	74.0	74.0	[99.2]	80.0
U.S. Institute of Peace	22.1	22.0	25.0	33.0
PL 480 Title II	729.0	666.5	1,211.0	109.5
Development Assistance (DA)	400.7	407.1	439.4	146.6
International Disaster Assistance (IDA)	280.1	165.0	430.0	–[c]
Transition Initiatives (TI)	39.6	40.0	45.0	40.0
Economic Support Fund (ESF)	1,731.5	3,577.1	3,213.3	1,892.3
Assistance for Eastern Europe and the Baltic States (AEEB)	117.3	326.1	175.0	306.0
Assistance for the Independent States of ex-USSR (FSA)	171.1	164.4	129.0	495.0
Democracy Fund	94.0	354.1	162.7	–[d]
International Narcotics Control and Law Enforcement (INCLE)	256.6	511.1	415.1	429.6
Migration and Refugee Assistance (MRA)	551.6	641.2	490.0	433.4
Emergency Refugee and Migration Assistance (ERMA)	29.7	110.0	45.0	45.0
Foreign Military Financing (FMF)	155.3	600.1	112.0	172.0
Peacekeeping Operations (PKO)	351.3	438.8	226.0	225.8

International Military Education and Training (IMET)	14.0	15.5	16.5	17.8
Total	6,167.3	9,849.2	8,833.0	6,171.9

ªFunding for PL 480 Title II and following accounts includes funding only for countries in or emerging from conflict; includes supplemental appropriations.

ᵇData provided by S/CRS; funds used in FY 2006 came from FY 2005 supplemental funds.

ᶜIDA is requested by region and not by country.

ᵈIn FY 2008 appropriated as part of Democracy Fund; administration did not request funding under the Democracy Fund.

Sources: FY 2006 actual drawn from Congressional Budget Justification, Foreign Operations for FY 2008, available at http://www.usaid.gov/policy/budget/cbj2008/fy2008cbj_full.pdf; FY 2007 actual, FY 2008 estimate, FY 2009 request drawn from Congressional Budget Justification, Foreign Operations for FY 2009, available at http://www.usaid.gov/policy/budget/cbj2009/101368.pdf.

The stabilization elements of the 050 function are fewer in number and heavily concentrated on Iraq and Afghanistan. The 050 figure for FY 2007 is $15.4 billion, falling to $9.4 billion in FY 2008 (including supplementals), because of a sharp drop in funding for the Iraqi and Afghanistan security forces.

Table 8.3
Peace-Building in the 050 Function

Peace-building account ($ million)	FY 2006 actual	FY 2007 actual	FY 2008 estimate	FY 2009 request
Operations and Maintenance— Army				
Commander's Emergency Response Program (CERP)	900.0	1,000.0	1,727.0	1,700.0
Iraq Security Forces Fund (ISFF)	3,000.0	5,500.0	3,000.0	2,000.0
Industry Revitalization (Iraq Freedom Fund)	–	–	50.0	50.0
Afghanistan Security Forces Fund (ASFF)	1,900.0	7,400.0	2,750.0	3,700.0
Operations and Maintenance— Defense-wide				
Global Train and Equip (Sec. 1206)ª	–	300.0	272.0	–
Security and Stabilization Assistance (Sec. 1207)ᵇ	10.0	99.5	100.0	200.0

Combatant Commander's Initiative Fund (CCIF)	–	–	25.0	50.0
Overseas Humanitarian, Disaster Assistance and Civic Assistance (OHDACA)[c]	45.1	45.0	45.7	83.2
Coalition Support	900.0	1,100.0	1,100.0	250.0
Lift & Sustain[d]	254.0	–	300.0	450.0
Total	7,009.1	15,444.5	9,369.7	8,483.2

[a] DOD reprogrammed $300 million from other parts of the budget after Congress eliminated it from the FY 2007 supplemental. See DOD FY 2009 Budget Request Summary, "Building Partnership Capacity," 101.

[b] No specific authorization in FY 2008 consolidated. DOD allocated $100 million from O&M —Defense-wide.

[c] Includes humanitarian mine action, humanitarian assistance program, but not disaster relief.

[d] Senate Appropriations deleted $100 million from FY 2007 supplemental. H.R. 2764 authorizes use of FY 2008 O&M for lift (Sec. 607) but appropriated no money.

Sources: FY 2006 actual. CRS Report for Congress, FY 2007 Supplemental Appropriations for Defense, Foreign Affairs and Other Purposes (updated July 2, 2007); Defense Security Cooperation Agency, Global War on Terror/Regional War on Terror, Operations and Maintenance, Defense-wide, DSCA-73 through 77. FY 2007 actual equals the sum of Revised Continuing Appropriations Resolution, 2007 H.J.Res. 20 (PL 110-5) and FY 2007 Supplemental 1 H.R. 2206 (PL 110-5). FY 2008 estimate equals the sum of H.R. 2764 (PL 110-161) and the FY 2008 Supplemental H.R. 2642 (PL 110-252). FY 2009 request is drawn from Presidential Request for FY 2009 Supplemental Appropriation, FY 2009 Emergency Proposals, p. 10; Office of the Secretary of Defense, Operations and Maintenance Overview, February 2008, FY 2009 Budget Estimates; DSCA, FY 2009 Supplemental Request, Operations and Maintenance, Defense-wide, Support for Coalition Forces, DSCA-55. For 2004–2006 figures for O&M Army, see also Congressional Research Service, Report to Congress, FY 2007 Supplemental Appropriations for Defense, Foreign Affairs and Other Purposes (updated July 20, 2007).

Combining the two functions brings the total to $25.3 billion in FY 2007 and an estimated $18.2 billion in FY 2008.

Table 8.4
An Approximation of Total U.S. Peace-Building Funding

Function	$ million			
	FY 2006	FY 2007	FY 2008	FY 2009 request
150	6,167.3	9,849.2	8,833.0	6,171.9
050	7,009.1	15,444.5	9,369.7	8,483.2
Total	13,176.4	25,293.7	18,202.7	14,655.1

Table 8.5
An Approximation of U.S. Peace-Building Funding, Excluding Iraq and Afghanistan

Function	$ million			
	FY 2006 actual	FY 2007 actual	FY 2008 estimate	FY 2009 request
150	4,390.6	6,129.2	5,829.7	4,543.7
050	55.1	144.5	170.7	358.2
Total	4,445.7	6,273.7	6,000.4	4,901.9

The picture changes if Iraq and Afghanistan are removed from the equation. For the 150 function the total was $6.1 billion in FY 2007. The 050 function falls away, at least in that year by 99 percent to $144.5 million. The total reached $6.3 billion in FY 2007 and slightly more than $6 billion in FY 2008.

FUTURE FUNDING ISSUES FOR PEACE-BUILDING

The reorganization and amalgamation of the Function 150 budget process for State and USAID have created greater coherence in assistance programming for peace-building. Much of that programming takes place under the "peace and security" objective. However, that objective does not supply an accurate measurement of funding for peace-building because it includes funding for states which have not experienced civil conflict in recent years and excludes other accounts like CIPA. In fact, there has been a proliferation of accounts that play a role in peace-building. A few like CIPA, Peacekeeping Operations, TI, and the USIP have been exclusively focused on peace-building. The FY 2009 budget request included for the first time major funding for the S/CRS. The bulk of the accounts used in peace-building are "dual-use"; they support additional functions such as development, narcotics interdiction, humanitarian relief, refugee aid, democratization, and strengthening of security forces. Most of these functions are an integral part of the overall peace-building process and play a useful role in its effectiveness.

Function 050 has been drawn into peace-building activity, particularly because of the conflicts in Afghanistan and Iraq. ISFF and ASFF flows for building the security forces in Iraq and Afghanistan respectively have been major instruments for reaching stability in both countries, and the CERP became the key mechanism for reconstruction projects carried out by the PRTs. Other accounts evolved to assist U.S. allies in both theaters. The Coalition Support, Train & Equip (Sec. 1206), and Lift & Sustain accounts impinge on the State Department's policy leadership and administrative management of U.S. military assistance. If Iraq- and Afghanistan-related assistance is removed from assistance calculations, the peace-building involvement of Function 050 becomes much more modest—a global CCIF and OHDACA, each accounting for about $100 million. The 050 account involvement in peace-building will diminish further, if S/CRS acquires its own substantial project funding stream out of Function 150, eliminating the need for Sec. 1207. There is a bipartisan view in both Houses of Congress that the U.S. military is overstretched and that the civilian agencies involved in national security should be strengthened both in numbers of personnel and budget. Those committees involved with national defense are unwilling to extend the Defense Department permanent authority in the military assistance area.

Such a diminution will not be welcomed by those in the defense community who advocate an expansive military role in R&S as essential to improved performance in crises where U.S. troops are committed. If stability operations continue to be enshrined in military doctrine as a core mission, the military leadership will likely argue for a level of budget resources to match this role.[71] They will seek to build on recent successes in creating new security assistance accounts in the Defense budget. As recommended by Williams and Adams, the Obama administration—with Congressional input—should carry out a thorough review of the current range of State and Defense Department security assistance programs with a view to their consolidation under the policy leadership of the State Department with full Defense Department participation.[72]

The future of Congressional funding for a "whole of government" approach to R&S is unsettled, even though there has been strong bipartisan support in the authorizing committees. Despite strong rhetorical support for the S/CRS Office, including in the President's 2007 State of the Union message, the Bush administration did not make a major effort to secure the required funding until $249 million for the Civilian Stabilization Initiative was included in the lame-duck FY 2009 budget. The 2008 Supplemental Appropriation Act ("the war supplemental") appropriated bridge funding of $55 million—$30 million for State and $25 million for USAID—to help launch in a modest way a "Response Readiness Corps" (active and standby components), but not the Civilian Response Corps. The question of permanent funding for a civilian expeditionary capacity was left to the 111th Congress at a time when severe recession and anticipated expanded funding of domestic programs are driving careful Congressional scrutiny of expensive new foreign operations programs.

CHAPTER 9

THE FUTURE OF U.S. PEACE-BUILDING

> The Bush Administration's system for managing reconstruction and stabilization is creating skill sets, doctrine, and institutions. But we must not lose sight of the fact that you have to work at the high-level political game to effect a settlement of the underlying struggle. S/CRS offers an answer to the tactical problem, not how you deal with the strategic threat. That requires diplomacy. The retail approach is necessary but not sufficient.
> —James Jeffrey[1]

The past two decades have generated a vast range of internal conflicts around the world requiring U.S. attention. That frequency has afforded an opportunity to test a variety of approaches, including how to array and coordinate different U.S. government agencies regarding conflicts of different intensity and of varying interest, to U.S. foreign policy and national security objectives. Most of these conflicts have been dealt with through U.S. diplomacy, usually in consultation with governments in the region, the United Nations, and regional organizations. In these cases, the United States has often looked to another donor government to take the lead in finding a solution, for example, Australia for East Timor and France for Cote d'Ivoire. In cases engaging broader U.S. interests, Washington has allocated significant amounts of assistance from Function 150 accounts, involving both USAID and State Department programs, to strengthen regional or UN peacekeeping initiatives undertaken with its diplomatic support. Examples include Sudan and the Democratic Republic of the Congo. In a few cases, the United States has deployed American military forces, either as part of a UN contingent or in a "coalition of the willing" in enforcement action, in concert with post-conflict assistance programs. Except in the Balkans and in the special cases of Afghanistan and Iraq, the military deployments have been brief (Somalia 1992–93, Haiti 1994, and Liberia 2003). All three administrations examined in this study have followed a somewhat similar overall pattern of interagency involvement, despite their very different orientations to peace-building. The George H. W. Bush administration was reluctant to lead on peace-building in internal conflicts. The Clinton administration gyrated between activism and noninvolvement until the Bosnian crisis set it on a leadership track. The George W. Bush administration, scornful of "nation-building," set aside the Clinton administration processes, only to establish an even more elaborate formal machinery of its own.

NATIONAL SECURITY REVIEW

The arrival in Washington of a new administration offers an opportunity to review in detail the U.S. approach to peace-building—to modify or fine-tune strategy, to confirm the mechanisms and institutions that work, and to repair or discard those that don't. It is essential that such a review operate with a clear understanding of the experience of the past two decades.

1. A thorough review of U.S. peace-building doctrine, mechanisms, and inter-agency coordination should be a major part of a new Quadrennial National Security Review.

Such a review should not take place in isolation from other aspects of U.S. national security. For that reason, it would be desirable for the administration to make it part of an overall evaluation of the U.S. national security posture. Recent studies have called for the inauguration of a "Quadrennial National Security Review" (QNSR), along the lines of the Quadrennial Defense Review mandated by the 1996 National Defense Authorization Act.[2] The quadrennial review would precede and become responsible for the National Security Strategy statement required by the Congress since the late 1980s. The Bush administration transformed the "boilerplate" quality of earlier submissions by developing a significant Strategy statement in 2002, updated in 2006. A new quadrennial review could build on this advance.

To give it bureaucratic heft, the President should make clear at the outset to his Secretaries of State and Defense and his NSA that the review is a top priority. Conflict prevention and resolution should be a major element of the quadrennial review, more explicit than in the two strategy statements issued by the Bush White House. A major question to be addressed at the outset is whether high priority should be accorded approaches to peace-building and interagency mechanisms to support it. This study suggests a positive answer to that question. Conflict management and resolution have become increasingly important since 1990, and the international dynamic behind that salience is unlikely to change in the coming decade.

2. A national security budget should be developed which gives careful attention to the sources and accounts used to fund the range of peace-building activities mounted by the U.S. government.

The national security review should become the basis for an even more fundamental appraisal: the balance of resources in the federal budget between the Defense Department and U.S. civilian agencies in support of national security goals and objectives. There is widespread agreement within the Congress and among scholars and decision-makers that the existing 13 to 1 ratio badly shortchanges the civilian side. Recommendations for the development of a national security budget are an integral part of the proposal for a national security quadrennial review. The balance between the existing Function 150 budget and the Function 050 budget would be evaluated in a national security budget, along with the current design of accounts having a bearing on peace-building. Since Congress will have the final say on a national security budget, it would be desirable to include key members of Congress in a consultative process as preparation of a national security budget gets underway.

That review should take into account and benefit from the experience of the Bush administration in creating a better integrated USAID and State budget.[3] It resulted in a process in which funds are allocated, not against agency programs but against strategic program objectives. The review needs to keep in mind that the accounts aggregated under the "peace and security" objective do not include major aspects of post-conflict reconstruction like funds for UN peacekeeping, humanitarian assistance, and democratization. The review would provide a banner opportunity to consider the recent balance between State and Defense accounts in the allocation of military assistance. New Function 050 instruments, including quick-disbursing CERP and CCIF, as well as "coalition support," "train and equip," and "lift and sustain," have muddied traditional State Department authority to determine the recipients and nature of military assistance provided.

3. The National Security Advisor and Deputies should give attention to the ranking and placement of the NSC official charged with responsibility for the interagency process for peace-building, stabilization, and reconstruction to ensure that person is well-positioned to help drive the interagency bureaucratic process.

A successful strategic review of peace-building strategy necessitates a central role by the NSC. The NSC must be the driver of the review process and will need to ensure that each relevant agency plays a constructive role in the process—prodding them, as necessary, with the authority of the President.

With regard to NSC organization, a significant decision for a new administration will be the positioning and rank of the person filling the role as Director of Stability Operations. Under the Bush administration that officer was placed initially in the Defense Directorate and then in the Directorate for Relief, Stabilization and Development. The latter reported to the Deputy National Security Advisor for International Economics and was primarily concerned with the nature and level of strategically important foreign assistance. The Director of Stability Operations has operated with some autonomy and flexibility, but had the disadvantages of being formally outside the main channel of NSC communications to the Defense Department and of being of relatively low rank in dealing with assistant secretaries or their equivalent in the Defense and State Departments. One possibility would be to modify the position of DNSA for Combating Terrorism into a DNSA for Combating Terrorism and Building Peace, placing under that official the existing Senior Director for Combating Terrorism Strategy and a Senior Director for Stability Operations and Peace-Building.

STRENGTHENING AGENCY OPERATIONS FOR PEACE-BUILDING

State Department

4. The Obama administration should confirm through presidential executive order that the Secretary of State will continue to carry the responsibility for leading and coordinating post-conflict reconstruction activities.

The principal locus of peace-building in the U.S. government is the State Department. That is because diplomacy is at the heart of conflict prevention, conflict resolution, and most post-conflict reconstruction. Most conflicts in the post–Cold War period are rooted in specific regional contexts, involving governments, disaffected elements within a state, and neighboring countries affected by the violence. Within the U.S. government, embassies and the State Department geographic bureaus they report to—aided by the intelligence community—are the storehouses of expertise not only about the political and security situation in the afflicted state but on past and present modes of U.S. operation there. They are therefore in the best position to make a judgment about the seriousness of a potential conflict and appropriate U.S. actions. When conflict has broken out, they are on the front lines of formulating the U.S. response—noninvolvement, consultation with other states and international organizations, providing good offices, or supporting the good offices of other states. Even when a peace agreement has been concluded, those State Department elements are intimately involved in the diplomacy of developing the mechanism of R&S, as well as the diplomacy of sustaining and modifying its format.

The fact that the State Department is the institution out of which most U.S. peace-building emerges has a bearing on but is not decisive of the debate about where policy leadership in that area should reside. The major options which have been suggested are three: NSC, Defense Department, and State Department. The case for the NSC is essentially that peace-building calls for a serious commitment on the part of a number of U.S. government agencies; that one cabinet secretary is not in a position to dictate to another department how it will allocate its personnel and budget; and that only the NSC is in a position to secure true interagency coordination for peace-building. The case for the Defense Department is basically that only the Pentagon has the operational planning capacity, the budget and personnel numbers to do post-conflict reconstruction effectively. We have seen that the Clinton White House informally divided the responsibility between NSC and State. The Bush administration, reflecting on the initial failure of DOD-led R&S in Afghanistan and Iraq, vested in the Secretary of State leadership and coordination responsibilities for R&S activities (NSPD 44). The decision recognized that the R&S are more closely tied to both foreign policy leadership and diplomacy than to military operations. NSPD 44 also reflected a consensus view that the NSC, as part of the White House staff, should not be "operational." It should be the driver of the bureaucratic process and ensure interagency coordination, drawing on presidential authority. Operational responsibility for coordinating the substantive process of R&S was placed with the State Department.

The wisdom of that placement rests not only on a judgment about the disadvantages of alternative approaches but also on the capacity of the State Department to operate programs. A number of critics, particularly those associated with the Defense Department and USAID, argue that the State Department lacks an "operational" bureaucratic culture.[4] According to this view, Foreign Service Officers are good at representation, reporting, and policy planning but are not equipped by orientation and training to manage complex programs. That, it is argued, is the province of the military, with its focus on operational planning and logistics, and USAID officers, with their long experience in planning and managing projects. In rebuttal, this study has argued that such a portrait of the State Department is outdated. Over the past three decades the State Department has become increasingly operational in fields related to post-conflict reconstruction, including human rights and democracy programs, refugee programs, and civilian police programs. The creation of an office charged with R&S adds an additional major program to this program management portfolio.

5. The State Department should require that political officers complete a training module on conflict during mid-career. Promotion precepts for entry into the Senior Foreign Service should include the completion of that module and at least one assignment in a conflict zone. The Bureau of Personnel should take positively into account experience in one or more countries troubled by political violence in negotiating with the regional bureaus assignments as deputy chief of mission and country director.[5]

Although State's geographic bureaus are naturally equipped to take the lead in peace-building diplomacy, they do not necessarily do so effectively. They may, of course, overlook key factors in the conflict. They may misjudge the capacity of the local government or rebellious movements. They may exercise bad judgment in proposing a U.S. response, sometimes ignoring cogent dissenting views. The diplomacy of peace-building is a necessarily imperfect art.

The State Department should invest an important effort in strengthening the peace-building capacity of the geographic bureaus through training and adjustment of promotion incentives. Officers in the political cone should be required to complete a training program on conflict prevention, conflict resolution, and post-conflict reconstruction. Promotion precepts should ensure that political officers do not cross the threshold to the Senior Foreign Service without conflict zone assignments. Such assignments should also be taken into account in assigning officers to senior positions, overseas and in Washington.

S/CRS: The Appropriate Secretariat to Coordinate Interagency Peace-Building?

6. The Secretary of State should confirm that staffing and operational support for her R&S leadership will be exercised through an office like that of the present Coordinator for Reconstruction and Stabilization. However, the State Department should undertake, in coordination with the NSC, Defense, and USAID, a thorough evaluation of the contribution and potential of that office, including its interface with the geographic bureaus and other agencies, its staffing needs—especially how to ensure a truly interagency staff—and its budget requirements. The objective would be to create a fully integrated State-USAID operation, with some staffing from the military and additional civilian agencies as well. There should be recognition that the ability of the office to play a major role in future crises will depend on the extent of support it receives from the Secretary, if and when the leaders of the geographic bureaus seek to limit it to a marginal role. The evaluation should also consider how the office might be calibrated to a more thoroughgoing multilateral approach to conflict management, in particular the desirable division of labor between S/CRS and analogous units in the UN secretariat and allied governments.

Even if it is conceded that operational leadership in peace-building—including R&S—belongs in the State Department, the proximate question is whether the major institutional mechanisms for exercising that leadership are up to the task. The most significant institutional initiative of the George W. Bush administration in peace-building was the creation of the S/CRS. S/CRS was established as the formal staffing and operational arm—the secretariat—of the Secretary of State in her new R&S policy responsibility. Since its creation S/CRS has logically divided its focus organizationally between conflict transformation and conflict prevention and has accumulated a 100-person staff, equivalent in size to a small bureau. It has had limited success in its efforts to create an interagency staff: a USAID principal deputy coordinator, two military officers, and one Department of Justice representative; the rest are from State. The absence of significant role in Iraq and Afghanistan, as well as in more recent crises like Lebanon and Kosovo, leave unanswered important questions about its potential in future crises. Nevertheless, the work of a handful of S/CRS Active Response Component personnel deployed to crisis spots like Darfur, Kosovo, Nepal, and Lebanon, R&S projects in a dozen countries, and planning exercises involving Zimbabwe and the Congo are building blocks for a wider post-conflict role.

One constraint on S/CRS effectiveness has been the unwillingness of the geographic bureaus to cede to S/CRS a major role in dealing with high-priority conflicts. S/CRS was largely excluded from decisions on the U.S. government response to the Lebanon and Somalia crises in 2006 and 2007, respectively. Most of the geographic bureaus now agree that S/CRS can play a useful role in modestly augmenting embassy resources through deployment of Active Response Component personnel, a success for S/CRS to build on in its future engagement with the bureaus. However, the issue of the balance between geographic bureaus and S/CRS is likely to be rejoined if Congress approves creation of a civilian reserve. The geographic bureaus may be reluctant to agree to a significant number of personnel in the field with institutional loyalties to S/CRS, rather than to them. To facilitate effective cooperation between S/CRS and the bureaus in major crises will require leadership from the Secretary of State. Depriving the bureaus of their primary diplomatic role would generate bureaucratic foot dragging. Moreover, short-circuiting the sources of regional expertise and experience is likely to lead to critical mistakes in practice. A useful rule of thumb would be to assign primacy in foreign policy guidance to the geographic bureaus and primacy in program design and implementation to S/CRS. Since these two responsibilities overlap in practice, a practical *modus operandi* would need to be worked out in each case.

The second major constraint has been the absence of substantial appropriated funds for S/CRS until very late in the Bush administration. Its only real source of program funds has been a transfer from the Defense Department (Sec. 1207). Not only can S/CRS not count on continued Congressional acquiescence in Sec. 1207 transfers, but such funding on a permanent basis would be inappropriate. S/CRS should be directly accountable to Congress for its major R&S projects.

7. In evaluating the future shape and mandate of S/CRS, the administration should reexamine—in at least informal consultation with Congress—the dimensions of the need for a civilian "surge" capacity, including the balance between additional full-time positions for State and USAID and a reserve cadre, to meet rapidly developing additional human resource and skill requirements.

Congress decided in a 2008 supplemental bill to "forward fund" $30 million to launch the civilian stabilization initiative, against the $249 million request for FY 2009. The FY 2009 Omnibus Appropriations Act, passed in March 2009, added an additional $75 million for a coordinated civilian response capacity at State and USAID, indicating that the new Congress was positively disposed toward—if not completely sold on—the R&S enterprise.

Prospects for adequate long-term funding for S/CRS will rest to a considerable extent on the fate of the proposed civilian reserve. That concept should be scrutinized carefully by the Obama administration, in consultation with the Congress. While supported by the authorizing committees, the civilian reserve has limited appeal for the appropriators. An evaluation of the proposed program should include a judgment about the nature and frequency of future conflicts engaging U.S. interests. It should look into the trade-offs between providing personnel for a surge capacity and increasing full-time employees for the State Department and USAID. There is sympathy in Congress for an increase in full-time State (and USAID) positions. The evaluation should also look into the possibilities of closer collaboration between the United States, the United Nations, and key allies building up post-conflict response capabilities like Canada, the United Kingdom, and other European states—and a desirable division of labor with these partners.

Defense

8. As part of the Quadrennial National Security Review, DOD should evaluate the results of Directive 3000.05, including its September 2009 revision, with a view to strengthening its integration into military operations.

The most important peace-building reversal of the George W. Bush administration was belated recognition of the importance of nation-building at the DOD. The elevation of stability operations to the importance of combat operations in Defense Directive 3000.05 was revolutionary. It may be hard to believe that the uniformed military fully accepts that theoretical equivalence, but the message of the high importance of R&S has been widely accepted. The administration should quickly reaffirm that importance in a new directive as one of the outcomes of a quadrennial national security review.

9. Pentagon leadership should seek to ensure that an interagency approach to stability operations is imbedded in the operational guidance, in particular, for the Joint Chiefs of Staff, JFCOM, the regional combatant commands, and the OSD.

Assigning responsibility for compliance with Directive 3000.05 to a wide spectrum of commands and offices helped gain acceptance of the importance of stability operations to military success. The OSD reorganized extensively to deal with the requirements of a "whole of government" approach. Defense's reissuance of the directive, confirming stability operations as "a core military mission to be conducted with the same proficiency as combat operations" is a welcome step, but further attention to the concept is warranted in the next QDR.

Assignment of a major role to JFCOM as the lead in developing the concept of stability operations was felicitous. It marks the logical extension of the idea of jointness to collaboration with the civilian agencies. Over the past three years, JFCOM has become a valued partner of S/CRS.

Integrating stability operations into ongoing service operations has been uneven. Army and Marines, obliged to work closely with civilian agencies in Afghanistan and Iraq, have devoted most attention to the concept. The Army has integrated stability operations into the new version of its Field Operations Manual.

In the end, successful integration of stability operations into overall military operations will depend on implementation by the combatant commands. CENTCOM has developed a working model and laboratory for interagency stability operations in the PRTs. CENTCOM was the first to develop, back in 2001, a Joint Interagency Coordination Group (JIACG) for interagency consultation in each command. That mechanism now exists in all the geographic commands, but its effective engagement with the issue of the division of labor for R&S seems limited.

10. The administration should place future responsibility for U.S. training of police in post-conflict situations in the hands of the State Department, working with the Department of Justice.

While training of the military forces is a legitimate DOD stabilization role, the wisdom of giving the U.S. military a lead role in training police even in conflicts where U.S. forces are heavily engaged is doubtful. Pentagon success in wresting that role from the State Department in Iraq did not produce a relatively incorrupt and non-factionalized Iraqi police, often contrasted unfavorably with the new U.S.-trained Iraqi army. Police training in Afghanistan has also been dismal. Training for military police and civilian police is quite different. Although it is probably too late to shift police training responsibility to the State Department in Iraq and Afghanistan, any U.S. CIVPOL training role in future conflict situations, including those where the U.S. military is deployed, should be the responsibility of the State Department, working with the Department of Justice. In most instances, the United States should encourage allies with national police forces to take over the police training function.

11. The administration should recognize that with respect to most violent internal conflicts engaging U.S. interests, the role of the U.S. military is likely to be limited to coordination with peacekeeping forces from other countries, logistical support, and occasional training of reformed military forces in a newly stabilized state.

Despite the recent attention given to stability operations at the Pentagon, the involvement of the U.S. military in American peace-building efforts in internal conflicts abroad is likely to remain limited. DOD will participate fully in interagency deliberations, if the IMS or a comparable system is activated. The relevant combatant commands would host an IPC dispatched in tandem with the ACT augmenting the embassy. It would provide intelligence and possibly limited logistic support for the ACT. However, DOD will resist proposals to use American forces for peacekeeping—as it did in the case of Liberia in 2003, until overruled by the President—let alone for peace enforcement operations. Only in cases involving a major U.S. national security interest—rising to the level of an Afghanistan or a Bosnia—will the Defense Department be comfortable with the deployment of large numbers of troops over a substantial period. In most cases, peacekeepers or peace enforcers will come from elsewhere, as authorized by the United Nations or regional organizations. U.S. combatant commands will certainly coordinate with those forces and perhaps provide lift, training, or other military assistance. In a few cases, similar to Liberia, the U.S. military might take responsibility for training the military forces of a stabilizing state.

The intense interagency activity generated by NSPD 44 and Directive 3000.05 has revealed in dramatic fashion the mismatch in numbers and budget between the Defense Department and the civilian agencies. S/CRS's budget problems and its limited engagement with the most serious conflicts faced by the U.S. government have bred or increased cynicism about civilian capacity for R&S. Some Defense officials have suggested that if the State Department and USAID prove incapable of managing post-conflict reconstruction, the Defense Department will be obliged to take over the task, even creating its own cadre of civilian specialists.

A lead Pentagon role in R&S in future major conflicts involving the United States would be dangerous. It would provide further ammunition for a widespread international view that U.S. foreign policy is excessively militarized. It would feed the conception that the U.S. approach to peace-building relies primarily on military occupation. It would exacerbate fears that the military, already overstretched in manpower and readiness, would be asked to assume new responsibilities with unclear parameters. It would lead to an even greater imbalance in funding resources allocated between military and civilian agencies of the U.S. government. Those points reinforce the argument that the Secretary of State should retain leadership of a "whole of government" approach to R&S.

USAID

12. The Obama administration should retain the principle of an integrated State-USAID Function 150 foreign operations budget by strategic objectives, which helps concentrate resources to be made available for peace-building. The 2005 reform should be consolidated by bringing hitherto separate foreign assistance programs under its umbrella and by mandating that OMB budget the same way for Function 150.

The integration of the USAID and State Department foreign operations budget under Function 150 and budgeting against strategic objectives are important, but incomplete moves toward coherence in the foreign policy process. Application of the principle of budgeting against strategic objectives, such as peace and security, governing justly and democratically, and humanitarian assistance, rather than for individual agencies is particularly helpful to peace-building. The process is incomplete, however, because OMB has not yet adopted the same kind of budgeting to objectives reform. A new administration has an opportunity to consolidate the reform and to work with OMB and the Congress to apply it to the entire gamut of the Function 150 budget process.

The reengagement of USAID in peace-building, a process which began under the Clinton administration and advanced under the Bush administration, is a positive development. Given the high incidence of internal conflict in the Global South, an understanding of how conflict impacts development programs and how development programs can contribute to conflict resolution is important both to development and to peace-building. Geographic bureau initiation and management of projects using development assistance to resolve conflicts in unstable areas are justified.

13. The Secretary of State and USAID Administrator should institute a study to determine how to amalgamate certain USAID conflict management and transformation functions into an integrated State/USAID Coordinator's Office. In particular, consideration should be given to transferring DCHA's Office of Conflict Management and Mitigation to S/CRS to take over the conflict prevention function. Consideration should likewise be given to integrating OTI into S/CRS as the foundation of the Active Component of the Civilian Response Corps.

Reconfiguring the Bureau of Humanitarian Response to create a Bureau of Democracy, Conflict and Humanitarian Assistance as the peace-building center of USAID and subsequently establishing S/CRS generated areas of duplication and overlap that have not been resolved. Specifically, the S/CRS Office for Conflict Prevention and USAID's CMM appear to have overlapping functions. If the new administration decides to continue with and strengthen S/CRS, modest alterations in USAID's architecture for R&S should be considered, in particular, integrating CMM into S/CRS. The case for doing so would be reinforced, if an intensified effort is undertaken to make S/CRS a more interagency office through the introduction of new slots for USAID officers.

A second integration issue involves OTI, an expeditionary group which facilitates transitions to democracy or peace, using funding mechanisms for local NGOs, business, and government. If Congress funds a civilian reserve program, will a continued independent role for OTI be justified? One option would be to transform OTI into S/CRS's Active Response Component. The fit would be awkward since the latter has exercised a primarily diplomatic liaison and reporting function, while OTI has had a mandate broader than peace-building and has taken on an "investment financing" role. The USAID Administrator, S/CRS Coordinator, and DCHA leadership should explore the desirability and modalities of integrating OTI into S/CRS, exercising care to avoid crippling an existing effective peace-building cadre.

U.S. Institute of Peace

14. The administration should explore the possibility of giving USIP the mandate to take over much of the function of training in the peace-building field. In assuming such a role, USIP should collaborate closely with S/CRS, FSI, and the National Defense University.

The transformation of USIP to a "think and do" tank has made this independent, nonpartisan body an important player among U.S. government peace-building agencies. It has achieved that role, despite its slender budget, by making itself relevant to U.S. government R&S programs in the Balkans, Iraq, and Afghanistan. USIP has effectively used its "convening" function to bring together government decision-makers, scholars, and civil society for dialogue on policy among sharply contending parties, as for example with the Iraq Study Group. The Institute provided valuable assistance to S/CRS in its start-up phase. The 2005 reorganization of USIP to cover the "life cycle of conflict"—prevention, resolution, and post-conflict reconstruction— should enable the Institute to interact with the U.S. government in a more coordinated manner. There is consensus among peace-building scholars and practitioners that greater attention to and funding for conflict prevention activities would save lives and money. Unfortunately, conflict prevention studies and activities receive less attention and government funding, and USIP has made less progress in this area than the other two. The fledgling partnership between USIP and S/CRS in conflict prevention, including cooperation on the ICAF, could be useful to both agencies.

USIP's two decades of experience have made it the paramount institution for training on conflict and peace-building in the U.S. government. The acquisition of two buildings adjacent to its new headquarters for an expanded ETC provides the administration with an excellent opportunity to strengthen and consolidate training for conflict prevention, resolution, stabilization, and reconstruction in place of the presently fragmented system operated by the FSI and the National Defense University.

USIP will come of age when it occupies that new $100 million headquarters on the National Mall. Its mandate to "think and do," as well as educate and train, and the relative size of its budget are appropriate for its place in the current array of U.S. government agencies concerned with peace. It will also be busy for the next several years consolidating its recent reorganization around the contours of the "life cycle of conflict."

Afterword

The Peace Corps

The first agency in the U.S. government to bear the word "peace" in its name was the Peace Corps. I have not included it in this survey of the U.S. government agencies most engaged with violent conflict, however. With very few exceptions, Peace Corps Volunteers (PCVs) have not worked on resolving violent conflict. As an agency, the Peace Corps operates largely independently of the other executive departments. PCVs are not considered employees of the U.S. mission overseas, although the Peace Corps director is a member of the country team. The Peace Corps does work closely with the State Department and, on occasion, the U.S. military, when violent conflict warrants the evacuation of PCVs from a crisis zone. Despite its outsider status in the interagency process for conflict, the Peace Corps was originally designed by its founders to play a peace-building role. I therefore could not end without a brief treatment of its place in U.S. peacefare.

The Peace Corps emerged from the 1960 presidential campaign of John F. Kennedy. Arriving after midnight at the Student Union at the University of Michigan, the candidate improvised a question for the enthusiastic crowd. "How many of you would be willing to spend your days working"—as teachers, doctors, and engineers—"in Ghana?" When the audience bellowed a positive response, Kennedy continued, "On your willingness ... to serve one or two years in the service [and] contribute part of your life to this country, I think will [determine] whether we as a free society can compete in the Cold War world." A few weeks later in a foreign policy speech in San Francisco, he proposed "a Peace Corps of talented young men [*sic*] willing and able to serve their country as an alternative to peace-time selective service." He clarified that the volunteers would need to be qualified in the local languages, acquire familiarity with local customs, and become skilled in their assigned tasks.[1] Kennedy saw the deployment of young American volunteers as a mode of "soft power" competition which would help diminish Soviet influence in the Global South and therefore, hopefully, the danger of war between the superpowers.

The Peace Corps was derided by the Republicans. Richard Nixon, Kennedy's opponent, called it the "kiddie corps"; President Eisenhower referred to it as "a juvenile experiment." But the idea caught the imagination of the American people, especially the generation emerging from college. I and the young woman who was to become my wife were captivated. We wrote for information about joining. Thirty months later we were on an aircraft heading for Addis Ababa, Ethiopia.

Being a PCV was a life-changing experience. A desire to contribute in some modest way to peace and development became a factor in our career plans. Judy taught English and journalism in African universities and in District of Columbia high schools. After a career of 30 plus years in the Foreign Service, I worked as president of the National Peace Corps Association, the private organization of returned volunteers and former Peace Corps staff, from 1999 to 2003.

There was debate from the outset about how to do the Peace Corps. The day after the inauguration Kennedy telephoned Sargent Shriver, his brother-in-law and a key member of his campaign staff, and asked him to figure out how to do the program. Shriver was reluctant, but Kennedy told him, at least according to legend, that if the program turned out to be a fiasco, it was easier to fire a relative than a political ally. The choice was brilliant. Shriver was a genius at mobilizing the best minds to put together a project and working them relentlessly until objectives and structure emerged.

A major question was its fit among the constellation of existing agencies. White House aides, doubtful about its viability, advocated a small experimental program under the wings of an existing foreign policy agency—either the State Department or the International Cooperation Administration (ICA), predecessor of USAID. However, Shriver was persuaded that the program needed to start big—with thousands of volunteers in large programs in major countries like Nigeria, the Philippines, India, and Pakistan—and be independent of other agencies. Otherwise, it would wither on the vine.[2] The idea of an independent agency temporarily won out, when Kennedy signed an Executive Order in early 1961, creating the Peace Corps with Shriver as its first director. The battle over independence was not settled until months later, however. When another bureaucratic assault seemed to portend Peace Corps' absorption into the ICA, Shriver and his deputy, Bill Moyers, enlisted the help of Vice President Lyndon Johnson. According to Shriver's biographer, Scott Stossel, Johnson "badgered" Kennedy until he came down on the side of independence.[3] The first volunteers arrived in Ghana in August, and by 1966 there were more than 15,000 of them, the high-water mark for the agency.

THE PEACE CORPS PHILOSOPHY

The philosophy behind the new agency is contained in the "Congressional declaration of purpose" in the Peace Corps Act of 1961.

[I]t is the policy of the United States and the purpose of this Act to promote world peace and friendship through a Peace Corps, which shall make available to interested countries and areas men and women of the United States qualified for service abroad and willing to serve, under conditions of hardship if necessary, to help the peoples of such countries and areas in meeting their needs for trained manpower, particularly in meeting the basic needs of those living in the poorest areas of such countries, and to help promote a better understanding of the American people on the part of the peoples served and a better understanding of other peoples on the part of the American people.[4]

The Kennedy administration was very much concerned with the broad implications of global competition with the Soviet Union. Under Khrushchev the Soviets had ardently embraced the decolonization struggle, supporting the demands for independence of the vanguard African colonies like Ghana and Guinea. American foreign policy analysts were concerned that the recently decolonized and decolonizing countries might be drawn into the Soviet orbit, rather than that of "the free world." These fears were heightened by suspicion that "nonalignment," to which many of them were drawn, was a facade for *entente* with Moscow and Beijing, because its rhetoric and economics seemed to lean strongly toward a Marxist analysis of the international system. Kennedy's foreign policy team wanted to avert a radical shift in favor of the Soviet side which could endanger international peace. The Peace Corps represents part of an impulse by the Kennedy administration to demonstrate that the United States could establish positive relations with decolonized countries, at one and the same time superseding the patronizing ties left over from colonialism and undercutting the blandishments of Moscow.[5]

The three "goals" mentioned in the second part of the declaration reveal more of the theory behind the Peace Corps. The first is to help the developing countries "meet their needs for trained manpower." In the late 1940s and 1950s, development was considered to derive in large part from the transfer of technical capacity to the developing countries. Low levels of education meant that they had insufficient teachers, doctors, engineers, and agricultural experts. By making available Americans with basic educational or technical qualifications, the Peace Corps could accelerate the process of technical transfer and development. Development, in turn, would enhance the likelihood of stability and peace in the Global South.

The second goal was to "help promote a better understanding of the American people" by host country nationals. Volunteers were expected to live at a standard approximately equal to that of people doing the same kind of work in the host country. For the most part, the volunteers were assigned outside the capital city in secondary cities, towns, or even large villages. They were expected to learn the local language and encouraged to develop close contacts with the local people. It was hoped this contact with the local population—far more intimate than that of embassy officers or USAID development specialists—would pay dividends in friendship—and ultimately in enhanced international peace and security—for the United States.

The third goal was to promote a better understanding of other peoples on the part of Americans through the leaven of returned Peace Corps Volunteers (RPCVs). The legislative architects of the Peace Corps correctly perceived that U.S. foreign policy would derive benefits from a better informed public. They also hoped that a public more sympathetic to the needs and achievements of the Global South would be more likely to eschew advocacy of bellicose policy positions based on racial and ethnic stereotypes.

THE EVOLUTION OF PEACE CORPS PROGRAMS

The Peace Corps declined under the Nixon administration. Republicans tended to regard it as a "Democrat" agency in the 1960s and 1970s, but its basic popularity protected it from elimination. Volunteer numbers shrank during the 1970s and stayed at a level of about 5,000 for most of the 1980s. Loret Ruppe, President Reagan's appointee as Peace Corps Director—and now, together with Sargent Shriver, an agency icon—effected a remarkable turnabout in Republican attitudes in Congress. She persuaded lawmakers that volunteers were a cost-effective way of providing overseas assistance. At the end of the Cold War there was a new demand for volunteers from countries in Eastern Europe and the former Soviet Union making the transition from communism to market economies.[6]

As the Peace Corps approaches its 50th anniversary, it has sent volunteers to 139 countries and enjoys widespread popularity. Presidents Clinton and Bush proposed significant increases in the number of volunteers. Neither came close to achieving his goals. Clinton pledged 10,000 but reached 7,000; Bush called for a doubling to 14,000 but reached slightly more than 8,000 in 2008. Funding for the Peace Corps increased annually during the Bush administration, but huge expenditures on Iraq and the GWOT discouraged appropriators from pumping in the funds required for the major increase proposed.

Although the vast majority of early volunteers were teachers, today's volunteers are more diversified, working in five general areas:

- Education is still the largest program (35%), with a focus on English, math and science, and business. Some work in curriculum development and some in teacher training. Several programs do outreach to at-risk youth (an additional 5%). A few volunteers do vocational education in construction skills usable in building schools, health centers, and markets.
- Health and HIV/AIDS (22%). Over the past decade, the Peace Corps health program has evolved toward heavy concentration on HIV/AIDS education and prevention, particularly in Africa. All health volunteers assigned to Africa work in this area, and all non-health volunteers sent to Africa are trained about HIV/AIDS and are expected to devote some nonworking hours to the crisis.

- Environment (14%). The emphasis is on environmental education, often through the establishment of environmental centers in rural areas partly staffed by PCVs. National park management and water management are often part of these programs.
- Business development (15%). Since the late 1980s, volunteers have been working in small business development in many parts of the world. The basic idea is to collaborate with individuals and communities to promote economic opportunities at the grassroots level.
- Agriculture (5%) is one of the original programs. Agriculture volunteers often work in support of environmentally friendly projects.[7]
- Information technology. In the last 10 years a number of volunteers are advancing the computer and Internet revolution in developing countries. PCVs are teaching computer skills and data processing. They bring the Internet into the classroom, link entrepreneurs with new business opportunities, and expand farmers' access to information on markets.

WHAT'S PEACE GOT TO DO WITH IT? PROGRESS TOWARD PEACE CORPS GOALS

The Peace Corps plays an ongoing role in the *transfer of skills* between educated and/or experienced Americans and their host country counterparts or students. The economic progress of countries in the Global South over the previous 50 years has been remarkable. There have been striking increases in life expectancy, adult literacy, and other social yardsticks, impressive by historical standards. The Peace Corps has provided a low-cost way for the United States to contribute to this valuable technology transfer, particularly through its largest sector—education. For example, there is no doubt that the presence of PCVs in Ethiopia and Eritrea in the 1960s and early 1970s had the effect of vastly increasing literacy and the number of students in middle and secondary schools. Volunteers teaching business in Eastern Europe in 1991 helped transfer skills important for the market economies under construction. In a 2003 evaluation, Lex Rieffel concluded that the first goal has generally been a success.

Over the past forty years, virtually all developing countries have established education systems that produce well prepared university graduates. All have sent students to the United States and elsewhere who have met the high standards of professional schools and have successfully competed in the global marketplace. . . . Hosting Peace Corps volunteers is a cost-effective way for developing countries to have early access to the cutting edge of modern life, including mastery of the English language.[8]

But, aside from education, has the Peace Corps been an effective development agency? There is no doubt that individual volunteers—highly motivated, resourceful, and able to communicate in the local language—have stimulated significant local advances in access to potable water, soil conservation, and primary health care in many different countries. Sometimes they achieve remarkable results with their development projects. As an agency, however, the Peace Corps has never placed high priority on the development task. Until 2007 it did not develop a strategic planning capacity which would examine systematically what has worked developmentally in the sectors where volunteers are present and what has not. It has never put into place a serious evaluation process to obtain systematic feedback from volunteers and the communities they work in about their development impact nor shaped that feedback into lessons learned and best practices.[9] It has not collaborated with development NGOs working in the field. And, absent a mechanism within the agency for promoting and monitoring the developmental task of volunteers, it has not made Peace Corps directors and staff accountable for the development success of their programs. Perhaps the most important development constraint at the local level is the failure of the Peace Corps to develop ways to promote continuity between the work of a departing volunteer and her successor.[10] Given training and assignment sequences, there is often a gap. The hiatus may not be a serious problem in a formal classroom, but in sectors like small business or agroforestry, the new volunteer regularly starts from scratch in figuring out the most appropriate approach.[11] So the Peace Corps contribution to development, though substantial in some countries, has not been large overall.

The Peace Corps has *promoted friendship* for the United States among those populations directly touched by PCVs. Numerous Americans traveling overseas have been approached by local people inquiring whether they know PCVs who taught them, perhaps decades before. I accompanied to Iran in 2002 a group of former volunteers who had served there in the 1960s. There were several moving reunions between the visitors and Iranians who had known them decades before. Students, coworkers, and townspeople in places where volunteers resided tend to have positive images of the Peace Corps. A Peace Corps couple assigned to Peru in the 1960s befriended a shoeshine boy, encouraged his education, and helped him get a scholarship to San Francisco State University. The shine boy, Alejandro Toledo, Stanford PhD and World Bank economist, was elected President of Peru in 2001, the first person of native Peruvian descent to reach that office.

Rieffel argues that fostering personal relationships "has been the greatest success of the Peace Corps."[12] I agree. At a time when polling indicates that foreign publics harbor great doubt and suspicion about the intentions of the United States, the Peace Corps is a countervailing force which reduces hostility toward the U.S. presence and contributes to a more peaceable atmosphere for Americans to work in. Increasing the size of the Peace Corps should be part of an overall U.S. peace-building strategy.[13]

RPCVs have *improved American understanding* of the Global South. Their numbers have almost reached 200,000 and are found in every state. In 2008, there were five members of Congress and one governor. Returned volunteers, well represented in USAID and the Foreign Service, have strengthened both agencies' understanding of Africa, Asia, Latin America, and Eurasia. NGOs working on international issues are heavily staffed by former volunteers. Many RPCVs have become professors in American universities. Many more have taught American children. Nevertheless, 200,000 is a small leaven in a population of 300 million. They haven't had a major impact on the way Americans in general regard the rest of the world. Progress toward the "third goal" has been significant but not transformative.

CRISIS CORPS BECOMES PEACE CORPS RESPONSE

In 1996 Peace Corps Director Mark Gearen created the Crisis Corps. The idea was to recruit former volunteers, particularly those who had recently finished their tours, for three- to six-month assignments in crisis situations where unseasoned volunteers might fail. In the early years, fewer than ten volunteers were deployed annually. With the increased frequency of hurricane disasters in the Caribbean, the numbers began to rise. As of mid-2008, 650 Crisis Corps Volunteers had served in 40 countries in Latin America, Africa, the Pacific, Asia, and Eastern Europe.

The same year the Peace Corps changed the name of the program to Peace Corps Response, recognizing that it is rarely an emergency response to crisis.[14] The work is divided, somewhat arbitrarily, into five general categories:

1. *Natural disaster relief and reconstruction* was the initial task of the Crisis Corps. An early example was a project to deal with flooding in Paraguay in 1997–98. Larger programs grew from the experience of Hurricane Mitch in 1999, which led to the dispatch of volunteers to Honduras, Guatemala, and Nicaragua. In response to the 2004 tsunami, the Crisis Corps sent more than 70 volunteers to Sri Lanka and Thailand, working on potable water and shelter design. In 2005 the Peace Corps deployed domestically for the first time, when 272 Crisis Corps Volunteers assisted recovery efforts in the Gulf states.

2. *Disaster preparedness and mitigation* is considered a second category, despite its close relationship to disaster relief. Major programs were mounted in 2004 and 2005 to assist Jamaica and El Salvador in strengthening housing and public buildings against seasonal storms. Volunteers worked in Micronesia to improve planning for cyclones and in Malawi to systematize preparations for annual outbreaks of cholera.

3. *HIV/AIDS.* As the pandemic moved toward the top of the U.S. humanitarian agenda, Crisis Corps increasingly targeted the crisis in Africa. During the 2001–2004 period, 80 percent of total deployments were for this purpose. Programming continues in coordination with the President's Emergency Program for AIDS Relief (PEPFAR), launched in 2003 and reauthorized in 2008.

4. *Humanitarian assistance*, something of a catchall, constitutes the largest single Peace Corps Response activity. The Peace Corps states that "projects must meet a critical and discrete need identified in the host country." Assignments have included technical assistance to food security and food for work projects in crisis zones. Other projects like health promotion and training, strategic planning, and program assessment appear unconnected with current "crises."

5. The last category, and the one most relevant to this study, is *post-conflict relief and reconstruction*.

The classic deployment was 20 volunteers sent to Bosnia-Herzegovina and Serbia in 2001. The program targeted Bosnian Muslims, Croats, and Serbs. Assignments included working with municipal governments to develop information technology for local courts, law seminars aimed at revising legislation, assistance to returned refugees, alleviating food insecurity, and increasing local farm income. A second in war-ravaged eastern Congo in 1998 was quickly shut down because the security risk to the volunteers proved too high.

Two other projects not formally placed in this category can be considered R&S efforts. One of the earliest Crisis Corps deployments was a "humanitarian assistance" project in the Forest Region of Guinea. The volunteers worked with refugees who fled to Guinea in massive numbers in the 1980s because of violent conflict in Liberia and Sierra Leone. A second project, just getting underway at the end of 2008 with 18 volunteers, mobilized Peace Corps Response to help rebuild the education and health services in Liberia. It responded to a personal request for experienced volunteers from Liberian President Ellen Johnson Sirleaf.

Through Peace Corps Response, therefore, the Peace Corps has initiated an explicit peace-building program, but one of very modest dimensions. A former director of Peace Corps Response has expressed doubt that post-conflict activities will expand in the future. She pointed out that regular Peace Corps programs are rarely found—or rarely continue—in countries in serious crises. Thus creation of a modest-sized Peace Corps Response program in such countries entails high overhead costs. Moreover, the Peace Corps faces major difficulties deploying volunteers to conflict areas because of strong Congressional concerns about general volunteer safety.[15] The sensitivity appears to be greater for volunteers, even Peace Corps veterans, than it is for overseas employees of the Defense and State Departments and for most NGOs that work abroad in theaters of conflict.

THE FUTURE OF THE PEACE CORPS

In one of his last speeches, Sargent Shriver suggested addition of a fourth goal to the Peace Corps mandate: "to bind all human beings together in a common cause to assure peace and survival for all." Congressman Sam Farr, a returned volunteer and Peace Corps champion on Capitol Hill, has advanced a more specific formulation: "to help promote global acceptance of the principles of international peace and non-violent coexistence among peoples of diverse cultures and systems of government." Adding a goal of this nature to the Peace Corps legislative charter should be carefully considered. The agency has presented a friendly and constructive American face to the world for almost 50 years. To give it an explicit peace-building goal would be logical and good public diplomacy.[16]

To add the goal without related adjustments to the Peace Corps program would be an empty gesture, however. I suggest four substantive steps to involve volunteers more directly in peace-building:

1. *Strengthen the development thrust of Peace Corps service.*

Adding a strategic planning capacity to the agency focused on the role of volunteers in development should be combined with accountability of Peace Corps staff overseas for supporting PCVs in their development role. Specifically, establishing a system for publicizing lessons learned and best practices, both in-country and generally, would help overcome the lack of continuity between volunteers at a single site. An enhanced development impact at the local level would work synergistically to make more friends for the United States and to ease to some degree tension in U.S. relations with the Global South. Legislation proposed by Senator Christopher Dodd in 2007, including a provision to double the number of volunteers with at least five years of experience in sectors relevant to Peace Corps work, would reinforce its development impact.[17]

2. *Provide Peace Corps trainees with basic training in conflict management and peace-building.*

Volunteers are trained to develop sensitivity to the specific cultures in which they find themselves as a basic building block for integrating into the communities to which they are assigned. They likewise receive training in the general development discipline to which they are assigned. However, they receive little guidance on how to deal with conflict. The Peace Corps should consider integrating into all its basic training programs a module on the theory and practice of conflict management. Such training would better equip volunteers to cope with conflicts which may arise at their assignment sites and to discuss violence prevention and peace-building (in a nonpolitical way) with their host country nationals.[18]

My third and fourth suggestions rely heavily on expanded use of RPCVs. The 200,000 Peace Corps alumni are an enormously underutilized resource. Even assuming that the vast majority of the total are not available for service at any given time because of health concerns, job or family commitments, disinterest, or because they are already in international careers, it is likely that the right institutional arrangements could persuade up to 10,000 (just over 5%) to make themselves available for further service. The group is continually being replenished—and even expanded—by graduation to alumni status of currently-serving volunteers. As a group, returned volunteers would bring special qualities to renewed service: experience, capability in both local and world languages, and skills in working effectively with local cultures, plus traits of adaptability, resourcefulness, and initiative.

3. *Expand Peace Corps Response, particularly post-conflict relief and reconstruction.*

Some Peace Corps officials are optimistic about the future growth of Peace Corps Response, seeing the new Liberia program as a model. In new countries, or countries where the Peace Corps is returning after an interval because of instability, a Peace Corps Response program with Peace Corps veterans can pave the way for creation of a regular program. The agency's current returned volunteer database of about 3,500 is too small to permit a major expansion of Peace Corps Response recruitment, however. The Peace Corps should invest in database expansion through an effective publicity campaign. It could partner for that purpose with the National Peace Corps Association. With expansion should come a closer look at post-conflict programs in countries where the Peace Corps has worked previously and enjoys a positive reputation. With regard to security, Peace Corps Response should not be saddled with standards more restrictive than those applying to State Department, USAID, and NGO appointments in the field. Some kind of waiver process might be considered (coupled with adequate life and health insurance arrangements) by which experienced volunteers heading for interesting post-conflict roles might absolve the agency of responsibility if tragedy should strike, except in the case of malfeasance.

4. Collaborate with the interagency peace-building process by facilitating access to RPCVs for the Civilian Reserve Corps.

If the U.S. government is serious about creating a Civilian Reserve Corps as part of a surge capacity for R&S, a database of returned volunteers could become an important tool. S/CRS should be empowered to work with the Peace Corps so that it might draw on the returned volunteer database. S/CRS might logically share in the cost of expanding it.

Essential to strengthening the Peace Corps for a more explicit role in U.S. peacefare is a major expansion of funding. The FY 2008 Peace Corps appropriation of $330 million accounted for less than 1 percent of the overall international affairs function. A doubling of the Peace Corps budget over the next four years would be highly desirable—and would scarcely be noticed in Function 150.[19] Only with a dramatic increase in budget can the Peace Corps be revitalized and enhanced as an instrument of American soft power and peace-building. There appears to be a bipartisan consensus in favor of expanding international programs, like public diplomacy and the Peace Corps, which present a positive American image to the rest of the world. The administration should rally support for an expanded and strengthened Peace Corps by doubling its budget and by facilitating the use of former volunteers in peace-building roles.

Notes

PREFACE

1. R2P originated with the 2001 report of the International Commission on Intervention and State Sovereignty, *The Responsibility to Protect*. It was included in the recommendations of the UN High-Level Panel, *A More Secure World*, in 2004. Secretary-General Kofi Annan endorsed R2P in his 2005 report, *In Larger Freedom*. See also Gareth Evans, ed., *Responsibility to Protect: Ending Mass Atrocity Crimes Once and for All* (Washington: Brookings Institution, 2008).

2. The definitions which follow draw on Mohammed Abu-Nimer, "A Framework: Issues and Challenges to Consider in Peace-Building Interventions," in *Leadership and Building State Capacity: Combining the Skills of Diplomats and Trainers* (Washington: Woodrow Wilson International Center for Scholars, 2005), available at www .wilsoncenter.org/topics/pubs/training_final.pdf, and, except for "peace-building," are close to those in the Army Field Operations Manual 3.0 (2008), Sec. 2-34 to 2-40, and in Boutros Boutros-Ghali, *An Agenda for Peace: Report of the Secretary-General, A/47/277-S24111* (June 17, 1992), available at http://www.un.org/Docs/SG/ agpeace.html.

3. Peace-building in this study is broader than that in the *Report of the Panel on UN Peace Operations* (the Brahimi Report), A/55/305-S/2000/809, August 21, 2000, which defines it as "activities undertaken on the far side of conflict to reassemble the foundations of peace and provide the tools for building on those foundations something that is more than just the absence of war." The Brahimi Report definition is close to what in official U.S. parlance is referred to as "post-conflict reconstruction" or "R&S."

4. The definition comes from Robert C. Orr, ed., *Winning the Peace: An American Strategy for Post-Conflict Reconstruction* (Washington: CSIS, 2004), 10–11.

5. James Dobbins revives the term "nation-building" in *America's Role in Nation-Building from Germany to Iraq* (Santa Monica, CA: Rand Corporation, 2003), 1.

CHAPTER 1

1. See Charles A. Kupchan, *The End of the American Era: U.S. Foreign Policy and the Geopolitics of the Twenty-First Century* (New York: Vintage Books, 2002), 163–166.

2. *The Selected Writings of Benjamin Rush* (New York: Philosophical Library, 1947), 19–23. A devout Christian, Rush opposed slavery and capital punishment and urged repeal of all laws creating militias.

3. The United States was in effect aligning itself with British policy for the region. The Monroe administration had turned aside a British suggestion for a joint statement of this nature and decided to issue it unilaterally. It was British "no transfer" policy, backed by the British navy, which kept the other European powers on the sidelines, at least until French and Austrian involvement in Mexico in the 1860s.

4. William H. Seward to the Marquis de Montholon, February 12, 1866, in *House Ex. Doc.* (1261), 39th Congress, 1st Session, No. 93, 589–598. See also Walter Lafeber, *The American Age: United States Foreign Policy at Home and Abroad* (New York: W. W. Norton & Company, 1994), 152–153.

5. Samuel F. Bemis, *A Diplomatic History of the United States* (New York: Holt, Rinehart and Winston, 1965), 758–759.

6. Ibid., 394.

7. Annual Message to Congress, December 6, 1904, *Roosevelt Almanac*, http://www .theodore-roosevelt.com/trmdcorollary.html. The assertion of the corollary followed the shelling of Venezuela by German and British gunboats and a successful Roosevelt ultimatum to Germany, persuading Berlin to seek arbitration of its claims. Edmund Morris, *Theodore Rex* (New York: Random House, 2001), 182–192, 207–208, 325–326.

8. In addition, Japan's "predominant interests" in Korea were recognized. Tokyo gave up its demand for an indemnity and agreed to accept half, rather than all, of Sakhalin Island, disputed among China, Russia, and Japan. Alexander DeConde, *A History of American Foreign Policy* (New York: Charles Scribner's Sons, 1963), 367–369.

9. Morris, *Theodore Rex*, 386–414.

10. Bemis, *Diplomatic History*, 585. See also Morris, *Theodore Rex*, 430, 440–442, on Roosevelt's diplomatic and peace-building skills in this crisis.

11. Speech, July 14, 1914, *The Papers of Woodrow Wilson*, XXX (Library of Congress), 255, cited in Thomas J. Knock, *To End All Wars: Woodrow Wilson and the Quest for New World Order* (New York: Oxford University Press, 1992), 20.

12. President Wilson's War Message, April 2, 1917. See http://historymatters .gmu.edu/d/4943/.

13. See Ruhl Bartlett, *Policy and Power: Two Centuries of American Foreign Relations* (New York: Hill and Wang, 1963), 151–153.

14. Address to the Senate, January 22, 1917, *PWW*, XL, 533–539, cited in Knock, *To End*, 113. See also p. 232 on Wilson's use of that argument with the Senate.

15. See Walter Russell Mead, *Special Providence: American Foreign Policy and How It Changed the World* (New York: Routledge, 2002), 9.

16. Initially the United States, the United Kingdom, and the USSR occupied Germany, but France joined after the Potsdam Conference.

17. The discussion of Germany draws heavily on Dobbins et al., *America's Role*, 3–23.

18. The Far Eastern Commission, made up of the 11 countries which had fought against Japan, and the smaller Allied Council for Japan (China, USSR, the United Kingdom, and the United States) served essentially as advisory bodies and were largely ignored.

19. Paragraph 10 stated, "The Japanese Government shall remove all obstacles to the revival and strengthening of democratic tendencies among the Japanese people. Freedom of speech, of religion, and of thought, as well as respect for fundamental human rights shall be established." The proclamation was signed July 26, 1945. Department of State *Bulletin*, Vol. XII, 137–138.

20. John W. Dower, *Embracing Defeat: Japan in the Wake of World War II* (New York: Norton, 1999), argues that the "true sentiment of ordinary Japanese revealed itself to be closer to mild attachment, resignation, even indifference about the imperial system," 303.

21. The discussion on Japan also draws heavily on Dobbins, *America's Role*, 25–53.

22. Humanitarian assistance was initially expected to be a major factor in Iraq but did not become important.

23. The Pearl Harbor attack helped precipitate the rise of Republicans favorable to that view, including Wendell Willkie and Thomas E. Dewey, the Republican presidential candidates in 1940 and 1944.

24. Townsend Hoopes and Douglas Brinkley, *FDR and the Creation of the U.N.* (New Haven: Yale University Press, 1997), especially 17–20, 62–63, 68–74.

25. See Inis Claude, *From Swords into Plowshares* (New York: Random House, 1964), 197–199.

26. Except in the case of enforcement action under Chapter 7. See below.

27. For more detailed discussion of this point, see Claude, *Swords*, 197–208.

28. The British initially wanted the Council to have sole responsibility for settling disputes, a position resisted by the United States. Subsequently, the United Kingdom and the United States took the position, opposed by the Soviet Union, that the General Assembly should be able to discuss disputes, even if only the Council was empowered to make final decisions. Ruth B. Russell, *A History of the United Nations Charter* (Washington: Brookings Institution, 1958), 401, 441.

29. The idea of peacekeeping and the principles underlying it—neutrality (no members of the force from the UN Security Council permanent five), impartiality, nonuse of force, unarmed—were developed by former Canadian Prime Minister Lester Pearson and Secretary-General Dag Hammarskjold in connection with that crisis. Doyle and Sambanis distinguish between this kind of "first generation peacekeeping," used primarily in interstate crises and depending strictly on the consent of both sides, and "multidimensional peacekeeping," designed to create the basis for a sustained peace and used primarily in post–civil war situations. Michael W. Doyle and Nicholas Sambanis, *Making War and Building Peace: United Nations Peace Operations* (Princeton: Princeton University Press, 2006), 12–14.

30. Report of the Panel on UN Peace Operations (the Brahimi Report) (A/55/305; S/2000/809, August 17, 2000), 10.

31. Hoopes and Brinkley, *FDR*, 39, 46, 59.

32. The Act of Chapultepec, signed at a meeting the Latin Americans insisted on holding the month before UNCIO, called for creation of a treaty "establishing procedures whereby . . . threats or acts [of aggression] may be met by [*inter alia*] . . . armed force to prevent or repel aggression." Inter-American Conference on Problems of War and Peace, March 6, 1945, in Department of State Publication 2497, Conference Series No. 85, 72–75. See also Bartlett, *Policy and Power*, 212.

33. On August 10, 1945, as the war with Japan was ending, the United States decided to occupy the Korean Peninsula at the 38th parallel, fearing that the USSR, which had just began attacking Japanese forces in northern Korea, would occupy the

entire peninsula. The Soviets raised no objections. U.S. and Soviet administration of the peninsula continued until 1948 when the Republic of Korea was established in Seoul and the Democratic People's Republic of Korea in Pyongyang. The failure of France to reestablish control of Vietnam led to the 1954 Geneva Agreement on the Cessation of Hostilities in Vietnam between France and the Democratic Republic of Vietnam. It provided for temporary division of Vietnam at roughly the 17th parallel, provisional northern (Communist) and southern (non-Communist) zone governments, and a 1956 election to bring the zones under a unified government. The South Vietnamese government rejected the third provision and in 1955 declared itself the Republic of Vietnam.

34. Security Council Resolution (hereafter S/Res.) 83 and S/Res. 84 of June 27 and July 7, 1950; General Assembly Resolution 377A (V) of November 3, 1950. The Uniting for Peace Resolution permits the Security Council to call a Special Emergency Session of the Assembly under a procedural resolution, to which a veto cannot be applied.

35. The formal character of UN involvement was preserved in the signature of the armistice by American LTG William K. Harrison, Jr., as Senior Delegate of the UN Command. General Assembly Resolution 811 (IX), December 11, 1954, after the armistice, cited the "continued objective" of the United Nations as the "achievement by peaceful means of a unified, independent and democratic Korea under a representative form of government."

36. "Developments under U Thant, 1961–1971," Encyclopedia of the Nations: United Nations: The Secretary-General, www.nationsencyclopedia.com.

37. Doyle and Sambanis, *Making War and Building Peace*, 11.

38. Saadia Touval and I. William Zartman, "International Mediation in the Post-Cold War Era," in Chester T. Crocker et al., *Turbulent Peace: The Challenges of Managing International Conflict* (Washington: U.S. Institute of Peace, 2001), 429.

39. S/Res. 143 (1960) of July 14, 1960 was approved with affirmative votes from both the United States and the USSR.

40. S/Reses. 161 (1961) and 169 (1961). U.S. intelligence colluded in Lumumba's detention by Belgian and Congolese opposition forces, and numerous writers have charged the U.S. government with responsibility for his death. Georges Nzongola-Ntalaja, *The Congo from Leopold to Kabila: A People's History* (London: Zed Books, 2002), 109, concludes that despite U.S. indirect involvement, "the Belgian ruling class and its representatives in the Congo were directly responsible for Lumumba's assassination" in January 1961.

41. S/Res. 199 of December 30, 1964, after the airdrop, requested all states to refrain from intervention and called on the OAU to pursue a solution. The United States voted affirmatively.

42. S/Res. 186(1964), March 4, 1964.

43. USAID, "Cyprus Country Profile," http://www.usaid.gov/locations/europe_eurasia/countries/cy/cyprus.pdf. The situation remained deadlocked for more than two decades but has seemed to become more susceptible to a settlement since the 1990s with an easing of tension between the two communities and Turkish interest in joining the European Union. U.S. attention to the problem also revived. In 1998, President Clinton appointed Richard Holbrooke as special envoy, and the Bush administration strongly supported UN efforts to achieve a settlement.

44. General Assembly Resolution 390A, December 2, 1950. John H. Spencer, the American legal counselor to the Emperor, reported that after the UN Commission on Eritrea deadlocked on Eritrea's future, the compromise federation approach was

worked out in confidential negotiations in New York involving representatives of the United States, the United Kingdom, Italy, and the leadership of the General Assembly. *Ethiopia at Bay: A Personal Account of the Haile Selassie Years* (Algonac, MI: Reference Publications, 1984), 232–233. The UN's Eritrea decision proved an anomaly. With very few exceptions, normally involving referenda, colonies came to independence within their colonial borders, not as parts of larger states.

45. See Richard Greenfield, *Ethiopia: A New Political History* (New York: Praeger, 1965), 298–306, and Michaela Wrong, *"I Didn't Do It for You": How the World Betrayed a Small African Nation* (New York: Harper Collins, 2005), 177–196.

46. The final report of the UN Commissioner for Eritrea stated, "If it were necessary either to amend or to interpret the Federal Act, only the General Assembly, as the author of that instrument, would be competent to take a decision. Similarly, if the Federal Act were violated, the General Assembly could be seized of the matter." Final Report of the UN Commissioner in Eritrea, General Assembly, 7th Session, Supplement No. 15 (A-2188), Vol. 4, p. 4, cited in Wrong, *"I Didn't Do It,"* 73.

47. The scales were only partly balanced by the British decision to continue traditional and defensive arms sales to the FMG, thus excluding bombs, aircraft, heavy artillery, and tanks.

48. Joseph Palmer, 2d, "Magnitude and Complexity of the Nigerian Problem," *Department of State Bulletin*, Vol. 59 (1968), 357–358.

49. Under Secretary of State Nicholas Katzenbach, "The Tragedy of Nigeria" (Address at Brown University, December 3, 1968), *Department of State Bulletin*, Vol. 59, 656.

50. OAU, Assembly of Heads of State and Government, 4th Ordinary Session, Kinshasa, September 11–19, 1967, AHG/Res. 51(IV).

51. Peace talks were also held under Commonwealth auspices in Uganda in 1968 but were not fruitful.

52. Four African states (Tanzania, Zambia, Cote d'Ivoire, and Gabon) recognized Biafra and sought without success a more neutral OAU stance.

53. Address to Joint Session of Congress, September 11, 1990.

54. Authorizes UN member states "to use all necessary means to uphold and implement resolution 660 [calling on Iraq to withdraw from Kuwait] and all subsequent relevant resolutions and to restore international peace and security in the area."

55. Peter W. Galbraith, *The End of Iraq: How American Incompetence Created a War without End* (New York: Simon and Schuster, 2006), 58.

56. Derek Chollet and James Goldgeier, *America between the Wars: From 11/9 to 9/11* (New York: Public Affairs Press, 2008), 12.

57. Herman J. Cohen, *Intervening in Africa: Superpower Peacemaking in a Troubled Continent* (London: Macmillan, 2000), 138–144.

58. UNITAF replaced UNOSOM I, a Chapter VI peacekeeping force designed to facilitate delivery of humanitarian assistance but too small to be effective. UNITAF was endorsed by the Security Council with a Chapter VII mandate but was not a "blue helmet" operation (S/Res. 794, December 3, 1992). The United States assumed about 75 percent of the costs. Karin von Hippel, *Democracy by Force: U.S. Military Intervention in the Post-Cold War World* (Cambridge: Cambridge University Press, 2000), 60–63.

59. The Europeans sponsored a team led by David Owen, former British foreign minister, and Cyrus Vance, former American secretary of state, with Washington giving qualified support.

60. It became fashionable for members of Congress to proclaim their disinterest in the rest of the world, some boasting they did not possess a U.S. passport. Chollet and Goldgeier, *America*, 109.

61. Chester Crocker, "Intervention: Toward Best Practices and a Holistic View," in *Turbulent Peace*, 245–246. Subsequently, U.S. intelligence found evidence of al-Qa'ida support for the Aideed forces.

62. Robert E. Gribbin, *In the Aftermath of Genocide: The US Role in Rwanda* (Lincoln, NE: iUniverse, 2005), 100, 261.

63. The Cedras government signed the Governor's Island Agreement, mediated by UN Special Envoy Dante Caputo, in July 1993. The UN Mission in Haiti was created by S/Res. 862 (August 31, 1993).

64. S/Res. 940, July 31, 1994.

65. Chollet and Goldgeier, *America*, 98.

66. Ivo Daalder, *Getting to Dayton: The Making of America's Bosnia Policy* (Washington: Brookings Institution, 2000), 63–80. Chollet and Goldgeier term the Srebrenica massacre "the worst war crime in Europe since the Second World War." *America*, 127.

67. Chester A. Crocker, Fen Osler Hampson, and Pamela Aall, *Taming Intractable Conflicts* (Washington: USIP, 2007), 34–35.

68. Ibid., 117–161.

69. IFOR was almost halved to 32,000 and renamed SFOR after a year.

70. There were still 2,000 American soldiers there as late as 2005. http://www.usaid.gov/locations/europe_eurasia/countries/ko/kosovo.pdf.

71. Chollet and Goldgeier, *America*, 131–132.

72. The author was given this role 1995–96, followed by Howard F. Jeter, 1997–99.

73. "I think we have to be very careful when we commit our troops." Presidential Debate, October 3, 2000, cited in Kupchan, *End*, 232.

74. The Northern Alliance suffered a very serious blow on the eve of 9/11 with the assassination of its legendary leader Ahmed Shah Massoud.

75. S/Res. 1441, November 8, 2002; Bob Woodward, *Bush at War* (New York: Simon and Schuster, 2002), 344–357. In his September 2002 address to the General Assembly, Bush said that Iraq posed a clear-cut challenge to the legitimacy of the United Nations: "the United Nations [faces] a difficult and defining moment. Are Security Council resolutions to be honored and enforced, or cast aside without consequence? Will the United Nations serve the purpose of its founding, or will it be irrelevant?" The White House, President's Remarks at the UN General Assembly, September 12, 2002. See Howard Lafranchi, "Bush Gives UN an Ultimatum," *Christian Science Monitor*, September 13, 2002.

76. However, making use of an incipient civil conflict was also a factor. As a result of the 1990 Gulf War and subsequent measures imposed by the United Nations, international restraints were already in place which created a potential platform for internal resistance to Saddam Hussein's rule. The northern "no-fly zone" extending north from the 36th parallel and "Operation Provide Comfort," a U.S.-led post-conflict reconstruction effort, had already created an autonomous Kurdistan. A southern no-fly zone below the 33rd parallel had also been established to limit regime control of the predominantly Shi'ite south. The Bush administration hoped to use these divisions to create civil war against the dictator, while U.S. forces shattered the Iraqi army.

77. See Galbraith, *End of Iraq*, 89.

78. The Clinton administration had a hostile relationship with Khartoum but did not get involved in resolving the civil war. It had pressured Sudan to expel Osama bin Laden, resident there 1990–96, and attacked an alleged chemical weapons factory in Khartoum with a cruise missile after the bombings of the U.S. embassies in Nairobi and Dar es Salaam in 1998.

79. On American exceptionalism, see *inter alia* Dorothy L. Madsen, *American Exceptionalism* (Jackson: University Press of Mississippi, 1998).

CHAPTER 2

1. *Running the World: The Inside Story of the National Security Council and the Architects of American Power* (New York: Public Affairs, 2005), 21.

2. See *inter alia* H. Jefferson Powell, *The President's Authority over Foreign Affairs: An Essay in Constitutional Interpretation* (Durham, NC: Carolina Academic Press, 2002).

3. The Act also created the position of Secretary of Defense, the Air Force, the Joint Chiefs of Staff, and the Central Intelligence Agency. Pub. L. No. 235, 80 Cong., 61 Stat. 496 (July 26, 1947).

4. Originally called *Special* Assistant to the President. The adjective was dropped during the Reagan administration.

5. Ivo H. Daalder and I. M. Destler, *A New NSC for a New Administration* (Washington: Brookings, 2000).

6. Rothkopf, *Running the World*, 218.

7. Report of the President's Special Review Board (1987) in Karl F. Inderfurth and Loch K. Johnson, eds., *Fateful Decisions: Inside the National Security Council* (New York: Oxford University Press, 2004), 308–315.

8. Rothkopf, *Running the World*, 267.

9. George H. W. Bush and Brent Scowcroft, *A World Transformed* (New York: Alfred A. Knopf, 1998); Rothkopf, *Running the World*, 267.

10. Balkans policy was stalemated until 1995, when NSA Anthony Lake persuaded Clinton to endorse a coercive diplomatic approach. On the Clinton approach during his first term, see Rothkopf, *Running the World*, 314–333.

11. Woodward, *Bush at War*. Woodward provides dates and usually the start times of all the meetings. The major players were CIA Director George Tenant, who came up with the most persuasive approach, Defense Secretary Donald Rumsfeld who struggled to find a quick mode of operation for U.S. forces, primarily Special Forces, and Secretary of State Colin Powell who took charge of the diplomacy with Pakistan and rallied the coalition.

12. The President does not attend meetings of the Principals Committee. The Deputies Committee met four times between the end of May and August to come up with a paper, "A Liberation Strategy," submitted to the principals in August. That process had not reached fruition before the 9/11 attacks. Woodward, *Plan of Attack* (New York: Simon & Schuster, 2004), 13–23.

13. When Richard Haass, State Department Director of Policy Planning, met with Rice in July 2002 to go over a list of the downside risks of attacking Saddam, she told him, "Don't waste your breath. The President has already made the decision." Marcus Mabry, *Twice as Good: Condoleezza Rice and Her Path to Power* (New York: Modern Times, 2007), 184.

14. Marcus Mabry writes, "The president had brought together strong-willed men with a wealth of experienced but discordant views, but then, according to several White House staffers, for whatever reason, he didn't want to manage the discord. Bush was uninterested in having Rice haul his senior advisers into the Oval Office to adjudicate their disputes." *Twice as Good*, 202.

15. Rothkopf, *Running the World*, 261–263.

16. Daalder, *Getting to Dayton*, 81–116.

17. She was initially Director for Soviet and East European Affairs in 1989 but was promoted to Senior Director and Special Assistant to the President in 1990.

18. Woodward, *Bush at War*, 254.

19. On Powell's position with the President, Cheney, and Rumsfeld, see Woodward, *Plan of Attack*, 79. NSC spokesman Sean McCormick told the press in May 2003 that Rice "didn't think refereeing intramural squabbles was her job." Mabry, *Twice as Good*, 195.

20. *The Confidante: Condoleezza Rice and the Creation of the Bush Legacy* (New York: St. Martin's Press, 2007). See also Mabry, *Twice as Good*, 169–172.

21. Deputy Secretary of State Richard Armitage told Rice that the NSC system was dysfunctional and that policy was not sufficiently coordinated, debated, and resolved. Woodward, *Plan of Attack*, 414. The other criticism related to Rice's role as counselor to the President. Why hadn't she communicated to the President in advance what might go wrong?

22. Thomas E. Ricks, *Fiasco: The American Military Adventure in Iraq* (New York: Penguin, 2006), 254–255.

23. Rice's more operational role in Iraq is documented by Woodward, *State of Denial* (New York: Simon & Schuster, 2006), 240–312; Ricks, *Fiasco*, 254–255; and Mabry, *Twice as Good*, 203–237.

24. *Running the World*, 388, and more generally 419–427.

25. Woodward, *Plan of Attack*, 48–49.

26. Lawrence B. Wilkerson, former chief of staff to Secretary of State Powell, has charged that Cheney and Rumsfeld constituted a secret cabal to influence the President at the expense of Powell. "The White House Cabal," *Los Angeles Times*, October 25, 2005.

27. Senate Historical Office, *Vice Presidents of the United States: John Nance Garner*, 4.

28. Rothkopf, *Running the World*, 311.

29. Libby resigned when indicted by Special Prosecutor Patrick Fitzgerald October 28, 2005 on five counts of perjury, making false statements to the FBI, and obstruction of justice. Libby was convicted on four counts March 6, 2007. His prison sentence was commuted by President Bush July 2, 2007. On Cheney's loss of influence in the second term, see Barton Gelman, *Angler: The Cheney Vice Presidency* (New York: Penguin Press, 2008), 364.

30. Daalder and Destler, *A New NSC*. The NSC senior staff may also serve on certain U.S. delegations to high-level negotiations.

31. LTG Donald Kerrick. The Clinton administration also elevated the position of NSC staff director to DNSA status for Nancy Soderberg and her successor Mara Rudman.

32. Although the Bush administration left standing the National Economic Council created by Clinton, it sought to integrate it more closely with the NSC through creation of a DNSA for international economics, with the rank of Deputy Assistant to the President. A second DNSA/Deputy Assistant was created for communications.

Elliott Abrams was named Deputy Assistant to the President and DNSA for Global Democracy. Abrams had joined the Bush 43 team in 2001 as Senior Director for Democracy, Human Rights and International Operations and then became Senior Director for Near East and North African Affairs in 2002. The DNSA slot combined both functions. In March 2005 National Security Advisor Stephen Hadley, who had succeeded Rice, issued a formal directive aligning the five DNSA/Deputy Assistant to the President positions with the President's priorities: combating terrorism, Iraq/Afghanistan, "the freedom agenda, particularly in the greater Middle East," "the prosperity agenda," and "explaining the President's strategy at home and abroad." Two of these DNSAs also were directed to report to a second supervisor in addition to the NSA; for example, terrorism to the Assistant to the President for Homeland Security and Counter Terrorism and international economics to the Assistant to the President for Economic Policy. "National Security Council Staff Reorganization," March 28, 2005.

33. Interview with Leonard R. Hawley, September 7, 2007.

34. "Organization of the National Security Council," Presidential Decision Directive 1 (February 13, 2001).

35. "Grand Strategy in the Second Term," *Foreign Policy* (January–February 2005), 2. Interestingly, Gaddis did not refer to the strategy document but rather primarily to Bush's 2002 State of the Union message.

36. *Twice as Good*, 188–190.

37. *The National Security Strategy of the United States of America*, September 2002, 1, available at www.whitehouse.gov/nsc/nss/2002/nss.pdf.

38. The 2002 strategy does not use one term to refer to the eight "tasks," "objectives," or "demands," which are at the heart of the strategy. The 2006 revised strategy refers consistently to "tasks." "Task" is used here for both documents.

39. Interview with Leonard R. Hawley, September 7, 2007.

40. The principal drafter of the Haiti plan was Michèle Flournoy, Deputy Assistant Secretary of Defense for Strategy. Richard A. Clarke, NSC Senior Director for Global Affairs, then asked Flournoy in late 1995 to try her hand at a PDD. It was written and drawn on in 1996, but not finalized until May 1997. Interview with Michèle Flournoy, October 11, 2007.

41. Interview with Matthew McLean, January 18, 2007.

42. There was also criticism that the detailed and highly structured format of the NSPD was not well suited to engaging the attention of policymakers.

43. The Stabilization and Reconstruction Civilian Management Act of 2004, passed unanimously by the Committee and included, with some modifications, as Title VII in S. 600, the Foreign Relations Authorization Act of 2006 and 2007. Amb. James Dobbins, a member of the Advisory Group who had served as Bush administration special envoy for Afghanistan, wrote a memo containing the proposal for State Department leadership, at the request of Robert Pearson, then Director-General of the Foreign Service.

44. Clark A. Murdock, Michèle A. Flournoy, et al., *Beyond Goldwater-Nichols: Defense Reform for a New Strategic Era Phase I Report* (Washington: CSIS, 2004).

45. Some argued that an executive order was needed, but the Vice President's Counsel argued for an NSPD, asserting the issue did not rise to the legal importance of an executive order. The former countered that the NSPD approach suggested the White House preferred not to publicize creation of S/CRS because it implicitly admitted mistakes in Iraq R&S.

46. The military were sometimes more accommodating than Pentagon civilians. Chairman of the Joint Chiefs of Staff, Gen. Peter Pace, is reported to have favored a strong role for State as coordinator for civilian-military activities, not just civilian activities.

47. The NSPD says "may use" S/CRS for this purpose.

48. My italics. That section was reportedly particularly difficult to draft, but not the subject of bitter wrangling.

49. Interview with J. Clint Williamson, January 3, 2007.

50. Humanitarian assistance, often a part of U.S. conflict response, has been handled by the Director for Humanitarian and Disaster Response in the same directorate, not by the Director for Stability Operations.

51. Woodward, *State of Denial*, 264.

52. Although Lute was referred to as the "war czar," veteran bureaucrats point out that as a "three-star," he had some difficulty ensuring that four-star generals working on Iraq complied with his instructions.

53. *The Iraq Study Group Report* (New York: Vintage, 2006), xvi, 51.

54. Fred Barnes, "How Bush Decided on the Surge," *The Weekly Standard*, February 4, 2008. See Thomas E. Ricks, *The Gamble: General David Petraeus and the American Military Adventure in Iraq, 2006–2008* (New York: The Penguin Press, 2009), for the impact of advocacy by certain "insurgent" military officers on Bush's thinking.

55. By then, however, it was too late to secure significant funding in that budget because the NSC had not engaged at a senior level with OMB to reverse its cuts to the S/CRS request. Interview with Laura A. Hall, January 17, 2009. Funding was eventually included in the FY 2009 budget request and partial supplemental appropriations were made in 2008 and early 2009. (See Chapters 4 and 8.)

56. State Department Bureau of Western Hemisphere Affairs, "Plan Colombia" Fact Sheet, March 14, 2001.

57. An alternative version of the story that Aristide was abducted and put on the plane by 20 uniformed U.S. troops "in full battle gear" was initially current among critics of U.S. policy, including Trans-Africa leader Randall Robinson and the Congressional Black Caucus. For both stories, see *New York Times*, March 2, 2004.

58. Interview with John F. Maisto, October 2, 2007.

59. The Clinton administration had pressured Khartoum to expel Osama bin Laden, resident there 1990–96, and attacked an alleged chemical weapons factory in Khartoum with a cruise missile after the bombings of the U.S. embassies in Nairobi and Dar es Salaam in 1998.

60. Asteris Huliaras, "Evangelists, Oil Companies, and Terrorists: The Bush Administration's Policy towards Sudan," *Orbis* 50:4 (Autumn 2006), 709–724.

61. Danforth was not the first choice. When the White House consulted with Secretary Powell, the name of Chester Crocker emerged first. Crocker, Assistant Secretary for Africa under the Reagan administration, was the architect of the settlement which brought independence to Namibia. Only after Crocker turned down the assignment did Danforth's name emerge. Back in May 2001, Andrew Natsios, Administrator of USAID, was named concurrently Special Humanitarian Coordinator for Sudan.

62. Interviews with Charles Snyder, September 22, 2006; Matthew McLean, January 18, 2007.

63. Chester A. Crocker, Fen Osler Hampson, and Pamela Aall, *Taming Intractable Conflicts* (Washington: U.S. Institute of Peace, 2004), 108. Egypt did not play a major role but was kept in the loop.

64. Khartoum's chief negotiator, Vice President Ali Osman Mohamed Taha, was heavily engaged in the Sudanese government response to the rebellion.

65. S/Res. 1769 of July 31, 2007.

66. Interview with Richard S. Williamson, November 20, 2008.

67. Interview with Michael J. Green, ex-NSC senior director, August 30, 2007.

68. Sen. Patrick Leahy's (D-VT) amendment, Sec. 592 of the State, Foreign Operations, Export Financing, & Related Programs Appropriations Act 2005 (H.R. 3057).

69. One former NSC staffer suggests that the regional directorate planning process is weak and the directorates spend too much time tracking down details that should be handled by a coordination function in State.

CHAPTER 3

1. *Arts of Power: Statecraft and Diplomacy* (Washington: USIP Press, 1997), 129.

2. See Harry W. Kopp and Charles A. Gillespie's very useful discussion of "what diplomats do" in *Career Diplomacy: Life and Work in the U.S. Foreign Service* (Washington: Georgetown University Press, 2008), 58–63.

3. Other strategic priorities under that peace and security objective were counterterrorism, weapons of mass destruction, international crime and drugs, "homeland security," and protecting American citizens, all outside the scope of this study.

4. At that early date Iraq was largely ignored under regional stability, with the focus for that conflict placed instead on democratization and economic growth.

5. Recognizing that the relationship between these State/USAID "strategic goals" and the "tasks" set forth in the National Security Strategy might not be self-evident, the 2007 Strategic Plan provided a chart purporting to demonstrate how its "goals" support "tasks." For example, "achieving peace and security" was deemed to support all the Strategy tasks except "championing aspirations for human dignity," "igniting a new era of global economic growth through free markets and free trade," and "expanding the circle of development by opening societies and building the structure of democracy." Since reviving an economy, building the infrastructure of democracy, and championing human dignity through just and democratic government are integral parts of post-conflict reconstruction, it is reasonable to conclude the Strategic Plan was not basically driven by the Strategy. Rather, the State/USAID Plan was a basically independent effort which accommodated the Strategy as best it could, seeking to avoid glaring inconsistencies.

6. The other priorities under peace and security remained counterterrorism, weapons of mass destruction, and transnational crime, but dropped homeland security and protection of American citizens.

7. There was general but not complete consistency between the Strategy and the Plan in conflict priorities. Indonesia was mentioned in the Strategy, but not in the Plan. The Plan highlighted Sudan, Nepal, and Sri Lanka, which did not merit mention in the Strategy. There is a similar slight inconsistency between the 2006 Strategy update and the 2007–2012 Plan. The Strategy treated Iraq and Afghanistan under the strategic task of "defeating global terrorism," and identified particular challenges in Darfur, Colombia, Uganda, and Nepal. The Plan avoided reference to specific

countries under strategic objectives and strategic priorities but under "regional priorities" cited Iraq, Afghanistan, Sudan, Liberia, Congo, Nepal, and Sri Lanka.

8. Woodward, *Plan of Attack*, 148–153.

9. Ibid., 221–227, 309–312.

10. Testimony before the SFRC, September 9, 2004.

11. Marcus Mabry suggests that Rice was basically going through the motions of humanitarian interest, but "the Administration sought no greater involvement in the humanitarian crisis." *Twice as Good*, 266. The quotation disregarded the President's personal interest in the crisis and his frustration about the inability of the administration to find a solution.

12. *Twice as Good*, 240; Kessler, *The Confidante*, 23–24.

13. *Twice as Good*, 287–292. S/Res. 1701, August 11, 2006.

14. Numerous observers have commented that the Annapolis Conference would not have occurred without Rice's efforts. Helene Cooper, "Rice's Way: Restraint in Quest of Peace," *New York Times*, November 29, 2007.

15. The DPA was never implemented basically because only one of the Darfur rebel groups signed it. Zoellick reportedly did not feel he was a success in the role. Richard S. Williamson, Special Sudan Envoy in 2008, has described the DPA as "an embarrassment to the United States." Interview with Williamson, November 20, 2008. One biographer suggests that in 2007 Rice effectively turned the Iraq issue over to Deputy Secretary John Negroponte, former ambassador to that country. Elisabeth Bumiller, *Condoleezza Rice: An American Life*, 304. That assertion was disputed by the Iraq Coordinator's Office. Interview with Barbara Stephenson, February 1, 2008.

16. S/Res. 1368 of September 12, 2001, S/Res. 1373 of September 28, 2001, and S/Res. 1378 of November 14, 2001.

17. Interview with A. Elizabeth Jones, November 9, 2007.

18. Interview with James Dobbins, December 1, 2006; see also a State Department biographic sketch for Dobbins, http://www.state.gov/www/about_state/biography/dobbins_james.html.

19. The Bonn Agreement, http://www.afghan-web.com/politics/bonn_agreement_2001.html.

20. S/Res. 1386 of December 20, 2002.

21. Dobbins interview.

22. Dobbins interview.

23. David T. Johnson, 2002–2003, William B. Taylor, Jr., 2003–2004, Maureen Quinn, 2004–2006, John A. Gastright, 2006–2007, and Patrick Moon, 2008. The Coordinators did not have the title of Special Envoy. Ronald E. Neumann, Ambassador to Afghanistan 2005–2007, told the author that when approached about the ambassador position, he responded that he would not serve, if a Special Envoy was named. Interview December 18, 2007.

24. Woodward, *Plan of Attack*, 282–283.

25. See George Packer, *The Assassins' Gate: America in Iraq* (New York: Farrar, Straus, & Giroux, 2005), 66; National Security Archive, New State Department Releases on the "Future of Iraq" Project, September 1, 2006. http://www.gwu.edu/~nsarchiv/NSAEBB/NSAEBB198/index.htm.

26. *Plan of Attack*, 283–284.

27. Respectively George Ward, Lew Lucke, and Michael Mobbs, former law partner of Under Secretary Douglas Feith.

28. David Dunford, Robin Raphel, Timothy M. Carney, and John W. Limbert, respectively. Barbara Bodine was administrator of central Iraq, including Baghdad. Raphel later replaced Mobbs as head of civil administration and governance. See *The Assassins' Gate*, 120–135.

29. There was no announcement of the establishment of the CPA or of the elimination of ORHA—or of the resignation of ORHA chief Gen. Jay Garner. L. Elaine Halchin, *The Coalition Provisional Authority (CPA): Origin, Characteristics, and Institutional Author-ities* (Congressional Research Service Report to Congress RL32370, April 29, 2004).

30. *State of Denial*, 236.

31. Departing ORHA Director Garner, according to Bob Woodward, thought that "though Rumsfeld had been eager to ensure that the Defense Department controlled the postwar effort, almost everyone in a position of power within Bremer's new CPA came from the State Department." *State of Denial*, 208. Bremer writes, "The CPA almost certainly had more junior, mid-grade and senior Foreign Service officers and retired ambassadors working in Iraq than anywhere else but the State Department itself." *My Year in Baghdad: The Struggle to Build a Future of Hope* (New York: Thresh-old Editions, 2006), 187.

32. In 2004 Kerik was nominated as Secretary of Homeland Security but withdrew. In 2009 he pleaded guilty to a multi-count indictment for conspiracy, mail fraud, wire fraud, and lying to the Internal Revenue Service. Another controversial appointee was the replacement of a senior USAID official, Frederick M. Burkle, Jr., a physician and professor at Johns Hopkins School of Public Health, with an international reputation on disaster response, serving as senior advisor to the Ministry of Health, by James Haveman, a community health leader from Michigan who had directed a Christian adoption agency. Rajiv Chandrasekaran, "Ties to GOP Trumped Know-How Among Staff Sent to Rebuild Iraq: Early U.S. Missteps in the Green Zone," *Washington Post*, September 17, 2006.

33. Marc Grossman, Under Secretary of State for Political Affairs, "The Imminent Transfer of Sovereignty in Iraq," Testimony to the House International Relations Committee, May 13, 2004, http://www.america.gov/st/washfile-english/2004/May/20040513183840cpataruk0.8424036.html.

34. Deputy Coordinator Barbara Stephenson had primary contact with the Iraqi Minister of Provincial Affairs.

35. Interview with Barbara Stephenson, February 1, 2008.

36. See John H. Esterline and Robert B. Black's 1975 study, *Inside Foreign Policy: The Department of State Political System and Its Subsystems* (Palo Alto: Mayfield), 47. Their comments about the role of the regional bureaus are generally still applicable today.

37. The exceptions are the Offices of Russian Affairs and Chinese Affairs which involve only one country.

38. Liberians United for Reconciliation & Democracy was a largely Mandingo (Muslim) faction, with close ties to the neighboring Government of Guinea.

39. Bush called on Taylor to leave Liberia, announcing that the United States would not assist Liberia until he did. It was not clear why such a statement was expected to push Taylor out the door.

40. Marcus Mabry cites NSC Africa Director Jendayi Frazer as reporting that Rice sided with Powell. "She said, 'Okay, now I think the Marines may need to go in' and the decision was made," *Twice as Good*, 205.

41. Interview with Jendayi Frazer, January 24, 2008.

42. It consisted of the Iwo Jima Amphibious Ready Group and the 26th Marine Expeditionary Unit. Until 2008, when the African unified combatant command (AFRICOM) became active, the European unified combatant command (EUCOM) handled operational military responsibilities for that part of Africa.

43. The LURD representative signed the agreement at the residence of the U.S. ambassador in Guinea, who faxed the signed document back to Accra. Interview with Ambassador Barry Walkley, September 28, 2004.

44. The Lusaka Agreement was concluded in August 1999. After a series of failed meetings in 2001 at different sites, under the mediation of former Botswana President Ketumile Masire, the South Africans sponsored a series of negotiations in 2002–2003 promoting the "Congolese National Dialogue" in Sun City, South Africa. These discussions resulted in Agreement on the Transition in the Democratic Republic of the Congo, which created a transitional constitution, recognized Joseph Kabila as transitional president, and brought the other factions into the government. It did not essentially change the problem of the Interahamwe and Rwandan intervention in eastern Congo to control that group.

45. Interview with Donald Y. Yamamoto, October 2, 2006.

46. Christine A. Terada, Washington File Staff Writer, "U.S. Deputy Assistant Secretary of State Discusses Meeting of Joint Commission," November 8, 2005.

47. The appointment of William L. Swing, a former U.S. ambassador to the Congo, as the Special Representative of UN Secretary-General Kofi Annan led to strengthened UN and MONUC performance, aided at a critical point by special French forces. On Swing's role, see Philip Roessler and John Prendergast, "Democratic Republic of the Congo," in William J. Durch, ed., *Twenty-First-Century Peace Operations* (Washington: USIP & Stimson Center, 2006), 287.

48. In 2005 the United States actually proposed deactivating the Commission but was dissuaded by the parties and interested European states. Under the auspices of the Commission, Rwanda and Congo signed an agreement in November 2007 to end threats to peace and stability in both countries and the region. Kigali agreed to submit a list of those accused of orchestrating the genocide in Rwanda in 1994 and believed to be in the Congo; Kinshasa promised to prepare a detailed plan to disarm the Rwandan Hutu rebels in the eastern Congo. Apparent progress toward that goal was finally made in early 2009, when President Kabila invited Rwandan troops to enter the Congo and join Congolese troops in combating the Hutu rebels.

49. The Moro National Liberation Front, from which the MILF split in 1977, was no longer a significant threat by the 1990s. The Communist New People's Army, a residue of the Hukbalahap rebellion of the 1930s and 1940s, seeks a Communist revolution but is largely inactive. It is listed by the United States as a Foreign Terrorist Organization.

50. Interview with James A. Kelly, January 17, 2008.

51. Benedicto R. Bacani, *The Mindanao Peace Talks: Another Opportunity to Resolve the Moro Conflict in the Philippines* (USIP Special Report No. 131, 2005).

52. Solomon was also Ambassador to the Philippines 1992–93.

53. Interview with Michael J. Green, August 30, 2007.

54. In October 2003, Secretary Powell announced that the Philippines had been designated as a Major Non-NATO Ally, making the country eligible for special deals on surplus military commodities, preferable defense equipment financing, and training. However, this announcement was largely a public relations effort, "a deliverable" generated for the official visit to Washington that year of Philippine President Gloria Macapagal-Arroyo. Already a U.S. ally, the Philippines had access to these U.S. facilities.

55. Direct action was reportedly advocated by Deputy Defense Secretary Wolfowitz but did not gain the support of Secretary Rumsfeld. GlobalSecurity.org, Operation Enduring Freedom—Philippines: Balikatan 2002-I, http://www.globalsecurity .org/military/ops/balikatan_02-1.htm.

56. The rest of the contingent included Navy Seabees, Marine Corps engineers, Air Force search and rescue personnel, and Army helicopter crews to ferry supplies. Jim Garamone, "Basilan: Before. After. After That?" American Foreign Press Service, June 4, 2002.

57. Fiona Hill, "Une stratégie incertaine: la politique des Etats-Unis dans le Caucase et en Asie centrale depuis 1991," *Politique étrangère* (February 2001), www .brookings.edu/articles/2001/02foreignpolicy_hill.aspx.

58. Responsibility for Caspian Energy Diplomacy was subsequently split off from Steven Mann and divided among up to six different officials at the end of the Bush 43 administration. Mann remained Eurasian Energy Coordinator.

59. The Andean Counterdrug Initiative (ACI) is the primary U.S. program that supports Plan Colombia, but it provides assistance to additional Andean countries.

60. Congressional Research Service, *Plan Colombia: A Progress Report* (RL32774, January 11, 2006), http://digital.library.unt.edu/govdocs/crs/permalink/meta-crs-8270:1.

61. Interview with Thomas Bruneau, NPS, December 9, 2008.

62. Kopp and Gillespie, *Career Diplomacy*, 32–33. As Kopp and Gillespie point out, a key reason for the State Department's failure to match the military in training for its personnel is that the number of FSOs relative to jobs is too small to create a sufficient "float" to enable its personnel to take regular time for training.

63. As of the beginning of 2009, the FSI Web site mentioned training in "foreign affairs tradecraft" to include area and cultural studies, consular affairs, information technology, resource management, security, economics, public diplomacy, political reporting and leadership but without mention of conflict. Only when the reader pursues the question into the course catalog do courses for "Reconstruction, Stabilization and Conflict Transformation" emerge.

64. Considerations of space preclude treatment of the Bureau of Population, Refugees and Migration (PRM), which enjoys a generally harmonious relationship with other bureaus involved in peace-building. PRM manages refugee protection programs funded by the United States. Most of this funding is allocated to support persons fleeing states afflicted by civil conflict. An approximate value of annual refugee funding devoted to support for peace-building and stabilization is $700 million, coming from the Migration and Refugee Assistance (MRA), for ongoing refugee crises, and U.S. ERMA, for unforeseen crises. PRM does not operate refugee camps or provide aid directly to refugees, but works through the United Nations High Commission for Refugees, other international organizations, and NGOs. Voluntary refugee repatriation is a major part of post-conflict reconstruction programs.

65. A recess appointment occurs when the President fills a vacant federal position during a recess of the Senate. It is sometimes made, as in the Bolton case, when the nominee faces serious obstacles to confirmation. It expires with the Congressional session.

66. As of October 2008, the United States was providing 298, of which all but 22 were police. Contributors to United Nations Peacekeeping Operations, Monthly Summary of Contributions (Police, Military Observers and Troops), as of October 31, 2008, available at http://www.un.org/Depts/dpko/dpko/contributors/2008/oct08_1.pdf. In early 1995, by contrast, the United States had several thousand troops

deployed in Somalia and Haiti. *U.S. Participation in the United Nations 1995*, available at http://www.state.gov/www/issues/unpart/1995/part1.html#997555.

67. Interview with Kim Holmes, former IO Assistant Secretary of State, November 28, 2006.

68. A number of the functional bureaus function as the interface for diplomacy with other government agencies. For example, the EEB provides a basic interface for the State Department with agencies such as the Treasury, Energy, Commerce, and Agriculture Departments and with the Office of the U.S. Trade Representative, which have a major interest in the international arena. Treasury and Agriculture sometimes play a role in major post-conflict reconstruction activity, but it is rarely a major interest of those departments.

69. Interview with Leonard R. Hawley, former NSC director and deputy assistant secretary of state, September 7, 2007. In a partial refutation of the conventional wisdom that plans simply gather dust on a shelf, Hawley discovered they had been downloaded into a database used by the State Department's Office of the Coordinator for Reconstruction and Stabilization during the Bush 43 administration.

70. Interview with Bloomfield, November 8, 2007.

71. The Office of Contingency Planning and Peacekeeping was renamed the Office of Plans, Policy and Analysis, but did not continue its role of planning for complex emergencies.

72. Interview with Bloomfield.

73. Known as *gendarmes* in French and "constabulary police" in English.

74. See Chapter 8 for details on this account, formally known as Peacekeeping Operations (PKO), within the Function 150 budget.

75. Congressional Research Service, *The Global Peace Operations Initiative: Background and Issues for Congress* (June 11, 2007), summary page.

76. Rumsfeld wanted the United States to provide the conceptual leadership and the Europeans to provide most of the funding. The NSC did not believe that claiming diplomatic leadership of the initiative, while foisting off the financial responsibility, would put the President in a positive light at a U.S.-based summit. NSA Rice telephoned Rumsfeld and persuaded him to ease the DOD demand. Of course, since the money was coming out of the Department of State peacekeeping budget, it was a concession without cost to the Defense Department. Interview with Matthew McLean, ex-NSC director, January 18, 2007.

77. Congressional Research Service, *The Global Peace Operations Initiative* (Report RL32773, updated June 11, 2007), 17, 21–23.

78. In 1974, following human rights abuses by foreign police forces which included graduates from USAID's Office of Public Security's police training program, Congress banned U.S. assistance to foreign police. Bayley, "U.S. Aid for Foreign Justice and Police," 469–479.

79. U.S. Department of State, "Civilian Police and Rule of Law Programs" (Fact Sheet, January 2, 2008).

80. Inspectors-General of the Defense and State Departments, Interagency Assessment of Afghanistan Police Training and Readiness, November 2006, 7.

81. UN Office of Drugs and Crime, World Drug Report 2007, 11.

82. Anthony H. Cordesman, *Losing the Afghan-Pakistan War? The Rising Threat*, Center for Strategic and International Studies, updated October 21, 2008, available at http://www.csis.org/index.php?option=com_csis_pubs&task=view&id=4885.

83. NATO News, October 16, 2008, available at http://www.nato.int/docu/update/2008/10-october/e1010b.html.

84. Interview with Christopher McMullen, Deputy Assistant Secretary of State for Western Hemisphere Affairs, December 12, 2007.

85. U.S. Department of State, "Civilian Police and Rule of Law Programs" (Fact Sheet, January 2, 2008).

CHAPTER 4

1. From his remarks introducing on February 25, 2004, the Stabilization & Reconstruction Civilian Management Act of 2004, http://foreign.senate.gov/testimony/2004/LugarStatement040303.pdf.

2. Congress endorsed S/CRS in the Consolidated Appropriations Act 2005 (Division B, Title IV, Sec. 408, H.R. 4818, PL 108–447), signed into law by President Bush December 8, 2004. The law directed that the Coordinator report directly to the Secretary of State and outlined the office's functions:

- Catalog the nonmilitary capabilities of U.S. agencies to deal with conflict in countries or regions that are in, or are in transition from, conflict crises;
- Monitor instability worldwide to anticipate the need for U.S. and international assistance;
- Assess the crises and determine the appropriate nonmilitary U.S. response;
- Plan the response;
- Coordinate interagency contingency planning and action; and
- Coordinate training of civilian personnel for R&S.

3. And, to a lesser extent, the Bureau of Democracy, Human Rights, and Labor, which manages the State-administered grants of the Human Rights and Democracy Fund (HRDF). (Since 2006 Congress has appropriated HRDF as part of the "Democracy Fund," which also includes the National Endowment for Democracy. Some DRL-supervised projects are used in countries in conflict.)

4. Prime Minister Meles Zenawi, a U.S. ally, was incensed to learn that Ethiopia was on the list. Interview with Constance B. Newman, July 17, 2007.

5. "Draft Planning Framework for Stabilization, Reconstruction and Conflict Transformation." The document was revised in 2007, incorporating feedback and lessons learned from planning exercises on Sudan, Chad, Haiti, Kosovo, Zimbabwe, and Nepal.

6. Interview with Barbara J. Stephenson, ex-S/CRS Director of Planning, October 3, 2006.

7. The "Post-Conflict Reconstruction Essential Tasks Matrix" is a detailed, 50 plus-page checklist of "to do" items. It divides the tasks into five basic functions: security, governance and participation, humanitarian assistance and social well-being (including health and education), economic stabilization and infrastructure (including legal and regulatory reform), justice, and reconciliation. Both the Planning Framework and the Essential Tasks Matrix were based on the *Post-Conflict Reconstruction Task Framework* developed jointly by the Center for Strategic and International Studies and the Association of the U.S. Army, found at Appendix 1 of Orr, *Winning the Peace*, 306–327.

8. For example, for the objective "sustainable security established," a metric might be "episodes of political violence with more than 4 deaths." Metrics are to be reassessed on a continuing basis.

9. Stephen D. Krasner and Carlos Pascual, "Addressing State Failure," *Foreign Affairs*, July–August 2005, 161.

10. Stephenson interview.

11. Theresa Johnson, "What Difference Can a Diplomat Make? Carlos Pascual Nurtures a New Ukraine," *Stanford Magazine*, July–August 2003.

12. The planning group, convoked by the NSC, was called a Country Reconstruction and Stabilization Group (CRSG), the body formalized in the 2007 approval of the IMS.

13. Stephenson interview.

14. S. 1042 National Defense Authorization Act for Fiscal Year 2006. See also "Defense Department Seeks More Aid Capability," *Washington Post*, October 29, 2005.

15. "Transformational Diplomacy," January 18, 2006, http://www.actfl.org/i4a/pages/Index.cfm?pageID=4259.

16. The new position made him formally third in rank in the State Department behind Deputy Secretary Robert Zoellick.

17. Tobias did not have charge of the entire 150 function, but of the foreign operations portion involving State and USAID. That did not include the State Department diplomatic and consular affairs account.

18. Statement to a roundtable of experts, July 18, 2007. Dane F. Smith, Jr., *Roundtable on Proposed Civilian Reserve Corps* (a Center for Strategic and International Studies PCR Project Special Briefing), November 2007, 1.

19. The direct formal relationship with the Secretary is indicated by the office prefix S in S/CRS. The State Department organizational chart has also linked S/CRS to the Secretary rather than to F.

20. Smith, *Roundtable*, 1.

21. An "experimental" CRSG took place in January 2008 to test the new mechanism. The subject and results are classified. Interview with Jonathan Benton, Director, S/CRS Office of Civilian Readiness and Response, December 7, 2007. Before approval of the IMS, a CRSG was established for implementation in southern Sudan of the CPA, and S/CRS cochaired meetings on Haiti and Cuba transition in the mode of a CRSG. As a follow-up to planning on post-Castro Cuba, an IPC was dispatched to the Southern Command.

22. Benton interview, December 5, 2008.

23. John E. Herbst, "Stabilization and Reconstruction Operations: Learning from the Provincial Reconstruction Team (PRT) Experience," Statement before the House Armed Services Subcommittee on Oversight and Investigations, October 30, 2007. Herbst was presumably seeking to clarify a criticism by the GAO that there was not a clear definition of R&S operations which distinguished them from other types of military or civilian activities such as counterterrorism, counterinsurgency, or development assistance, thereby creating confusion about when the framework would be applied. Government Accountability Office, *Stabilization and Reconstruction: Actions Needed to Improve Governmentwide Planning and Capabilities for Future Operations* (GAO-08-228, October 30, 2007), 8. It seems clear the IMS could be used to deal with a counterterrorism or counterinsurgency situation, if the other criteria applied and R&S activities were warranted. The IMS could generate a strategic plan that would include various kinds of short-term assistance, but development assistance would be handled under existing USAID procedures.

24. The Principal Deputy also supervises a Resource Management Office that handles personnel, finance and budget, technology, and general services.

25. Much of the section on planning reflects an interview with Oscar de Soto, S/CRS Director of Planning, December 10, 2007.

26. Although the first and second sequence would normally be separate, the strategic planning team may develop the MME strategies as well.

27. The triggers and planning sequences are described in detail in Department of State/U.S. Joint Forces Command, *US Government Draft Planning Framework for Reconstruction, Stabilization and Conflict Transformation* (2005), 12–34.

28. The views of the chief of mission, channeled through the geographic bureau and assistant secretary, would presumably be taken into account throughout the policy and strategic planning process.

29. Since Cuba does not have violent internal conflict, it is not dealt with in this study, even though S/CRS has become involved in post-Castro planning. Cuban planning under S/CRS auspices emerged from earlier work by the Commission for a Free Cuba (CAFC). At the end of 2006, S/CRS, at the request of WHA, became the secretariat for an integrated planning approach to post-Castro Cuba.

30. Benton interview, December 7, 2007.

31. Stephenson interview.

32. When the civilian surge was launched in 2007 to accompany the military surge in Iraq, senior military were disappointed to discover that the much discussed civilian reserve did not yet exist, four years after the creation of S/CRS, and that the military would initially have to put reservists into those positions.

33. Interview with L. Celeste Ward, Deputy Assistant Secretary of Defense for Stability Operations Capabilities, December 1, 2008.

34. De Soto interview.

35. Government Accountability Office, *Stabilization and Reconstruction: Actions Are Needed to Develop a Planning and Coordination Framework and Establish the Civilian Reserve Corps*, November 2007, 13.

36. In its response to the GAO report, the State Department stated that "S/CRS works to complement the existing roles of the regional bureaus at State, USAID and other agencies working in R&S. S/CRS may, depending on the circumstance, assist with conflict assessment and planning processes for reconstruction and stabilization in conjunction with its interagency partners." GAO, *Stabilization and Reconstruction*, Annex 3, 5.

37. For analysis of both, see Stewart Patrick and Kaysie Brown, *Greater than the Sum of Its Parts: Assessing "Whole of Government" Approaches to Fragile States* (International Peace Academy, 2007), 27–30, 67–73. In 2007 S/CRS had one non-American staff member, but from the European Union, not from the Stabilisation Unit or START.

38. Interview with Marcia Wong, ex-Deputy Coordinator, S/CRS, January 10, 2007.

39. Until 2008 CRC-A was called the "active response corps."

40. Interview with John E. Herbst, January 30, 2007.

41. Interview with Ann Bodine, Chief, and Eythan Sontag, member, Active Response Corps, November 1, 2007.

42. Previously called Standby Response Corps.

43. The S/CRS Web site as of December 2007 seemed to imply CRC-S deployments to Lebanon, Haiti, Kosovo, Iraq, Nepal, and Afghanistan, but those additional deployments did not occur.

44. Benton interview, December 2007.

45. The appropriation included $30 million for S/CRS and $25 million for USAID for the same purpose. H.R. 2642 (PL 110–252) Supplemental Appropriations Act 2008. The FY 2009 Omnibus Appropriations Act of March 2009 added a total of $75 million for State and USAID.

46. Interview with Christopher Hoh, Associate Dean, Foreign Service Institute, December 4, 2008.

47. Testimony by Carlos Pascual, "Stabilization and Reconstruction: Building Peace in a Hostile Environment," Hearing before the Committee on Foreign Relations, United States Senate, 109th Congress, June 16, 2005.

48. The ICAF is built on but should not be confused with the Conflict Assessment Framework (CAF) developed by USAID's CMM. See Chapter 6.

49. See *Principles of the Interagency Conflict Assessment Framework*, 8, available at http://www.crs.state.gov/index.cfm?fuseaction=public.display&shortcut=CJ2R.

50. Nina M. Serafino, *Department of Defense "Section 1207" Security and Stabilization Assistance: A Fact Sheet* (Congressional Research Service RS22871, November 25, 2008). A $5 million project for Colombia was held up at least temporarily because of a hold imposed by House State, Foreign Operations and Related Programs Subcommittee Chair Nita Lowey.

51. As advertised on the S/CRS Web site, http://www.crs.state.gov/index.cfm?fuseaction=public.display&shortcut=CKIH.

52. S/CRS was told not to come back in the future with the same arguments to justify the reserve. Stephenson interview. There was speculation that Subcommittee Chair James Kolbe (R-AZ) was influenced by former USAID Administrator Andrew Natsios, who reportedly opposed the creation of S/CRS.

53. Sen. Coburn, a relentless critic of the State Department and admirer of the Defense Department, is ranking minority member of Subcommittee on Federal Financial Management, Government Information, and International Security of the Homeland Security and Governmental Affairs Committee.

54. Karen DeYoung, "Diplomats Give Rice Low Marks," *Washington Post*, January 8, 2008.

55. The Duncan Hunter National Defense Authorization Act for Fiscal Year 2009 (S. 30010) authorized S/CRS, the Response Readiness Corps (active and standby components), and Civilian Reserve Corps. The Coburn hold was circumvented by placing the legislation in the Defense Authorization bill, which he did not want to oppose.

56. Both the Consolidated Appropriations Act 2004 and the National Defense Authorization Act of 2008 stipulate that the Coordinator reports directly to the Secretary.

57. President Bush proposed increasing the two services by a total of 92,000 in his State of the Union message, January 23, 2007. The proposed FY 2009 budget included an increase in State Department employees by 726, net of those required for the Civilian Stabilization Initiative, and 300 more for USAID.

CHAPTER 5

1. Interview with James Dobbins, December 1, 2006, 3. See Chapter 2.

2. Gen. William L. Nash, who commanded NATO peacekeeping forces in Bosnia, recalls Sen. Ted Stevens of the Armed Services Committee asking him during a visit, "You're not doing that nation-building stuff are you?" Interview, January 12, 2007.

3. Second Presidential Debate, Wake Forest University, October 11, 2000.

4. Quoted by Michael R. Gordon, "The 2000 Campaign: The Military; Bush Would Stop U.S. Peacekeeping in Balkan Fights," *New York Times*, October 21, 2000.

5. Joint Chiefs of Staff Chairman, Gen. Hugh Shelton, responded, "It is naive to think that the military will become involved in only those areas that affect our vital national interests." *New York Times*, December 17, 2000, A7, courtesy of Tammy Schultz, "Ten Years Each Week: The Warrior's Transformation to Win the Peace," PhD Dissertation, Georgetown University, 2005, 2.

6. *Power, Terror, Peace and War: America's Grand Strategy in a World of Risk* (New York: Vintage, 2004), 42.

7. Summary and Highlights: International Affairs Function 150, Fiscal Year 2009 Budget Request, 47. Allocation decisions are worked out between the Political-Military Affairs Bureau and the geographic bureaus in the State Department, since security assistance is funded out of the international affairs budget, rather than the Defense budget. See Chapter 8 for details on IMET funding for conflict countries.

8. Chas. W. Freeman, Jr., writes that "training and joint exercises demonstrate effective partnership and give deterrent credibility to alliance." *Arts of Power*, 54.

9. Ibid., 54.

10. Summary and Highlights: International Affairs Function 150, Fiscal Year 2009 Budget Request, 44. State's PM bureau determines policy for FMF; the Defense Department's DSCA manages the movement of military equipment financed by it.

11. *Arts of Power*, 53.

12. See Army Field Manual 100-15 Corps Operations, Chapter 9 OOTW. Interview with Capt. Jon Padfield, April 3, 2007, 3.

13. The Road Map for National Security: Imperative for Change: The Phase 3 Report of the U.S. Commission on National Security/21st Century (usually referred to as the Hart-Rudman Report) (Wilkes-Barre, PA: Kallisti Publishers, 2002), 77, courtesy of Dr. Tammy Schultz.

14. Joseph R. Collins interview, March 16, 2007.

15. See Schultz, "Ten Years Each Week," 24–26.

16. With the Assistant Secretary/SOLIC position unfilled during 2003, Collins found himself reporting directly to Under Secretary for Policy, Douglas Feith.

17. Collins also gives credit to his staffer Mustafa Popal, an Afghan-American.

18. Casie Vinall, "Joe Collins: Career Officer, Deputy Assistant Secretary," Armed Forces Press Service, June 23, 2003.

19. James Dobbins et al., *After the War: Nation-Building from FDR to George W. Bush* (Santa Monica, DA: Rand, 2008), 90.

20. Wolfowitz said on *Face the Nation* November 18, 2001 that "one of the lessons of Afghanistan's history . . . is if you're a foreigner, try not to go in. If you do go in, don't stay too long, because they don't tend to like any foreigners who stay too long." Quoted by Lawrence Freedman, "Using Force for Peace in an Age of Terror," in Crocker, Hampson, and Aall, *Leashing the Dogs of War: Conflict Management in a Divided World* (Washington: USIP Press, 2007), 255.

21. Collins interview; see also Milan Vaishnav, "The Chimera of the Light Footprint" in Robert C. Orr, ed., *Winning the Peace: An American Strategy for Post-Conflict*

Reconstruction (Washington: CSIS Press, 2004), 244–262.

22. S/Res. 1368, September 12, 2001. Barnett Rubin, *Afghanistan's Uncertain Transition from Turmoil to Normalcy* (Washington: USIP, 2006), 5.

23. S/Res. 1386, December 20, 2001.

24. Dobbins et al., *America's Role*, 136.

25. The origin of the PRT is not clear. Credit has been imputed to a British officer, Nick Carter, working with U.S. forces. James Dobbins, Special Bush Administration Envoy for Afghanistan 2001–2002, reports that in his role as envoy he sought DOD agreement to colocate civilians with the military in urban units. The original term was "joint regional team," rejected by President Ahmed Karzai, who said there was no word for "joint" in Pashtu or Dari and that "regional" would be linked to warlords in the public mind. Interview with Joseph R. Collins, March 16, 2007.

26. Danny Hall, "The Very Model of a Modern . . . ," *Foreign Service Journal* (March 2007), 40–41. See also Michael J. Dziedzic and Colonel Michael K. Seidl, *Provincial Reconstruction Teams: Military Relations with International and Nongovernmental Organizations in Afghanistan* (Washington: U.S. Institute of Peace, Special Report #147, August 2005).

27. Marcus Gausker, *Provincial Reconstruction Teams in Afghanistan* (George C. Marshall European Center for Security Studies, Occasional Paper 16, January 2008), including the useful comparison of national teams on p. 56.

28. Coalition members deploying over 1,000 troops originally included Britain, Italy, Spain, Netherlands, Korea, and Ukraine. A couple of dozen other countries provided less than 1,000.

29. Statement of Defense Under Secretary for Policy Douglas Feith, February 11, 2003 available at http://www.sourcewatch.org/index.php?title=Office_of_Reconstruction_and_Humanitarian_Assistance.

30. Packer, *The Assassins' Gate*, 129.

31. See James Dobbins in "What to Do in Iraq: A Roundtable," *Foreign Affairs* 85:4 (July–August 2006), 150–169, and Galbraith, *End of Iraq*, 116–117.

32. The use of the seized funds was deemed admissible under international law and did not require Congressional appropriation.

33. There were only 10 PRTs by the end of 2006, but they rapidly expanded in 2007 and 2008, in parallel with the U.S. "surge," to reach 31 teams, 28 led by American personnel. In 2008, personnel in Iraq PRTs from U.S. civilian agencies began to outnumber military personnel for the first time. Government Accountability Office, *Provincial Reconstruction Teams in Afghanistan and Iraq* (October 1, 2008), 4–5,12, available at http://www.gao.gov/new.items/do986r.odf.

34. An analysis of the effectiveness of PRTs in Iraq is beyond the scope of this study, although aspects of the PRTs are explored in Chapters 2 to 4. In his final report, the Special Inspector for Iraq Reconstruction details the difficulties of PRT organization in Iraq, including personnel recruitment and budget, but concludes that "when violence is pervasive, soft programs—like those . . . [of] the Provincial Reconstruction Teams—are especially important in advancing U.S. goals." SIGIR, *Hard Lessons: The Iraq Reconstruction Experience* (Washington: Government Printing Office, 2009), 332.

35. See Chapter 2.

36. Jeffrey Nadaner, Remarks at the Center for Strategic and International Studies, December 11, 2006.

37. Defense Science Board, *2004 Summer Study on Transition to and from Hostilities* (published December 2004). Supporting documents for the study included a historical

review of emergence from hostilities, which concludes that "enhancing stabilization and reconstruction (S&R) capabilities is vital to U.S. interests." Defense Science Board, *2004 Summer Study on Transition to and from Hostilities: Supporting Documents* (published January 2005). Although the study is often associated with William Schneider, Board Chair at the time of release, Fields was the principal author, according to a former senior OSD official. The study builds to some extent on the Lugar-Biden Bill (see Chapter 2), which the study recommended that the Defense Department endorse.

38. Giambastiani claims he persuaded Deputy Secretary Gordon England to sign the Directive, since Rumsfeld did not have time to look at the details, although he supported the concept behind it. Interview with Adm. (Ret.) Giambastiani, December 11, 2008.

39. Noting that "military-civilian teams are a critical . . . stability operations tool," the Directive states that DOD shall continue "*to lead* and support the development of military-civilian teams."

40. The Goldwater-Nichols Department of Defense Reorganization Act of 1986 (PL 99-433) transformed the chain of command to run directly from the President and the Secretary of Defense to the commanders of the unified combatant commands, which may be either functional or geographic in nature. The other unified functional combatant commands are the Strategic Command (STRATCOM), the Special Operations Command (SOCOM), and the Transportation Command (TRANSCOM).

41. "Military doctrine is what is believed to be the best way to conduct military affairs. . . . [T]he principal source of doctrine is experience." Dennis Drew and Don Snow, "Military Doctrine," from *Making Strategy: An Introduction to National Security Processes and Problems* (Maxwell, AL: Air University Press, 2006), 210. More formally, doctrine provides the "fundamental principles by which the military forces or elements thereof guide their actions in support of national objectives." *DOD Dictionary of Military and Associated Terms*, as amended through August 19, 2009, available at http://www.dtic.mil/doctrine/dod_dictionary/.

42. Giambastiani interview.

43. The military refers to integration with interagency, NGO, international organization, and multinational partners as "unified action."

44. Department of Defense, Capstone Concept for Joint Operations, Version 2 (August 2005). See also JFCOM, "Joint Operations Concepts (JOpsC)," available at http://www.jfcom.mil/about/fact_jopsc.htm. JOpsCs are referred to variously as "Joint Operating Concepts" and "Joint Operations Concepts."

45. JFCOM also tasked its Joint Center of Operational Analysis, set up at the beginning of the war in Iraq, to examine how stability operations should be integrated into operations. Additional work has been done on experimentation on "unified action." "Unified action is something broadly acknowledged now where military action as an instrument alone cannot handle the problems we face. It must do it in concert with the United States government, multinational elements and coalition partners, and inter-agencies and multi-agencies." LTG Bob Wood, Deputy Commander JFCOM, May 10, 2006, http://www.jfcom.mil/newslink/storyarchive/2006/pa051006.htm.

46. Department of Defense, *Support for Security, Stabilization, Transition, Reconstruction Operations Joint Operating Concept*, Version 2, December 2006.

47. Capstone Concept, 8.

48. Ibid., 9–10.

49. Ibid., 17.

50. Ibid., 12.

51. Interview with LTC Steven Leonard, October 31, 2008. The manual states, "[Stability operations] postures the military to perform *a role common throughout history*—ensuring the safety and security of the local populace, assisting with reconstruction, and providing basic sustenance and public services." (My italics)

52. Speech before Global Leadership Campaign, July 15, 2008, available at www.defenselink.mil/speeches/speech.aspx?speechid=1262.

53. Interview with James Benn, Deputy Director for Doctrine Development, Army Combined Arms Center, Fort Leavenworth, October 16, 2008. See also pp. 1–14 and 6–2 of AFM 3.07.

54. AFM 3.07, 3–7 to 14.

55. LTC Leonard interview.

56. Full spectrum includes offensive operations, defensive operations, stability operations, and operations in support of civil authorities in natural disaster situations. Army Field Manual 3.0 Operations, February 27, 2008, 3–7 to 19.

57. Interview with Michael McNerney, Director, International Capacity Building, April 25, 2007.

58. It also relates strategy and policies to counterinsurgency, foreign internal defense, de-mining, and foreign health disaster response. DASD Celeste Ward emphasized that the mandate of Stability Operations Capabilities is not just the 3000.05 implementing office. Its mandate is "to help create a general purpose force to deal with irregular challenges." Interview, December 1, 2008.

59. McNerney interview.

60. The virtually incomprehensible mission statement for Stability Operations Capabilities found on an OSD organizational chart dated April 2007 suggests some of the confusion: "Develop stability operations capabilities' vision and strategy for own future joint force and warfighters for SECDEF consideration. Formulate and coordinate stability operations capabilities policies and missions in support of SECDEF strategic objectives. Oversee interdependent operational execution and force development of SECDEF-approved stability operations capabilities policies for: Security, Stability, Transition, and Reconstruction (SSTR) capabilities."

61. GSP was known as INMA, International Negotiations and Multilateral Affairs, until mid-2006.

62. Posture Statement of General Peter Pace, USMC, Chairman of the Joint Chiefs of Staff before the 110th Congress, Senate Armed Services Committee, February 6, 2007, 9. My italics.

63. The European Command (EUCOM), the Central Command (CENTCOM), the Southern Command (SOUTHCOM), the Pacific Command (PACOM), the Africa Command (AFRICOM), created in 2008, and the Northern Command (NORTHCOM). Since NORTHCOM is responsible for the U.S. homeland (except for Hawaii), Canada, Mexico, and adjacent waters, it is not discussed in this study. For reasons of space, and since the geographic COCOMs are by nature focused on overseas operations, this section does not attempt an exhaustive survey of the evolution of their handling of stability operations.

64. This requirement appears to imply a vast military intelligence effort, overlapping with the data embassies and the CIA collect. The post-9/11 period shift in military intelligence away from what the enemy military is doing to focus more on the society where conflict is taking place is also reflected in detail in chapter 3 of the Army Counterinsurgency Field Manual 3.24 (2007).

65. All combatant commands are endowed with Joint Interagency Coordination Groups (JIACGs). Originally created during the Clinton administration to facilitate interagency dialogue with the military, they were downgraded by the incoming Bush administration. After 9/11, Gen. Tommy Franks, CENTCOM Commander, requested an "interagency coordination cell" to work directly with various agencies involved in Operation Enduring Freedom in Afghanistan. JIACGs were then revived by the NSC and reimposed on the combatant commands by the Secretary of Defense to integrate information sharing in support of the GWOT. State, Justice, and Treasury have been the main participants. Since the JIACGs are primarily concerned with terrorism and not peace-building, they are not further analyzed in this study.

66. In the European Command the Coordinating Authority was originally under the Operations Directorate (J-3), but in 2007 the position migrated to J-5.

67. A description of the UJTL and EMTL in pre-Matrix versions is found in Chairman of the Joint Chiefs of Staff, Universal Joint Task List Manual, July 2002, and Chairman of the Joint Chiefs of Staff, Joint Mission Essential Task List (JMETL) Development Handbook, September 2002.

68. Sgt. Sara Wood, "CENTCOM Coordination Center Represents Strong Coalition," Armed Forces Information Services, March 7, 2007, http://www.globalsecurity.org/military/library/news/2007/03/mil-070316-afps01.htm.

69. Telephone interview with Col. Lindsay Gudridge, SSTR Branch Chief, CENTCOM J-5/Plans Division, April 13, 2007, 2.

70. Charles F. Wald, "New Thinking at EUCOM: The Zero Campaign," *Joint Forces Quarterly* 43 (4th quarter 2006), 73. In military "phasing" terminology, Phase IV was considered to be "transition," that is, the follow on to decisive military operations. At the beginning of the Iraq war in 2003, R&S were viewed as being part of a vague Phase IV. EUCOM's Phase Zero is focused on prevention, therefore, rather than R&S.

71. Ricks, *Fiasco*, 162–163.

72. GAO's other criticisms that (a) Defense had not yet fully identified and prioritized stability operations capabilities, and for that reason, the individual services are pursuing initiatives that may not provide the comprehensive set of capabilities that combatant commanders need to accomplish stability operations in the future; (b) DOD had not advanced very far in developing the measures of effectiveness required by Directive 3000.05, making progress hard to measure; and (c) the military did not currently have a process to incorporate lessons were largely outdated by the time the report appeared in October 2007. The writing of the report was actually launched in 2006 a few months after Directive 3000.05 was issued. With respect to lessons learned, DOD probably does better in systematically incorporating lessons learned from past operations than any other federal agency. GAO, Stabilization and Reconstruction: Actions Needed to Improve Governmentwide Planning and Capabilities for Future Operations, Testimony before the Subcommittee on Oversight and Investigations, Committee on Armed Services, House of Representatives, October 30, 2007 (GAO-08-228T0), especially 13–16. See Chapter 4 for treatment of the report's criticism of S/CRS.

73. http://ccoportal.org/page/about; Spencer Ackerman, "Civilians Missing from Action," Sixth in a Series: "The Rise of the Counterinsurgents," *The Washington Independent*, May 13, 2008, available at http://washingtonindependent.com/1371/civilians-missing-from-action.

74. Kopp and Gillespie, *Career Diplomacy*, 40, 42.

75. Armed Forces Strength Figures for September 30, 2008, available at http://siadapp.dmdc.osd.mil/personnel/MILITARY/ms0.pdf and http://siadapp.dmdc.osd.mil/personnel/MILITARY/rg0809.pdf; Government Accountability Office, *The Department of Defense's Civilian Human Capital Strategic Plan Does Not Meet Most Statutory Requirements* (February 8, 2008), 1.

76. Interview with Janine Davidson, ex-Stability Operations Capabilities officer and ex-Director, Consortium for Complex Operations, November 29, 2008.

77. Interview with Hans J. Binnendijk, Director, Center for Technology & National Security Policy, National Defense University, January 16, 2007, 3.

78. Remarks at the Center for Strategic and International Studies, December 11, 2006.

79. *To the Point with Warren Olney*, February 13, 2008, available at http://media.kcrw.com/podcast/enc/audio/tp/tp0802. At CAC Caldwell immediately succeeded then LTG David Petraeus, who oversaw publication of the joint Army-Marine manual on counterinsurgency, before becoming commanding general in Iraq.

80. Interview, December 1, 2008.

CHAPTER 6

1. See, for example, on the USAID Web site, "USAID Primer," http://www.usaid.gov/about_usaid/primer.html.

2. The objectives are identically stated in both the 2002 and the 2006 versions. "Expand the circle of development" is listed as Objective VII in the National Security Strategy. "Champion aspirations for human dignity" is listed as Objective II. Objective IV "Work with Others to Defuse Regional Conflicts" states that "we will continue to pursue foreign assistance reforms that allow the President to draw on the skills of agencies across the U.S. Government." However, that section emphasizes the State Department's S/CRS office, not USAID. Sec. VI—Promote global growth through free markets and free trade—is largely the responsibility of Treasury and the Office of the U.S. Special Trade Representative (USTR).

3. My italics. USAID Primer, http://www.usaid.gov/about_usaid/primer.html.

4. *The Four Horsemen of the Apocalypse: Humanitarian Relief in Complex Emergencies* (Washington: Center for Strategic and International Studies, 1997).

5. USAID, *Foreign Aid in the National Interest: Promoting Freedom, Security & Opportunity* (2002), 96–110.

6. USAID, *White Paper: U.S. Foreign Aid Meeting the Challenges of the Twenty-first Century* (2004), 3, 5.

7. USAID, *Fragile States Strategy* (2005), 2.

8. USAID, *At Freedom's Frontiers: A Democracy and Governance Strategic Framework* (December 2005), 6.

9. Following ambiguous results in Iraqi elections and particularly after elections in Palestine in 2006, which brought Hamas to power, some U.S. officials have been questioning emphasis on elections as a key element in post-conflict reconstruction, or at least insisting that proper preparations and timing are an essential element of success. Craig Cohen asks, "What conditions must be met before elections can effectively substitute for force in determining who governs?" in *Measuring Progress in Stabilization and Reconstruction* (Washington: USIP, 2006), 5.

10. *Democracy and Governance Strategic Framework*, 3, 13.

11. For reasonably stable developing countries, the United States will promote "far-reaching, fundamental changes in governance and institutions, human capacity, and economic structure" through access to the new Millennium Challenge Account. For strategic allies, the United States will provide assistance—more extensive or focused on key policy goals–from the Economic Support Fund account, which is managed by State.

12. USAID, *Policy Framework for Bilateral Foreign Aid: Implementing Transformational Diplomacy through Development* (2006), 1–2. Although the 2002 document cited these goals as key "issues" of development assistance, they were framed as "goals." The 2006 listing does include some functional goals, such as "provide humanitarian relief and address global issues and other special, self-standing concerns," along with promoting transformational development in reasonably stable developing countries and supporting strategic states.

13. See also Chapter 4.

14. A senior USAID official expressed the view that Tobias saw the Failed States Strategy as an independent effort to create a new policy of foreign assistance, thereby undermining the new union between USAID and State under the Secretary of State and himself. Interview with James R. Kunder, Acting Deputy Administrator, September 6, 2007.

15. The Failed States Strategy also talked about "fragile, failing, failed and recovering" states.

16. DCHA also includes the offices of American Schools and Hospitals Abroad and Private and Voluntary Cooperation.

17. Interview with Carlos Pascual, the first Coordinator, November 8, 2006.

18. Interviews with Robert W. Jenkins, Acting Director, DCHA/OTI, October 26, 2007, and Frederick B. Barton, first director of OTI, October 2, 2006.

19. OTI's Web site actually cites three types of transitions: democracy, peace, and what it calls "pivotal political events." http://www.usaid.gov/our_work/cross-cutting_programs/transition_initiatives/.

20. Interview with Michael E. Hess, May 11, 2007.

21. Barton interview.

22. "Criteria for Engagement," http://www.usaid.gov/our_work/cross-cutting_programs/transition_initiatives/aboutoti3.html.

23. In contrast with S/CRS, for which the Department of State did not set aside a discrete level of funding from its Diplomatic and Consular Program Funds, but simply asked Congress for money in a supplemental. Congress was not receptive, at least not until 2008.

24. "Notwithstanding" authority is reluctantly and rarely used, but provides the OTI director with leverage in securing funds when needed. OTI claims to have created an innovative contracting mechanism that preserves the principle of competition while allowing quick start-up in new countries and direct grants to small, indigenous organizations.

25. USAID Office of Transition Initiatives, *Advancing Peaceful, Democratic Change* (1999), 10.

26. OTI's purpose in Somalia was to promote the National Reconciliation Congress, in particular by strengthening the capacity of the National Governance and Reconciliation Committee to organize it. USAID/OTI Somalia Fact Sheet, July 2007, available at http://www.usaid.gov/our_work/cross-cutting_programs/transition_initaitves/country/somalia/fact0707.html. However, the Congress excluded those

Somali parties which opposed Ethiopian intervention, and little reconciliation was achieved. That unsatisfactory outcome presumably precipitated OTI's early departure from the project. In 2002 OTI began a program in Venezuela, after military restoration of Hugo Chavez to the presidency and launch of an internationally and regionally promoted "national reconciliation" process. The OTI program, operating out of the U.S. Embassy, was aimed not at conflict resolution, but rather "to provide critical and timely assistance to maintain democratic stability and strengthen the country's fragile democratic institutions."

27. S/Res. 940 (1994) authorized member states "to use all necessary means to facilitate the departure of Haiti's military leadership and restore Haiti's constitutionally elected government."

28. Social Impact, *USAID/OTI Afghanistan Final Evaluation*, August 15, 2005, 9, 14.34, 35, 49–50.

29. Social Impact, Inc., *Strategy and Impact of the Iraq Transition Initiative: OTI in Iraq (2003–2006), Final Evaluation Report* (September 30, 2006), 1. There is some confusion about the total amount since $417.6 million is used in another part of the report for 5,200 projects. Acting OTI Director Robert W. Jenkins used the figure $419 million in an October 27, 2006 interview to cover both project and administrative expenses.

30. USAID/OTI, Iraq Transition Initiative (2005), http://www.usaid.gov/our_-work/cross-cutting_programs/transition_initiatives/country/iraq/progdesc.html.

31. The breakdown of Americans included 6 "direct hire" USAID employees, 62 personal services contractors, and 8 persons from institutional contractors. Foreign partner staff for its projects numbered over 400.

32. Figures on personnel and funding courtesy of Frederick Barton, Codirector, Post-Conflict Reconstruction Project, Center for Strategic and International Studies.

33. Robert Rotberg, *The First Ten Years: An Assessment of the Office of Transition Initiatives* (Program on Intrastate Conflict and Conflict Resolution, Belfer Center for Science and International Affairs, John F. Kennedy School of Government, Harvard University) (2005), 7, 12–13. Rotberg described OTI's mandate as follows: "OTI's founding and continuing mandate was to steer fragile, war-torn, post-conflict countries along a democratic path; to help turn incipient into real democracies; to jump-start destroyed economies; to create or re-create viable political, social, and economic institutions; and—in a general sense and in several specific real senses —to make a substantial difference at the very inception of an emerging nation's life. *OTI was also charged with mitigating existing or renewed conflict and with promoting reconciliation—with helping to heal and permanently bandage a society's wounds.*" My italics.

34. In Serbia OTI saw an "opening" in the existence of a "well-organized and broad-based opposition," supported by a popular majority and seeking power in a constitutional and nonviolent manner. Sitting in the U.S. Embassy in Budapest, OTI networked via e-mail with Serbians resident in Belgrade and Novi Sad. OTI gave support to Otpor (resistance), an organization of youths who mobilized almost single-handedly the massive demonstrations in Belgrade in October 2000, which forced Slobodan Milosevic from office. The Otpor candidate Vojislav Kostunica won the elections and remained Serbia's president during most of the period until 2008.

35. Social Impact, *Afghanistan*, 34.

36. Ibid., 7–11.

37. Social Impact, Inc., *OTI in Iraq*, vi.

38. SIGIR, *Hard Lessons: The Iraq Reconstruction Experience* (February 2, 2009), 238. SIGIR laments that the decision of the USAID mission to phase out OTI led to a slow down in contracting for projects and diminished results (281–282).

39. Ibid., 281.

40. Interview with Robert W. Jenkins, October 27, 2006, 1. See also Jason Peckenpaugh, "On the Heels of Disaster," *Government Executive*, January 15, 2004, available at www.govexec.com/features/0104/0104s4.htm.

41. In a presentation to U.S. Government Counterinsurgency Conference, Washington D.C., September 28, 2006. Col. McMaster's reputation from his command in Tal Afar soared after he was profiled by George Packer in "The Lesson of Tal Afar," *The New Yorker*, April 10, 2006.

42. Sharon Morris, author of the CAF, reports that she strongly opposed including a checklist, which she believed would routinize country-level analysis of conflict and undermine critical thinking.

43. See especially Mats Berdal and David Malone, eds., *Greed and Grievance: Economic Agendas in Civil Wars* (2000).

44. USAID, *Conducting a Conflict Assessment: A Framework for Strategy and Program Development* (2005; hereafter cited as *CAF*), 16.

45. In London the Department for International Development (DFID)—through its Conflict and Humanitarian Affairs Department (now Conflict, Humanitarian and Security Department [CHASE])—produced "Conducting Conflict Assessments: Guidance Notes" in January 2002.

46. Ibrahim Elbadawi and Nicholas Sambanis, *How Much War Will We See? Estimating the Incidence of War in 161 Countries* (World Bank, 2000). See also Ted Robert Gurr, "Peoples Against States: Ethnopolitical Conflict and the Changing World," *International Studies Quarterly* 38 (1994), 347–377.

47. Finally, the CAF asks users to identify "windows" of vulnerability or opportunity, which might include plans for major economic reforms or elections, as well as natural disasters. This last section includes questions on historical capacity of central and local governments to respond to political crises, factors that seem better placed in the "institutional capacity" section. *CAF*, 40.

48. Interview with Alexa Courtney, USAID/DCHA/CMM, May 11, 2007, 1.

49. The TCAF was authored by James Derleth of CMM.

50. Interview with Michael E. Hess, May 11, 2007.

51. The ICAF was approved by the NSC's Reconstruction and Stabilization Policy Coordination Committee July 18, 2008.

52. USAID, *Youth & Conflict: A Toolkit for Intervention* (2005), Http:// www.usaid.gov/our_work/cross-cutting_programs/conflict/publications/docs/ CMM_Youth_and_Conflict_Toolkit_April_2005.pdf. The highly regarded toolkit on youth and conflict was originally drafted by Prof. Jack Goldstone, Director of the Center for Global Policy and senior professor of public policy at George Mason University. Goldstone was part of the brain trust on which CMM drew for its CAF. For the land toolkit, CMM asked David Bledsoe, senior attorney and specialist in land law at the Rural Development Institute, to do the initial drafting, http:// www.usaid.gov/our_work/cross-cutting_programs/conflict/publications/docs/ CMM_Land_and_Conflict_Toolkit_April_2005.pdf. The International Center for Forestry Research (CIFOR), headquartered in Indonesia, and Adelphi Research, an independent German development think tank, played major roles in the minerals and forests toolkits, http://www.usaid.gov/our_work/cross-cutting_programs/

conflict/publications/docs/CMM_Minerals_and_Conflict_Toolkit_April_2005.pdf
and http://www.usaid.gov/our_work/cross-cutting_programs/conflict/publications/
docs/CMM_Forests_and_Conflict_2005.pdf.

53. See Chapter 4.

54. The lists are developed under contract with the University of Maryland's Center
for International Development and Conflict Management and ARD, Inc. An approximation of the lists may be found in the Center's biennial publication, J. Joseph Hewitt,
Jonathan Wilkenfeld, and Ted Robert Gurr, *Peace and Conflict 2008* (2007).

55. Telephone conversation with Mark Hannafin, DCHA/CMM, January 21, 2009.

56. USAID/CMM, Prioritizing Prevention: Recommendations for Elevating USG
Engagement in At-Risk Countries (Draft Outline for Transition White Paper, n.d.).

57. The FY 2009 Omnibus Appropriations Act, enacted in March 2009, added an
additional $75 million for a coordinated civilian response capacity at State and
USAID, including $30 million for USAID.

58. The White House, *The National Security Strategy of the United States of America*,
March 2006, 1.

59. USAID Democracy & Governance Web site, http://www.usaid.gov/our_work/
democracy_and_governance/.

60. See, for example, Paul Gottfried, "The Invincible Wilsonian Matrix: Universal
Human Rights Once Again," *Orbis* 51:2 (2007), 239–250.

61. Interview with Michael Miklaucic, former senior program officer DCHA/DG,
July 31, 2007.

62. USAID, *At Freedom's Frontiers*, 6.

63. Miklaucic interview.

64. A Washington-based NGO, now known simply as IFES, which styles itself "the
world's premiere election assistance organization."

65. http://www.usaid.gov/our_work/humanitarian_assistance/disaster_assistance/.

66. In FY 2006, OFDA funding went 57 percent to NGOs, 18 percent to UN agencies, 13 percent to other U.S. government agencies, and 3 percent to other
international organizations. USAID, *Office of Foreign Disaster Assistance: Annual Report
for FY2006*, 1, http://www.usaid.gov/our_work/humanitarian_assistance/disaster
_assistance/publications/annual_reports/pdf/AR2006.pdf.

67. USAID, *Office of U.S. Foreign Disaster Assistance: Annual Report for Fiscal Year
2003*, 72.

68. Interview with Ky Luu, Director, USAID/DCHA/OFDA, August 7, 2007. Luu
was particularly indignant about an Oxfam press release (July 30, 2007), "8 Million
Iraqis in Need of Aid," asserting that the numbers were "pulled out of the air."

69. The Agricultural Trade Development and Assistance Act of 1954.

70. In 2007, 15.6 percent of Emergency Title II food aid went through NGOs, the
rest through WFP. American NGOs included Adventist Development and Relief
Agency, Catholic Relief Services, CARE, Food for the Hungry International, Save
the Children Foundation, supplemented by Norwegian Peoples Aid, Save the
Children-UK, and a handful of NGOs from the recipient countries. USAID, *U.S.
International Food Assistance Report 2007*, 22–25.

71. USAID, *Sudan—Complex Emergency*, Situation Report #5, Fiscal Year (FY)
2007, December 1, 2006.

72. USAID, *U.S. International Food Assistance Report 2006*, 9 and Appendix 5:
USAID Title II Emergency Activities, http://www.usaid.gov/our_work/humanitaria-
n_assistance/ffp/cr_food_aid.pdf.

73. The Bush administration proposed using limited amounts of Title II emergency funds to purchase local food supplies in areas of need, which in certain circumstances could give a stabilizing boost to rural income in conflict regions. The relevant appropriation subcommittees, dominated by farm state representatives, have been resistant, but the FY 2008 supplemental for the first time set aside $50 million for that purpose. The local food purchase issue is only a very small part of the broader issue of a conflict between U.S. farm interests and U.S. foreign policy interests, including the question of whether U.S. farm subsidies damage agricultural development in the Global South.

74. Kunder interview.

75. One assistant administrator suggested that the Bush administration tended to view policy problems as rooted in coordination and therefore as requiring a new "coordinator," for example, coordinators for PEPFAR (HIV/AIDS Relief), Cuba, and Reconstruction and Stabilization. He argued that excessive concern with coordination led to fragmentation—even "feudalism"—in assistance, with the result that the foreign affairs bureaucracy is "meetinged to death." The appointment of multiple coordinators also perhaps grated on "Republican" sensibilities favorable to simplicity, streamlining, and clear lines of bureaucratic authority.

76. Interview with Constance Newman, ex-Assistant Administrator for Africa, July 17, 2007.

77. Interview with Sharon Isralow, USAID/AFR/SD/CPG, June 26, 2007.

78. Division of Communications, Peacebuilding & Governance in the Office of Sustainable Development (AFR/SD/CPG).

79. Interview with Kent R. Hill, August 1, 2007. The projects were the Boston University-led Tolerance Project and Fostering Religious Harmony in Albania (2004–2006).

80. Governance & Economic Management Assistance Program, 2005–2009.

81. See S. 613, Reconstruction and Stabilization Civilian Management Act of 2007. The bill provides in Section 618, "If the President determines that it is important to the national interests of the United States for United States civilian agencies ... to assist in stabilizing and reconstructing a country or region that is at risk of, in, or is in transition from, conflict or civil strife, the President may ... furnish assistance to respond to the crisis."

82. See the policy paper by InterAction, the umbrella organization of U.S. humanitarian and development organizations, "Why the U.S. Needs a Cabinet-Level Department for Global and Human Development" (June 2008), available at http://interaction.org/files.cgi/6304_Cabinet-level_summary.pdf.

CHAPTER 7

1. "The Growth of a Unique Federal Agency: Reflections on the Past and Thoughts about the Future of the United States Institute of Peace," August 4, 2004.

2. The United States Institute of Peace Act (Title XVII of the Defense Authorization Act of 1985), Sec. 1702(a)(6).

3. As noted in Chapter 1, Benjamin Rush, a delegate to the 1787 Constitutional Convention, proposed a "peace-office" which he thought should have been included in the U.S. Constitution.

4. Rhoda Miller, *Institutionalizing Peace: The Concept of the USIP and Its Role in American Political Thought* (Jefferson, NC: McFarland, 1994), 51–57.

5. *To Establish the United States Academy of Peace: Report of the Commission on Proposals for the National Academy of Peace and Conflict Resolution to the President of the United States and the Senate and the House of Representatives of the United States Congress* (Washington: U.S. Government Printing Office, 1981), 169.

6. Initially the ACDA Director was a statutory member. With the abolition of ACDA, the USIP President became a nonvoting member of the board.

7. Interview with Chester A. Crocker, April 24, 2008.

8. That proved less of a weapon than it seemed at first blush. Congress established the Institute with "no-year" funding; funds appropriated for one fiscal year, if not used, carry over to the following year. USIP was eventually able to use all of the initial $10 million. For the historical background and debate over the creation of USIP, see Miller, *Institutionalizing Peace*, and Mary E. Montgomery, "Working for Peace While Preparing for War: The Creation of the United States Institute of Peace," *Journal of Peace Research* 40:4 (2003), 479–496.

9. Interview with Daniel Serwer, Vice President and Director of the Center for Post-Conflict Peace and Stability Operations, October 20, 2006.

10. In 2008, $333,000 was allocated to each country. Interview with Steven Heydeman, Vice President for Grants and Fellowships, March 31, 2008.

11. The compendia have been undertaken under the leadership of Chester A. Crocker, Chairman of the USIP Board 1992–2004 and senior professor at Georgetown University. Scholar and practitioner, Crocker, as Assistant Secretary of State for African Affairs, was a key actor in the diplomatic settlement of 1988 which brought Namibia to independence and secured the withdrawal of Cuban forces from Angola.

12. Interviews with Crocker and Paul Stares, April 8, 2008.

13. The centers of innovation also include the Virtual Diplomacy Initiative, which examines the role of information and communications technology in conflict management. Possible future additions may be Economies of Conflict and Media and Conflict. These are currently only tangentially engaged with the interagency process and are therefore not covered in this survey.

14. Each center expert draws up an annual plan for projects with suggested budget. The center vice president consolidates the proposals into a center plan. Center plans are in turn vetted and refined into a plan for the institute within the framework of the expected Congressional appropriations, plus grants and revenues from other sources.

15. Interview with Lawrence Woocher, Center for Conflict Analysis and Prevention, February 21, 2008.

16. In 2008 this Center had six program officers and three program assistants supporting them, plus a couple of research assistants drawn from local graduate students.

17. African specialist Dorina Bekoe seized a segment of the Sudan problem to launch a prevention study and exercise for the Eastern Sudan. See Bekoe, *The Eastern Sudan Peace Agreement: Taking Stock and Moving Forward*, USIPeace Briefing (October 2007). The North-South problem and Darfur are under the jurisdiction of the other two major centers.

18. Interview with Abiodun Williams, December 18, 2008.

19. The original hope was to model the initiative somewhat on the Balkans Initiative, which had led to extensive USIP projects in that part of the world. Stares interview.

20. The Syria Working Group included State participants. Heydeman interview. See Mona Yacoubian, *Promoting Middle East Democracy II: Arab Initiatives*, Special

Report (May 2005); Yacoubian, *Engaging Islamists and Promoting Democracy: A Preliminary Assessment*, Special Report (September 2007); Scott Lasensky and Mona Yacoubian, *Syria and Political Change*, USIPeace Briefing (December 2005, March 2006). After the terrorist bombings in Madrid and London in 2004 and 2005, the initiative cosponsored a series of workshops in Europe, based on the presumption that Europe had become an important battleground in the war on terrorism.

21. Williams interview.

22. The two institutes are, along with the Center for International Private Enterprise and the American Center for International Labor Solidarity, the four core units of the National Endowment for Democracy (NED). The NED was created by the Congress in 1983 and receives an annual appropriation to provide grants to pro-democracy groups around the world. It is governed by an independent, nonpartisan board of directors.

23. The G-8 consists of Canada, France, Germany, Italy, Japan, Russia, the United Kingdom, and the United States.

24. Center for Eurasian Strategic Studies (ASAM).

25. *The Marmara Declaration: Iraq and Its Neighbors Dialogue*, Istanbul, March 23, 2007. The name was taken from the hotel in Istanbul where the meeting took place. Names and positions of participants were not made public.

26. The project had five subgroups, focusing on early warning, precrisis engagement, preventive diplomacy, military options, and international institutions.

27. *Preventing Genocide: A Blueprint for the U.S. Government* (Washington: United States Holocaust Memorial Museum, The American Academy of Diplomacy, and the Endowment of the United States Institute of Peace, 2008).

28. Interview with David Smock, February 19, 2008.

29. The original rebels were the Sudan Liberation Movement/Sudan Liberation Army, modeled after John Garang's Sudan Peoples' Liberation Movement/Army. The Justice & Equality Movement (JEM) represented Darfur Africans linked with Islamist leader Hassan al-Turabi and purged from the government in 1999 at the time of his ouster from the ruling party. The Zaghawa-led military wing of the SLA split off from the Fur-led political wing in 2005, at the time of the signing of the abortive DPA. By 2007 as many as a dozen groups claimed the mantle of rebel leadership.

30. In "The Back Channel," *The New Yorker* (March 2, 2009), Steve Coll reported on two years of back-channel negotiations to demilitarize Kashmir as an autonomous region covering both sides of the disputed border. He concluded that the talks stalled in 2007 and were abandoned with the fall of Pakistani President Parvez Musharraf. The work of USIP and its partners was linked loosely to this negotiation.

31. Smock interview.

32. The ongoing work is referred to as the Alexandria Process. The Declaration is found at "The Alexandria Process: Israeli and Palestinian Religious Leaders in Support of the Middle East Peace Process" at http://www.usip.org/programs/projects/alexandria-process.

33. See Chapter 6.

34. "USAID Conflict Management," available at http://www.usaid.gov/our_work/cross-cutting_programs/conflict/focus_areas/peace_building.html; http://www.usaid.gov/locations/sub-saharan_africa/countries/nigeria/index.html.

35. Over a career of more than 40 years in development, religion, and conflict resolution, Smock has authored or coauthored more than 20 books.

36. The PFP was brought under the CMCR in 2006, when the center was established, but operated in a generally autonomous manner until the project was terminated.

37. Thirty million dollars was appropriated from the 2003 Iraq supplemental, including $3 million for USIP expenses and $27 million for USAID projects in Mindanao, if an agreement were achieved and implemented. G. Eugene Martin and Astrid S. Tuminez, *Toward Peace in the Southern Philippines: A Summary and Assessment of the USIP Philippine Facilitation Project*, 2003–2007 (Washington: USIP, 2008), 4.

38. Board chair Chester Crocker, retired Gen. Anthony Zinni (Special Envoy to the Middle East 2002–2003), and other former ambassadors to Manila, including Stephen Bosworth, Nicholas Platt, Frank Wisner, and Richard Murphy.

39. Interview with Michael J. Green, August 30, 2007.

40. Martin and Tuminez, *Toward Peace*, 15.

41. Project director Martin suggests that a special envoy might usefully have been appointed to supplant the PFP at that point, but there was no interest in such an approach either in Manila or in Washington. The use of a special envoy would have marked a shift from unofficial to official "facilitation" of the peace process.

42. USIP President Solomon praised Martin's "fabulous job of innovating." Interview April 5, 2008.

43. Ibid., 14.

44. Ancestral domain was apparently the third part of a settlement package, reached after accord had already been achieved on security and economic development. USIP, "Philippines Agreement in Question," September 18, 2008, available at http://www.usip.org/on_the_issues/philippines.html.

45. Clashes between Philippine military forces and the MILF were reported beginning December 2008, along with rumors that talks would be renewed. See, for example, Carlos H. Conde, "10 Killed as Separatists Fight Troops in Southern Philippines," *New York Times*, December 9, 2008.

46. The project report also suggests that the United States could "spearhead" an international coalition of "Friends of Mindanao" to focus on a political solution to the conflict. Martin and Tuminez, *Toward Peace*, 16.

47. Interview with Beth Ellen Cole, Senior Program Officer, Center for Post-Conflict Peace and Security Operations, February 19, 2008.

48. Daniel Serwer, the main proponent of an active USIP role in the Balkans, reports he initially held back from involvement in Afghanistan, doubting that a successful program could be put together "with illiterate warlords."

49. Minister-Counselor is a Senior Foreign Service rank equivalent to that of two stars in the military. Those with that rank are involuntarily retired when their "time-in-class" in that and the previous rank total 12 years.

50. Serwer interview. The USIP charter provides under Sec. 1705 (e) "The Institute may respond to the request of a department or agency of the United States Government to investigate, examine, study, and report on any issue within the Institute's competence" and Sec. 1705 (h)(1) "the Institute may obtain grants and contracts, including contracts for classified research for the Department of State, the Department of Defense . . . and the intelligence community."

51. Robert Perito, Michael Dziedzic, and Beth DeGrasse, *Building Civilian Capacity for U.S. Stability Operations: The Rule of Law Component* (USIP Special Report No. 118, April 2004). See Chapter 2 on the origins of S/CRS.

52. Pascual interview.

53. Cole interview. See Chapter 2 on NSPD 44.

54. The $2.9 million includes the $1.2 million mentioned above under grants to USIP from the State Department.

55. "Many international NGOs ... claim that the U.S.-led coalition OEF, in particular, has deliberately blurred the distinction between military and humanitarian groups. The U.S. military has openly said it can 'use' humanitarian actors as 'force extenders' for its own ends, and spokespersons for the Coalition have said repeatedly that the military and NGOs 'share the same goals.' " Lara Olsen, "Fighting for Humanitarian Space: NGOs in Afghanistan," *Journal of Military and Strategic Studies* 9 (Fall 2006), 13, http://www.jmss.org/2006/2006fall/articles/olson_ngo-afghanistan.pdf.

56. See Chapter 5.

57. Dafna Linzer, "Think Tank Is Moving Up in the World: With Work on Iraq, USIP Has New Stature, Building," *Washington Post*, January 27, 2005. USIP Senior Program Officer Robert Perito warned the Pentagon's Defense Policy Board in February 2003 that there would be looting and civil disorder after the U.S. military captured Baghdad. Michael Gordon and Gen. Bernard E. Trainor, *Cobra II: The Inside Story of the Invasion and Occupation of Iraq* (New York: Pantheon, 2006), 158.

58. Sen. John Warner (R-VA), Chairman of the Senate Armed Services Committee, was widely reported to be a "silent partner" in the Wolf initiative. Robert Dreyfuss, "A Higher Power: James Baker Puts George Bush's Iraq Policy into Rehab," *Washington Monthly* (September 2006).

59. The Center for Strategic and International Studies, the Center for the Study of the Presidency, and the Baker Institute for Public Policy at Rice University provided logistic support.

60. *The Washington Post* reported April 6, 2008 that Hamilton wished to repeat the exercise in 2008, but that the White House discouraged Baker from participation. Instead, the experts who advised the Study Group were reassembled by USIP. Their report conceded absence of consensus, but laid out four options, including two variants within the existing policy: (1) Instead of trying to resolve basic issues relating to the Iraqi state, focus on capacity building at provincial and local levels, cultivating new local leaders, as a basis for future national political reconciliation (bottom-up approach); (2) Bring together all factions into a wide-ranging negotiation about the nature of the Iraqi state, centering around revision of the constitution (grand bargain); (3) Condition future U.S. support for the Iraqi government on achieving a few minimal political goals, leading to a decentralized system and weak central government with a sharply reduced U.S. presence (reduced conditional commitment); (4) redeploy all U.S. forces from Iraq but strengthen the U.S. security presence in the region, invigorate regional diplomacy, and continue political support to the Government of Iraq (unconditional, near-total reduction of U.S. military commitment).

61. Interview, May 5, 2008.

62. As of 2008 the permanent name of the training facility had not yet been determined. "The Academy of Conflict Management" is favored by influential board members, but some view that term as "grandiose" and too "academic." Solomon has said he does not envisage a multiyear academic program, particularly not one on the model of the military service academies.

63. Interview February 26, 2008.

64. Political Research Associates, Rightweb, September 1990, http://rightweb.irc-online.org/gw/2814.html.

65. Michael Barker, "A Force More Powerful: Promoting 'Democracy' through Civil Disobedience," *State of Nature* (Winter 2007).

66. "Birds of a Feather Flock Together," Commentary by Howard Phillips, The Constitutional Government Blog, A Project of the Constitutional Caucus, June 28, 2007.

67. During his brief tenure Pipes scathingly—and publicly—criticized USIP for hosting a conference with the Center for the Study of Islam and Democracy, which he termed an employer of Muslim "radicals." Daniel Pipes, "The U.S. Institute of Peace Stumbles," *New York Sun*, March 23, 2004.

CHAPTER 8

1. *Congressional Budget Justification: Foreign Operations, FY 2009*, xxiii.

2. The chapter covers the budget process and Congressional action basically through the end of 2008.

3. For FY 2008 a 21st function, Overseas Deployments and Other Activities, was added in response to the GWOT. That function did not appear in the FY 2009 budget request, however.

4. Most of the Defense spending on Afghanistan and Iraq has come from supplemental appropriations; thus previous proposed Defense budgets have significantly understated the impact on the federal budget.

5. In the State Department the key action office was the Bureau of Resource Management (RM), which provided guidance to the other bureaus about assembling and defending their administrative and program budgets. The geographic bureaus would divide up the ESF and negotiate with PM to come up with a budget for FMF and IMET. INL would collaborate with most of the same bureaus to create a budget for civilian police programs. RM would then finalize a consolidated State Department budget for the approval of the Secretary of State. In USAID the Bureau of Policy and Program Coordination (PPC) managed the budget process through a series of formal bureau reviews to determine the request level for the major categories—development assistance, childhood survival and health programs, international disaster and famine assistance, and USAID operational expenses. The USAID administrator was heavily engaged in the final stages of the USAID budget, which also required formal approval of the Secretary of State before forwarding to the White House.

6. Even as the Congress is reviewing the budget request for the next fiscal year, the executive branch is putting together the budget request for the year after that and overseeing implementation of appropriations for the current fiscal year.

7. During the first iteration of the F budget process for FY 2008, the missions played a limited role. The second iteration for FY 2009 was much more inclusive of the field.

8. The bureau budget was set forth at two levels: "constrained" (usually based on the level of the previous year) and "unconstrained" (including desired increases to cover special initiatives or to enhance existing programs). F guidance provided that "unconstrained" levels should be realistic and not "blue-sky" aspirations. In the past the geographic bureaus of State and USAID did not match. USAID had one bureau for Asia, while State had three: Near East/North Africa, South Asia, and East Asia and the Pacific. In 2007, USAID subdivided its Asia operation into a Middle East and an Asia Bureau. Although the alignment is still imperfect, recent changes have facilitated the amalgamation of the foreign assistance budget.

9. The functional bureaus, such as PM or INL, also come up with their proposed budgets at this time; they are not based on an MSP but usually reflect consultations with those overseas missions where their major activities are located.

10. There have been six senior reviews, covering the six geographic bureaus. The functional bureaus have had their Senior Reviews with the Deputy Secretary (i.e., one level above F). Interview with Dan Corle, F Peace & Security Sector Group, April 2, 2008.

11. During a presidential election year, the process changes considerably, particularly in the case of a "lame-duck" president. For the FY 2010 budget, OMB prepared a "budget database" with a "current services baseline." It also developed estimates of the costs of current services for the next fiscal year. The agencies provided OMB with information for the database and current services baseline but did not submit a formal budget request to OMB. Instead they prepared informal budget requests with background data to provide to the presidential Transition Team after the election. Jim Nussle, Director, Office of Management and Budget, Requirements for the FY 2010 Budget Process; Memorandum for the Heads of Departments and Agencies, April 7, 2008.

12. Barton Gelman reports that in the Bush White House, such appeals never reached the President. *Angler*, 259–261.

13. Budget calendar for agencies, interview with John Moore, ex-OMB official, November 20, 2005.

14. See Stimson Foundation, "US 'Cap' on UN Peacekeeping Funding" (2007), available at http://www.stimson.org/fopo/?SN=FP200607251040.

15. In the early 1990s the average duration was two to three years, by the late 1990s five to six years. James Dobbins, "Nation-Building after Iraq," presentation at the Center for Strategic and International Studies, June 4, 2008.

16. Executive Office of the President, *Summary and Highlights, International Affairs Function 150 Fiscal Year 2009 Budget Request*, 45.

17. The force was created following the 1979 signature of the Egypt-Israel Peace Treaty but because of the threat of a Soviet veto was created outside the framework of the United Nations. PKO includes funding for two counterterrorism initiatives— the Trans-Sahel Counter-Terrorism Initiative and the East African Regional Security Initiative—which this study has not included within the ambit of peace-building activities.

18. Interview with Richard H. Solomon, President of USIP, May 5, 2008.

19. Rebuilding countries for purposes of the FY 2009 budget were Côte d'Ivoire, Democratic Republic of the Congo, Liberia, Sierra Leone, Somalia, Sudan, Kosovo, Iraq, Lebanon, Afghanistan, Nepal, Colombia, and Haiti. The list of "restrictive" countries is classified.

20. Enacted 1989 and 1991, respectively. The two accounts are now called Assistance for Eastern Europe and the Baltic States and Assistance for the Independent States.

21. Interview with John Underriner, Deputy Director, EUR/Regional Political-Military Affairs, July 17, 2008.

22. If the large Afghanistan program ($250 million proposed), heavily focused on poppy eradication and the expansion and training of the Counternarcotics Police, is included, the percentage rises to 64 percent.

23. As of 2008, only Haiti was in the "rebuilding" category. Sri Lanka, Timor-Leste, and Philippines were considered "transforming," and Chad, Guinea-Bissau, and Uganda were considered "developing."

24. USAID, Office of Foreign Disaster Assistance, Annual Reports for 2006 and 2007.

25. U.S. contributions (through Title II) for the WFP are listed by that organization as $1,123.1 million in FY 2006 and $1.183.1 million in FY 2007.

26. The funding process for HRDF and NED is confusing because of the difference between how the money has been requested and how it has been appropriated. Through the FY 2009 budget request, HRDF funding has been proposed under ESF, while NED money has been requested from State Department Diplomatic and Consular Program funding. Under that approach, HRDF but not NED has been subject to the F process, since the latter has not been considered part of "foreign operations." However, beginning in FY 2006, Congress appropriated funds for both HRDF and NED under a separate "Democracy Fund" account.

27. Because of the sensitivity created for some recipients, for example, in Venezuela or Iran, a comprehensive list has not recently been made public. For an analysis of the current approach to funding, see Freedom House, *A Legacy of Support for Freedom: An Analysis of the Bush Administration's 2009 Budget Request for Democracy and Human Rights* (June 2008), 4, 9.

28. Bureau of Democracy, Human Rights, and Labor, *Fact Sheet: FY 2005–2006 Human Rights and Democracy Fund Projects*, December 6, 2005; *Summary and Highlights, International Affairs Function 150 Fiscal Year 2008 Budget Request*, 1, 10, available at http://www.usaid.gov/policy/budget/cbj2008/fy2008cbj_highlights.pdf.

29. White House, *National Strategy for Victory in Iraq* (November 2005), 18, available at http://www.whitehouse.gov/infocus/iraq/iraq_national_strategy_2005 1130.pdf.

30. The FY 2007 supplemental required a report to Congress on the use of the funds. See, for example, MNSTC-I, *Section 3303 Report to Congress*, January 7, 2008.

31. Coalition Provisional Authority, Memo of June 16, 2003, cited in Mark S. Martins, "The Commander's Emergency Response Program," *Joint Forces Quarterly*, no. 37 (2005), 47.

32. President's Request for Fiscal Year 2006 Supplemental Appropriations, February 16, 2006, 82.

33. Special Inspector-General for Iraq Reconstruction, Memorandum to the Deputy Secretary of Defense, Management of Commanders' [*sic*] Emergency Response Program for Fiscal Year 2004 (Report No. SIGIR 05-014, October 13, 2005), 2.

34. DOD Financial Management Regulation, Vol. 12, Ch. 27, 3–4.

35. The actual amounts for CERP are not found in the language of the supplemental, where the figure is buried in O&M—Army, but only in the General Provisions at the end of the supplemental bill.

36. FY 2009 National Defense Authorization Act (H.R. 5658), Sec. 1214 limited authorization to $1.7 billion in FY 2008 and $1.5 billion in FY 2009.

37. Cindy Williams and Gordon Adams, *Strengthening Statecraft and Security: Reforming U.S. Planning and Resource Allocation* (Cambridge: MIT Security Studies, Occasional Paper, June 2008), 68.

38. Open source information on the Iraq Freedom Fund is difficult to find. The fund appears to have been available for military operations broadly and flexibly construed. A letter from President Bush dated May 12, 2004 requesting $25 billion for the Fund says they would be "available to the Department of Defense and classified programs to support operations in Iraq and Afghanistan and would only be available

if the President makes an emergency determination that additional resources are needed for essential war costs. Funds would be available for all service operation and maintenance accounts as well as emerging needs." See www.whitehouse.gov/omb/budget/amendments/amendment_5_12_04.pdf.

39. Projects have been vetted by a working level committee involving the OSD, the Joint Chiefs of Staff, and State's Political-Military Bureau.

40. In FY 2007 a separate line item was eliminated in the appropriating and funds were taken generally from O&M—Defense-wide. In FY 2008, $1.1 billion was appropriated. The request for FY 2009 sought authority for $750 million but budgeted only $500 million.

41. Congressional Research Service, *Section 1206 of the National Defense Authorization Act for FY2006: A Fact Sheet on Department of Defense Authority to Train and Equip Foreign Military Forces* (updated May 15, 2008), Table 1.

42. DOD FY 2009 Budget Request Summary Justification, 105.

43. DOD, *Fiscal Year (FY) 2007 Budget Estimates, Overseas Humanitarian, Disaster, and Civic Aid (OHDACA)*, 3.

44. For FY 2008 DOD requested an additional $40 million to build "partnership capacity" in dealing with disasters. That amount was appropriated but is not considered part of funding for stability operations.

45. Government Accountability Office, *Stabilizing and Rebuilding Iraq Coalition Support and International Donor Commitments*, March 9, 2007, 3–4. Funds for Poland were also for the countries under its command, including Armenia, Slovakia, Denmark, El Salvador, Ukraine, Romania, Lithuania, Latvia, Mongolia, Kazakhstan, and Bosnia-Herzegovina. "Lift and Sustain" is distinguished from "global lift and sustain" by the former's use in connection with Iraq and Afghanistan. The latter is used in connection with support of allies in the GWOT and is not included in the calculation of Function 050 peacebuilding.

46. Congressional Research Service, *CRS Report for Congress; The Congressional Appropriations Process: An Introduction* (Order Code 97-684, updated February 22, 2007), 24.

47. It was called the House Committee on International Relations 1995–2007.

48. The SFRC and CFA have a staff of regional and functional experts, but at the subcommittee level, only the chairman and ranking minority have staff aides.

49. In the case of the USIP, the SFRC and CFA claim oversight, but the Senate Health, Education, Labor and Pensions Committee and the House Education and Labor Committee are the authorizers. No USIP formal testimony has been required in recent years.

50. "Secretary Rice's Testimony before House Armed Services Committee" (joint testimony with Defense Secretary Gates), April 15, 2008, http://www.america.gov/st/texttrans-english/2008/April/20080415171000eaifas0.7060358.html.

51. Before 2006 the House Appropriations Committee dealt with appropriations for the State Department operations and UN peacekeeping under the Commerce, Justice, State and Related Agencies Subcommittee. In 2006 these accounts were brought under the slightly realigned Science, State, Justice Commerce Subcommittee. The House subsequently realigned its subcommittees to consolidate State operations and UN peacekeeping under the Subcommittee for State, Foreign Operations and Related Programs, the same name as the counterpart subcommittee in the Senate. For international agriculture programs it is the Agriculture, Rural Development, Food and Drug Administration, and Related Agencies Subcommittee in both Houses.

52. In 1995 there was an impasse over appropriations between the Republican majority in Congress and the Clinton White House, and for an interval no CRs were passed. Some parts of the government shut down, except for essential operations. The shutdown proved unpopular politically and was widely credited for helping Clinton win reelection the following year.

53. Under the Budget Enforcement Act (BEA) of 1990, which expired in 2002, "emergency" supplementals could trigger lifting discretionary spending caps for both the budget authority and outlays without offsetting rescissions. Supplemental spending became identified with "emergency spending." OMB Watch, a private OMB watchdog sited in Washington D.C., charges that since 2002 "supplemental spending . . . has, in effect become a way for the federal government to evade annual budget limits and fiscal responsibility controls while increasing spending." OMB Watch, *Background Brief: Supplemental Appropriations* (March 2007), 2, www.ombwatch.org/budget/supplementalbackgrounder.pdf.

54. Ibid., 5.

55. See Chapter 4.

56. The House passed a bill authorizing an Active Response Corps (H.R. 2601—July 20, 2005) without funding and without authorizing S/CRS.

57. H.R. 109-486, the report accompanying the foreign operations appropriation bill for 2007. The Congressional Research Service commented that "Congress has long resisted the provision of 'blank check' pots of money as an abdication of constitutional appropriation and oversight powers," although it has done so in the case of the ERMA. Congressional Research Service, *Peacekeeping and Conflict Transitions: Background and Congressional Action on Civilian Capabilities* (Updated September 18, 2006), 19.

58. Sec. 1605, the Duncan Hunter National Defense Authorization Act (S. 3001), which became PL 110-417 October 14, 2008.

59. One staffer expressed annoyance at being bombarded with too much USIP material. Another suggested that USIP's recent prominence stemmed from its moving into the gap on Iraq left by a "dysfunctional" administration.

60. H.R. 2642 Supplemental Appropriations Act 2008 ("the War Supplemental").

61. Strong media attention to the "global food crisis" stemming from increased food commodity prices induced the subcommittee to set aside $50 million in the second 2008 supplemental for local food purchases in areas targeted for emergency feeding, the first time the Congress has responded to an administration request for local purchase authority.

62. See Congressional Research Service, *Military Operations: Precedents for Funding Contingency Operations in Regular or Supplemental Appropriation Bills* (June 13, 2006). In each case the funding in the latter stages was shifted to the regular budget.

63. Defense authorizers have been less troubled by ISFF. That may be in part because ISFF has been limited to supplemental appropriations, has therefore not been subject to the normal authorization process, and therefore has received less scrutiny.

64. Senator Ted Stevens, ranking member of the Senate Appropriations Subcommittee, reportedly indicated dissatisfaction with Secretary Gates about the types of projects undertaken and the quality of DOD reporting, while Senator Levin, Chairman of the Senate Armed Services Committee, indicated reservations about the breadth of the Iraq program.

65. Although the provision was not enacted, the House version of the Defense Authorization Bill for 2009 established a matching requirement: American CERP for Iraq should not exceed twice the amount of Iraq-CERP. H.R. 5658, Sec. 1214(b).

66. Letter from Deputy Assistant Secretary of Defense Jeffrey M. Nadaner to the staff of the House Committee on Armed Services, April 24, 2008.

67. That discussion can be considered related to a broader debate over the balance in U.S. foreign assistance between DOD on the one hand and State and USAID on the other. A widely publicized report by Refugees International asserts that "Between 1998 and 2005, the percentage of Official Development Assistance the Pentagon controlled exploded from 3.5% to nearly 22%, while the percentage controlled by the U.S. Agency for International Development (USAID) shrunk from 65% to 40%." *U.S. Civil-Military Imbalance for Global Engagement: Lessons from the Operational Level in Africa* (July 2008), Executive Summary.

68. There appears to be more support for DOD screening of Sec. 1207 projects among the appropriators in both chambers.

69. In FY 2007 no amount was included in the budget. In the FY 2008 Defense Authorization Act, the account was capped at $400 million.

70. The comprehensive list of ESF countries in FY 2008 also included Benin, Djibouti, Ethiopia, Guinea, Kenya, Madagascar, Malawi, Mali, Mauritania, Mozambique, Namibia, Niger, Nigeria, Senegal, Zambia, Zimbabwe, Burma, Cambodia, Laos, North Korea, Vietnam, Iran, Morocco, Yemen, Pakistan, Bolivia, Cuba, Guatemala, Peru, and Venezuela.

71. In September 2009 the Defense Department reissued and revised Directive 3000.05 terming stability operations "a core U.S. military mission that the Department of Defense shall be prepared to conduct with proficiency equivalent to combat operations." Stability Operations, Department of Defense Instruction Number 3000.05, September 16, 2009, available at www.dtic.mil/whs/directives/corres/pdf/300005p.pdf.

72. Williams and Adams, *Strengthening Statecraft*, 71.

CHAPTER 9

1. Deputy National Security Advisor, interview, December 13, 2007.

2. Clark Murdock and Michele Flournoy, lead investigators, *Beyond Goldwater-Nichols: U.S. Government and Defense Reform for a New Strategic Era*, Phase 2 Report, Center for Strategic and International Studies, July 2005, and Flournoy and Shawn W. Brimley, "Strategic Planning for National Security: A New Project Solarium," *Joint Forces Quarterly*, no. 41 (2nd Quarter 2006), 80–86, available at http://www.dtic.mil/doctrine/jel/jfq_pubs/4119.pdf. Secretary of State Clinton ordered in 2009 a "Quadrennial Diplomacy and Development Review" modeled on DOD's Quadrennial Defense Review. While potentially valuable in its own right, a review limited to State and USAID would not have the "whole-of-government" scope of a QNSR.

3. That progress is ignored in the otherwise informative report by the Congressional Research Service, *Organizing the U.S. Government for National Security: Overview of the Interagency Reform Debates* (April 18, 2008), 34, in the statement, "The categories of the President's annual budget request to Congress are based on agencies, such as the Departments of State and Defense . . . [not] functional areas, such as 'national security' or 'foreign assistance.' "

4. Interview with Andrew S. Natsios, former Administrator of USAID and former Special Envoy for Sudan, April 28, 2008.

5. It should also be taken into account in selection of ambassadors to conflict zones. However, since the selection of an ambassador involves at the outset a choice between a political and a career appointee, that position is not included in the recommendation.

AFTERWORD

1. Scott Stossel, *Sarge: The Life and Times of Sargent Shriver* (Washington: Smithsonian Books, 2004), 169–171. The original idea of a program of government-sponsored voluntary service abroad came from then Sen. Hubert Humphrey and Congressman Henry Reuss of Wisconsin, who had proposed legislation to explore the feasibility of a program under which "young *men* [would] assist the peoples of the underdeveloped areas of the world to combat poverty, disease, illiteracy, and hunger."

2. Shriver was particularly influenced by a report entitled "The Towering Task," by two rising stars in the ICA, Warren Wiggins and Bill Josephson. Ibid., 200–203.

3. Ibid., 225. Moyers had been Johnson's chief aide in the Senate.

4. Title 22 United States Code, Sec. 2501(a).

5. The same impulse was a major part of the rationale for creating USAID out of the International Cooperation Agency.

6. Lex Rieffel, *Reconsidering the Peace Corps* (Washington: Brookings Policy Brief 127, 2003), 2.

7. Figures as of 2008, available from http://www.peacecorps.gov/index.cfm?shell=learn.

8. Rieffel, *Reconsidering*, 4.

9. There is a biennial survey of volunteers but it is not linked to feedback from the host country.

10. In 2008, 59 percent of PCVs were female.

11. See the critique of Robert L. Strauss, "Think Again: The Peace Corps," *Foreign Policy*, April 2008. Detailed recommendations related to these weaknesses are included in Chuck Ludlam and Paula Hirschoff, Testimony Regarding the Peace Corps Volunteer Empowerment Act (S. 732), March 1, 2007, before the Subcommittee on the Western Hemisphere, Peace Corps, and Narcotics Affairs of the Senate Foreign Relations Committee, available at http://foreign.senate.gov/testimony/2007/Hirschoff-Testimony070725.pdf; and a recommendation for "a well-funded strategic planning in unit" in Dane F. Smith, "A Peace Corps Charter for the 21st Century," June 25, 2002, before the same subcommittee.

12. Rieffel, *Reconsidering*, 4.

13. A serious effort to expand the Peace Corps should be integrally related to strengthening training for volunteers, site selection for Peace Corps assignments, and project programming, as recommended in "Draft Memorandum to the Director-Designate: Plan to Strengthen and Expand the Peace Corps: Priorities for President Obama's First Term," Chuck Ludlam/Paula Hirschoff, April 2009.

14. Interview with Mary Angelini, Director of Peace Corps Response, August 19, 2008.

15. For a discussion of general Congressional concern about PCV security, see Curt Tarnoff, *The Peace Corps: Current Issues* (CRS Report for Congress RS21168, updated October 19, 2005), 4–5.

16. Rieffel endorses this idea. "The Peace Corps is uniquely positioned to deliver this message [of peace]. A fresh vision could both invigorate the Peace Corps and enhance our national security."

17. Peace Corps Volunteer Empowerment Act (S. 732), introduced March 1, 2007, especially Sec. 104. Peace Corps Director Ronald Tschetter launched in 2007 a 50+ program to appeal to baby boomers to join the Peace Corps in larger numbers.

18. I am indebted to Paula Hirschoff and Chuck Ludlam for this recommendation.

19. The Dodd bill calls for a budget increase from $336 million in FY 2008 to $618 million in FY 2011 (84%). Despite presidential calls for doubling the number of volunteers, the Peace Corps budget has inched up slowly during the Clinton and Bush administrations. In real terms it has risen only 10.9 percent in 15 years, or an average of less than 1 percent per year.

The budget for the Peace Corps fell outside the F process, described in Chapter 8. The Peace Corps comes up for Congressional reauthorization every four years. It is under the oversight of the Subcommittee on the Western Hemisphere, Peace Corps, and Narcotics Affairs of the Senate Foreign Relations Committee. Its appropriation is handled by the Subcommittee on State, Foreign Operations and Related Programs in both chambers of Congress.

Bibliography

BOOKS

Bacani, Benedicto R., *The Mindanao Peace Talks: Another Opportunity to Resolve the Moro Conflict in the Philippines* (Washington: USIP Special Report No. 131, 2005).

Bartlett, Ruhl, *Policy and Power: Two Centuries of American Foreign Relations* (New York: Hill and Wang, 1963).

Bekoe, Dorina A., *The Eastern Sudan Peace Agreement: Taking Stock and Moving Forward* (Washington: USIPeace Briefing, October 2007).

Bemis, Samuel F., *A Diplomatic History of the United States* (New York: Holt, Rinehart and Winston, 1965).

Bremer, L. Paul, *My Year in Baghdad: The Struggle to Build a Future of Hope* (New York: Threshold Editions, 2006).

Bush, George H. W. and Brent Scowcroft, *A World Transformed* (New York: Alfred A. Knopf, 1998).

Chollet, Derek and James Goldgeier, *America between the Wars: From 11/9 to 9/11* (New York: Public Affairs Press, 2008).

Claude, Inis, *From Swords into Plowshares: The Problems and Progress of International Organization* (New York: Random House, 1964).

Cohen, Craig, *Measuring Progress in Stabilization and Reconstruction* (Washington: USIP, March 2006).

Cohen, Herman J., *Intervening in Africa: Superpower Peacemaking in a Troubled Continent* (London: Macmillan, 2000).

Collier, Paul, et al., *Breaking the Conflict Trap: Civil War and Development Policy* (Washington: World Bank Policy Research Report, 2003).

Cordesman, Anthony H., *Losing the Afghan-Pakistan War? The Rising Threat* (Washington: CSIS, updated October 21, 2008).

Crocker, Chester A., Fen Osler Hampson, and Pamela Aall, *Leashing the Dogs of War: Conflict Management in a Divided World* (Washington: USIP, 2007).

———, *Taming Intractable Conflicts* (Washington: USIP, 2007).

Daalder, Ivo H., *Getting to Dayton: The Making of America's Bosnia Policy* (Washington: Brookings, 2000).

Daalder, Ivo H. and I. M. Destler, *A New NSC for a New Administration* (Washington: Brookings, 2000).

DeConde, Alexander, *A History of American Foreign Policy* (New York: Charles Scribner's Sons, 1963).

Dobbins, James, et al., *After the War: Nation-Building from FDR to George W. Bush* (Santa Monica: Rand, 2008).

———, *America's Role in Nation-Building: From Germany to Iraq* (Santa Monica: Rand, 2003).

Dower, John W., *Embracing Defeat: Japan in the Wake of World War II* (New York: Norton, 1999).

Doyle, Michael W. and Nicholas Sambanis, *Making War and Building Peace: United Nations Peace Operations* (Princeton: Princeton University Press, 2006).

Durch, William J., ed., *Twenty-First-Century Peace Operations* (Washington: USIP & Stimson Center, 2006).

Dziedzic, Michael J. and Colonel Michael K. Seidl, *Provincial Reconstruction Teams: Military Relations with International and Nongovernmental Organizations in Afghanistan* (Washington: USIP Special Report #147, August 2005).

Esterline, John H. and Robert B. Black, *Inside Foreign Policy: The Department of State System and Its Subsystems* (Palo Alto, CA: Mayfield, 1975).

Freedom House, *A Legacy of Support for Freedom: An Analysis of the Bush Administration's 2009 Budget Request for Democracy and Human Rights* (June 2008).

Freeman, Chas. W., Jr., *Arts of Power: Statecraft and Diplomacy* (Washington: USIP, 1997).

Galbraith, Peter W., *The End of Iraq: How American Incompetence Created a War without End* (New York: Simon & Schuster, 2006).

Gausker, Marcus, *Provincial Reconstruction Teams in Afghanistan* (Garmisch-Partenkirchen: George C. Marshall European Center for Security Studies, Occasional Paper 16, January 2008).

Greenfield, Richard, *Ethiopia: A New Political History* (New York: Praeger, 1965).

Gribbin, Robert E., *In the Aftermath of Genocide: The US Role in Rwanda* (Lincoln, NE: iUniverse, 2005).

Hewitt, J. Joseph, Jonathan Wilkenfeld, and Ted Robert Gurr, *Peace and Conflict 2008* (College Park: University of Maryland Center for International Development and Conflict Management, 2007).

Hoopes, Townsend and Douglas Brinkley, *FDR and the Creation of the U.N.* (New Haven: Yale University Press, 1997).

Inderfurth, Karl F. and Loch K. Johnson, eds., *Fateful Decisions: Inside the National Security Council* (New York: Oxford University Press, 2004).

InterAction, *Why the U.S. Needs a Cabinet-Level Department for Global and Human Development* (Washington: InterAction, 2008).

Kessler, Glenn, *The Confidante: Condoleezza Rice and the Creation of the Bush Legacy* (New York: St. Martin's Press, 2007).

Knock, Thomas J., *To End All Wars: Woodrow Wilson and the Quest for New World Order* (New York: Oxford University Press, 1992).

Kopp, Harry W. and Charles A. Gillespie, *Career Diplomacy: Life and Work in the U.S. Foreign Service* (Washington: Georgetown University Press, 2008).

Kupchan, Charles A., *The End of the American Era: U.S. Foreign Policy and the Geopolitics of the Twenty-First Century* (New York: Vintage Books, 2002).

Lafeber, Walter, *The American Age: United States Foreign Policy at Home and Abroad* (New York: Norton, 1994).

Lasensky, Scott and Mona Yacoubian, *Syria and Political Change* (Washington: USIPeace Briefing, December 2005).

Mabry, Marcus, *Twice as Good: Condoleezza Rice and Her Path to Power* (New York: Modern Times, 2007).

Madsen, Dorothy L., *American Exceptionalism* (Jackson: University Press of Mississippi, 1998).

Martin, G. Eugene and Astrid S. Tuminez, *Toward Peace in the Southern Philippines: A Summary and Assessment of the USIP Philippine Facilitation Project, 2003–2007* (Washington: USIP, 2008).

Mead, Walter Russell, *Power, Terror, Peace and War: America's Grand Strategy in a World of Risk* (New York: Vintage, 2004).

——, *Special Providence: American Foreign Policy and How It Changed the World* (New York: Routledge, 2002).

Miller, Rhoda, *Institutionalizing Peace: The Concept of the USIP and Its Role in American Political Thought* (Jefferson, NC: McFarland, 1994).

Morris, Edmund, *Theodore Rex* (New York: Random House, 2001).

Murdock, Clark A., Michèle A. Flournoy, et al., *Beyond Goldwater-Nichols: Defense Reform for a New Strategic Era Phase I Report* (Washington: CSIS, 2004).

Natsios, Andrew S., *The Four Horsemen of the Apocalypse: Humanitarian Relief in Complex Emergencies* (Washington: CSIS, 1997).

Nzongola-Ntalaja, Georges, *The Congo from Leopold to Kabila: A People's History* (London: Zed Books, 2002).

Orr, Robert C., ed., *Winning the Peace: An American Strategy for Post-Conflict Reconstruction* (Washington: CSIS, 2004).

Packer, George, *The Assassins' Gate: America in Iraq* (New York: Farrar, Straus, & Giroux, 2005).

Patrick, Stewart and Kaysie Brown, *Greater than the Sum of Its Parts: Assessing "Whole of Government" Approaches to Fragile States* (New York: International Peace Academy, 2007).

Perito, Robert M., Michael Dziedzic, and Beth DeGrasse, *Building Civilian Capacity for U.S. Stability Operations: The Rule of Law Component* (Washington: USIP Special Report No. 118, April 2004).

Powell, H. Jefferson, *The President's Authority over Foreign Affairs: An Essay in Constitutional Interpretation* (Durham, NC: Carolina Academic Press, 2002).

Preventing Genocide: A Blueprint for the U.S. Government (Washington: United States Holocaust Memorial Museum/American Academy of Diplomacy/Endowment of the United States Institute of Peace, 2008).

Ricks, Thomas E., *Fiasco: The American Military Adventure in Iraq* (New York: Penguin, 2006).

Rotberg, Robert, *The First Ten Years: An Assessment of the Office of Transition Initiatives* (Program on Intrastate Conflict and Conflict Resolution, Belfer Center for Science and International Affairs, John F. Kennedy School of Government, Harvard University, 2005).

Rothkopf, David, *Running the World: The Inside Story of the National Security Council and the Architects of American Power* (New York: Public Affairs, 2005).

Rubin, Barnett, *Afghanistan's Uncertain Transition from Turmoil to Normalcy* (Washington: USIP, 2006).

Russell, Ruth B., *A History of the United Nations Charter* (Washington: Brookings, 1958).

Smith, Dane F., Jr., *Roundtable on Proposed Civilian Reserve Corps* (A CSIS PCR Project Special Briefing), November 2007.

Spencer, John H., *Ethiopia at Bay: A Personal Account of the Haile Selassie Years* (Algonac, MI: Reference Publications, 1984).

von Hippel, Karin, *Democracy by Force: U.S. Military Intervention in the Post-Cold War World* (Cambridge: Cambridge University Press, 2000).

Williams, Cindy and Gordon Adams, *Strengthening Statecraft and Security: Reforming U.S. Planning and Resource Allocation* (Cambridge: MIT Security Studies Program Occasional Paper, June 2008).

Woodward, Bob, *Bush at War* (New York: Simon & Schuster, 2002).

——, *Plan of Attack* (New York: Simon & Schuster, 2004).

——, *State of Denial* (New York: Simon & Schuster, 2006).

Wrong, Michaela, *"I Didn't Do It for You": How the World Betrayed a Small African Nation* (New York: Harper Collins, 2005).

Yacoubian, Mona, *Promoting Middle East Democracy II: Arab Initiatives* (Washington: USIP Special Report, May 2005).

——, *Engaging Islamists and Promoting Democracy: A Preliminary Assessment* (Washington: USIP Special Report, September 2007).

ARTICLES

Barnes, Fred, "How Bush Decided on the Surge," *The Weekly Standard* (February 4, 2008).

Bayley, David H., "U.S. Aid for Foreign Justice and Police," *Orbis* 30:3 (2006), 469–479.

Coll, Steve, "The Back Channel," *The New Yorker* (March 2, 2009).

Cooper, Helene, "Rice's Way: Restraint in Quest of Peace," *New York Times* (November 29, 2007).

DeYoung, Karen, "Diplomats Give Rice Low Marks," *Washington Post* (January 8, 2008).

Drew, Dennis and Don Snow, "Military Doctrine" in *Making Strategy: An Introduction to National Security Processes and Problems* (Maxwell, AL: Air University Press, 2006).

Dreyfuss, Robert, "A Higher Power: James Baker Puts George Bush's Iraq Policy into Rehab," *Washington Monthly* (September 2006).

Gaddis, John Lewis, "Grand Strategy in the Second Term," *Foreign Policy* (January–February 2005).

Gottfried, Paul, "The Invincible Wilsonian Matrix: Universal Human Rights Once Again," *Orbis* 51:2 (2007), 239–250.

Hill, Fiona, *"Une stratégie incertaine: la politique des Etats-Unis dans le Caucase et en Asie centrale depuis 1991,"* *Politique étrangère* (February 2001).

Huliaras, Asteris, "Evangelists, Oil Companies, and Terrorists: The Bush Administration's Policy towards Sudan," *Orbis* 50:4 (Autumn 2006), 709–724.

Krasner, Stephen D. and Carlos Pascual, "Addressing State Failure," *Foreign Affairs* (July–August 2005).

Lafranchi, Howard, "Bush Gives UN an Ultimatum," *Christian Science Monitor* (September 13, 2002).

Martins, Mark S., "The Commander's Emergency Response Program," *Joint Forces Quarterly*, no. 37 (2005).

Montgomery, Mary E., "Working for Peace while Preparing for War: The Creation of the United States Institute of Peace," *Journal of Peace Research* 40:4 (2003), 479–496.

Olsen, Lara, "Fighting for Humanitarian Space: NGOs in Afghanistan," *Journal of Military and Strategic Studies* 9 (Fall 2006).

Touval, Saadia and I. William Zartman, "International Mediation in the Post-Cold War Era" in Chester T. Crocker, et al., *Turbulent Peace: The Challenges of Managing International Conflict* (Washington: USIP, 2001), 427–443.

Wald, Charles F., "New Thinking at EUCOM: The Zero Campaign," *Joint Forces Quarterly* 43 (4th quarter 2006).

INTERVIEWS (PARTIAL LISTING)

Title indicates whether the person interviewed was in the position at the time of the interview or before the interview.

Defense Department

Adams, Clark, Director, USG Capabilities, OSD-Stability Operations, November 11, 2006.

Agoglia, John, Director, Peacekeeping and Stability Operations Institute, Army War College, October 23, 2006.

Benn, James, Deputy Director for Doctrine Development, Knowledge Directorate, Army Combined Arms Center, October 16, 2008.

Binnendijk, Hans J., Director Center for Technology and National Security Policy, National Defense University, January 16, 2007.

Brineman, Elena, Senior Advisor, Peacekeeping and Stability Operations Institute, Army War College, November 7, 2008.

Carreau, Bernard, Senior Research Fellow, Center for Technology and National Security Policy, National Defense University, January 16, 2007.

Cheek, Marc, Director, OSD/Stability Operations/Office of Policy and Integration, April 19, 2007.

Collins, Joseph R., ex-Deputy Assistant Secretary of Defense for Peacekeeping and Stability Operations, March 16, 2007.

Davenport, Dan W., RADM, Director, Joint Concept Development and Experimentation Directorate (J-9), Joint Forces Command, December 23, 2008.

Davidson, Janine, OSD-Policy/Stability Operations/Office of U.S. Government Capabilities, October 24, 2006.

Flournoy, Michèle, ex-Principal Deputy Assistant Secretary for Strategy and Threat Reduction, October 11, 2007.

Giambastiani, Edmund, Adm. (Ret.), ex-Vice Chief of the Joint Chiefs of Staff, December 11, 2008.

Gudridge, Col. Lindsay, Chief, SSTR Branch/Plans Division/CENTCOM/J-5, April 13, 2007.

Hand, Bailey S., OSD/Office of Stability Operations, June 20, 2007.
Hirst, Col. Barbara, Chief, Strategy and Policy Division, J-5, Joint Forces Command, March 29, 2007.
Leonard, LTC Steven, Office of Doctrine Development, Knowledge Directorate, Army Combined Arms Center, October 31, 2008.
McNerney, Michael, OSD/Stability Operations/Director Office of International Capabilities, October 25, 2006; and as OSD/Global Security/Partnership Strategy/Director for International Capacity Building, April 25, 2007.
Padfield, Jon, Capt., JCS/J-5/Deputy Directorate for Global Security Partnerships/ Director of Stability Operations, April 3, 2007.
Seaward, LTC George, European Command/J-5/Plans/Stability Plans Branch, April 16, 2007.
Ward, L. Celeste, Deputy Assistant Secretary of Defense for Stability Operations Capabilities, December 1, 2008.

National Security Council

Courville, Cindy L., ex-Senior Director for Africa, October 19, 2007.
Daalder, Ivo, ex-Director for European Affairs, September 25, 2007.
Feaver, Peter, ex-Special Advisor for Strategic Planning and Institutional Reform, November 13, 2007.
Green, Michael J., ex-Senior Director for Asian Affairs, August 30, 2007.
Hall, Laura A., Director for Stabilization, January 25, 2008.
Inboden, William C., ex-Senior Director for Strategic Planning, November 14, 2007.
Jeffrey, James F., Deputy National Security Adviser, December 13, 2007.
Maisto, John F., ex-Senior Director for Western Hemisphere Affairs, October 2, 2007.
McLean, Matthew, ex-Director, Planning and Contingency Operations, ex-Director for Africa, January 18, 2007.
Williamson, John Clint, ex-Acting Senior Director for Relief, Stabilization and Development, January 3, 2007.

Office of Management and Budget

Calbos, Philip, Chief, Operations & Support Branch, National Security Division, National Security Programs, June 5, 2008.
Capozzola, Christa, Chief, Economic Affairs Branch, National Security Programs, International Affairs Division, May 16, 2008.

Peace Corps

Angelini, Mary, Director of Peace Corps Response, August 19, 2008.
Olsen, Jody, Deputy Director, September 9, 2008.

State Department

Benton, Jonathan, CRS/Director of Civilian Readiness and Response, December 7, 2007.
Bloomfield, Lincoln, ex-Assistant Secretary of State for Political Military Affairs, November 8, 2007.

Charles, Robert C. (Bobby), ex-Assistant Secretary for International Narcotics and Law Enforcement Affairs, December 19, 2007.

Corle, Dan, F/Peace and Security Sector Group, April 2, 2008.

Danforth, The Honorable John, ex-Special Envoy for Sudan, November 13, 2008.

de Soto, Oscar, S/CRS Director of Planning, December 20, 2007.

Dobbins, Ambassador James, ex-Special Envoy for Somalia, Haiti, Bosnia, Kosovo, and the Afghan Opposition, December 1, 2006.

Field, Kimberly, LTC, S/CRS Senior Military Advisor, November 10, 2008.

Frazer, Jendayi, Assistant Secretary of State for African Affairs, January 16, 2008.

Hawley, Leonard R., ex-Deputy Assistant Secretary for Political Military Affairs, September 7, 2007.

Herbst, John E., Ambassador, Coordinator for Reconstruction and Stabilization, January 30, 2007.

Hoh, Christopher, Associate Dean, Foreign Service Institute, December 4, 2008.

Holmes, Kim, ex-Assistant Secretary of State for International Organization Affairs, November 28, 2006.

Jones, A. Elizabeth, Ambassador, ex-Assistant Secretary of State for European and Eurasian Affairs, November 9, 2007.

Kelly, James A., ex-Assistant Secretary for East Asia and Pacific Affairs, November 17, 2008.

Krasner, Stephen D., Director of Policy Planning, December 5, 2006.

McMullen, Christopher, Deputy Assistant Secretary for Western Hemisphere Affairs, December 12, 2007.

Milligan, T. Christopher, F/Head of NEA Team, April 17, 2008.

Moore, Thomas, S/CRS Director of Conflict Prevention, December 7, 2007.

Neumann, Ronald E., ex-Ambassador to Afghanistan, December 18, 2007.

Pascual, Carlos, Ambassador, ex-Coordinator for Reconstruction and Stabilization, November 8, 2006.

Raphel, Robin L., Ambassador, ex-Coordinator for Reconstruction for Iraq, December 10, 2007.

Ray, Wilna, Director, CRS Office of Resource Management.

Ryan, Timothy G., Deputy Director, Caribbean Affairs, Bureau of Western Hemisphere Affairs, February 22, 2008.

Shortley, Timothy R., Senior Advisor on Conflict Resolution, Bureau of African Affairs, June 24, 2008.

Snyder, Charles R., Deputy Assistant Secretary of State for African Affairs, September 22, 2006.

Sontag, Eythan, S/CRC Active Response Corps, November 1, 2007.

Stephenson, Barbara, Deputy Coordinator for Iraq (S/I), October 3, 2006 and February 1, 2008.

Underriner, John, Deputy Director, Regional Political Military Affairs, Bureau of Europe and Eurasian Affairs, July 15, 2008.

Williamson, Richard S., Ambassador, Special Presidential Envoy for Sudan, November 20, 2008.

Wong, Marcia, ex-Deputy Coordinator for Reconstruction and Stabilization, January 10, 2007.

Yamamoto, Donald Y., Ambassador, Deputy Assistant Secretary of State for African Affairs, October 2, 2006.

USAID

Baltazar, Thomas, Director, DCHA/Office of Military Affairs, May 8, 2007.

Barton, Frederick D., ex-Director, Office of Transition Initiatives, October 3, 2006.

Carter, Sharon, LAC/RSD/Chief, Democracy and Human Rights, July 6, 2007.

Courtney, Alexa, DCHA/Office of Conflict Management and Mitigation, May 11, 2007.

Fertig-Dykes, Susan, Europe and Eurasia/DGST/Chief Democracy and Government, July 20, 2007.

Franco, Adolfo, ex-Assistant Administrator for Latin America and the Caribbean, July 30, 2007.

Gold, Ricki, Asia and the Near East, NE/TS/Leader of Democracy and Government Technical Team, July 6, 2007.

Hannifin, Mark, Office of Conflict Management and Mitigation, January 21, 2009.

Hill, Kent, ex-Assistant Administrator for Europe and Eurasia, August 1, 2007.

Isralow, Sharon, Chief, Communication, Peace-Building and Governance, Bureau for Africa, June 26, 2007.

Jenkins, Robert W., Acting Director, DCHA/Office of Transition Initiatives, October 27, 2006.

Kunder, James R., Acting Deputy Administrator, September 6, 2007.

Kvitashvili, Elisabeth, Director, DCHA/Office of Conflict Management and Mitigation, October 26, 2006.

Luu, Ky, Director, DCHA/Office of Foreign Disaster Assistance, August 7, 2007.

Miklaucic, Michael, ex-DCHA/Democracy and Governance Senior Program Officer, July 31, 2007.

Morris, Sharon, ex-Senior Advisor, Office of Conflict Management and Mitigation, July 9, 2007.

Natsios, Andrew S., The Honorable, ex-Administrator (also ex-Special Envoy for Sudan), April 28, 2008.

Newman, Constance, ex-Assistant Administrator for Africa (and ex-Assistant Secretary of State for African Affairs), July 17, 2007.

Pierson, Lloyd O., ex-Assistant Administrator for Africa, June 13, 2007.

Smith, Zeric, Division of Communication, Peace-Building and Governance, Bureau for Africa, July 12, 2007.

Walker, S. Tjip, Director, Warning and Analysis Team, Office of Conflict Management and Mitigation, September 28, 2006 and February 11, 2009.

U.S. Congress

Higgins, Craig, Majority Staff, House Appropriations Committee, State and Foreign Operations Subcommittee, May 16, 2008.

Kojac, Christine, Minority Staff, House Appropriations Committee, State, Foreign Operations and Related Programs Subcommittee, June 20, 2008.

Phelan, Michael V., Minority Staff, Senate Foreign Relations Committee, June 5, 2008.

Sanok, Stephanie, Minority Staff, House Armed Services Committee, July 14, 2008.

Veillette, Connie, Minority Staff, Senate Foreign Relations Committee, June 5, 2008.

U.S. Institute of Peace

Aall, Pamela, Vice President for Domestic Programs, Education and Training Center, February 26, 2008.

Bekoe, Dorina, Senior Research Associate, Center for Conflict Analysis and Prevention, March 31, 2008.
Cole, Beth Ellen, Senior Program Officer, Center for Post-Conflict Peace and Stability Operations, February 19, 2008 and May 7, 2008.
Coyne, A. Heather, Center for Mediation and Conflict Resolution, February 19, 2008.
Crocker, Chester A., ex-Chairman, Board Member, April 24, 2008.
Hayward, Susan, Program Officer, USIP Religion and Peacemaking Program, February 19, 2008.
Heim, Laurie Schultz, Director for Congressional Relations, July 29, 2008.
Huda, Qamar-ul, Senior Program Officer, Religion and Peacemaking Center of Innovation, April 25, 2008.
Lasensky, Scott B., Acting Director, Center for Analysis and Prevention, April 30, 2008.
Martin, G. Eugene, ex-Director Philippine Facilitation Project, April 10, 2008.
Nelson, Charles E. (Chick), Vice President for the Headquarters Project, March 5, 2008.
Perito, Robert M., Senior Program Officer, Center for Post-Conflict Peace and Security (ex-Director ICITAP, Justice Department), March 20, 2007.
Serwer, Daniel P., Vice President and Director of the Center for Post-Conflict Peace and Stability Operations, October 20, 2006.
Smock, David R., Vice President and Director, Center for Mediation and Conflict Resolution, February 19, 2008.
Solomon, Richard H., President, May 5 and 16, 2008.
Stares, Paul, ex-Vice President and Director, Center for Conflict Analysis and Prevention, April 7, 2008.
Thomson, Patricia P., Executive Vice President and Chief Operating Officer, March 24, 2008.
Ward, George F., ex-Director of Training, April 22, 2008.
Williams, Abiodun, Vice President and Director, Center for Conflict Analysis and Prevention, December 18, 2008.
Woocher, Lawrence, Program Officer, Center for Conflict Analysis and Prevention, February 21, 2008.

Other

Destler, I. M., Director, Program on International Security and Economic policy, School of Public Policy, University of Maryland, College Park, October 5, 2007.
Nash, William L., MG (Ret.), Director, Center for Preventive Action, Council on Foreign Relations, January 12, 2007.

DOCUMENTS OF GOVERNMENT AND INTERNATIONAL ORGANIZATIONS

Army Field Manual 3.0 Operations (2008).
Army Field Manual 3.24 Counterinsurgency (2007).
Army Field Manual 3.7 Stability Operations (2008).

Congressional Research Service, *The Congressional Appropriations Process: An Introduction* (Order Code 97-684, updated February 22, 2007).

———, *The Global Peace Operations Initiative: Background and Issues for Congress* (June 11, 2007).

———, *Military Operations: Precedents for Funding Contingency Operations in Regular or Supplemental Appropriation Bills* (June 13, 2006).

———, *Organizing the U.S. Government for National Security: Overview of the Interagency Reform Debates* (April 18, 2008).

———, *Peacekeeping and Conflict Transitions: Background and Congressional Action on Civilian Capabilities* (updated September 18, 2006).

———, *Plan Colombia: A Progress Report* (RL32774, January 11, 2006), http://digital.library.unt.edu/govdocs/crs/permalink/meta-crs-8270:1.

———, *Security and Stabilization Assistance: A Fact Sheet* (RS22871, November 25, 2008).

Crocker, Chester A., "The Growth of a Unique Federal Agency: Reflections on the Past and Thoughts about the Future of the United States Institute of Peace," August 4, 2004.

Department of Defense, Capstone Concept for Joint Operations, Version 2 (August 2005).

———, *Support for Security, Stabilization, Transition, Reconstruction Operations Joint Operating Concept*, Version 2 (December 2006).

Department of State/U.S. Joint Forces Command, *US Government Draft Planning Framework for Reconstruction, Stabilization and Conflict Transformation* (2005).

Government Accountability Office, *Provincial Reconstruction Teams in Afghanistan and Iraq* (October 1, 2008).

———, *Stabilization and Reconstruction: Actions Are Needed to Develop a Planning and Coordination Framework and Establish the Civilian Reserve Corps* (November 2007).

———, *Stabilization and Reconstruction: Actions Needed to Improve Governmentwide Planning and Capabilities for Future Operations* (GAO-08-228, October 30, 2007).

———, *Stabilizing and Rebuilding Iraq Coalition Support and International Donor Commitments* (March 9, 2007).

Halchin, L. Elaine, *The Coalition Provisional Authority (CPA): Origin, Characteristics, and Institutional Authorities* (Congressional Research Service Report to Congress, RL32370, April 29, 2004).

The Iraq Study Group Report (New York: Vintage, 2006).

Organization of the National Security Council, Presidential Decision Directive 1 (February 13, 2001).

Report of the Panel on United Nations Peace Operations (the Brahimi Report) (A/55/305; S/2000/809, August 17, 2000).

Serafino, Nina M., *Department of Defense "Section 1207": Security and Stabilization: A Fact Sheet*, CRS Report for Congress (November 25, 2008).

Social Impact, Inc., *Strategy and Impact of the Iraq Transition Initiative: OTI in Iraq (2003–2006), Final Evaluation Report* (September 30, 2006).

———, *USAID/OTI Afghanistan Final Evaluation* (August 15, 2005).

Special Inspector General for Iraq Reconstruction, *Hard Lessons: The Iraq Reconstruction Experience* (Washington: Government Printing Office, 2009).

To Establish the United States Academy of Peace: Report of the Commission on Proposals for the National Academy of Peace and Conflict Resolution to the President of the United

States and the Senate and the House of Representatives of the United States Congress (Washington D.C.: U.S. Government Printing Office, 1981).

USAID, *At Freedom's Frontiers: A Democracy and Governance Strategic Framework* (2005).

———, *Conducting a Conflict Assessment: A Framework for Strategy and Program Development* (2005).

———, *Foreign Aid in the National Interest: Promoting Freedom, Security & Opportunity* (2002).

———, *Fragile States Strategy* (2005).

———, *Policy Framework for Bilateral Foreign Aid: Implementing Transformational Diplomacy through Development* (2006).

———, *White Paper: U.S. Foreign Aid Meeting the Challenges of the Twenty-First Century* (2004).

USAID, Office of Conflict Management and Mitigation, *Forests and Conflict: A Tool for Intervention* (2005).

———, *Land and Conflict: A Toolkit for Intervention* (2005).

———, *Livelihoods and Conflict: A Tool for Intervention* (2005).

———, *Minerals and Conflict: A Toolkit for Intervention* (2004).

———, *Women and Conflict: A Tool for Intervention* (2006).

———, *Youth & Conflict: A Toolkit for Intervention* (2005).

USAID, Office of Transition Initiatives, *Advancing Peaceful, Democratic Change* (1999).

———, *Iraq Transition Initiative* (2005).

White House, *The National Security Strategy of the United States of America* (September 2002)

———, *The National Security Strategy of the United States of America* (March 2006).

UNPUBLISHED DOCUMENTS

Tammy Schultz, "Ten Years Each Week: The Warrior's Transformation to Win the Peace," PhD Dissertation, Georgetown University, 2005.

Index

About the Author

DANE F. SMITH, Jr., is currently Senior Associate at the Center for Strategic and International Studies and Adjunct Professor at American University. From 1999 to 2003 he served as President of the National Peace Corps Association. He was U.S. Ambassador to Senegal 1996–99, Special Presidential Envoy for Liberia 1995–96, and Ambassador to Guinea 1990–93. Dr. Smith received his AB from Harvard College and PhD from the Fletcher School of Law and Diplomacy, and also studied at the Union Theological Seminary in New York. He and his wife Judy live in Washington D.C.